I0528442

www.ingramcontent.com/pod-product-compliance
Lightning Source LLC
Chambersburg PA
CBHW051315120626
46547CB00015B/2242

ישעיהו

THE
ISRAEL
BIBLE

ISAIAH

EDITED BY

Rabbi Tuly Weisz

The Israel Bible: Isaiah

First Edition, 2021

The Israel Bible was produced by Israel365 in cooperation with Teach for Israel and is used with permission from Teach for Israel. All rights reserved. The English translation was adapted by Israel365 from the JPS Tanakh. Copyright © 1985 by the Jewish Publication Society. All rights reserved.

Cover images used under license from Shutterstock.com

ISBN 978-1-957109-35-0

A CIP catalogue record for this title is available from the British Library

The Israel Bible: Isaiah is a holy book that contains the name of God and should be treated with respect.

Table of Contents

Introduction

The Hebrew Bible is commonly known as the *Tanakh* which stands for *Torah* (the Five Books of Moses), *Neviim* (the Prophets) and *Ketuvim* (the Writings). The *Tanakh* consists of 24 books that are considered by Jews to be the word of God. While these books have been referred to as the "Old Testament," many Jews reject this label since it implies the replacement of the Hebrew Bible with something newer and prefer the more authentic Jewish name.

The *Tanakh* is not only the most important book known to man, it is God's word that is perfect and absolute. It is therefore a daunting undertaking to publish an edition of the *Tanakh*, and the responsibilities are awesome. There is no room for error or carelessness in dealing with the eternal word of God. Further, upon embarking on such a serious initiative, we ask ourselves if our efforts are gratuitous. Considering the many editions of the Bible in print, is there truly a need for yet another one?

While there are numerous Bibles in circulation today, its most central aspect – the Land of Israel – has often been overlooked. References to Israel appear on nearly every page, and the city of Jerusalem is specifically referred to hundreds of times throughout the Bible. The essential link between Israel and *Torah* is emphasized repeatedly in verses such as, "For instruction (*Torah*) shall come forth from *Tzion*, the word of *Hashem* from *Yerushalayim*" (Micah 4:2).

The miraculous return of the People of Israel to the Land of Israel in our own generation provides the perfect moment for a new volume to fill this void in biblical literature. *The Israel Bible* includes many special features elucidating God's focus on Israel throughout *Tanakh* and there are many additional, multimedia features available on our website **www.theisraelbible.com**.

Ordering and Presentation – In presenting *The Israel Bible*, our goal is to spread awareness of the biblical significance of the Land of Israel as well as the Jewish people's eternal connection to the land, based on the text of the *Tanakh*, the Hebrew Bible. We aim to honor "the God, the People and the Land of Israel" from an Orthodox Jewish perspective. To that end, *The Israel Bible* follows the traditional Jewish ordering of the books and the customary Hebrew division of chapters. Therefore, for example, we count 24 books of *Tanakh* with *Sefer Divrei Hayamim* (Chronicles) appearing last. It is our hope that our rich content will speak to all Jews and non-Jews who appreciate Israel as the God given land of the Jewish people.

English Translation – Throughout history, Jews have studied the Bible in Hebrew, as any form of translation would miss much of the nuance of the original holy tongue in which *Torah* has been transmitted since the days of Moses. However, as many Jews settled in America in the 19th Century, the need for an English translation became necessary. To be sure, there were already English translations prepared over the centuries by Christians, but in the words of the original editors of the Jewish Publication Society (JPS), "The Jew cannot afford to have his Bible translation prepared for him by others. He cannot have it as a gift, even as he cannot borrow his soul from others."

JPS set out in the late 1800s to publish an authoritative English translation "in the spirit of Jewish tradition." It was compiled over decades by some of the leading Jewish scholars of the time. They formed committees and subcommittees to compare existing English versions, considering medieval and modern Jewish commentators. The monumental JPS translation, originally published in 1917, has been updated in recent years, and *The Israel Bible* is proud to utilize the 1984 New Jewish Publication Society (NJPS) version with its modern, clear language, as well as its wide-ranging acceptance as an accurate and high-quality translation. We applied the NJPS translation verbatim, except for a select list of nouns which we replaced with their traditional Hebrew names. This is true even when we found the NJPS translation to be different than the popular translation of a word or phrase and when the NJPS switched the order of the text for the sake of clarity (see, for example, Ezekiel 24:22–24).

Hebrew Transliteration – To give our readers an authentic *Tanakh* experience, every verse that has commentary is transliterated from Hebrew into English. The Hebrew alphabet chart includes our standards for transliteration and pronunciation of Hebrew verses, enabling readers of *The Israel Bible* to decipher key biblical passages in the holy language. Readers can hear the entire Bible read in Hebrew on our website **www.theisraelbible.com**.

There are various standards when it comes to transliterating Hebrew words into English letters. While we have relied primarily on the classical Hebrew transliteration, we have occasionally deviated for the sake of simplicity, clarity and to reflect common usage.

In addition to whole verses, we have also transliterated many proper nouns in the English translation so that our readers can learn the names of key biblical figures and locations in their Hebrew form. As a rule, we chose to transliterate names of people that were central in the establishment and functioning of the nation of Israel, as well as significant places in the Holy Land. Therefore, regarding Adam's sons, for example, only *Shet* (Seth) is transliterated since it was from him that *Noach* (Noah), and ultimately *Avraham* (Abraham), descended. For this reason, there might be verses or sections of *The Israel Bible* that contains multiple names and only some of them are transliterated.

For the same reason, we have transliterated the names of the books of *Tanakh* when referring to them in our introductions and commentary. When referencing a specific chapter or verse, however, we use the English names of the books in our citations for clarity. We also transliterated ideas and concepts that are central to Judaism such as *Shabbat* (Sabbath), the names of the Jewish holidays and the *Beit Hamikdash* (Temple), as well as biblical measurements. Finally, the name of God is transliterated. Out of respect, Orthodox Jews generally refer to the Lord as *Hashem*, which literally means 'the Name.' Referring to God as *Hashem* reminds us that we feel close to Him but also recognize our distance at the same time. To stress this moniker, we transliterated both the Tetragrammaton as well as the name *Elohim* as *Hashem*.

Study Notes – Our unique commentary was compiled by Orthodox Jewish scholars who live in Israel. It is an anthology in the sense that most of the commentary is not original, but draws from traditional teachings of early Jewish Sages and modern rabbinic commentators. We also include quotations from individuals who have played a significant part in the past century of modern Israeli history including Israeli prime ministers, poets and military leaders.

Our commentary can be broken into four categories, three of which are identified by an icon at the beginning of the study note:

 Israel lessons are indicated with an icon bearing the map of Israel and focus on the Land of Israel and the modern State of Israel.

 Jewish lessons are indicated with a *Torah* scroll and teach a concept in Judaism or a classic idea from rabbinic thought.

 Hebrew lessons are represented by an icon bearing the letter *aleph* and focus on the meaning of a Hebrew word or phrase.

All other comments are considered general comments and are not assigned an icon.

Supplemental Material – In addition to our unique translation and original commentary, *The Israel Bible* offers supplementary material to enrich the learning experience of our readers. Before every book of *Tanakh,* we provide an introduction, as well as information, generally in the form of a map, a chart or a list, which is central to the specific book.

Maps – As the purpose of *The Israel Bible* is to highlight the biblical significance of the Land of Israel, significant time was spent researching and preparing maps to bring the physical contours of the holy land to life with great accuracy. However, since there is a lack of information regarding the precise locations of certain ancient cities, some of the places on our maps are approximate or subject to debate. In these cases, we followed the opinion that we are most comfortable with, but acknowledge that there is room for disagreement. We continue to produce new maps, which are available on our website **www.theisraelbible.com/maps**.

Torah **Readings** – The *Torah* is not just a work that is studied privately, it is also read out loud in synagogue. Every *Shabbat* and holiday a portion of the *Torah* is read, as well as a related section from *Neviim*, the prophets, called the *haftarah*. We included the blessings recited before and after the reading of the *Torah*, a list of the weekly *Torah* portions and their corresponding *haftarot*, and a chart of the *Torah* readings for special days with their corresponding *haftarot*. Readers can always find the current week's *Torah* portion by visiting **www.theisraelbible.com/weekly-torah-portion**. In this volume, we indicate where a new *Torah* portion begins by highlighting the Hebrew verse number with a gray box so readers can follow along with the communal *Torah* readings. Furthermore, we have included prayers for the State of Israel and the soldiers of the Israel Defense Forces (IDF) that are generally recited following the *Torah* reading in synagogue. It is our constant prayer that God watch over the State of Israel and the members of the IDF, who defend Israel every hour of every day.

In 1948, the State of Israel was created providing a modern answer to Isaiah's ancient question, "Is a nation born all at once?" (Isaiah 66:8). *The Israel Bible* was first published in the 70th year of God's miraculous restoration of the People of Israel to the Land of Israel. Jewish wisdom teaches that 70 is a significant number: *Moshe* (Moses) translated the *Torah* into 70 languages for all 70 nations of the world. From our very origins, the Jewish people were meant to be a light unto the 70 nations, spreading God's truth to the masses.

In the seven decades since the modern rebirth of the State of Israel, God's plan has been unfolding with unprecedented speed, dramatic highs and heartbreaking lows. Never has Israel been at the forefront of the world's attention as it is in our generation. Efforts to vilify the Jewish State seem to spread every day across the globe. At the same time, so does the growing movement of millions of non-Jewish biblical Zionists who stand with the nation of Israel as an expression of their commitment to God's word. As we seek to understand the clash of these two conflicting worldviews, the need for *The Israel Bible* has never been so important.

Standing on the great shoulders of those who came before us and emanating from the land that has always served as the birthplace for the Bible, we conclude with a heartfelt prayer: May the Almighty bless our efforts in offering this *Tanakh* to influence the hearts, minds and actions of its readers. In this way, it is our hope to spread God's name so that the publication of *The Israel Bible* brings us one step closer to the final redemption of Israel and the entire world.

Rabbi Tuly Weisz
Editor, *The Israel Bible*

Foreword

The mandate to study God's word daily is interestingly not found in the Five Books of Moses (Pentateuch), but rather in the first book of our prophetic writings: "Let not this Book of the Teaching cease from your lips, but recite it day and night, so that you may observe faithfully all that is written in it. Only then will you prosper in your undertakings and only then will you be successful" (Joshua 1:8). Charged with bringing the Israelites into the land covenantally promised to Abraham, Isaac and Jacob, God ensures Joshua of His protection if the nation observes His ways as dictated in the Divine constitution known as the *Torah*.

In Jewish tradition, Joshua (1:8) is directly linked with Deuteronomy (11:14), "You shall gather in your new grain and wine, and oil."[1] Our Sages deduced from this scriptural combination the importance of merging *Torah* study with a profession. Completely dedicating oneself to the study of *Torah* without having the financial means to sustain this lifestyle can lead one to eventually straying from observance of God's will. Poverty and crime can have an intimate relationship.

We must also be careful that our work does not affect our daily study of Scripture. The addiction of becoming a workaholic and not making *Torah* study a priority can also lead one into temptations that can violate our personal relationship with Him as well as our fellow human beings. The goal is to achieve a healthy balance between our study of God's word and our daily work.

The Deuteronomic verse quoted above is part of the second section of the Shema[2] that discusses the concept of reward and punishment. Sanctifying God by fulfilling His commandments results in the Land of Israel practically benefitting from rains that occur in the right season and reaping the abundance from the fields. However, if the nation follows pagan gods and practices, the consequences are devastating – famine and death. The Land of Israel is intrinsically linked with the keeping of the *Torah*. Covenant Land comes with covenant responsibility.

---

1. Talmud Bavli Berachot 35b
2. Consisting of three sections within the Five Books of Moses (Deut. 6:4–8; 11:13–22 and Numbers 15:37–42), the *Shema* is proclamation of accepting God's Kingdom in our lives, loyalty to His commandments and remembering His redemptive act of liberating us from Egypt. Jews recite the *Shema* twice a day as stated in Deut. 6:7.

Born into slavery, Joshua is now leading His people into the Promised Land. More than 500 years separates him from his ancestral forefather Abraham. The historical narratives that took place between Abraham leaving everything behind to follow God in Genesis 12 and the death of Moses in the last chapter of Deuteronomy are filled with intrigue, suspense, joy, sorrow and hope. What began as a family is now a nation actualizing its mission to be a kingdom of priests to the world. However, for the Israelites to succeed in the Land of Israel, they must see the *Torah* as the only compass to direct their lives.

The biblical episodes after our first entry into the land are well known. Our ancestors' triumphs and sins are all on public record. We learned the harsh reality of Leviticus (18:28) "So let not the land spew you out for defiling it as it spewed out the nation that came before you." Twice, we lost the privilege to be stewards of the Land of Israel and to fulfill our nation state mandate to be a light to the world. However, when the annals of history were ready to archive the Jewish people after the Holocaust, God kept His covenantal promise and gathered us from the four corners of the globe to come home. The year 1948 was a game changer. Biblical prophecies were and are being realized. We are now living in the birth pangs of the messianic era.

In our morning prayers, we recite a series of blessings over the *Torah* that include petitioning God to have a sweet tooth for His word, to study it without any ulterior motive and to have Him to teach it to us. They are some congregations that invoke the following liturgical prayer after the completion of these blessings: *May the Torah be my faith and El Shaddai my help. Blessed be the name of His glorious kingdom forever and all time.*

According to Jewish tradition, the neglect of not blessing the *Torah* before engaging in its study was one of the reasons for the destruction of the Temple.[3] This is deduced from the redundancy of words in Jeremiah (9:12) that talks about Israel not following God: "… Because they forsook the teaching I had set before them. They did not obey Me and they did not follow it [did not make a blessing before studying it]." Our inability to properly cherish God's greatest gift to the world, the *Torah*, led to our eventual exile from our land.

On Israel's Independence Day, Jews around the world recite Psalms 113–118 to express our gratitude to God for His Divine hand in helping establish the State of Israel. We have learned from our past and realize the privilege to see firsthand the land, people and *Torah* operating all together in our generation.

---

3. Babylonian Talmud Nedarim 81a

When Rabbi Tuly Weisz approached me about his intent to publish *The Israel Bible* that would highlight commentary about the special relationship between the land and people, I saw this project as another way to publicly demonstrate our appreciation to God for having the State of Israel. In addition, it is another educational tool to ensure biblical literacy. If we are to truly enjoy the Land of Israel, it is incumbent upon us to continually study the *Torah*. Isaiah once prophesied that the Jewish people would return to Zion with songs, "crowned with everlasting joy" (35:10). *The Israel Bible* provides us the lyrical content to express our joy in living in the land that God calls holy.

Rabbi Shlomo Riskin
Chief Rabbi of Efrat
Founder of the Center for Jewish-Christian
Understanding & Cooperation (cjcuc)

Introduction to Sefer Yeshayahu
The Book of Isaiah

Introduction and commentary by Rabbi Yaakov Beasley

Sefer Yeshayahu (Isaiah) is the first and the longest of the books of the Latter Prophets. *Yeshayahu*'s prophecies are recorded in both prose and poetry, and his imagery is considered among the most beautiful in the Bible.

Yeshayahu prophesies during the reigns of at least four kings of *Yehuda* in the second half of the eighth century BCE: *Uzziyahu* (769–733), *Yotam* (758–743 as regent), *Achaz* (743–733 as regent; 733–727), and *Chizkiyahu* (727–698). It appears that his prophecies also continue into the reign of the next king, *Menashe*.

During his lifetime, *Yeshayahu* sees the fortunes of the two kingdoms in Israel, *Shomron* in the north and *Yehuda* in the south, decline dramatically. When he begins his prophetic career, the two kingdoms live in prosperity, harmony, and stability. Within fifty years, the ten tribes of the northern kingdom are a distant memory, exiled to the edges of the Assyrian Empire in 722 BCE. The fortunes of southern kingdom of *Yehuda* are only slightly better; most of its cities are destroyed in the Assyrian invasion of 701 BCE.

Yeshayahu is given the task of explaining why the tragedies are occurring and advising what changes need to be made. Although he uttered many pronouncements of rebuke, *Yeshayahu* is most well-known for his prophecies of consolation and hope. Despite the bleak circumstances of the present, *Yeshayahu* is always able to describe a brighter future which features return and redemption, with the Jewish people living peacefully in their land. These images remain an integral part of Israel's consciousness until today.

The political quiet that exists at the beginning of his life is disturbed with the emergence of the rapacious Assyrian Empire in the east. The kings of the region face two options – either submit to the might of the Assyrians, or attempt to form alliances to oppose the behemoth rising against them. In fact, the kings of Aram and *Yisrael* invade *Yehuda* in 733, in an attempt to pressure King *Achaz* into joining their coalition against Assyria. Instead of supporting them, *Achaz* chooses to ask the Assyrian king *Tiglat-Pileser* for assistance, a decision that would prove nearly fatal for the Jewish people. *Yeshayahu* condemns this decision.

More important to *Yeshayahu*, however, is his attempt to change the people's focus from politics to morality. While they are engaged in political intrigue, the people perform their ritual obligations almost robotically, without passion, and they fail to maintain a just and moral society. Indeed, other prophets among *Yeshayahu's* contemporaries (*Micha, Hoshea,* and *Amos*) also rail against these failures. Their message is clear: If the people can improve their personal lives, live in justice and peace with each other and serve *Hashem* with sincerity, then the political turmoil will disappear.

The structure of the book reflects these messages. The first section (chapters 1–6) serves as an introduction to the entire book, contrasting the present sinful state of the people with the wonderful potential future that awaits them. The next section (chapters 7–12) describes the immediate threat of the Assyrian invasion, and then its ultimate defeat by a son of *David* who will bring peace and righteousness to Israel. Chapters 13–23 describe a series of judgments against the nations, and chapters 24–27 describe judgments against *Yehuda*. After eight more chapters discussing the woes of Israel and other nations, there is a four-chapter historical summary of the events of *Yeshayahu's* time (chapters 36–39). Finally, there is a long section of prophecies of consolation that spans from the relief of immediate troubles into the future beyond the horizon, when the People of Israel will return from exile and dwell again in the Land of Israel.

Chart of the Empires that Ruled the Land of Israel

Yeshayahu lived during the period when the Assyrian Empire controlled the region. At this time, the Assyrians captured the Kingdom of *Yisrael* and exiled its inhabitants, causing….the ten tribes of 5–8 Israel to be "lost." *Yeshayahu* also witnessed the capture of some of the cities of the Kingdom of *Yehuda* and the attempt by the Assyrian army to capture *Yerushalayim*. If not for God's intervention, the Kingdom of *Yehuda* would also have fallen to the Assyrians. The Assyrian Empire was just one of many empires that controlled all or parts of the Holy Land over the ages. The following is a list of the major empires that controlled the Land of Israel throughout history, and some of the significant events that occurred during their reigns.

Empire	Years	Significant Events in the Land of Israel	Relevant Verses
Canaanite	c. 15th century BCE–1273 BCE	*Avraham* arrives in the land of Canaan. *Hashem* promises that his descendants, through *Yitzchak*, will inherit the land.	Genesis 12:1–9, 13:14–17, 15:18–21, 17:8, 21:12
Israelite	1273–586 BCE	*Yehoshua* conquers the Land of Israel from the Canaanites, fulfilling *Hashem*'s promise to give it to *Avraham*'s descendants. The Children of Israel live and rule in the Land of Israel until the Babylonian exile.	The events of this time are described throughout the books of the Prophets.
Assyrian	740–c. 625 BCE	Assyrian captivity of parts of the kingdom of *Yisrael* begins in approximately 740 BCE. In 721 BCE, the entire kingdom of *Yisrael* is captured by the Assyrians. The ten tribes that belonged to the kingdom are exiled and "lost." Sennacherib captures some cities belonging to the kingdom *Yehuda* and lays siege around *Yerushalayim* in approximately 701 BCE, but is not successful in conquering the capital city.	II Kings 15:29, I Chronicles 5:26, II Kings 17:1–6, II Kings 18:9–12, II Kings 18:13–19:37, Isaiah 36–37
Egyptian	609–605 BCE	King *Yoshiyahu* of the kingdom of *Yehuda* refuses to let Pharaoh Neco pass through his land on his way to fight with the Assyrians against the Babylonians at Carchemish. Instead, the Judeans fight against the Egyptians at *Megiddo* and *Yoshiyahu* is killed in 609 BCE. The kingdom of *Yehuda* becomes subordinate to the Egyptians.	II Kings 23:29–30, II Chronicles 35:20–25
Babylonian	605–538 BCE	The Babylonian Empire takes control of the kingdom of *Yehuda*. Ignoring *Yirmiyahu*'s call to accept the reign of the Babylonians, the people of *Yehuda* try to free themselves of Babylonian rule. This angers Nebuchadnezzar and leads to the exile. The exile of the artisans and craftsmen takes place in 597 BCE, followed by the destruction of the first *Beit Hamikdash* and the exile of the rest of the people in 586 BCE.	II Kings 24–25
Persian	538–333 BCE	Cyrus of Persia defeats the Babylonians and declares that the Jews can return to the Land of Israel and rebuild the *Beit Hamikdash* in 538 BCE. Construction of the Second Temple is completed in the 6th year of King Darius.	Ezra 1:1–3, 6:13–15
Seleucid	333–142 BCE	Alexander the Great conquers the region in 333 BCE. During the reign of King Antiochus IV, the *Beit Hamikdash* is desecrated, leading to the Maccabean revolt. As a result, the Second Temple is cleansed and re-dedicated, and the Maccabees establish semi-autonomy in 142 BCE.	
Hasmonean	142–63 BCE	The Hasmonean dynasty, established by the Maccabbees, becomes semi-autonomous in 142 BCE, and eventually gains independence from the disintegrating Seleucid empire. The Jews thus regain full control of the Land of Israel for the first time since the Babylonian exile.	

Empire	Years	Significant Events in the Land of Israel	Relevant Verses
Roman	63 BCE–313 CE	The Land of Israel came under Roman rule in 63 BCE. The second *Beit Hamikdash* is destroyed by the Romans in 70 CE, and the *Bar Kochba* revolt takes place in 132 CE.	
Byzantine	313–637	In response to religious persecution, a fixed Hebrew calendar is established in approximately 360 CE. The Jerusalem Talmud is completed in approximately 400 CE.	
Muslim	638–1099	The Dome of the Rock is built on the site of the Holy Temple in 688–691 CE. Jewish scribes, known as the Masorites, create the Masoretic text of the Bible working mainly in *Tiveria* (Tiberias) and *Yerushalayim*.	
Crusaders	1099–1291	The Crusaders come from Europe to capture the Holy Land, following an appeal by Pope Urbani II. On their way, they massacre those who are not Christian. Thousands of Jews are killed.	
Mamluk	1291–1517	In the 1400s, the Sephardic community established by the Ramban (Nachmanides) moves inside the city walls of *Yerushalayim* and establishes the Ramban Synagogue, which still exists today. After the expulsion from Spain in 1492, more Jews begin migrating to the Land of Israel. Many settle the city of *Tzfat*, which eventually becomes the center of *Kabbalah* (Jewish mysticism).	
Ottoman	1517–1917	Under Sultan Suleiman the Magnificent, the walls of Jerusalem are rebuilt in 1535–1538. These are the current walls of Jerusalem's Old City. Also during Ottoman rule, the First *Aliyah* (wave of immigration to Israel) and Second *Aliyah* both take place, in 1882–1903 and 1904–1914 respectively.	
British	1917–1948	While the Land of Israel is under British control, the world experiences World War II and the Holocaust. In addition, more waves of immigration to the Land of Israel take place, namely the Third *Aliyah* in 1919–1923, the Fourth *Aliyah* in 1924–1928, the Fifth *Aliyah* in 1929–1939 and *Aliyah Bet*, in 1934–1948.	
Jewish	1948–Present	The declaration of the State of Israel on May 14, 1948 (the 5th of *Iyar* 5708) begins the return of Jewish sovereignty to the Land of Israel for the first time in approximately 2,000 years.	

1 ¹ The prophecies of *Yeshayahu* son of *Amotz*, who prophesied concerning *Yehuda* and *Yerushalayim* in the reigns of *Uzziyahu, Yotam, Achaz,* and *Chizkiyahu,* kings of *Yehuda*.

א חֲזוֹן יְשַׁעְיָהוּ בֶן־אָמוֹץ אֲשֶׁר חָזָה עַל־יְהוּדָה וִירוּשָׁלֻם בִּימֵי עֻזִּיָּהוּ יוֹתָם אָחָז יְחִזְקִיָּהוּ מַלְכֵי יְהוּדָה:

² Hear, O heavens, and give ear, O earth, For *Hashem* has spoken: "I reared children and brought them up – And they have rebelled against Me!

ב שִׁמְעוּ שָׁמַיִם וְהַאֲזִינִי אֶרֶץ כִּי יְהוָה דִּבֵּר בָּנִים גִּדַּלְתִּי וְרוֹמַמְתִּי וְהֵם פָּשְׁעוּ בִי:

³ An ox knows its owner, An ass its master's crib: *Yisrael* does not know, My people takes no thought."

ג יָדַע שׁוֹר קֹנֵהוּ וַחֲמוֹר אֵבוּס בְּעָלָיו יִשְׂרָאֵל לֹא יָדַע עַמִּי לֹא הִתְבּוֹנָן:

⁴ Ah, sinful nation! People laden with iniquity! Brood of evildoers! Depraved children! They have forsaken *Hashem,* Spurned the Holy One of *Yisrael,* Turned their backs [on Him].

ד הוֹי גּוֹי חֹטֵא עַם כֶּבֶד עָוֹן זֶרַע מְרֵעִים בָּנִים מַשְׁחִיתִים עָזְבוּ אֶת־יְהוָה נִאֲצוּ אֶת־קְדוֹשׁ יִשְׂרָאֵל נָזֹרוּ אָחוֹר:

⁵ Why do you seek further beatings, That you continue to offend? Every head is ailing, And every heart is sick.

ה עַל מֶה תֻכּוּ עוֹד תּוֹסִיפוּ סָרָה כָּל־רֹאשׁ לָחֳלִי וְכָל־לֵבָב דַּוָּי:

⁶ From head to foot No spot is sound: All bruises, and welts, And festering sores – Not pressed out, not bound up, Not softened with oil.

ו מִכַּף־רֶגֶל וְעַד־רֹאשׁ אֵין־בּוֹ מְתֹם פֶּצַע וְחַבּוּרָה וּמַכָּה טְרִיָּה לֹא־זֹרוּ וְלֹא חֻבָּשׁוּ וְלֹא רֻכְּכָה בַּשָּׁמֶן:

⁷ Your land is a waste, Your cities burnt down; Before your eyes, the yield of your soil Is consumed by strangers – A wasteland as overthrown by strangers!

ז אַרְצְכֶם שְׁמָמָה עָרֵיכֶם שְׂרֻפוֹת אֵשׁ אַדְמַתְכֶם לְנֶגְדְּכֶם זָרִים אֹכְלִים אֹתָהּ וּשְׁמָמָה כְּמַהְפֵּכַת זָרִים:

⁸ Fair *Tzion* is left Like a booth in a vineyard, Like a hut in a cucumber field, Like a city beleaguered.

ח וְנוֹתְרָה בַת־צִיּוֹן כְּסֻכָּה בְכָרֶם כִּמְלוּנָה בְמִקְשָׁה כְּעִיר נְצוּרָה:

⁹ Had not the Lᴏʀᴅ of Hosts Left us some survivors, We should be like Sodom, Another Gomorrah.

ט לוּלֵי יְהוָה צְבָאוֹת הוֹתִיר לָנוּ שָׂרִיד כִּמְעַט כִּסְדֹם הָיִינוּ לַעֲמֹרָה דָּמִינוּ:

lu-LAY a-do-NAI tz'-va-OT ho-TEER LA-nu sa-REED kim-AT kis-DOM ha-YEE-nu la-a-mo-RAH da-MEE-nu

¹⁰ Hear the word of *Hashem,* You chieftains of Sodom; Give ear to our God's instruction, You folk of Gomorrah!

י שִׁמְעוּ דְבַר־יְהוָה קְצִינֵי סְדֹם הַאֲזִינוּ תּוֹרַת אֱלֹהֵינוּ עַם עֲמֹרָה:

Mount Sodom on the coast of the Dead Sea

1:9 We should be like Sodom, another Gomorrah The first chapter of *Sefer Yeshayahu* begins with a description of the devastation caused to *Yehuda* during the Assyrian invasion of 701 BCE. Only through *Hashem*'s kindness and mercy, and not through their own merit and strength, do the Jewish people merit to remain in the land. The people remark that they were nearly wiped out, as were Sodom and Gomorrah in times of old. By way of allusion, in verse 10 the prophet begins to convey the message that the reason for this was because they had adopted the ways of Sodom and Gomorrah, oppressing the poor while feigning piety. In order to remain in the Land of Israel, they must learn to behave towards everyone with genuine piety.

11 "What need have I of all your sacrifices?" Says *Hashem*. "I am sated with burnt offerings of rams, And suet of fatlings, And blood of bulls; And I have no delight In lambs and he-goats.

יא לָמָּה־לִּי רֹב־זִבְחֵיכֶם יֹאמַר יְהֹוָה שָׂבַעְתִּי עֹלוֹת אֵילִים וְחֵלֶב מְרִיאִים וְדַם פָּרִים וּכְבָשִׂים וְעַתּוּדִים לֹא חָפָצְתִּי:

12 That you come to appear before Me – Who asked that of you? Trample My courts

יב כִּי תָבֹאוּ לֵרָאוֹת פָּנָי מִי־בִקֵּשׁ זֹאת מִיֶּדְכֶם רְמֹס חֲצֵרָי:

13 no more; Bringing oblations is futile, Incense is offensive to Me. New moon and *Shabbat*, Proclaiming of solemnities, Assemblies with iniquity, I cannot abide.

יג לֹא תוֹסִיפוּ הָבִיא מִנְחַת־שָׁוְא קְטֹרֶת תּוֹעֵבָה הִיא לִי חֹדֶשׁ וְשַׁבָּת קְרֹא מִקְרָא לֹא־אוּכַל אָוֶן וַעֲצָרָה:

14 Your new moons and fixed seasons Fill Me with loathing; They are become a burden to Me, I cannot endure them.

יד חָדְשֵׁיכֶם וּמוֹעֲדֵיכֶם שָׂנְאָה נַפְשִׁי הָיוּ עָלַי לָטֹרַח נִלְאֵיתִי נְשֹׂא:

15 And when you lift up your hands, I will turn My eyes away from you; Though you pray at length, I will not listen. Your hands are stained with crime –

טו וּבְפָרִשְׂכֶם כַּפֵּיכֶם אַעְלִים עֵינַי מִכֶּם גַּם כִּי־תַרְבּוּ תְפִלָּה אֵינֶנִּי שֹׁמֵעַ יְדֵיכֶם דָּמִים מָלֵאוּ:

16 Wash yourselves clean; Put your evil doings Away from My sight. Cease to do evil;

טז רַחֲצוּ הִזַּכּוּ הָסִירוּ רֹעַ מַעַלְלֵיכֶם מִנֶּגֶד עֵינָי חִדְלוּ הָרֵעַ:

17 Learn to do good. Devote yourselves to justice; Aid the wronged. Uphold the rights of the orphan; Defend the cause of the widow.

יז לִמְדוּ הֵיטֵב דִּרְשׁוּ מִשְׁפָּט אַשְּׁרוּ חָמוֹץ שִׁפְטוּ יָתוֹם רִיבוּ אַלְמָנָה:

18 "Come, let us reach an understanding, – says *Hashem*. Be your sins like crimson, They can turn snow-white; Be they red as dyed wool, They can become like fleece."

יח לְכוּ־נָא וְנִוָּכְחָה יֹאמַר יְהֹוָה אִם־יִהְיוּ חֲטָאֵיכֶם כַּשָּׁנִים כַּשֶּׁלֶג יַלְבִּינוּ אִם־יַאְדִּימוּ כַתּוֹלָע כַּצֶּמֶר יִהְיוּ:

19 If, then, you agree and give heed, You will eat the good things of the earth;

יט אִם־תֹּאבוּ וּשְׁמַעְתֶּם טוּב הָאָרֶץ תֹּאכֵלוּ:

20 But if you refuse and disobey, You will be devoured [by] the sword. – For it was *Hashem* who spoke.

כ וְאִם־תְּמָאֲנוּ וּמְרִיתֶם חֶרֶב תְּאֻכְּלוּ כִּי פִּי יְהֹוָה דִּבֵּר:

21 Alas, she has become a harlot, The faithful city That was filled with justice, Where righteousness dwelt – But now murderers.

כא אֵיכָה הָיְתָה לְזוֹנָה קִרְיָה נֶאֱמָנָה מְלֵאֲתִי מִשְׁפָּט צֶדֶק יָלִין בָּהּ וְעַתָּה מְרַצְּחִים:

22 Your silver has turned to dross; Your wine is cut with water.

כב כַּסְפֵּךְ הָיָה לְסִיגִים סָבְאֵךְ מָהוּל בַּמָּיִם:

23 Your rulers are rogues And cronies of thieves, Every one avid for presents And greedy for gifts; They do not judge the case of the orphan, And the widow's cause never reaches them.

כג שָׂרַיִךְ סוֹרְרִים וְחַבְרֵי גַּנָּבִים כֻּלּוֹ אֹהֵב שֹׁחַד וְרֹדֵף שַׁלְמֹנִים יָתוֹם לֹא יִשְׁפֹּטוּ וְרִיב אַלְמָנָה לֹא־יָבוֹא אֲלֵיהֶם:

24 Assuredly, this is the declaration Of the Sovereign, the LORD of Hosts, The Mighty One of *Yisrael*: "Ah, I will get satisfaction from My foes; I will wreak vengeance on My enemies!

כד לָכֵן נְאֻם הָאָדוֹן יְהֹוָה צְבָאוֹת אֲבִיר יִשְׂרָאֵל הוֹי אֶנָּחֵם מִצָּרַי וְאִנָּקְמָה מֵאוֹיְבָי:

²⁵ I will turn My hand against you, And smelt out your dross as with lye, And remove all your slag:

כה וְאָשִׁיבָה יָדִי עָלַיִךְ וְאֶצְרֹף כַּבֹּר סִיגָיִךְ וְאָסִירָה כָּל־בְּדִילָיִךְ:

²⁶ I will restore your magistrates as of old, And your counselors as of yore. After that you shall be called City of Righteousness, Faithful City."

כו וְאָשִׁיבָה שֹׁפְטַיִךְ כְּבָרִאשֹׁנָה וְיֹעֲצַיִךְ כְּבַתְּחִלָּה אַחֲרֵי־כֵן יִקָּרֵא לָךְ עִיר הַצֶּדֶק קִרְיָה נֶאֱמָנָה:

²⁷ *Tzion* shall be saved in the judgment; Her repentant ones, in the retribution.

כז צִיּוֹן בְּמִשְׁפָּט תִּפָּדֶה וְשָׁבֶיהָ בִּצְדָקָה:

²⁸ But rebels and sinners shall all be crushed, And those who forsake *Hashem* shall perish.

כח וְשֶׁבֶר פֹּשְׁעִים וְחַטָּאִים יַחְדָּו וְעֹזְבֵי יְהֹוָה יִכְלוּ:

²⁹ Truly, you shall be shamed Because of the terebinths you desired, And you shall be confounded Because of the gardens you coveted.

כט כִּי יֵבֹשׁוּ מֵאֵילִים אֲשֶׁר חֲמַדְתֶּם וְתַחְפְּרוּ מֵהַגַּנּוֹת אֲשֶׁר בְּחַרְתֶּם:

³⁰ For you shall be like a terebinth Wilted of leaf, And like a garden That has no water,

ל כִּי תִהְיוּ כְּאֵלָה נֹבֶלֶת עָלֶהָ וּכְגַנָּה אֲשֶׁר־מַיִם אֵין לָהּ:

³¹ Stored wealth shall become as tow, And he who amassed it a spark; And the two shall burn together, With none to quench.

לא וְהָיָה הֶחָסֹן לִנְעֹרֶת וּפֹעֲלוֹ לְנִיצוֹץ וּבָעֲרוּ שְׁנֵיהֶם יַחְדָּו וְאֵין מְכַבֶּה:

2 ¹ The word that *Yeshayahu* son of *Amotz* prophesied concerning *Yehuda* and *Yerushalayim*.

ב א הַדָּבָר אֲשֶׁר חָזָה יְשַׁעְיָהוּ בֶּן־אָמוֹץ עַל־יְהוּדָה וִירוּשָׁלָ͏ִם:

² In the days to come, The Mount of *Hashem*'s House Shall stand firm above the mountains And tower above the hills; And all the nations Shall gaze on it with joy.

ב וְהָיָה בְּאַחֲרִית הַיָּמִים נָכוֹן יִהְיֶה הַר בֵּית־יְהֹוָה בְּרֹאשׁ הֶהָרִים וְנִשָּׂא מִגְּבָעוֹת וְנָהֲרוּ אֵלָיו כָּל־הַגּוֹיִם:

³ And the many peoples shall go and say: "Come, Let us go up to the Mount of *Hashem*, To the House of the God of *Yaakov*; That He may instruct us in His ways, And that we may walk in His paths." For instruction shall come forth from *Tzion*, The word of *Hashem* from *Yerushalayim*.

ג וְהָלְכוּ עַמִּים רַבִּים וְאָמְרוּ לְכוּ וְנַעֲלֶה אֶל־הַר־יְהֹוָה אֶל־בֵּית אֱלֹהֵי יַעֲקֹב וְיֹרֵנוּ מִדְּרָכָיו וְנֵלְכָה בְּאֹרְחֹתָיו כִּי מִצִּיּוֹן תֵּצֵא תוֹרָה וּדְבַר־יְהֹוָה מִירוּשָׁלָ͏ִם:

v'-ha-l'-KHU a-MEEM ra-BEEM v'-a-m'-RU l'-KHU v'-na-a-LEH
el har a-do-NAI el BAYT e-lo-HAY ya-a-KOV v'-yo-RAY-nu
mi-d'-ra-KHAV v'-nay-l'-KHAH b'-o-r'-kho-TAV KEE mi-tzi-YON
tay-TZAY to-RAH ud-var a-do-NAI mee-ru-sha-LA-im

 2:3 And the many peoples shall go and say According to Rabbi Joseph Rosen, a great nineteenth-century *Torah* scholar, the job of awakening the will of *Hashem* to rebuild the *Beit Hamikdash* is not limited to the Jewish people. Rather, the third Temple will be built by all of mankind. And if the *Beit Hamikdash* is to be built through prayers and good deeds, as Jewish tradition teaches, it is the prayers and good deeds of all of humanity that will rouse *Hashem* to build it. Once built, it will be a house of God for all nations. People of all backgrounds will visit there in order to learn God's *Torah* and walk in His ways. Our generation is blessed to see this promise being fulfilled, with millions of non-Jews realizing that "from *Tzion* shall come forth the *Torah* and the word of *Hashem* from *Yerushalayim*."

Rabbi Tuly Weisz welcomes Christian tourists to Israel

⁴ Thus He will judge among the nations And arbitrate for the many peoples, And they shall beat their swords into plowshares And their spears into pruning hooks: Nation shall not take up Sword against nation; They shall never again know war.

ד וְשָׁפַט בֵּין הַגּוֹיִם וְהוֹכִיחַ לְעַמִּים רַבִּים וְכִתְּתוּ חַרְבוֹתָם לְאִתִּים וַחֲנִיתוֹתֵיהֶם לְמַזְמֵרוֹת לֹא־יִשָּׂא גוֹי אֶל־גּוֹי חֶרֶב וְלֹא־יִלְמְדוּ עוֹד מִלְחָמָה:

⁵ O House of *Yaakov!* Come, let us walk By the light of *Hashem.*

ה בֵּית יַעֲקֹב לְכוּ וְנֵלְכָה בְּאוֹר יְהֹוָה:

⁶ For you have forsaken [the ways of] your people, O House of *Yaakov!* For they are full [of practices] from the East, And of soothsaying like the Philistines; They abound in customs of the aliens.

ו כִּי נָטַשְׁתָּה עַמְּךָ בֵּית יַעֲקֹב כִּי מָלְאוּ מִקֶּדֶם וְעֹנְנִים כַּפְּלִשְׁתִּים וּבְיַלְדֵי נָכְרִים יַשְׂפִּיקוּ:

⁷ Their land is full of silver and gold, There is no limit to their treasures; Their land is full of horses, There is no limit to their chariots.

ז וַתִּמָּלֵא אַרְצוֹ כֶּסֶף וְזָהָב וְאֵין קֵצֶה לְאֹצְרֹתָיו וַתִּמָּלֵא אַרְצוֹ סוּסִים וְאֵין קֵצֶה לְמַרְכְּבֹתָיו:

⁸ And their land is full of idols; They bow down to the work of their hands, To what their own fingers have wrought.

ח וַתִּמָּלֵא אַרְצוֹ אֱלִילִים לְמַעֲשֵׂה יָדָיו יִשְׁתַּחֲווּ לַאֲשֶׁר עָשׂוּ אֶצְבְּעֹתָיו:

⁹ But man shall be humbled, And mortal brought low – Oh, do not forgive them!

ט וַיִּשַּׁח אָדָם וַיִּשְׁפַּל־אִישׁ וְאַל־תִּשָּׂא לָהֶם:

¹⁰ Go deep into the rock, Bury yourselves in the ground, Before the terror of *Hashem* And His dread majesty!

י בּוֹא בַצּוּר וְהִטָּמֵן בֶּעָפָר מִפְּנֵי פַּחַד יְהֹוָה וּמֵהֲדַר גְּאֹנוֹ:

¹¹ Man's haughty look shall be brought low, And the pride of mortals shall be humbled. None but *Hashem* shall be Exalted in that day.

יא עֵינֵי גַבְהוּת אָדָם שָׁפֵל וְשַׁח רוּם אֲנָשִׁים וְנִשְׂגַּב יְהֹוָה לְבַדּוֹ בַּיּוֹם הַהוּא:

¹² For the LORD of Hosts has ready a day Against all that is proud and arrogant, Against all that is lofty – so that it is brought low:

יב כִּי יוֹם לַיהֹוָה צְבָאוֹת עַל כָּל־גֵּאֶה וָרָם וְעַל כָּל־נִשָּׂא וְשָׁפֵל:

¹³ Against all the cedars of Lebanon, Tall and stately, And all the oaks of Bashan;

יג וְעַל כָּל־אַרְזֵי הַלְּבָנוֹן הָרָמִים וְהַנִּשָּׂאִים וְעַל כָּל־אַלּוֹנֵי הַבָּשָׁן:

¹⁴ Against all the high mountains And all the lofty hills;

יד וְעַל כָּל־הֶהָרִים הָרָמִים וְעַל כָּל־הַגְּבָעוֹת הַנִּשָּׂאוֹת:

¹⁵ Against every soaring tower And every mighty wall;

טו וְעַל כָּל־מִגְדָּל גָּבֹהַ וְעַל כָּל־חוֹמָה בְצוּרָה:

¹⁶ Against all the ships of Tarshish And all the gallant barks.

טז וְעַל כָּל־אֳנִיּוֹת תַּרְשִׁישׁ וְעַל כָּל־שְׂכִיּוֹת הַחֶמְדָּה:

¹⁷ Then man's haughtiness shall be humbled And the pride of man brought low. None but *Hashem* shall be Exalted in that day.

יז וְשַׁח גַּבְהוּת הָאָדָם וְשָׁפֵל רוּם אֲנָשִׁים וְנִשְׂגַּב יְהֹוָה לְבַדּוֹ בַּיּוֹם הַהוּא:

¹⁸ As for idols, they shall vanish completely.

יח וְהָאֱלִילִים כָּלִיל יַחֲלֹף:

Isaiah

19 And men shall enter caverns in the rock And hollows in the ground – Before the terror of *Hashem* And His dread majesty, When He comes forth to overawe the earth.

יט וּבָאוּ בִּמְעָרוֹת צֻרִים וּבִמְחִלּוֹת עָפָר מִפְּנֵי פַּחַד יְהֹוָה וּמֵהֲדַר גְּאוֹנוֹ בְּקוּמוֹ לַעֲרֹץ הָאָרֶץ:

20 On that day, men shall fling away, To the flying foxes and the bats, The idols of silver And the idols of gold Which they made for worshiping.

כ בַּיּוֹם הַהוּא יַשְׁלִיךְ הָאָדָם אֵת אֱלִילֵי כַסְפּוֹ וְאֵת אֱלִילֵי זְהָבוֹ אֲשֶׁר עָשׂוּ־לוֹ לְהִשְׁתַּחֲוֹת לַחְפֹּר פֵּרוֹת וְלָעֲטַלֵּפִים:

21 And they shall enter the clefts in the rocks And the crevices in the cliffs, Before the terror of *Hashem* And His dread majesty, When He comes forth to overawe the earth.

כא לָבוֹא בְּנִקְרוֹת הַצֻּרִים וּבִסְעִפֵי הַסְּלָעִים מִפְּנֵי פַּחַד יְהֹוָה וּמֵהֲדַר גְּאוֹנוֹ בְּקוּמוֹ לַעֲרֹץ הָאָרֶץ:

22 Oh, cease to glorify man, Who has only a breath in his nostrils! For by what does he merit esteem?

כב חִדְלוּ לָכֶם מִן־הָאָדָם אֲשֶׁר נְשָׁמָה בְּאַפּוֹ כִּי־בַמֶּה נֶחְשָׁב הוּא:

3 **1** For lo! The Sovereign LORD of Hosts Will remove from *Yerushalayim* and from *Yehuda* Prop and stay, Every prop of food And every prop of water:

ג א כִּי הִנֵּה הָאָדוֹן יְהֹוָה צְבָאוֹת מֵסִיר מִירוּשָׁלַ͏ִם וּמִיהוּדָה מַשְׁעֵן וּמַשְׁעֵנָה כֹּל מִשְׁעַן־לֶחֶם וְכֹל מִשְׁעַן־מָיִם:

2 Soldier and warrior, Magistrate and *Navi*, Augur and elder;

ב גִּבּוֹר וְאִישׁ מִלְחָמָה שׁוֹפֵט וְנָבִיא וְקֹסֵם וְזָקֵן:

3 Captain of fifty, Magnate and counselor, Skilled artisan and expert enchanter;

ג שַׂר־חֲמִשִּׁים וּנְשׂוּא פָנִים וְיוֹעֵץ וַחֲכַם חֲרָשִׁים וּנְבוֹן לָחַשׁ:

4 And He will make boys their rulers, And babes shall govern them.

ד וְנָתַתִּי נְעָרִים שָׂרֵיהֶם וְתַעֲלוּלִים יִמְשְׁלוּ־בָם:

v'-na-ta-TEE n'-a-REEM sa-ray-HEM v'-ta-a-lu-LEEM yim-sh'-lu VAM

5 So the people shall oppress one another – Each oppressing his fellow: The young shall bully the old; And the despised [shall bully] the honored.

ה וְנִגַּשׂ הָעָם אִישׁ בְּאִישׁ וְאִישׁ בְּרֵעֵהוּ יִרְהֲבוּ הַנַּעַר בַּזָּקֵן וְהַנִּקְלֶה בַּנִּכְבָּד:

6 For should a man seize his brother, In whose father's house there is clothing: "Come, be a chief over us, And let this ruin be under your care,"

ו כִּי־יִתְפֹּשׂ אִישׁ בְּאָחִיו בֵּית אָבִיו שִׂמְלָה לְכָה קָצִין תִּהְיֶה־לָּנוּ וְהַמַּכְשֵׁלָה הַזֹּאת תַּחַת יָדֶךָ:

3:4 And He will make boys their rulers After the removal of the competent and qualified leadership of *Yehuda* (verses 1–3), young and inexperienced leaders will rule in their place. These rulers will lead the people even further astray from *Hashem*. The chapter describes a collapse of social order under their governance; the people oppress one another, there is a lack of respect between friends and the young behave with arrogance towards their elders, as the nation continues on its path of Sodom-like behavior (verse 9). In verses 10–11, *Yeshayahu* promises that *Hashem* will reward the righteous and punish the wicked. Leadership carries with it tremendous responsibility: A leader has the potential to carry his nation to great heights or to lead it to its downfall. Jewish leadership in the Land of Israel is charged with the responsibility to lead the nation in justice and morality. Anything less than that is intolerable in *Hashem*'s eyes, and will be punished.

Statue of King *David* in *Yerushalayim*

7 The other will thereupon protest, "I will not be a dresser of wounds, With no food or clothing in my own house. You shall not make me chief of a people!"

ז יִשָּׂא בַיּוֹם הַהוּא לֵאמֹר לֹא־אֶהְיֶה חֹבֵשׁ וּבְבֵיתִי אֵין לֶחֶם וְאֵין שִׂמְלָה לֹא תְשִׂימֻנִי קְצִין עָם:

8 Ah, *Yerushalayim* has stumbled, And *Yehuda* has fallen, Because by word and deed They insult *Hashem*, Defying His majestic glance.

ח כִּי כָשְׁלָה יְרוּשָׁלַםִ וִיהוּדָה נָפָל כִּי־לְשׁוֹנָם וּמַעַלְלֵיהֶם אֶל־יְהֹוָה לַמְרוֹת עֵנֵי כְבוֹדוֹ:

9 Their partiality in judgment accuses them; They avow their sins like Sodom, They do not conceal them. Woe to them! For ill Have they served themselves.

ט הַכָּרַת פְּנֵיהֶם עָנְתָה בָּם וְחַטָּאתָם כִּסְדֹם הִגִּידוּ לֹא כִחֵדוּ אוֹי לְנַפְשָׁם כִּי־גָמְלוּ לָהֶם רָעָה:

10 (Hail the just man, for he shall fare well; He shall eat the fruit of his works.

י אִמְרוּ צַדִּיק כִּי־טוֹב כִּי־פְרִי מַעַלְלֵיהֶם יֹאכֵלוּ:

11 Woe to the wicked man, for he shall fare ill; As his hands have dealt, so shall it be done to him.)

יא אוֹי לְרָשָׁע רָע כִּי־גְמוּל יָדָיו יֵעָשֶׂה לּוֹ:

12 My people's rulers are babes, It is governed by women. O my people! Your leaders are misleaders; They have confused the course of your paths.

יב עַמִּי נֹגְשָׂיו מְעוֹלֵל וְנָשִׁים מָשְׁלוּ בוֹ עַמִּי מְאַשְּׁרֶיךָ מַתְעִים וְדֶרֶךְ אֹרְחֹתֶיךָ בִּלֵּעוּ:

13 *Hashem* stands up to plead a cause, He rises to champion peoples.

יג נִצָּב לָרִיב יְהֹוָה וְעֹמֵד לָדִין עַמִּים:

14 *Hashem* will bring this charge Against the elders and officers of His people: "It is you who have ravaged the vineyard; That which was robbed from the poor is in your houses.

יד יְהֹוָה בְּמִשְׁפָּט יָבוֹא עִם־זִקְנֵי עַמּוֹ וְשָׂרָיו וְאַתֶּם בִּעַרְתֶּם הַכֶּרֶם גְּזֵלַת הֶעָנִי בְּבָתֵּיכֶם:

15 How dare you crush My people And grind the faces of the poor?" – says Hashem my God of Hosts.

טו מַלְּכֶם [מַה־] [לָּכֶם] תְּדַכְּאוּ עַמִּי וּפְנֵי עֲנִיִּים תִּטְחָנוּ נְאֻם־אֲדֹנָי יְהֹוִה צְבָאוֹת:

16 *Hashem* said: "Because the daughters of *Tzion* Are so vain And walk with heads thrown back, With roving eyes, And with mincing gait, Making a tinkling with their feet" –

טז וַיֹּאמֶר יְהֹוָה יַעַן כִּי גָבְהוּ בְּנוֹת צִיּוֹן וַתֵּלַכְנָה נטוות [נְטוּיוֹת] גָּרוֹן וּמְשַׂקְּרוֹת עֵינָיִם הָלוֹךְ וְטָפֹף תֵּלַכְנָה וּבְרַגְלֵיהֶם תְּעַכַּסְנָה:

17 My Lord will bare the pates Of the daughters of *Tzion*, *Hashem* will uncover their heads.

יז וְשִׂפַּח אֲדֹנָי קָדְקֹד בְּנוֹת צִיּוֹן וַיהֹוָה פָּתְהֵן יְעָרֶה:

18 In that day, *Hashem* will strip off the finery of the anklets, the fillets, and the crescents;

יח בַּיּוֹם הַהוּא יָסִיר אֲדֹנָי אֵת תִּפְאֶרֶת הָעֲכָסִים וְהַשְּׁבִיסִים וְהַשַּׂהֲרֹנִים:

19 of the eardrops, the bracelets, and the veils;

יט הַנְּטִיפוֹת וְהַשֵּׁירוֹת וְהָרְעָלוֹת:

20 the turbans, the armlets, and the sashes; of the talismans and the amulets;

כ הַפְּאֵרִים וְהַצְּעָדוֹת וְהַקִּשֻּׁרִים וּבָתֵּי הַנֶּפֶשׁ וְהַלְּחָשִׁים:

21 the signet rings and the nose rings;

כא הַטַּבָּעוֹת וְנִזְמֵי הָאָף:

22 of the festive robes, the mantles, and the shawls; the purses,

כב הַמַּחֲלָצוֹת וְהַמַּעֲטָפוֹת וְהַמִּטְפָּחוֹת וְהָחֲרִיטִים:

23 the lace gowns, and the linen vests; and the kerchiefs and the capes.

כג וְהַגִּלְיֹנִים וְהַסְּדִינִים וְהַצְּנִיפוֹת וְהָרְדִידִים:

24 And then – Instead of perfume, there shall be rot; And instead of an apron, a rope; Instead of a diadem of beaten-work, A shorn head; Instead of a rich robe, A girding of sackcloth; A burn instead of beauty.

כד וְהָיָה תַחַת בֹּשֶׂם מַק יִהְיֶה וְתַחַת חֲגוֹרָה נִקְפָּה וְתַחַת מַעֲשֶׂה מִקְשֶׁה קָרְחָה וְתַחַת פְּתִיגִיל מַחֲגֹרֶת שָׂק כִּי־תַחַת יֹפִי:

25 Her men shall fall by the sword, Her fighting manhood in battle;

כה מְתַיִךְ בַּחֶרֶב יִפֹּלוּ וּגְבוּרָתֵךְ בַּמִּלְחָמָה:

26 And her gates shall lament and mourn, And she shall be emptied, Shall sit on the ground.

כו וְאָנוּ וְאָבְלוּ פְּתָחֶיהָ וְנִקָּתָה לָאָרֶץ תֵּשֵׁב:

4 1 In that day, seven women shall take hold of one man, saying, "We will eat our own food And wear our own clothes; Only let us be called by your name – Take away our disgrace!"

ד א וְהֶחֱזִיקוּ שֶׁבַע נָשִׁים בְּאִישׁ אֶחָד בַּיּוֹם הַהוּא לֵאמֹר לַחְמֵנוּ נֹאכֵל וְשִׂמְלָתֵנוּ נִלְבָּשׁ רַק יִקָּרֵא שִׁמְךָ עָלֵינוּ אֱסֹף חֶרְפָּתֵנוּ:

2 In that day, The radiance of *Hashem* Will lend beauty and glory, And the splendor of the land [Will give] dignity and majesty, To the survivors of *Yisrael*.

ב בַּיּוֹם הַהוּא יִהְיֶה צֶמַח יְהוָה לִצְבִי וּלְכָבוֹד וּפְרִי הָאָרֶץ לְגָאוֹן וּלְתִפְאֶרֶת לִפְלֵיטַת יִשְׂרָאֵל:

ba-YOM ha-HU yih-YEH TZE-makh a-do-NAI litz-VEE ul-kha-VOD uf-REE ha-A-retz l'-ga-ON ul-tif-E-ret lif-lay-TAT yis-ra-AYL

3 And those who remain in *Tzion* And are left in *Yerushalayim* – All who are inscribed for life in *Yerushalayim* – Shall be called holy.

ג וְהָיָה הַנִּשְׁאָר בְּצִיּוֹן וְהַנּוֹתָר בִּירוּשָׁלַ͏ִם קָדוֹשׁ יֵאָמֶר לוֹ כָּל־הַכָּתוּב לַחַיִּים בִּירוּשָׁלָ͏ִם:

4 When my Lord has washed away The filth of the daughters of *Tzion*, And from *Yerushalayim*'s midst Has rinsed out her infamy – In a spirit of judgment And in a spirit of purging –

ד אִם רָחַץ אֲדֹנָי אֵת צֹאַת בְּנוֹת־צִיּוֹן וְאֶת־דְּמֵי יְרוּשָׁלַ͏ִם יָדִיחַ מִקִּרְבָּהּ בְּרוּחַ מִשְׁפָּט וּבְרוּחַ בָּעֵר:

5 *Hashem* will create over the whole shrine and meeting place of Mount *Tzion* cloud by day and smoke with a glow of flaming fire by night. Indeed, over all the glory shall hang a canopy,

ה וּבָרָא יְהוָה עַל כָּל־מְכוֹן הַר־צִיּוֹן וְעַל־מִקְרָאֶהָ עָנָן יוֹמָם וְעָשָׁן וְנֹגַהּ אֵשׁ לֶהָבָה לָיְלָה כִּי עַל־כָּל־כָּבוֹד חֻפָּה:

6 which shall serve as a pavilion for shade from heat by day and as a shelter for protection against drenching rain.

ו וְסֻכָּה תִּהְיֶה לְצֵל־יוֹמָם מֵחֹרֶב וּלְמַחְסֶה וּלְמִסְתּוֹר מִזֶּרֶם וּמִמָּטָר:

4:2 Dignity and majesty to the survivors of *Yisrael* *Ramban* writes that nowhere in the world would one find a land which is good and bountiful when settled by its people, but desolate when ruled by foreigners. However, this is exactly what *Hashem* promises regarding the Land of Israel, as it says in *Vayikra* (26:32), "I will make the land desolate, so that your enemies who settle in it shall be appalled by it." This guarantees that throughout the ages, *Eretz Yisrael* will not accept its enemies; it will prosper only for the Children of Israel. Today, one can see this blessing fulfilled, as her children have returned home. The land which lay desolate for centuries under foreign rule again flourishes and blooms, giving dignity and majesty to her people.

Field of flowers on an Israeli kibbutz

5

ה א אָשִׁירָה נָּא לִידִידִי שִׁירַת דּוֹדִי לְכַרְמוֹ
כֶּרֶם הָיָה לִידִידִי בְּקֶרֶן בֶּן־שָׁמֶן:

1 Let me sing for my beloved A song of my lover about his vineyard. My beloved had a vineyard On a fruitful hill.

*a-SHEE-ra NA lee-dee-DEE shee-RAT do-DEE l'-khar-MO
KE-rem ha-YAH lee-dee-DEE b'-KE-ren ben SHA-men*

ב וַיְעַזְּקֵהוּ וַיְסַקְּלֵהוּ וַיִּטָּעֵהוּ שֹׂרֵק וַיִּבֶן
מִגְדָּל בְּתוֹכוֹ וְגַם־יֶקֶב חָצֵב בּוֹ וַיְקַו
לַעֲשׂוֹת עֲנָבִים וַיַּעַשׂ בְּאֻשִׁים:

2 He broke the ground, cleared it of stones, And planted it with choice vines. He built a watchtower inside it, He even hewed a wine press in it; For he hoped it would yield grapes. Instead, it yielded wild grapes.

ג וְעַתָּה יוֹשֵׁב יְרוּשָׁלַם וְאִישׁ יְהוּדָה
שִׁפְטוּ־נָא בֵּינִי וּבֵין כַּרְמִי:

3 "Now, then, Dwellers of *Yerushalayim* And men of *Yehuda*, You be the judges Between Me and My vineyard:

ד מַה־לַּעֲשׂוֹת עוֹד לְכַרְמִי וְלֹא עָשִׂיתִי
בּוֹ מַדּוּעַ קִוֵּיתִי לַעֲשׂוֹת עֲנָבִים וַיַּעַשׂ
בְּאֻשִׁים:

4 What more could have been done for My vineyard That I failed to do in it? Why, when I hoped it would yield grapes, Did it yield wild grapes?

ה וְעַתָּה אוֹדִיעָה־נָּא אֶתְכֶם אֵת אֲשֶׁר־אֲנִי
עֹשֶׂה לְכַרְמִי הָסֵר מְשׂוּכָּתוֹ וְהָיָה לְבָעֵר
פָּרֹץ גְּדֵרוֹ וְהָיָה לְמִרְמָס:

5 "Now I am going to tell you What I will do to My vineyard: I will remove its hedge, That it may be ravaged; I will break down its wall, That it may be trampled.

ו וַאֲשִׁיתֵהוּ בָתָה לֹא יִזָּמֵר וְלֹא יֵעָדֵר
וְעָלָה שָׁמִיר וָשָׁיִת וְעַל הֶעָבִים אֲצַוֶּה
מֵהַמְטִיר עָלָיו מָטָר:

6 And I will make it a desolation; It shall not be pruned or hoed, And it shall be overgrown with briers and thistles. And I will command the clouds To drop no rain on it."

ז כִּי כֶרֶם יְהוָה צְבָאוֹת בֵּית יִשְׂרָאֵל וְאִישׁ
יְהוּדָה נְטַע שַׁעֲשׁוּעָיו וַיְקַו לְמִשְׁפָּט
וְהִנֵּה מִשְׂפָּח לִצְדָקָה וְהִנֵּה צְעָקָה:

7 For the vineyard of the LORD of Hosts Is the House of *Yisrael*, And the seedlings he lovingly tended Are the men of *Yehuda*. And He hoped for justice, But behold, injustice; For equity, But behold, iniquity!

ח הוֹי מַגִּיעֵי בַיִת בְּבַיִת שָׂדֶה בְשָׂדֶה
יַקְרִיבוּ עַד אֶפֶס מָקוֹם וְהוּשַׁבְתֶּם
לְבַדְּכֶם בְּקֶרֶב הָאָרֶץ:

8 Ah, Those who add house to house And join field to field, Till there is room for none but you To dwell in the land!

Isaiah

5:1 A song of my lover about his vineyard This chapter presents one of the most famous parables in the Bible, known as the song of the vineyard. *Yeshayahu* gathers the people together to pass judgment on a disobedient vineyard. Despite the owner's efforts to care for the vineyard that he loves (a metaphor for God's care for the Children of Israel), it produces unripe grapes. Therefore, the owner announces that he will tear down the walls that protect the vineyard from thorns and other dangers of the forest. With beautiful word-play, *Yeshayahu* states, though the men of *Yehuda* are "the seedlings He lovingly tended," instead of 'justice,' in He-

brew *mishpat* (משפט), they caused 'injustice,' *mispach* (משפח). Instead of 'equity,' *tzedaka* (צדקה), they caused 'iniquity,' *tza'aka* (צעקה) (verse 7). *Hashem* will therefore remove His protection from Israel and allow for its enemies to enter. The theme of injustice and oppression leading to destruction plays a prominent role in *Yeshayahu's* prophecies. Ultimately, *Tzion* will be redeemed through justice and righteousness (Isaiah 1:27).

צדקה
משפט

Ripe grapes on a vine in Kfar Tabor

9 In my hearing [said] the Lord of Hosts: Surely, great houses Shall lie forlorn, Spacious and splendid ones Without occupants.

ט בְּאָזְנָי יְהֹוָה צְבָאוֹת אִם־לֹא בָּתִּים רַבִּים לְשַׁמָּה יִהְיוּ גְּדֹלִים וְטוֹבִים מֵאֵין יוֹשֵׁב:

10 For ten acres of vineyard Shall yield just one *bat*, And a field sown with a *chomer* of seed Shall yield a mere *efah*.

י כִּי עֲשֶׂרֶת צִמְדֵּי־כֶרֶם יַעֲשׂוּ בַּת אֶחָת וְזֶרַע חֹמֶר יַעֲשֶׂה אֵיפָה:

11 Ah, Those who chase liquor From early in the morning, And till late in the evening Are inflamed by wine!

יא הוֹי מַשְׁכִּימֵי בַבֹּקֶר שֵׁכָר יִרְדֹּפוּ מְאַחֲרֵי בַנֶּשֶׁף יַיִן יַדְלִיקֵם:

12 Who, at their banquets, Have lyre and lute, Timbrel, flute, and wine; But who never give a thought To the plan of *Hashem*, And take no note Of what He is designing.

יב וְהָיָה כִנּוֹר וָנֶבֶל תֹּף וְחָלִיל וָיַיִן מִשְׁתֵּיהֶם וְאֵת פֹּעַל יְהֹוָה לֹא יַבִּיטוּ וּמַעֲשֵׂה יָדָיו לֹא רָאוּ:

13 Assuredly, My people will suffer exile For not giving heed, Its multitude victims of hunger And its masses parched with thirst.

יג לָכֵן גָּלָה עַמִּי מִבְּלִי־דָעַת וּכְבוֹדוֹ מְתֵי רָעָב וַהֲמוֹנוֹ צִחֵה צָמָא:

14 Assuredly, Sheol has opened wide its gullet And parted its jaws in a measureless gape; And down into it shall go, That splendor and tumult, That din and revelry.

יד לָכֵן הִרְחִיבָה שְּׁאוֹל נַפְשָׁהּ וּפָעֲרָה פִיהָ לִבְלִי־חֹק וְיָרַד הֲדָרָהּ וַהֲמוֹנָהּ וּשְׁאוֹנָהּ וְעָלֵז בָּהּ:

15 Yea, man is bowed, And mortal brought low; Brought low is the pride of the haughty.

טו וַיִּשַּׁח אָדָם וַיִּשְׁפַּל־אִישׁ וְעֵינֵי גְבֹהִים תִּשְׁפַּלְנָה:

16 And the Lord of Hosts is exalted by judgment, The Holy *Hashem* proved holy by retribution.

טז וַיִּגְבַּהּ יְהֹוָה צְבָאוֹת בַּמִּשְׁפָּט וְהָאֵל הַקָּדוֹשׁ נִקְדָּשׁ בִּצְדָקָה:

17 Then lambs shall graze As in their meadows, And strangers shall feed On the ruins of the stout.

יז וְרָעוּ כְבָשִׂים כְּדָבְרָם וְחָרְבוֹת מֵחִים גָּרִים יֹאכֵלוּ:

18 Ah, Those who haul sin with cords of falsehood And iniquity as with cart ropes!

יח הוֹי מֹשְׁכֵי הֶעָוֺן בְּחַבְלֵי הַשָּׁוְא וְכַעֲבוֹת הָעֲגָלָה חַטָּאָה:

19 Who say, "Let Him speed, let Him hasten His purpose, If we are to give thought; Let the plans of the Holy One of *Yisrael* Be quickly fulfilled, If we are to give heed."

יט הָאֹמְרִים יְמַהֵר יָחִישָׁה מַעֲשֵׂהוּ לְמַעַן נִרְאֶה וְתִקְרַב וְתָבוֹאָה עֲצַת קְדוֹשׁ יִשְׂרָאֵל וְנֵדָעָה:

20 Ah, Those who call evil good And good evil; Who present darkness as light And light as darkness; Who present bitter as sweet And sweet as bitter!

כ הוֹי הָאֹמְרִים לָרַע טוֹב וְלַטּוֹב רָע שָׂמִים חֹשֶׁךְ לְאוֹר וְאוֹר לְחֹשֶׁךְ שָׂמִים מַר לְמָתוֹק וּמָתוֹק לְמָר:

21 Ah, Those who are so wise – In their own opinion; So clever – In their own judgment!

כא הוֹי חֲכָמִים בְּעֵינֵיהֶם וְנֶגֶד פְּנֵיהֶם נְבֹנִים:

22 Ah, Those who are so doughty – As drinkers of wine, And so valiant – As mixers of drink!

כב הוֹי גִּבּוֹרִים לִשְׁתּוֹת יָיִן וְאַנְשֵׁי־חַיִל לִמְסֹךְ שֵׁכָר:

23 Who vindicate him who is in the wrong In return for a bribe, And withhold vindication From him who is in the right.

כג מַצְדִּיקֵי רָשָׁע עֵקֶב שֹׁחַד וְצִדְקַת צַדִּיקִים יָסִירוּ מִמֶּנּוּ:

9

24 Assuredly, As straw is consumed by a tongue of fire And hay shrivels as it burns, Their stock shall become like rot, And their buds shall blow away like dust. For they have rejected the instruction of the LORD of Hosts, Spurned the word of the Holy One of *Yisrael*.

כד לָכֵן כֶּאֱכֹל קַשׁ לְשׁוֹן אֵשׁ וַחֲשַׁשׁ לֶהָבָה יִרְפֶּה שָׁרְשָׁם כַּמָּק יִהְיֶה וּפִרְחָם כָּאָבָק יַעֲלֶה כִּי מָאֲסוּ אֵת תּוֹרַת יְהֹוָה צְבָאוֹת וְאֵת אִמְרַת קְדוֹשׁ־יִשְׂרָאֵל נִאֵצוּ:

25 That is why *Hashem*'s anger was roused Against His people, Why He stretched out His arm against it And struck it, So that the mountains quaked, And its corpses lay Like refuse in the streets. Yet his anger has not turned back, And His arm is outstretched still.

כה עַל־כֵּן חָרָה אַף־יְהֹוָה בְּעַמּוֹ וַיֵּט יָדוֹ עָלָיו וַיַּכֵּהוּ וַיִּרְגְּזוּ הֶהָרִים וַתְּהִי נִבְלָתָם כַּסּוּחָה בְּקֶרֶב חוּצוֹת בְּכָל־זֹאת לֹא־שָׁב אַפּוֹ וְעוֹד יָדוֹ נְטוּיָה:

26 He will raise an ensign to a nation afar, Whistle to one at the end of the earth. There it comes with lightning speed!

כו וְנָשָׂא־נֵס לַגּוֹיִם מֵרָחוֹק וְשָׁרַק לוֹ מִקְצֵה הָאָרֶץ וְהִנֵּה מְהֵרָה קַל יָבוֹא:

27 In its ranks, none is weary or stumbles, They never sleep or slumber; The belts on their waists do not come loose, Nor do the thongs of their sandals break.

כז אֵין־עָיֵף וְאֵין־כּוֹשֵׁל בּוֹ לֹא יָנוּם וְלֹא יִישָׁן וְלֹא נִפְתַּח אֵזוֹר חֲלָצָיו וְלֹא נִתַּק שְׂרוֹךְ נְעָלָיו:

28 Their arrows are sharpened, And all their bows are drawn. Their horses' hoofs are like flint, Their chariot wheels like the whirlwind.

כח אֲשֶׁר חִצָּיו שְׁנוּנִים וְכָל־קַשְּׁתֹתָיו דְּרֻכוֹת פַּרְסוֹת סוּסָיו כַּצַּר נֶחְשָׁבוּ וְגַלְגִּלָּיו כַּסּוּפָה:

29 Their roaring is like a lion's, They roar like the great beasts; When they growl and seize a prey, They carry it off and none can recover it.

כט שְׁאָגָה לוֹ כַּלָּבִיא [וְשָׁאַג] כַּכְּפִירִים וְיִנְהֹם וְיֹאחֵז טֶרֶף וְיַפְלִיט וְאֵין מַצִּיל:

30 But in that day, a roaring shall resound over him like that of the sea; and then he shall look below and, behold, Distressing darkness, with light; Darkness, in its lowering clouds.

ל וְיִנְהֹם עָלָיו בַּיּוֹם הַהוּא כְּנַהֲמַת־יָם וְנִבַּט לָאָרֶץ וְהִנֵּה־חֹשֶׁךְ צַר וָאוֹר חָשַׁךְ בַּעֲרִיפֶיהָ:

6 1 In the year that King *Uzziyahu* died, I beheld my Lord seated on a high and lofty throne; and the skirts of His robe filled the Temple.

ו א בִּשְׁנַת־מוֹת הַמֶּלֶךְ עֻזִּיָּהוּ וָאֶרְאֶה אֶת־אֲדֹנָי יֹשֵׁב עַל־כִּסֵּא רָם וְנִשָּׂא וְשׁוּלָיו מְלֵאִים אֶת־הַהֵיכָל:

*bish-nat MOT ha-ME-lekh u-zi-YA-hu va-er-EH et a-do-NAI yo-SHAYV
al ki-SAY RAM v'-ni-SA v'-shu-LAV m'-lay-EEM et ha-hay-KHAL*

6:1 I beheld my Lord seated on a high and lofty throne *Yeshayahu* sees *Hashem* sitting on His heavenly throne, with the base of the throne filling the Temple. Though He dwells on high, God is still intimately involved in this world, the manifestation of his presence emanating from the *Beit Hamikdash*. Rabbi Abraham Isaac Kook expressed a similar idea in the 1920s, when he wrote that the State of Israel will be an ideal state which will be "the pedestal of God's throne in this world, whose aim is that the Lord be acknowledged as one and His name as one."

Model of the Second *Beit Hamikdash* in *Yerushalayim*

2 Seraphs stood in attendance on Him. Each of them had six wings: with two he covered his face, with two he covered his legs, and with two he would fly.

ב שְׂרָפִים עֹמְדִים מִמַּעַל לוֹ שֵׁשׁ כְּנָפַיִם שֵׁשׁ כְּנָפַיִם לְאֶחָד בִּשְׁתַּיִם יְכַסֶּה פָנָיו וּבִשְׁתַּיִם יְכַסֶּה רַגְלָיו וּבִשְׁתַּיִם יְעוֹפֵף:

3 And one would call to the other, "Holy, holy, holy! the LORD of Hosts! His presence fills all the earth!"

ג וְקָרָא זֶה אֶל־זֶה וְאָמַר קָדוֹשׁ קָדוֹשׁ קָדוֹשׁ יְהֹוָה צְבָאוֹת מְלֹא כָל־הָאָרֶץ כְּבוֹדוֹ:

4 The doorposts would shake at the sound of the one who called, and the House kept filling with smoke.

ד וַיָּנֻעוּ אַמּוֹת הַסִּפִּים מִקּוֹל הַקּוֹרֵא וְהַבַּיִת יִמָּלֵא עָשָׁן:

5 I cried, "Woe is me; I am lost! For I am a man of unclean lips And I live among a people Of unclean lips; Yet my own eyes have beheld The King LORD of Hosts."

ה וָאֹמַר אוֹי־לִי כִי־נִדְמֵיתִי כִּי אִישׁ טְמֵא־שְׂפָתַיִם אָנֹכִי וּבְתוֹךְ עַם־טְמֵא שְׂפָתַיִם אָנֹכִי יוֹשֵׁב כִּי אֶת־הַמֶּלֶךְ יְהֹוָה צְבָאוֹת רָאוּ עֵינָי:

6 Then one of the seraphs flew over to me with a live coal, which he had taken from the *Mizbayach* with a pair of tongs.

ו וַיָּעָף אֵלַי אֶחָד מִן־הַשְּׂרָפִים וּבְיָדוֹ רִצְפָּה בְּמֶלְקַחַיִם לָקַח מֵעַל הַמִּזְבֵּחַ:

7 He touched it to my lips and declared, "Now that this has touched your lips, Your guilt shall depart And your sin be purged away."

ז וַיַּגַּע עַל־פִּי וַיֹּאמֶר הִנֵּה נָגַע זֶה עַל־שְׂפָתֶיךָ וְסָר עֲוֹנֶךָ וְחַטָּאתְךָ תְּכֻפָּר:

8 Then I heard the voice of my Lord saying, "Whom shall I send? Who will go for us?" And I said, "Here am I; send me."

ח וָאֶשְׁמַע אֶת־קוֹל אֲדֹנָי אֹמֵר אֶת־מִי אֶשְׁלַח וּמִי יֵלֶךְ־לָנוּ וָאֹמַר הִנְנִי שְׁלָחֵנִי:

9 And He said, "Go, say to that people: 'Hear, indeed, but do not understand; See, indeed, but do not grasp.'

ט וַיֹּאמֶר לֵךְ וְאָמַרְתָּ לָעָם הַזֶּה שִׁמְעוּ שָׁמוֹעַ וְאַל־תָּבִינוּ וּרְאוּ רָאוֹ וְאַל־תֵּדָעוּ:

10 Dull that people's mind, Stop its ears, And seal its eyes – Lest, seeing with its eyes And hearing with its ears, It also grasp with its mind, And repent and save itself."

י הַשְׁמֵן לֵב־הָעָם הַזֶּה וְאָזְנָיו הַכְבֵּד וְעֵינָיו הָשַׁע פֶּן־יִרְאֶה בְעֵינָיו וּבְאָזְנָיו יִשְׁמָע וּלְבָבוֹ יָבִין וָשָׁב וְרָפָא לוֹ:

11 I asked, "How long, my Lord?" And He replied: "Till towns lie waste without inhabitants And houses without people, And the ground lies waste and desolate –

יא וָאֹמַר עַד־מָתַי אֲדֹנָי וַיֹּאמֶר עַד אֲשֶׁר אִם־שָׁאוּ עָרִים מֵאֵין יוֹשֵׁב וּבָתִּים מֵאֵין אָדָם וְהָאֲדָמָה תִּשָּׁאֶה שְׁמָמָה:

12 For *Hashem* will banish the population – And deserted sites are many In the midst of the land.

יב וְרִחַק יְהֹוָה אֶת־הָאָדָם וְרַבָּה הָעֲזוּבָה בְּקֶרֶב הָאָרֶץ:

13 "But while a tenth part yet remains in it, it shall repent. It shall be ravaged like the terebinth and the oak, of which stumps are left even when they are felled: its stump shall be a holy seed."

יג וְעוֹד בָּהּ עֲשִׂרִיָּה וְשָׁבָה וְהָיְתָה לְבָעֵר כָּאֵלָה וְכָאַלּוֹן אֲשֶׁר בְּשַׁלֶּכֶת מַצֶּבֶת בָּם זֶרַע קֹדֶשׁ מַצַּבְתָּהּ:

7 1 In the reign of *Achaz* son of *Yotam* son of *Uzziyahu*, king of *Yehuda*, King Rezin of Aram and King *Pekach* son of Remaliah of *Yisrael* marched upon *Yerushalayim* to attack it; but they were not able to attack it.

ז א וַיְהִי בִּימֵי אָחָז בֶּן־יוֹתָם בֶּן־עֻזִּיָּהוּ מֶלֶךְ יְהוּדָה עָלָה רְצִין מֶלֶךְ־אֲרָם וּפֶקַח בֶּן־רְמַלְיָהוּ מֶלֶךְ־יִשְׂרָאֵל יְרוּשָׁלַ͏ִם לַמִּלְחָמָה עָלֶיהָ וְלֹא יָכֹל לְהִלָּחֵם עָלֶיהָ:

2 Now, when it was reported to the House of *David* that Aram had allied itself with *Efraim*, their hearts and the hearts of their people trembled as trees of the forest sway before a wind.

ב וַיֻּגַּד לְבֵית דָּוִד לֵאמֹר נָחָה אֲרָם עַל־אֶפְרָיִם וַיָּנַע לְבָבוֹ וּלְבַב עַמּוֹ כְּנוֹעַ עֲצֵי־יַעַר מִפְּנֵי־רוּחַ:

3 But *Hashem* said to *Yeshayahu*, "Go out with your son *Shear Yashuv* to meet *Achaz* at the end of the conduit of the Upper Pool, by the road of the Fuller's Field.

ג וַיֹּאמֶר יְהֹוָה אֶל־יְשַׁעְיָהוּ צֵא־נָא לִקְרַאת אָחָז אַתָּה וּשְׁאָר יָשׁוּב בְּנֶךָ אֶל־קְצֵה תְּעָלַת הַבְּרֵכָה הָעֶלְיוֹנָה אֶל־מְסִלַּת שְׂדֵה כוֹבֵס:

*va-YO-mer a-do-NAI el y'-sha-YA-hu tzay NA lik-RAT a-KHAZ
a-TAH ush-AR ya-SHUV b'-NE-kha el k'-TZAY t'-a-LAT
ha-b'-ray-KHAH ha-el-yo-NAH el m'-si-LAT s'-DAY kho-VAYS*

4 And say to him: Be firm and be calm. Do not be afraid and do not lose heart on account of those two smoking stubs of firebrands, on account of the raging of Rezin and his Arameans and the son of Remaliah.

ד וְאָמַרְתָּ אֵלָיו הִשָּׁמֵר וְהַשְׁקֵט אַל־תִּירָא וּלְבָבְךָ אַל־יֵרַךְ מִשְּׁנֵי זַנְבוֹת הָאוּדִים הָעֲשֵׁנִים הָאֵלֶּה בָּחֳרִי־אַף רְצִין וַאֲרָם וּבֶן־רְמַלְיָהוּ:

5 Because the Arameans – with *Efraim* and the son of Remaliah – have plotted against you, saying,

ה יַעַן כִּי־יָעַץ עָלֶיךָ אֲרָם רָעָה אֶפְרַיִם וּבֶן־רְמַלְיָהוּ לֵאמֹר:

6 'We will march against *Yehuda* and invade and conquer it, and we will set up as king in it the son of Tabeel,'

ו נַעֲלֶה בִיהוּדָה וּנְקִיצֶנָּה וְנַבְקִעֶנָּה אֵלֵינוּ וְנַמְלִיךְ מֶלֶךְ בְּתוֹכָהּ אֵת בֶּן־טָבְאַל:

7 thus said my God: It shall not succeed, It shall not come to pass.

ז כֹּה אָמַר אֲדֹנָי יְהֹוִה לֹא תָקוּם וְלֹא תִהְיֶה:

8 For the chief city of Aram is Damascus, And the chief of Damascus is Rezin;

ח כִּי רֹאשׁ אֲרָם דַּמֶּשֶׂק וְרֹאשׁ דַּמֶּשֶׂק רְצִין וּבְעוֹד שִׁשִּׁים וְחָמֵשׁ שָׁנָה יֵחַת אֶפְרַיִם מֵעָם:

9 The chief city of *Efraim* is *Shomron*, And the chief of *Shomron* is the son of Remaliah. And in another sixty-five years, *Efraim* shall be shattered as a people.* If you will not believe, for you cannot be trusted…"

ט וְרֹאשׁ אֶפְרַיִם שֹׁמְרוֹן וְרֹאשׁ שֹׁמְרוֹן בֶּן־רְמַלְיָהוּ אִם לֹא תַאֲמִינוּ כִּי לֹא תֵאָמֵנוּ:

---

* "And in another sixty-five years, *Efraim* shall be shattered as a people" brought down from verse 8 for clarity

7:3 At the end of the conduit of the Upper Pool *Yeshayahu* and his son *Shear-Yashuv* confront *Achaz*, then king of *Yehuda*, who was facing an invasion from Aram (Syria) and the northern kingdom of Israel. While *Achaz* fearfully refers to them as two powerful princes, *Yeshayahu* tries to assure him that they are only tails of smoking firebrands, meaning two kingdoms on their deathbeds. Therefore, says *Yeshayahu*, *Yehuda* has only to trust in *Hashem*, and nothing to fear. This meeting – a paradigmatic demonstration of faith in God – occurred at the Launderer's Pool. This pool of water is mentioned two other times in the Bible, and there are various opinions with regard to its exact location. One opinion is a location in the northeast of *Yerushalayim*, close to today's Lions' Gate, where a dam forms a pool carved into a riverbed. Another opinion suggests the pool was in the northwest of the city, where a channel of a riverbed was discovered. While it is unclear if one of these is the pool referred to in this verse, we do know that both of these pools were within the city limits during the time of the Second Temple, and were used by tens of thousands of pilgrims each year for drinking, cleaning and purification in preparation for their visit to the nearby *Beit Hamikdash*.

"Hezekiah's Pool" in *Yerushalayim*, a proposed location of the Upper Pool

10 *Hashem* spoke further to *Achaz*:

 י וַיּוֹסֶף יְהֹוָה דַּבֵּר אֶל־אָחָז לֵאמֹר:

11 "Ask for a sign from *Hashem* your God, anywhere down to Sheol or up to the sky."

יא שְׁאַל־לְךָ אוֹת מֵעִם יְהֹוָה אֱלֹהֶיךָ הַעְמֵק שְׁאָלָה אוֹ הַגְבֵּהַּ לְמָעְלָה:

12 But *Achaz* replied, "I will not ask, and I will not test *Hashem*."

יב וַיֹּאמֶר אָחָז לֹא־אֶשְׁאַל וְלֹא־אֲנַסֶּה אֶת־יְהֹוָה:

13 "Listen, House of *David*," [*Yeshayahu*] retorted, "is it not enough for you to treat men as helpless that you also treat my God as helpless?

יג וַיֹּאמֶר שִׁמְעוּ־נָא בֵּית דָּוִד הַמְעַט מִכֶּם הַלְאוֹת אֲנָשִׁים כִּי תַלְאוּ גַּם אֶת־אֱלֹהָי:

14 Assuredly, my Lord will give you a sign of His own accord! Look, the young woman is with child and about to give birth to a son. Let her name him *Imanu-El*.

יד לָכֵן יִתֵּן אֲדֹנָי הוּא לָכֶם אוֹת הִנֵּה הָעַלְמָה הָרָה וְיֹלֶדֶת בֵּן וְקָרָאת שְׁמוֹ עִמָּנוּ אֵל:

15 (By the time he learns to reject the bad and choose the good, people will be feeding on curds and honey.)

טו חֶמְאָה וּדְבַשׁ יֹאכֵל לְדַעְתּוֹ מָאוֹס בָּרָע וּבָחוֹר בַּטּוֹב:

16 For before the lad knows to reject the bad and choose the good, the ground whose two kings you dread shall be abandoned.

טז כִּי בְּטֶרֶם יֵדַע הַנַּעַר מָאֹס בָּרָע וּבָחֹר בַּטּוֹב תֵּעָזֵב הָאֲדָמָה אֲשֶׁר אַתָּה קָץ מִפְּנֵי שְׁנֵי מְלָכֶיהָ:

17 *Hashem* will cause to come upon you and your people and your ancestral house such days as never have come since *Efraim* turned away from *Yehuda* – that selfsame king of Assyria!

יז יָבִיא יְהֹוָה עָלֶיךָ וְעַל־עַמְּךָ וְעַל־בֵּית אָבִיךָ יָמִים אֲשֶׁר לֹא־בָאוּ לְמִיּוֹם סוּר־אֶפְרַיִם מֵעַל יְהוּדָה אֵת מֶלֶךְ אַשּׁוּר:

18 "In that day, *Hashem* will whistle to the flies at the ends of the water channels of Egypt and to the bees in the land of Assyria;

יח וְהָיָה בַּיּוֹם הַהוּא יִשְׁרֹק יְהֹוָה לַזְּבוּב אֲשֶׁר בִּקְצֵה יְאֹרֵי מִצְרָיִם וְלַדְּבוֹרָה אֲשֶׁר בְּאֶרֶץ אַשּׁוּר:

19 and they shall all come and alight in the rugged wadis, and in the clefts of the rocks, and in all the thornbrakes, and in all the watering places.

יט וּבָאוּ וְנָחוּ כֻלָּם בְּנַחֲלֵי הַבַּתּוֹת וּבִנְקִיקֵי הַסְּלָעִים וּבְכֹל הַנַּעֲצוּצִים וּבְכֹל הַנַּהֲלֹלִים:

20 "In that day, my Lord will cut away with the razor that is hired beyond the Euphrates – with the king of Assyria – the hair of the head and the hair of the legs, and it shall clip off the beard as well.

כ בַּיּוֹם הַהוּא יְגַלַּח אֲדֹנָי בְּתַעַר הַשְּׂכִירָה בְּעֶבְרֵי נָהָר בְּמֶלֶךְ אַשּׁוּר אֶת־הָרֹאשׁ וְשַׂעַר הָרַגְלָיִם וְגַם אֶת־הַזָּקָן תִּסְפֶּה:

21 And in that day, each man shall save alive a heifer of the herd and two animals of the flock.

כא וְהָיָה בַּיּוֹם הַהוּא יְחַיֶּה־אִישׁ עֶגְלַת בָּקָר וּשְׁתֵּי־צֹאן:

22 (And he shall obtain so much milk that he shall eat curds.) Thus everyone who is left in the land shall feed on curds and honey.

כב וְהָיָה מֵרֹב עֲשׂוֹת חָלָב יֹאכַל חֶמְאָה כִּי־חֶמְאָה וּדְבַשׁ יֹאכֵל כָּל־הַנּוֹתָר בְּקֶרֶב הָאָרֶץ:

23 "For in that day, every spot where there could stand a thousand vines worth a thousand *shekalim* of silver shall become a wilderness of thornbush and thistle.

כג וְהָיָה בַּיּוֹם הַהוּא יִהְיֶה כָל־מָקוֹם אֲשֶׁר יִהְיֶה־שָּׁם אֶלֶף גֶּפֶן בְּאֶלֶף כָּסֶף לַשָּׁמִיר וְלַשַּׁיִת יִהְיֶה:

²⁴ One will have to go there with bow and arrows, for the country shall be all thornbushes and thistles.

²⁵ But the perils of thornbush and thistle shall not spread to any of the hills that could only be tilled with a hoe; and here cattle shall be let loose, and sheep and goats shall tramp about."

8 ¹ *Hashem* said to me, "Get yourself a large sheet and write on it in common script 'For Maher-shalal-hash-baz';

² and call reliable witnesses, the *kohen Uriya* and *Zecharya* son of Je*Berechiah*, to witness for Me."

³ I was intimate with the *Neviah*, and she conceived and bore a son; and *Hashem* said to me, "Name him Maher-shalal-hash-baz.

⁴ For before the boy learns to call 'Father' and 'Mother,' the wealth of Damascus and the spoils of *Shomron*, and the delights of Rezin and of the son of Remaliah,* shall be carried off before the king of Assyria."

⁵ Again *Hashem* spoke to me, thus:

⁶ "Because that people has spurned The gently flowing waters of Siloam" –

⁷ Assuredly, My Lord will bring up against them The mighty, massive waters of the Euphrates, The king of Assyria and all his multitude. It shall rise above all its channels, And flow over all its beds,

⁸ And swirl through *Yehuda* like a flash flood Reaching up to the neck. But with us is *Hashem*, Whose wings are spread As wide as your land is broad!

⁹ Band together, O peoples – you shall be broken! Listen to this, you remotest parts of the earth: Gird yourselves – you shall be broken; Gird yourselves – you shall be broken!

¹⁰ Hatch a plot – it shall be foiled; Agree on action – it shall not succeed. For with us is *Hashem*!

¹¹ For this is what *Hashem* said to me, when He took me by the hand and charged me not to walk in the path of that people:

כד בַּחִצִּים וּבַקֶּשֶׁת יָבוֹא שָׁמָּה כִּי־שָׁמִיר וָשַׁיִת תִּהְיֶה כָל־הָאָרֶץ:

כה וְכֹל הֶהָרִים אֲשֶׁר בַּמַּעְדֵּר יֵעָדֵרוּן לֹא־תָבוֹא שָׁמָּה יִרְאַת שָׁמִיר וָשָׁיִת וְהָיָה לְמִשְׁלַח שׁוֹר וּלְמִרְמַס שֶׂה:

א וַיֹּאמֶר יְהֹוָה אֵלַי קַח־לְךָ גִּלָּיוֹן גָּדוֹל וּכְתֹב עָלָיו בְּחֶרֶט אֱנוֹשׁ לְמַהֵר שָׁלָל חָשׁ בַּז:

ב וְאָעִידָה לִּי עֵדִים נֶאֱמָנִים אֵת אוּרִיָּה הַכֹּהֵן וְאֶת־זְכַרְיָהוּ בֶּן יְבֶרֶכְיָהוּ:

ג וָאֶקְרַב אֶל־הַנְּבִיאָה וַתַּהַר וַתֵּלֶד בֵּן וַיֹּאמֶר יְהֹוָה אֵלַי קְרָא שְׁמוֹ מַהֵר שָׁלָל חָשׁ בַּז:

ד כִּי בְּטֶרֶם יֵדַע הַנַּעַר קְרֹא אָבִי וְאִמִּי יִשָּׂא אֶת־חֵיל דַּמֶּשֶׂק וְאֵת שְׁלַל שֹׁמְרוֹן לִפְנֵי מֶלֶךְ אַשּׁוּר:

ה וַיֹּסֶף יְהֹוָה דַּבֵּר אֵלַי עוֹד לֵאמֹר:

ו יַעַן כִּי מָאַס הָעָם הַזֶּה אֵת מֵי הַשִּׁלֹחַ הַהֹלְכִים לְאַט וּמְשׂוֹשׂ אֶת־רְצִין וּבֶן־רְמַלְיָהוּ:

ז וְלָכֵן הִנֵּה אֲדֹנָי מַעֲלֶה עֲלֵיהֶם אֶת־מֵי הַנָּהָר הָעֲצוּמִים וְהָרַבִּים אֶת־מֶלֶךְ אַשּׁוּר וְאֶת־כָּל־כְּבוֹדוֹ וְעָלָה עַל־כָּל־אֲפִיקָיו וְהָלַךְ עַל־כָּל־גְּדוֹתָיו:

ח וְחָלַף בִּיהוּדָה שָׁטַף וְעָבַר עַד־צַוָּאר יַגִּיעַ וְהָיָה מֻטּוֹת כְּנָפָיו מְלֹא רֹחַב־אַרְצְךָ עִמָּנוּ אֵל:

ט רֹעוּ עַמִּים וָחֹתּוּ וְהַאֲזִינוּ כֹּל מֶרְחַקֵּי־אָרֶץ הִתְאַזְּרוּ וָחֹתּוּ הִתְאַזְּרוּ וָחֹתּוּ:

י עֻצוּ עֵצָה וְתֻפָר דַּבְּרוּ דָבָר וְלֹא יָקוּם כִּי עִמָּנוּ אֵל:

יא כִּי כֹה אָמַר יְהֹוָה אֵלַי כְּחֶזְקַת הַיָּד וְיִסְּרֵנִי מִלֶּכֶת בְּדֶרֶךְ הָעָם־הַזֶּה לֵאמֹר:

---

* "and the delights of Rezin and of the son of Remaliah" brought up from verse 6 for clarity

12 "You must not call conspiracy All that that people calls conspiracy, Nor revere what it reveres, Nor hold it in awe.

יב לֹא־תֹאמְרוּן קֶשֶׁר לְכֹל אֲשֶׁר־יֹאמַר הָעָם הַזֶּה קָשֶׁר וְאֶת־מוֹרָאוֹ לֹא־תִירְאוּ וְלֹא תַעֲרִיצוּ:

13 None but the LORD of Hosts Shall you account holy; Give reverence to Him alone, Hold Him alone in awe.

יג אֶת־יְהוָה צְבָאוֹת אֹתוֹ תַקְדִּישׁוּ וְהוּא מוֹרַאֲכֶם וְהוּא מַעֲרִצְכֶם:

14 He shall be for a sanctuary, A stone men strike against: A rock men stumble over For the two Houses of *Yisrael*, And a trap and a snare for those Who dwell in *Yerushalayim*.

יד וְהָיָה לְמִקְדָּשׁ וּלְאֶבֶן נֶגֶף וּלְצוּר מִכְשׁוֹל לִשְׁנֵי בָתֵּי יִשְׂרָאֵל לְפַח וּלְמוֹקֵשׁ לְיוֹשֵׁב יְרוּשָׁלָם:

15 The masses shall trip over these And shall fall and be injured, Shall be snared and be caught.

טו וְכָשְׁלוּ בָם רַבִּים וְנָפְלוּ וְנִשְׁבָּרוּ וְנוֹקְשׁוּ וְנִלְכָּדוּ:

16 Bind up the message, Seal the instruction with My disciples."

טז צוֹר תְּעוּדָה חֲתוֹם תּוֹרָה בְּלִמֻּדָי:

17 So I will wait for *Hashem*, who is hiding His face from the House of *Yaakov*, and I will trust in Him.

יז וְחִכִּיתִי לַיהוָה הַמַּסְתִּיר פָּנָיו מִבֵּית יַעֲקֹב וְקִוֵּיתִי־לוֹ:

18 Here stand I and the children *Hashem* has given me as signs and portents in *Yisrael* from the LORD of Hosts, who dwells on Mount *Tzion*.

יח הִנֵּה אָנֹכִי וְהַיְלָדִים אֲשֶׁר נָתַן־לִי יְהוָה לְאֹתוֹת וּלְמוֹפְתִים בְּיִשְׂרָאֵל מֵעִם יְהוָה צְבָאוֹת הַשֹּׁכֵן בְּהַר צִיּוֹן:

hi-NAY a-no-KHEE v'-hai-la-DEEM a-SHER na-tan LEE
a-do-NAI l'-o-TOT ul-mof-TEEM b'-yis-ra-AYL may-IM
a-do-NAI tz'-va-OT ha-sho-KHAYN b'-HAR tzi-YON

19 Now, should people say to you, "Inquire of the ghosts and familiar spirits that chirp and moan; for a people may inquire of its divine beings – of the dead on behalf of the living –

יט וְכִי־יֹאמְרוּ אֲלֵיכֶם דִּרְשׁוּ אֶל־הָאֹבוֹת וְאֶל־הַיִּדְּעֹנִים הַמְצַפְצְפִים וְהַמַּהְגִּים הֲלוֹא־עַם אֶל־אֱלֹהָיו יִדְרֹשׁ בְּעַד הַחַיִּים אֶל־הַמֵּתִים:

20 for instruction and message," surely, for one who speaks thus there shall be no dawn.

כ לְתוֹרָה וְלִתְעוּדָה אִם־לֹא יֹאמְרוּ כַּדָּבָר הַזֶּה אֲשֶׁר אֵין־לוֹ שָׁחַר:

21 And he shall go about in it wretched and hungry; and when he is hungry, he shall rage and revolt against his king and his divine beings. He may turn his face upward

כא וְעָבַר בָּהּ נִקְשֶׁה וְרָעֵב וְהָיָה כִי־יִרְעַב וְהִתְקַצַּף וְקִלֵּל בְּמַלְכּוֹ וּבֵאלֹהָיו וּפָנָה לְמָעְלָה:

22 or he may look below, but behold, Distress and darkness, with no daybreak; Straitness and gloom, with no dawn.

כב וְאֶל־אֶרֶץ יַבִּיט וְהִנֵּה צָרָה וַחֲשֵׁכָה מְעוּף צוּקָה וַאֲפֵלָה מְנֻדָּח:

8:18 the LORD of Hosts, who dwells on Mount *Tzion* After describing the upcoming Assyrian invasion, the prophet takes steps to ensure that a small remnant of believers in *Hashem*'s salvation will remain. He goes so far as to name his children with names of hope and promise, as signs that the redemption will come. *Yeshayahu* points to the fact that God's presence continues to reside on Mount *Tzion*. Regarding the *Beit Hamikdash* and *Yerushalayim*, the *Rambam* states, "even though it is destroyed, it still possesses its holiness." This means that *Hashem* will never abandon His land or His people. Instead, He remains with His children even while they are in exile, and guarantees that He will redeem them at the right time (Deuteronomy 30:3–5).

The Temple Mount, Mount *Tzion*

Isaiah

²³ For if there were to be any break of day for that [land] which is in straits, only the former [king] would have brought abasement to the land of *Zevulun* and the land of *Naftali* – while the later one would have brought honor to the Way of the Sea, the other side of the *Yarden*, and Galilee of the Nations.

כג כִּי לֹא מוּעָף לַאֲשֶׁר מוּצָק לָהּ כָּעֵת הָרִאשׁוֹן הֵקַל אַרְצָה זְבֻלוּן וְאַרְצָה נַפְתָּלִי וְהָאַחֲרוֹן הִכְבִּיד דֶּרֶךְ הַיָּם עֵבֶר הַיַּרְדֵּן גְּלִיל הַגּוֹיִם:

ט ¹ The people that walked in darkness have seen a brilliant light; On those who dwelt in a land of gloom Light has dawned.

ט א הָעָם הַהֹלְכִים בַּחֹשֶׁךְ רָאוּ אוֹר גָּדוֹל יֹשְׁבֵי בְּאֶרֶץ צַלְמָוֶת אוֹר נָגַהּ עֲלֵיהֶם:

² You have magnified that nation, Have given it great joy; They have rejoiced before You As they rejoice at reaping time, As they exult When dividing spoil.

ב הִרְבִּיתָ הַגּוֹי לֹא [לוֹ] הִגְדַּלְתָּ הַשִּׂמְחָה שָׂמְחוּ לְפָנֶיךָ כְּשִׂמְחַת בַּקָּצִיר כַּאֲשֶׁר יָגִילוּ בְּחַלְּקָם שָׁלָל:

³ For the yoke that they bore And the stick on their back – The rod of their taskmaster – You have broken as on the day of Midian.

ג כִּי אֶת־עֹל סֻבֳּלוֹ וְאֵת מַטֵּה שִׁכְמוֹ שֵׁבֶט הַנֹּגֵשׂ בּוֹ הַחִתֹּתָ כְּיוֹם מִדְיָן:

⁴ Truly, all the boots put on to stamp with And all the garments donned in infamy Have been fed to the flames, Devoured by fire.

ד כִּי כָל־סְאוֹן סֹאֵן בְּרַעַשׁ וְשִׂמְלָה מְגוֹלָלָה בְדָמִים וְהָיְתָה לִשְׂרֵפָה מַאֲכֹלֶת אֵשׁ:

⁵ For a child has been born to us, A son has been given us. And authority has settled on his shoulders. He has been named "The Mighty *Hashem* is planning grace; The Eternal Father, a peaceable ruler" –

ה כִּי־יֶלֶד יֻלַּד־לָנוּ בֵּן נִתַּן־לָנוּ וַתְּהִי הַמִּשְׂרָה עַל־שִׁכְמוֹ וַיִּקְרָא שְׁמוֹ פֶּלֶא יוֹעֵץ אֵל גִּבּוֹר אֲבִיעַד שַׂר־שָׁלוֹם:

kee YE-led yu-lad LA-nu BEN ni-tan LA-nu va-t'-HEE ha-mis-RAH al shikh-MO va-yik-RA sh'-MO PE-le yo-AYTZ AYL gi-BOR a-vee AD sar sha-LOM

⁶ In token of abundant authority And of peace without limit Upon *David*'s throne and kingdom, That it may be firmly established In justice and in equity Now and evermore. The zeal of the LORD of Hosts Shall bring this to pass.

ו לְמַרְבֵּה [לְמַרְבֵּה] הַמִּשְׂרָה וּלְשָׁלוֹם אֵין־קֵץ עַל־כִּסֵּא דָוִד וְעַל־מַמְלַכְתּוֹ לְהָכִין אֹתָהּ וּלְסַעֲדָהּ בְּמִשְׁפָּט וּבִצְדָקָה מֵעַתָּה וְעַד־עוֹלָם קִנְאַת יְהֹוָה צְבָאוֹת תַּעֲשֶׂה־זֹּאת:

⁷ My Lord Let loose a word against *Yaakov* And it fell upon *Yisrael*.

ז דָּבָר שָׁלַח אֲדֹנָי בְּיַעֲקֹב וְנָפַל בְּיִשְׂרָאֵל:

⁸ But all the people noted – *Efraim* and the inhabitants of *Shomron* – In arrogance and haughtiness:

ח וְיָדְעוּ הָעָם כֻּלּוֹ אֶפְרַיִם וְיוֹשֵׁב שֹׁמְרוֹן בְּגַאֲוָה וּבְגֹדֶל לֵבָב לֵאמֹר:

9:5 For a child has been born to us *Yeshayahu*'s prophecy of the upcoming salvation of the people is combined with a vision regarding the birth of a child. Judging from the context of the prophecy, *Yeshayahu* appears to be referring to the righteous King *Chizkiyahu*, whom tradition credits with educating all the Children of Israel about the intricacies of *Hashem*'s laws. Over the last three chapters, *Yeshayahu* has combined prophecies of redemption with announcements of upcoming births. This signifies that even if the present may seem difficult, the future will always be brighter.

Mother and baby with the *Chanukah* lights

16

9 "Bricks have fallen – We'll rebuild with dressed stone; Sycamores have been felled – We'll grow cedars instead!"

ט לְבֵנִים נָפָלוּ וְגָזִית נִבְנֶה שִׁקְמִים גֻּדָּעוּ וַאֲרָזִים נַחֲלִיף:

10 So *Hashem* let the enemies of Rezin Triumph over it And stirred up its foes –

י וַיְשַׂגֵּב יְהוָה אֶת־צָרֵי רְצִין עָלָיו וְאֶת־אֹיְבָיו יְסַכְסֵךְ:

11 Aram from the east And Philistia from the west – Who devoured *Yisrael* With greedy mouths. Yet His anger has not turned back, And His arm is outstretched still.

יא אֲרָם מִקֶּדֶם וּפְלִשְׁתִּים מֵאָחוֹר וַיֹּאכְלוּ אֶת־יִשְׂרָאֵל בְּכָל־פֶּה בְּכָל־זֹאת לֹא־שָׁב אַפּוֹ וְעוֹד יָדוֹ נְטוּיָה:

12 For the people has not turned back To Him who struck it And has not sought the LORD of Hosts.

יב וְהָעָם לֹא־שָׁב עַד־הַמַּכֵּהוּ וְאֶת־יְהוָה צְבָאוֹת לֹא דָרָשׁוּ:

13 So *Hashem* will cut off from *Yisrael* Head and tail, Palm branch and reed, In a single day.

יג וַיַּכְרֵת יְהוָה מִיִּשְׂרָאֵל רֹאשׁ וְזָנָב כִּפָּה וְאַגְמוֹן יוֹם אֶחָד:

14 Elders and magnates – Such are the heads; *Neviim* who give false instruction, Such are the tails

יד זָקֵן וּנְשׂוּא־פָנִים הוּא הָרֹאשׁ וְנָבִיא מוֹרֶה־שֶּׁקֶר הוּא הַזָּנָב:

15 That people's leaders have been misleaders, So they that are led have been confused.

טו וַיִּהְיוּ מְאַשְּׁרֵי הָעָם־הַזֶּה מַתְעִים וּמְאֻשָּׁרָיו מְבֻלָּעִים:

16 That is why my Lord Will not spare their youths, Nor show compassion To their orphans and widows; For all are ungodly and wicked, And every mouth speaks impiety.

טז עַל־כֵּן עַל־בַּחוּרָיו לֹא־יִשְׂמַח אֲדֹנָי וְאֶת־יְתֹמָיו וְאֶת־אַלְמְנֹתָיו לֹא יְרַחֵם כִּי כֻלּוֹ חָנֵף וּמֵרַע וְכָל־פֶּה דֹּבֵר נְבָלָה בְּכָל־זֹאת לֹא־שָׁב אַפּוֹ וְעוֹד יָדוֹ נְטוּיָה:

17 Already wickedness has blazed forth like a fire Devouring thorn and thistle. It has kindled the thickets of the wood, Which have turned into billowing smoke. Yet His anger has not turned back, And His arm is outstretched still.*

יז כִּי־בָעֲרָה כָאֵשׁ רִשְׁעָה שָׁמִיר וָשַׁיִת תֹּאכֵל וַתִּצַּת בְּסִבְכֵי הַיַּעַר וַיִּתְאַבְּכוּ גֵּאוּת עָשָׁן:

18 By the fury of the LORD of Hosts, The earth was shaken. Next, the people became like devouring fire: No man spared his countryman.

יח בְּעֶבְרַת יְהוָה צְבָאוֹת נֶעְתַּם אָרֶץ וַיְהִי הָעָם כְּמַאֲכֹלֶת אֵשׁ אִישׁ אֶל־אָחִיו לֹא יַחְמֹלוּ:

19 They snatched on the right, but remained hungry, And consumed on the left without being sated. Each devoured the flesh of his own kindred –

יט וַיִּגְזֹר עַל־יָמִין וְרָעֵב וַיֹּאכַל עַל־שְׂמֹאול וְלֹא שָׂבֵעוּ אִישׁ בְּשַׂר־זְרֹעוֹ יֹאכֵלוּ:

20 *Menashe Efraim*'s, and *Efraim Menashe*'s, And both of them against *Yehuda*! Yet His anger has not turned back, And His arm is outstretched still.

כ מְנַשֶּׁה אֶת־אֶפְרַיִם וְאֶפְרַיִם אֶת־מְנַשֶּׁה יַחְדָּו הֵמָּה עַל־יְהוּדָה בְּכָל־זֹאת לֹא־שָׁב אַפּוֹ וְעוֹד יָדוֹ נְטוּיָה:

10

1 Ha! Those who write out evil writs And compose iniquitous documents,

פרק י

א הוֹי הַחֹקְקִים חִקְקֵי־אָוֶן וּמְכַתְּבִים עָמָל כִּתֵּבוּ:

2 To subvert the cause of the poor, To rob their rights the needy of My people; That widows may be their spoil, And fatherless children their booty!

ב לְהַטּוֹת מִדִּין דַּלִּים וְלִגְזֹל מִשְׁפַּט עֲנִיֵּי עַמִּי לִהְיוֹת אַלְמָנוֹת שְׁלָלָם וְאֶת־יְתוֹמִים יָבֹזּוּ:

---

* "Yet His anger has not turned back, And His arm is outstretched still" brought down from verse 16 for clarity

Isaiah

3 What will you do on the day of punishment, When the calamity comes from afar? To whom will you flee for help, And how will you save your carcasses

ג וּמַה־תַּעֲשׂוּ לְיוֹם פְּקֻדָּה וּלְשׁוֹאָה מִמֶּרְחָק תָּבוֹא עַל־מִי תָּנוּסוּ לְעֶזְרָה וְאָנָה תַעַזְבוּ כְּבוֹדְכֶם:

4 From collapsing under [fellow] prisoners, From falling beneath the slain? Yet His anger has not turned back, And his arm is outstretched still.

ד בִּלְתִּי כָרַע תַּחַת אַסִּיר וְתַחַת הֲרוּגִים יִפֹּלוּ בְּכָל־זֹאת לֹא־שָׁב אַפּוֹ וְעוֹד יָדוֹ נְטוּיָה:

5 Ha! Assyria, rod of My anger, In whose hand, as a staff, is My fury!

ה הוֹי אַשּׁוּר שֵׁבֶט אַפִּי וּמַטֶּה־הוּא בְיָדָם זַעְמִי:

HOY a-SHUR SHAY-vet a-PEE u-ma-teh HU v'-ya-DAM za-MEE

6 I send him against an ungodly nation, I charge him against a people that provokes Me, To take its spoil and to seize its booty And to make it a thing trampled Like the mire of the streets.

ו בְּגוֹי חָנֵף אֲשַׁלְּחֶנּוּ וְעַל־עַם עֶבְרָתִי אֲצַוֶּנּוּ לִשְׁלֹל שָׁלָל וְלָבֹז בַּז וּלְשִׂימוֹ [וּלְשׂוּמוֹ] מִרְמָס כְּחֹמֶר חוּצוֹת:

7 But he has evil plans, His mind harbors evil designs; For he means to destroy, To wipe out nations, not a few.

ז וְהוּא לֹא־כֵן יְדַמֶּה וּלְבָבוֹ לֹא־כֵן יַחְשֹׁב כִּי לְהַשְׁמִיד בִּלְבָבוֹ וּלְהַכְרִית גּוֹיִם לֹא מְעָט:

8 For he thinks, "After all, I have kings as my captains!

ח כִּי יֹאמַר הֲלֹא שָׂרַי יַחְדָּו מְלָכִים:

9 Was Calno any different from Carchemish? Or Hamath from Arpad? Or *Shomron* from Damascus?

ט הֲלֹא כְּכַרְכְּמִישׁ כַּלְנוֹ אִם־לֹא כְאַרְפַּד חֲמָת אִם־לֹא כְדַמֶּשֶׂק שֹׁמְרוֹן:

10 Since I was able to seize The insignificant kingdoms, Whose images exceeded *Yerushalayim*'s and *Shomron*'s,

י כַּאֲשֶׁר מָצְאָה יָדִי לְמַמְלְכֹת הָאֱלִיל וּפְסִילֵיהֶם מִירוּשָׁלַםִ וּמִשֹּׁמְרוֹן:

11 Shall I not do to *Yerushalayim* and her images What I did to *Shomron* and her idols?"

יא הֲלֹא כַּאֲשֶׁר עָשִׂיתִי לְשֹׁמְרוֹן וְלֶאֱלִילֶיהָ כֵּן אֶעֱשֶׂה לִירוּשָׁלַםִ וְלַעֲצַבֶּיהָ:

12 But when my Lord has carried out all his purpose on Mount *Tzion* and in *Yerushalayim*, He will punish the majestic pride and overbearing arrogance of the king of Assyria.

יב וְהָיָה כִּי־יְבַצַּע אֲדֹנָי אֶת־כָּל־מַעֲשֵׂהוּ בְּהַר צִיּוֹן וּבִירוּשָׁלָםִ אֶפְקֹד עַל־פְּרִי־גֹדֶל לְבַב מֶלֶךְ־אַשּׁוּר וְעַל־תִּפְאֶרֶת רוּם עֵינָיו:

10:5 Assyria, rod of My anger Ancient idol-worshippers believed that the fortunes of their countries were directly tied to the strength of their gods. Therefore, if another country was to conquer theirs, they would have no problem transferring their worship and loyalty to the invaders' gods, as these were clearly stronger. Against that background, what *Yeshayahu* says to the people in this verse is quite revolutionary: Not only are the Assyrian gods non-existent, but *Hashem* Himself controls the Assyrians, and is using them as an instrument to punish Israel. Should the People of Israel return to God and practice justice and righteousness, however, *Hashem* will break the Assyrian yoke of oppression and punish the Assyrians for their arrogance. *Yeshayahu*'s eternal message to the Children of Israel is that God is always the cause of everything that occurs to them, and the nature of their fortune will be determined only on the basis of their record of adherence to His laws.

A man holding a *Torah*, the book of God's laws, at the Western Wall

Isaiah

13 For he thought, "By the might of my hand have I wrought it, By my skill, for I am clever: I have erased the borders of peoples; I have plundered their treasures, And exiled their vast populations.

כִּי אָמַר בְּכֹחַ יָדִי עָשִׂיתִי וּבְחָכְמָתִי כִּי נְבֻנוֹתִי וְאָסִיר גְּבוּלֹת עַמִּים וַעֲתִידֹתֵיהֶם [וַעֲתוּדֹתֵיהֶם] שׁוֹשֵׂתִי וְאוֹרִיד כַּאבִּיר יוֹשְׁבִים:

14 I was able to seize, like a nest, The wealth of peoples; As one gathers abandoned eggs, So I gathered all the earth: Nothing so much as flapped a wing Or opened a mouth to peep."

וַתִּמְצָא כַקֵּן יָדִי לְחֵיל הָעַמִּים וְכֶאֱסֹף בֵּיצִים עֲזֻבוֹת כָּל־הָאָרֶץ אֲנִי אָסָפְתִּי וְלֹא הָיָה נֹדֵד כָּנָף וּפֹצֶה פֶה וּמְצַפְצֵף:

15 Does an ax boast over him who hews with it, Or a saw magnify itself above him who wields it? As though the rod raised him who lifts it, As though the staff lifted the man!

הֲיִתְפָּאֵר הַגַּרְזֶן עַל הַחֹצֵב בּוֹ אִם־יִתְגַּדֵּל הַמַּשּׂוֹר עַל־מְנִיפוֹ כְּהָנִיף שֵׁבֶט וְאֶת־מְרִימָיו כְּהָרִים מַטֶּה לֹא־עֵץ:

16 Assuredly, The Sovereign Lᴏʀᴅ of Hosts will send A wasting away in its fatness; And under its body shall burn A burning like that of fire, Destroying frame and flesh. It shall be like a sick man who pines away.*

לָכֵן יְשַׁלַּח הָאָדוֹן יְהוָה צְבָאוֹת בְּמִשְׁמַנָּיו רָזוֹן וְתַחַת כְּבֹדוֹ יֵקַד יְקֹד כִּיקוֹד אֵשׁ:

17 The Light of *Yisrael* will be fire And its Holy One flame. It will burn and consume its thorns And its thistles in a single day,

וְהָיָה אוֹר־יִשְׂרָאֵל לְאֵשׁ וּקְדוֹשׁוֹ לְלֶהָבָה וּבָעֲרָה וְאָכְלָה שִׁיתוֹ וּשְׁמִירוֹ בְּיוֹם אֶחָד:

18 And the mass of its scrub and its farm land.

וּכְבוֹד יַעְרוֹ וְכַרְמִלּוֹ מִנֶּפֶשׁ וְעַד־בָּשָׂר יְכַלֶּה וְהָיָה כִּמְסֹס נֹסֵס:

19 What trees remain of its scrub Shall be so few that a boy may record them.

וּשְׁאָר עֵץ יַעְרוֹ מִסְפָּר יִהְיוּ וְנַעַר יִכְתְּבֵם:

20 And in that day, The remnant of *Yisrael* And the escaped of the House of *Yaakov* Shall lean no more upon him that beats it, But shall lean sincerely On *Hashem*, the Holy One of *Yisrael*.

וְהָיָה בַּיּוֹם הַהוּא לֹא־יוֹסִיף עוֹד שְׁאָר יִשְׂרָאֵל וּפְלֵיטַת בֵּית־יַעֲקֹב לְהִשָּׁעֵן עַל־מַכֵּהוּ וְנִשְׁעַן עַל־יְהוָה קְדוֹשׁ יִשְׂרָאֵל בֶּאֱמֶת:

21 Only a remnant shall return, Only a remnant of *Yaakov*, To Mighty *Hashem*.

שְׁאָר יָשׁוּב שְׁאָר יַעֲקֹב אֶל־אֵל גִּבּוֹר:

22 Even if your people, O *Yisrael*, Should be as the sands of the sea, Only a remnant of it shall return. Destruction is decreed; Retribution comes like a flood!

כִּי אִם־יִהְיֶה עַמְּךָ יִשְׂרָאֵל כְּחוֹל הַיָּם שְׁאָר יָשׁוּב בּוֹ כִּלָּיוֹן חָרוּץ שׁוֹטֵף צְדָקָה:

23 For my Lord God of Hosts is carrying out A decree of destruction upon all the land.

כִּי כָלָה וְנֶחֱרָצָה אֲדֹנָי יְהוִה צְבָאוֹת עֹשֶׂה בְּקֶרֶב כָּל־הָאָרֶץ:

24 Assuredly, thus said my Lord God of Hosts: "O My people that dwells in *Tzion*, have no fear of Assyria, who beats you with a rod and wields his staff over you as did the Egyptians.

לָכֵן כֹּה־אָמַר אֲדֹנָי יְהוִה צְבָאוֹת אַל־תִּירָא עַמִּי יֹשֵׁב צִיּוֹן מֵאַשּׁוּר בַּשֵּׁבֶט יַכֶּכָּה וּמַטֵּהוּ יִשָּׂא־עָלֶיךָ בְּדֶרֶךְ מִצְרָיִם:

---

* "Destroying frame and flesh. It shall be like a sick man who pines away" brought up from verse 18 for clarity

25 For very soon My wrath will have spent itself, and My anger that was bent on wasting them."

כה כִּי־עוֹד מְעַט מִזְעָר וְכָלָה זַעַם וְאַפִּי עַל־תַּבְלִיתָם:

26 The LORD of Hosts will brandish a scourge over him as when He beat Midian at the Rock of Oreb, and will wield His staff as He did over the Egyptians by the sea.

כו וְעוֹרֵר עָלָיו יְהֹוָה צְבָאוֹת שׁוֹט כְּמַכַּת מִדְיָן בְּצוּר עוֹרֵב וּמַטֵּהוּ עַל־הַיָּם וּנְשָׂאוֹ בְּדֶרֶךְ מִצְרָיִם:

27 And in that day, His burden shall drop from your back, And his yoke from your neck; The yoke shall be destroyed because of fatness.

כז וְהָיָה בַּיּוֹם הַהוּא יָסוּר סֻבֳּלוֹ מֵעַל שִׁכְמֶךָ וְעֻלּוֹ מֵעַל צַוָּארֶךָ וְחֻבַּל עֹל מִפְּנֵי־שָׁמֶן:

28 He advanced upon Aiath, He proceeded to Migron, At Michmas he deposited his baggage.

כח בָּא עַל־עַיַּת עָבַר בְּמִגְרוֹן לְמִכְמָשׂ יַפְקִיד כֵּלָיו:

29 They made the crossing; "Geba is to be our night quarters!" *Rama* was alarmed; *Giva* of *Shaul* took to flight.

כט עָבְרוּ מַעְבָּרָה גֶּבַע מָלוֹן לָנוּ חָרְדָה הָרָמָה גִּבְעַת שָׁאוּל נָסָה:

30 "Give a shrill cry, O Bath-gallim! Hearken, Laishah! Take up the cry, *Anatot!*"

ל צַהֲלִי קוֹלֵךְ בַּת־גַּלִּים הַקְשִׁיבִי לַיְשָׁה עֲנִיָּה עֲנָתוֹת:

31 Madmenah ran away; The dwellers of Gebim sought refuge.

לא נָדְדָה מַדְמֵנָה יֹשְׁבֵי הַגֵּבִים הֵעִיזוּ:

32 This same day at *Nov* He shall stand and wave his hand. O mount of Fair *Tzion!* O hill of *Yerushalayim!*

לב עוֹד הַיּוֹם בְּנֹב לַעֲמֹד יְנֹפֵף יָדוֹ הַר בֵּית־ [בַּת־] צִיּוֹן גִּבְעַת יְרוּשָׁלָיִם:

33 Lo! The Sovereign LORD of Hosts Will hew off the tree-crowns with an ax: The tall ones shall be felled, The lofty ones cut down:

לג הִנֵּה הָאָדוֹן יְהֹוָה צְבָאוֹת מְסָעֵף פֻּארָה בְּמַעֲרָצָה וְרָמֵי הַקּוֹמָה גְּדוּעִים וְהַגְּבֹהִים יִשְׁפָּלוּ:

34 The thickets of the forest shall be hacked away with iron, And the Lebanon trees shall fall in their majesty.

לד וְנִקַּף סִבְכֵי הַיַּעַר בַּבַּרְזֶל וְהַלְּבָנוֹן בְּאַדִּיר יִפּוֹל:

11 1 But a shoot shall grow out of the stump of *Yishai,* A twig shall sprout from his stock.

יא א וְיָצָא חֹטֶר מִגֵּזַע יִשָׁי וְנֵצֶר מִשָּׁרָשָׁיו יִפְרֶה:

2 The spirit of *Hashem* shall alight upon him: A spirit of wisdom and insight, A spirit of counsel and valor, A spirit of devotion and reverence for *Hashem.*

ב וְנָחָה עָלָיו רוּחַ יְהֹוָה רוּחַ חָכְמָה וּבִינָה רוּחַ עֵצָה וּגְבוּרָה רוּחַ דַּעַת וְיִרְאַת יְהֹוָה:

3 He shall sense the truth by his reverence for *Hashem:* He shall not judge by what his eyes behold, Nor decide by what his ears perceive.

ג וַהֲרִיחוֹ בְּיִרְאַת יְהֹוָה וְלֹא־לְמַרְאֵה עֵינָיו יִשְׁפּוֹט וְלֹא־לְמִשְׁמַע אָזְנָיו יוֹכִיחַ:

4 Thus he shall judge the poor with equity And decide with justice for the lowly of the land. He shall strike down a land with the rod of his mouth And slay the wicked with the breath of his lips.

ד וְשָׁפַט בְּצֶדֶק דַּלִּים וְהוֹכִיחַ בְּמִישׁוֹר לְעַנְוֵי־אָרֶץ וְהִכָּה־אֶרֶץ בְּשֵׁבֶט פִּיו וּבְרוּחַ שְׂפָתָיו יָמִית רָשָׁע:

5 Justice shall be the girdle of his loins, And faithfulness the girdle of his waist.

ה וְהָיָה צֶדֶק אֵזוֹר מָתְנָיו וְהָאֱמוּנָה אֵזוֹר חֲלָצָיו:

6 The wolf shall dwell with the lamb, The leopard lie down with the kid; The calf, the beast of prey, and the fatling together, With a little boy to herd them.

7 The cow and the bear shall graze, Their young shall lie down together; And the lion, like the ox, shall eat straw.

8 A babe shall play Over a viper's hole, And an infant pass his hand Over an adder's den.

9 In all of My sacred mount Nothing evil or vile shall be done; For the land shall be filled with devotion to *Hashem* As water covers the sea.

10 In that day, The stock of *Yishai* that has remained standing Shall become a standard to peoples – Nations shall seek his counsel And his abode shall be honored.

11 In that day, my Lord will apply His hand again to redeeming the other part of His people from Assyria – as also from Egypt, Pathros, Nubia, Elam, Shinar, Hamath, and the coastlands.

12 He will hold up a signal to the nations And assemble the banished of *Yisrael*, And gather the dispersed of *Yehuda* From the four corners of the earth.

v'-na-SA NAYS la-go-YIM v'-a-SAF nid-KHAY yis-ra-AYL un-fu-TZOT
y'-hu-DAH y'-ka-BAYTZ may-ar-BA kan-FOT ha-A-retz

13 Then *Efraim*'s envy shall cease And *Yehuda*'s harassment shall end; *Efraim* shall not envy *Yehuda*, And *Yehuda* shall not harass *Efraim*.

14 They shall pounce on the back of Philistia to the west, And together plunder the peoples of the east; Edom and Moab shall be subject to them And the children of Ammon shall obey them.

15 *Hashem* will dry up the tongue of the Egyptian sea. – He will raise His hand over the Euphrates with the might of His wind and break it into seven wadis, so that it can be trodden dry-shod.

ו וְגָ֤ר זְאֵב֙ עִם־כֶּ֔בֶשׂ וְנָמֵ֖ר עִם־גְּדִ֣י יִרְבָּ֑ץ וְעֵ֨גֶל וּכְפִ֤יר וּמְרִיא֙ יַחְדָּ֔ו וְנַ֥עַר קָטֹ֖ן נֹהֵ֥ג בָּֽם:

ז וּפָרָ֤ה וָדֹב֙ תִּרְעֶ֔ינָה יַחְדָּ֖ו יִרְבְּצ֣וּ יַלְדֵיהֶ֑ן וְאַרְיֵ֖ה כַּבָּקָ֥ר יֹֽאכַל־תֶּֽבֶן:

ח וְשִֽׁעֲשַׁ֥ע יוֹנֵ֖ק עַל־חֻ֣ר פָּ֑תֶן וְעַל֙ מְאוּרַ֣ת צִפְעוֹנִ֔י גָּמ֖וּל יָד֥וֹ הָדָֽה:

ט לֹֽא־יָרֵ֥עוּ וְלֹֽא־יַשְׁחִ֖יתוּ בְּכָל־הַ֣ר קָדְשִׁ֑י כִּֽי־מָלְאָ֣ה הָאָ֗רֶץ דֵּעָה֙ אֶת־יְהֹוָ֔ה כַּמַּ֖יִם לַיָּ֥ם מְכַסִּֽים:

י וְהָיָה֙ בַּיּ֣וֹם הַה֔וּא שֹׁ֣רֶשׁ יִשַׁ֗י אֲשֶׁ֤ר עֹמֵד֙ לְנֵ֣ס עַמִּ֔ים אֵלָ֖יו גּוֹיִ֣ם יִדְרֹ֑שׁוּ וְהָֽיְתָ֥ה מְנֻחָת֖וֹ כָּבֽוֹד:

יא וְהָיָ֣ה | בַּיּ֣וֹם הַה֗וּא יוֹסִ֨יף אֲדֹנָ֤י | שֵׁנִית֙ יָד֔וֹ לִקְנ֖וֹת אֶת־שְׁאָ֣ר עַמּ֑וֹ אֲשֶׁ֣ר יִשָּׁאֵר֩ מֵֽאַשּׁ֨וּר וּמִמִּצְרַ֜יִם וּמִפַּתְר֣וֹס וּמִכּ֗וּשׁ וּמֵֽעֵילָ֤ם וּמִשִּׁנְעָר֙ וּמֵ֣חֲמָ֔ת וּמֵֽאִיֵּ֖י הַיָּֽם:

יב וְנָשָׂ֥א נֵס֙ לַגּוֹיִ֔ם וְאָסַ֖ף נִדְחֵ֣י יִשְׂרָאֵ֑ל וּנְפֻצ֤וֹת יְהוּדָה֙ יְקַבֵּ֔ץ מֵֽאַרְבַּ֖ע כַּנְפ֥וֹת הָאָֽרֶץ:

יג וְסָ֨רָה֙ קִנְאַ֣ת אֶפְרַ֔יִם וְצֹֽרְרֵ֥י יְהוּדָ֖ה יִכָּרֵ֑תוּ אֶפְרַ֨יִם֙ לֹֽא־יְקַנֵּ֣א אֶת־יְהוּדָ֔ה וִֽיהוּדָ֖ה לֹֽא־יָצֹ֥ר אֶת־אֶפְרָֽיִם:

יד וְעָפ֨וּ בְכָתֵ֤ף פְּלִשְׁתִּים֙ יָ֔מָּה יַחְדָּ֖ו יָבֹ֣זּוּ אֶת־בְּנֵי־קֶ֑דֶם אֱד֤וֹם וּמוֹאָב֙ מִשְׁל֣וֹחַ יָדָ֔ם וּבְנֵ֥י עַמּ֖וֹן מִשְׁמַעְתָּֽם:

טו וְהֶֽחֱרִ֣ים יְהֹוָ֗ה אֵ֚ת לְשׁ֣וֹן יָֽם־מִצְרַ֔יִם וְהֵנִ֥יף יָד֛וֹ עַל־הַנָּהָ֖ר בַּֽעְיָ֣ם רוּח֑וֹ וְהִכָּ֨הוּ֙ לְשִׁבְעָ֣ה נְחָלִ֔ים וְהִדְרִ֖יךְ בַּנְּעָלִֽים:

11:12 And assemble the banished of *Yisrael* For thousands of years, Jews read these prophecies and believed them, yet wondered how and when they would actually take place. During the past century, Jews have returned to the Land of Israel from literally all parts of the earth: from Asia and Russia, Europe, North and South America, Australia and New Zealand. This section was chosen as the *Haftarah* portion to be read on Israel's Independence Day, expressing the hope and belief that the founding of the State of Israel is the beginning of the fulfillment of these prophecies.

New immigrants from France
arrive at Ben Gurion airport

Isaiah

16 Thus there shall be a highway for the other part of His people out of Assyria, such as there was for *Yisrael* when it left the land of Egypt.

טז וְהָיְתָה מְסִלָּה לִשְׁאָר עַמּוֹ אֲשֶׁר יִשָּׁאֵר מֵאַשּׁוּר כַּאֲשֶׁר הָיְתָה לְיִשְׂרָאֵל בְּיוֹם עֲלֹתוֹ מֵאֶרֶץ מִצְרָיִם:

12 1 In that day, you shall say: "I give thanks to You, *Hashem*! Although You were wroth with me, Your wrath has turned back and You comfort me,

יב א וְאָמַרְתָּ בַּיּוֹם הַהוּא אוֹדְךָ יְהֹוָה כִּי אָנַפְתָּ בִּי יָשֹׁב אַפְּךָ וּתְנַחֲמֵנִי:

2 Behold the God who gives me triumph! I am confident, unafraid; For Yah *Hashem* is my strength and might, And He has been my deliverance."

ב הִנֵּה אֵל יְשׁוּעָתִי אֶבְטַח וְלֹא אֶפְחָד כִּי־ עָזִּי וְזִמְרָת יָהּ יְהֹוָה וַיְהִי־לִי לִישׁוּעָה:

3 Joyfully shall you draw water From the fountains of triumph,

ג וּשְׁאַבְתֶּם־מַיִם בְּשָׂשׂוֹן מִמַּעַיְנֵי הַיְשׁוּעָה:

4 And you shall say on that day: "Praise *Hashem*, proclaim His name. Make His deeds known among the peoples; Declare that His name is exalted.

ד וַאֲמַרְתֶּם בַּיּוֹם הַהוּא הוֹדוּ לַיהֹוָה קִרְאוּ בִשְׁמוֹ הוֹדִיעוּ בָעַמִּים עֲלִילֹתָיו הַזְכִּירוּ כִּי נִשְׂגָּב שְׁמוֹ:

5 Hymn *Hashem*, For He has done gloriously; Let this be made known In all the world!

ה זַמְּרוּ יְהֹוָה כִּי גֵאוּת עָשָׂה מֵידַעַת [מוּדַעַת] זֹאת בְּכָל־הָאָרֶץ:

za-m'-RU a-do-NAI KEE gay-UT a-SAH mu-DA-at ZOT b'-khol ha-A-retz

6 Oh, shout for joy, You who dwell in *Tzion*! For great in your midst Is the Holy One of *Yisrael*."

ו צַהֲלִי וָרֹנִּי יוֹשֶׁבֶת צִיּוֹן כִּי־גָדוֹל בְּקִרְבֵּךְ קְדוֹשׁ יִשְׂרָאֵל:

13 1 The "Babylon" Pronouncement, a prophecy of *Yeshayahu* son of *Amotz*.

יג א מַשָּׂא בָּבֶל אֲשֶׁר חָזָה יְשַׁעְיָהוּ בֶּן־ אָמוֹץ:

2 "Raise a standard upon a bare hill, Cry aloud to them; Wave a hand, and let them enter The gates of the nobles!

ב עַל הַר־נִשְׁפֶּה שְׂאוּ־נֵס הָרִימוּ קוֹל לָהֶם הָנִיפוּ יָד וְיָבֹאוּ פִּתְחֵי נְדִיבִים:

AL har nish-PEH s'-u NAYS ha-REE-mu KOL la-HEM
ha-NEE-fu YAD v'-ya-VO-u pit-KHAY n'-dee-VEEM

12:5 Hymn *Hashem*, for He has done gloriously The Talmud (*Sanhedrin* 94a) states that after *Yehuda*'s miraculous deliverance from the Assyrian invasion, *Hashem* desired to crown the righteous king *Chizkiyahu* as the *Mashiach*. Only one thing was required – that *Chizkiyahu* sing a song of praise before Him. Instead, though, *Chizkiyahu* arose that morning, and continued with his regular daily routine, the study of the *Torah*, until *Yeshayahu* instructed him to sing. Unfortunately, as the song was not spontaneous but rather came as a response to a command, the opportunity was lost. In this verse, *Yeshayahu* teaches the importance of appreciating everything that occurs for us, and being able to sing praise for it before *Hashem*.

13:2 Raise a standard upon a bare hill *Yeshayahu* begins a series of prophecies against the nations (chapters 13–23) with a message to Baby-lon. He calls on *Hashem*'s army to assemble on a mountaintop against the Babylonians. The word that describes the mountain is *nish-peh* (נשפה), which means 'bare.' The selected moun-

Appreciating the beauty of God's world in northern Israel

taintop is bare and empty of trees – most likely so that the *nays* (נס), the 'standard' or signal for the warriors to gather, might be better seen from it. *Yeshayahu* contrasts the barren mountain of Babylon (which means 'gates of gods' in Ugaritic) with the genuine mountain of *Hashem* in *Yerushalayim* described in chapter 2, which is the source of knowledge and righteousness for the world.

3 I have summoned My purified guests To execute My wrath; Behold, I have called My stalwarts, My proudly exultant ones."

ג אֲנִי צִוֵּיתִי לִמְקֻדָּשָׁי גַּם קָרָאתִי גִבּוֹרַי לְאַפִּי עַלִּיזֵי גַּאֲוָתִי:

4 Hark! a tumult on the mountains – As of a mighty force; Hark! an uproar of kingdoms, Nations assembling! the Lord of Hosts is mustering A host for war.

ד קוֹל הָמוֹן בֶּהָרִים דְּמוּת עַם־רָב קוֹל שָׁאוֹן מַמְלְכוֹת גּוֹיִם נֶאֱסָפִים יְהֹוָה צְבָאוֹת מְפַקֵּד צְבָא מִלְחָמָה:

5 They come from a distant land, From the end of the sky – *Hashem* with the weapons of His wrath – To ravage all the earth!

ה בָּאִים מֵאֶרֶץ מֶרְחָק מִקְצֵה הַשָּׁמָיִם יְהֹוָה וּכְלֵי זַעְמוֹ לְחַבֵּל כָּל־הָאָרֶץ:

6 Howl! For the day of *Hashem* is near; It shall come like havoc from *Shaddai*.

ו הֵילִילוּ כִּי קָרוֹב יוֹם יְהֹוָה כְּשֹׁד מִשַּׁדַּי יָבוֹא:

7 Therefore all hands shall grow limp, And all men's hearts shall sink;

ז עַל־כֵּן כָּל־יָדַיִם תִּרְפֶּינָה וְכָל־לְבַב אֱנוֹשׁ יִמָּס:

8 And, overcome by terror, They shall be seized by pangs and throes, Writhe like a woman in travail. They shall gaze at each other in horror, Their faces livid with fright.

ח וְנִבְהָלוּ צִירִים וַחֲבָלִים יֹאחֵזוּן כַּיּוֹלֵדָה יְחִילוּן אִישׁ אֶל־רֵעֵהוּ יִתְמָהוּ פְּנֵי לְהָבִים פְּנֵיהֶם:

9 Lo! The day of *Hashem* is coming With pitiless fury and wrath, To make the earth a desolation, To wipe out the sinners upon it.

ט הִנֵּה יוֹם־יְהֹוָה בָּא אַכְזָרִי וְעֶבְרָה וַחֲרוֹן אָף לָשׂוּם הָאָרֶץ לְשַׁמָּה וְחַטָּאֶיהָ יַשְׁמִיד מִמֶּנָּה:

10 The stars and constellations of heaven Shall not give off their light; The sun shall be dark when it rises, And the moon shall diffuse no glow.

י כִּי־כוֹכְבֵי הַשָּׁמַיִם וּכְסִילֵיהֶם לֹא יָהֵלּוּ אוֹרָם חָשַׁךְ הַשֶּׁמֶשׁ בְּצֵאתוֹ וְיָרֵחַ לֹא־יַגִּיהַּ אוֹרוֹ:

11 "And I will requite to the world its evil, And to the wicked their iniquity; I will put an end to the pride of the arrogant And humble the haughtiness of tyrants.

יא וּפָקַדְתִּי עַל־תֵּבֵל רָעָה וְעַל־רְשָׁעִים עֲוֺנָם וְהִשְׁבַּתִּי גְּאוֹן זֵדִים וְגַאֲוַת עָרִיצִים אַשְׁפִּיל:

12 I will make people scarcer than fine gold, And men than gold of Ophir."

יב אוֹקִיר אֱנוֹשׁ מִפָּז וְאָדָם מִכֶּתֶם אוֹפִיר:

13 Therefore shall heaven be shaken, And earth leap out of its place, At the fury of the Lord of Hosts On the day of His burning wrath.

יג עַל־כֵּן שָׁמַיִם אַרְגִּיז וְתִרְעַשׁ הָאָרֶץ מִמְּקוֹמָהּ בְּעֶבְרַת יְהֹוָה צְבָאוֹת וּבְיוֹם חֲרוֹן אַפּוֹ:

14 Then like gazelles that are chased, And like sheep that no man gathers, Each man shall turn back to his people, They shall flee every one to his land.

יד וְהָיָה כִּצְבִי מֻדָּח וּכְצֹאן וְאֵין מְקַבֵּץ אִישׁ אֶל־עַמּוֹ יִפְנוּ וְאִישׁ אֶל־אַרְצוֹ יָנוּסוּ:

15 All who remain shall be pierced through, All who are caught Shall fall by the sword.

טו כָּל־הַנִּמְצָא יִדָּקֵר וְכָל־הַנִּסְפֶּה יִפּוֹל בֶּחָרֶב:

16 And their babes shall be dashed to pieces in their sight, Their homes shall be plundered, And their wives shall be raped.

טז וְעֹלְלֵיהֶם יְרֻטְּשׁוּ לְעֵינֵיהֶם יִשַּׁסּוּ בָּתֵּיהֶם וּנְשֵׁיהֶם תשגלנה [תִּשָּׁכַבְנָה]:

17	"Behold, I stir up the Medes against them, Who do not value silver Or delight in gold.	הִנְנִי מֵעִיר עֲלֵיהֶם אֶת־מָדָי אֲשֶׁר־כֶּסֶף לֹא יַחְשֹׁבוּ וְזָהָב לֹא יַחְפְּצוּ־בוֹ: יז
18	Their bows shall shatter the young; They shall show no pity to infants, They shall not spare the children."	וּקְשָׁתוֹת נְעָרִים תְּרַטַּשְׁנָה וּפְרִי־בֶטֶן לֹא יְרַחֵמוּ עַל־בָּנִים לֹא־תָחוּס עֵינָם: יח
19	And Babylon, glory of kingdoms, Proud splendor of the Chaldeans, Shall become like Sodom and Gomorrah Overturned by *Hashem*.	וְהָיְתָה בָבֶל צְבִי מַמְלָכוֹת תִּפְאֶרֶת גְּאוֹן כַּשְׂדִּים כְּמַהְפֵּכַת אֱלֹהִים אֶת־סְדֹם וְאֶת־עֲמֹרָה: יט
20	Nevermore shall it be settled Nor dwelt in through all the ages. No Arab shall pitch his tent there, No shepherds make flocks lie down there.	לֹא־תֵשֵׁב לָנֶצַח וְלֹא תִשְׁכֹּן עַד־דּוֹר וָדוֹר וְלֹא־יַהֵל שָׁם עֲרָבִי וְרֹעִים לֹא־יַרְבִּצוּ שָׁם: כ
21	But beasts shall lie down there, And the houses be filled with owls; There shall ostriches make their home, And there shall satyrs dance.	וְרָבְצוּ־שָׁם צִיִּים וּמָלְאוּ בָתֵּיהֶם אֹחִים וְשָׁכְנוּ שָׁם בְּנוֹת יַעֲנָה וּשְׂעִירִים יְרַקְּדוּ־שָׁם: כא
22	And jackals shall abide in its castles And dragons in the palaces of pleasure. Her hour is close at hand; Her days will not be long.	וְעָנָה אִיִּים בְּאַלְמְנוֹתָיו וְתַנִּים בְּהֵיכְלֵי עֹנֶג וְקָרוֹב לָבוֹא עִתָּהּ וְיָמֶיהָ לֹא יִמָּשֵׁכוּ: כב

Isaiah

14 1	But *Hashem* will pardon *Yaakov*, and will again choose *Yisrael*, and will settle them on their own soil. And strangers shall join them and shall cleave to the House of *Yaakov*.	כִּי יְרַחֵם יְהֹוָה אֶת־יַעֲקֹב וּבָחַר עוֹד בְּיִשְׂרָאֵל וְהִנִּיחָם עַל־אַדְמָתָם וְנִלְוָה הַגֵּר עֲלֵיהֶם וְנִסְפְּחוּ עַל־בֵּית יַעֲקֹב: א יד

KEE y'-ra-KHAYM a-do-NAI et ya-a-KOV u-va-KHAR OD
b'-yis-ra-AYL v'-hi-nee-KHAM al ad-ma-TAM v'-nil-VAH
ha-GAYR a-lay-HEM v'-nis-p'-KHU al BAYT ya-a-KOV

2	For peoples shall take them and bring them to their homeland; and the House of *Yisrael* shall possess them as slaves and handmaids on the soil of *Hashem*. They shall be captors of their captors and masters to their taskmasters.	וּלְקָחוּם עַמִּים וֶהֱבִיאוּם אֶל־מְקוֹמָם וְהִתְנַחֲלוּם בֵּית־יִשְׂרָאֵל עַל אַדְמַת יְהֹוָה לַעֲבָדִים וְלִשְׁפָחוֹת וְהָיוּ שֹׁבִים לְשֹׁבֵיהֶם וְרָדוּ בְּנֹגְשֵׂיהֶם: ב
3	And when *Hashem* has given you rest from your sorrow and trouble, and from the hard service that you were made to serve,	וְהָיָה בְּיוֹם הָנִיחַ יְהֹוָה לְךָ מֵעָצְבְּךָ וּמֵרָגְזֶךָ וּמִן־הָעֲבֹדָה הַקָּשָׁה אֲשֶׁר עֻבַּד־בָּךְ: ג
4	you shall recite this song of scorn over the king of Babylon: How is the taskmaster vanished, How is oppression ended!	וְנָשָׂאתָ הַמָּשָׁל הַזֶּה עַל־מֶלֶךְ בָּבֶל וְאָמָרְתָּ אֵיךְ שָׁבַת נֹגֵשׂ שָׁבְתָה מַדְהֵבָה: ד
5	*Hashem* has broken the staff of the wicked, The rod of tyrants,	שָׁבַר יְהֹוָה מַטֵּה רְשָׁעִים שֵׁבֶט מֹשְׁלִים: ה
6	That smote peoples in wrath With stroke unceasing, That belabored nations in fury In relentless pursuit.	מַכֶּה עַמִּים בְּעֶבְרָה מַכַּת בִּלְתִּי סָרָה רֹדֶה בָאַף גּוֹיִם מֻרְדָּף בְּלִי חָשָׂךְ: ו
7	All the earth is calm, untroubled; Loudly it cheers.	נָחָה שָׁקְטָה כָּל־הָאָרֶץ פָּצְחוּ רִנָּה: ז

8 Even pines rejoice at your fate, And cedars of Lebanon: "Now that you have lain down, None shall come up to fell us."

ח גַּם־בְּרוֹשִׁים שָׂמְחוּ לְךָ אַרְזֵי לְבָנוֹן מֵאָז שָׁכַבְתָּ לֹא־יַעֲלֶה הַכֹּרֵת עָלֵינוּ:

9 Sheol below was astir To greet your coming – Rousing for you the shades Of all earth's chieftains, Raising from their thrones All the kings of nations.

ט שְׁאוֹל מִתַּחַת רָגְזָה לְךָ לִקְרַאת בּוֹאֶךָ עוֹרֵר לְךָ רְפָאִים כָּל־עַתּוּדֵי אָרֶץ הֵקִים מִכִּסְאוֹתָם כֹּל מַלְכֵי גוֹיִם:

10 All speak up and say to you, "So you have been stricken as we were, You have become like us!

י כֻּלָּם יַעֲנוּ וְיֹאמְרוּ אֵלֶיךָ גַּם־אַתָּה חֻלֵּיתָ כָמוֹנוּ אֵלֵינוּ נִמְשָׁלְתָּ:

11 Your pomp is brought down to Sheol, And the strains of your lutes! Worms are to be your bed, Maggots your blanket!"

יא הוּרַד שְׁאוֹל גְּאוֹנֶךָ הֶמְיַת נְבָלֶיךָ תַּחְתֶּיךָ יֻצַּע רִמָּה וּמְכַסֶּיךָ תּוֹלֵעָה:

12 How are you fallen from heaven, O Shining One, son of Dawn! How are you felled to earth, O vanquisher of nations!

יב אֵיךְ נָפַלְתָּ מִשָּׁמַיִם הֵילֵל בֶּן־שָׁחַר נִגְדַּעְתָּ לָאָרֶץ חוֹלֵשׁ עַל־גּוֹיִם:

13 Once you thought in your heart, "I will climb to the sky; Higher than the stars of *Hashem* I will set my throne. I will sit in the mount of assembly, On the summit of Zaphon:

יג וְאַתָּה אָמַרְתָּ בִלְבָבְךָ הַשָּׁמַיִם אֶעֱלֶה מִמַּעַל לְכוֹכְבֵי־אֵל אָרִים כִּסְאִי וְאֵשֵׁב בְּהַר־מוֹעֵד בְּיַרְכְּתֵי צָפוֹן:

14 I will mount the back of a cloud – I will match the Most High."

יד אֶעֱלֶה עַל־בָּמֳתֵי עָב אֶדַּמֶּה לְעֶלְיוֹן:

e-e-LEH al BA-mo-tay av e-da-MEH l'-el-YON

15 Instead, you are brought down to Sheol, To the bottom of the Pit.

טו אַךְ אֶל־שְׁאוֹל תּוּרָד אֶל־יַרְכְּתֵי־בוֹר:

16 They who behold you stare; They peer at you closely: "Is this the man Who shook the earth, Who made realms tremble,

טז רֹאֶיךָ אֵלֶיךָ יַשְׁגִּיחוּ אֵלֶיךָ יִתְבּוֹנָנוּ הֲזֶה הָאִישׁ מַרְגִּיז הָאָרֶץ מַרְעִישׁ מַמְלָכוֹת:

17 Who made the world like a waste And wrecked its towns, Who never released his prisoners to their homes?"

יז שָׂם תֵּבֵל כַּמִּדְבָּר וְעָרָיו הָרָס אֲסִירָיו לֹא־פָתַח בָּיְתָה:

18 All the kings of nations Were laid, every one, in honor Each in his tomb;

יח כָּל־מַלְכֵי גוֹיִם כֻּלָּם שָׁכְבוּ בְכָבוֹד אִישׁ בְּבֵיתוֹ:

19 While you were left lying unburied, Like loathsome carrion, Like a trampled corpse [In] the clothing of slain gashed by the sword Who sink to the very stones of the Pit.

יט וְאַתָּה הָשְׁלַכְתָּ מִקִּבְרְךָ כְּנֵצֶר נִתְעָב לְבוּשׁ הֲרֻגִים מְטֹעֲנֵי חָרֶב יוֹרְדֵי אֶל־אַבְנֵי־בוֹר כְּפֶגֶר מוּבָס:

Man overlooking the colored sand stone at *HaMakhtesh HaGadol* in the Negev desert

אדם
אדמה

14:14 I will match the Most High The Hebrew word for 'man' is *adam* (אדם). Rabbi Yeshaya Horowitz, who lived in Prague in the sixteenth and seventeenth centuries and is better known by the acronym of his important work as "the *Shelah*", points out that the word *adam* may originate from the word *edameh* (אֶדַּמֶּה), 'I will match,' in this verse – indicating that man's mission in this world is *imitatio dei*, the imperative to imitate God by emulating His actions. At the same time, man should not become haughty due to his lofty task. This too is hinted at by the word *adam*, which may also be derived from the word *adama* (אֲדָמָה) 'earth,' reminding man of his lowly origins, as he was fashioned from the earth (Genesis 2:7).

20 You shall not have a burial like them; Because you destroyed your country, Murdered your people. Let the breed of evildoers Nevermore be named!

כ לֹא־תֵחַד אִתָּם בִּקְבוּרָה כִּי־אַרְצְךָ שִׁחַתָּ עַמְּךָ הָרָגְתָּ לֹא־יִקָּרֵא לְעוֹלָם זֶרַע מְרֵעִים:

21 Prepare a slaughtering block for his sons Because of the guilt of their father. Let them not arise to possess the earth! Then the world's face shall be covered with towns.

כא הָכִינוּ לְבָנָיו מַטְבֵּחַ בַּעֲוֺן אֲבוֹתָם בַּל־ יָקֻמוּ וְיָרְשׁוּ אָרֶץ וּמָלְאוּ פְנֵי־תֵבֵל עָרִים:

22 I will rise up against them – declares the LORD of Hosts – and will wipe out from Babylon name and remnant, kith and kin – declares *Hashem*

כב וְקַמְתִּי עֲלֵיהֶם נְאֻם יְהוָה צְבָאוֹת וְהִכְרַתִּי לְבָבֶל שֵׁם וּשְׁאָר וְנִין וָנֶכֶד נְאֻם־יְהוָה:

23 and I will make it a home of bitterns, pools of water. I will sweep it with a broom of extermination – declares the LORD of Hosts.

כג וְשַׂמְתִּיהָ לְמוֹרַשׁ קִפֹּד וְאַגְמֵי־מָיִם וְטֵאטֵאתִיהָ בְּמַטְאֲטֵא הַשְׁמֵד נְאֻם יְהוָה צְבָאוֹת:

24 the LORD of Hosts has sworn this oath: "As I have designed, so shall it happen; What I have planned, that shall come to pass:

כד נִשְׁבַּע יְהוָה צְבָאוֹת לֵאמֹר אִם־לֹא כַּאֲשֶׁר דִּמִּיתִי כֵּן הָיָתָה וְכַאֲשֶׁר יָעַצְתִּי הִיא תָקוּם:

25 To break Assyria in My land, To crush him on My mountain." And his yoke shall drop off them, And his burden shall drop from their backs.

כה לִשְׁבֹּר אַשּׁוּר בְּאַרְצִי וְעַל־הָרַי אֲבוּסֶנּוּ וְסָר מֵעֲלֵיהֶם עֻלּוֹ וְסֻבֳּלוֹ מֵעַל שִׁכְמוֹ יָסוּר:

26 That is the plan that is planned For all the earth; That is why an arm is poised Over all the nations.

כו זֹאת הָעֵצָה הַיְעוּצָה עַל־כָּל־הָאָרֶץ וְזֹאת הַיָּד הַנְּטוּיָה עַל־כָּל־הַגּוֹיִם:

27 For the LORD of Hosts has planned, Who then can foil it? It is His arm that is poised, And who can stay it?

כז כִּי־יְהוָה צְבָאוֹת יָעָץ וּמִי יָפֵר וְיָדוֹ הַנְּטוּיָה וּמִי יְשִׁיבֶנָּה:

28 This pronouncement was made in the year that King *Achaz* died:

כח בִּשְׁנַת־מוֹת הַמֶּלֶךְ אָחָז הָיָה הַמַּשָּׂא הַזֶּה:

29 Rejoice not, all Philistia, Because the staff of him that beat you is broken. For from the stock of a snake there sprouts an asp, A flying seraph branches out from it.

כט אַל־תִּשְׂמְחִי פְלֶשֶׁת כֻּלֵּךְ כִּי נִשְׁבַּר שֵׁבֶט מַכֵּךְ כִּי־מִשֹּׁרֶשׁ נָחָשׁ יֵצֵא צֶפַע וּפִרְיוֹ שָׂרָף מְעוֹפֵף:

30 The first-born of the poor shall graze And the destitute lie down secure. I will kill your stock by famine, And it shall slay the very last of you.

ל וְרָעוּ בְּכוֹרֵי דַלִּים וְאֶבְיוֹנִים לָבֶטַח יִרְבָּצוּ וְהֵמַתִּי בָרָעָב שָׁרְשֵׁךְ וּשְׁאֵרִיתֵךְ יַהֲרֹג:

31 Howl, O gate; cry out, O city; Quake, all Philistia! For a stout one is coming from the north And there is no straggler in his ranks.

לא הֵילִילִי שַׁעַר זַעֲקִי־עִיר נָמוֹג פְּלֶשֶׁת כֻּלֵּךְ כִּי מִצָּפוֹן עָשָׁן בָּא וְאֵין בּוֹדֵד בְּמוֹעָדָיו:

32 And what will he answer the messengers of any nation? That *Tzion* has been established by *Hashem*: In it, the needy of His people shall find shelter.

לב וּמַה־יַּעֲנֶה מַלְאֲכֵי־גוֹי כִּי יְהוָה יִסַּד צִיּוֹן וּבָהּ יֶחֱסוּ עֲנִיֵּי עַמּוֹ:

15 1 The "Moab" Pronouncement. Ah, in the night Ar was sacked, Moab was ruined; Ah, in the night Kir was sacked, Moab was ruined.

טו א מַשָּׂא מוֹאָב כִּי בְּלֵיל שֻׁדַּד עָר מוֹאָב נִדְמָה כִּי בְּלֵיל שֻׁדַּד קִיר־מוֹאָב נִדְמָה:

Isaiah

2 He went up to the temple to weep, Dibon [went] to the outdoor shrines. Over Nebo and Medeba Moab is wailing; On every head is baldness, Every beard is shorn.

ב עָלָה הַבַּיִת וְדִיבֹן הַבָּמוֹת לְבֶכִי עַל־נְבוֹ וְעַל מֵידְבָא מוֹאָב יְיֵלִיל בְּכָל־רָאשָׁיו קָרְחָה כָּל־זָקָן גְּרוּעָה:

3 In its streets, they are girt with sackcloth; On its roofs, in its squares, Everyone is wailing, Streaming with tears.

ג בְּחוּצֹתָיו חָגְרוּ שָׂק עַל גַּגּוֹתֶיהָ וּבִרְחֹבֹתֶיהָ כֻּלֹּה יְיֵלִיל יֹרֵד בַּבֶּכִי:

4 Heshbon and Elealeh cry out, Their voice carries to Jahaz. Therefore, The shock troops of Moab shout, His body is convulsed.

ד וַתִּזְעַק חֶשְׁבּוֹן וְאֶלְעָלֵה עַד־יַהַץ נִשְׁמַע קוֹלָם עַל־כֵּן חֲלֻצֵי מוֹאָב יָרִיעוּ נַפְשׁוֹ יָרְעָה לּוֹ:

5 My heart cries out for Moab – His fugitives flee down to Zoar, To Eglath-shelishiyah. For the ascent of Luhith They ascend with weeping; On the road to Horonaim They raise a cry of anguish.

ה לִבִּי לְמוֹאָב יִזְעָק בְּרִיחֶהָ עַד־צֹעַר עֶגְלַת שְׁלִשִׁיָּה כִּי מַעֲלֵה הַלּוּחִית בִּבְכִי יַעֲלֶה־בּוֹ כִּי דֶּרֶךְ חוֹרֹנַיִם זַעֲקַת־שֶׁבֶר יְעֹעֵרוּ:

li-BEE l'-mo-AV yiz-AK b'-ree-KHE-ha ad TZO-ar eg-LAT
sh'-li-shi-YAH KEE ma-a-LAY ha-lu-KHEET biv-KHEE ya-a-leh BO
KEE DE-rekh kho-ro-NA-yim za-a-kat SHE-ver y'-o-AY-ru

6 Ah, the waters of Nimrim Are become a desolation; The grass is sear, The herbage is gone, Vegetation is vanished.

ו כִּי־מֵי נִמְרִים מְשַׁמּוֹת יִהְיוּ כִּי־יָבֵשׁ חָצִיר כָּלָה דֶשֶׁא יֶרֶק לֹא הָיָה:

7 Therefore, The gains they have made, and their stores, They carry to the Wadi of Willows.

ז עַל־כֵּן יִתְרָה עָשָׂה וּפְקֻדָּתָם עַל נַחַל הָעֲרָבִים יִשָּׂאוּם:

8 Ah, the cry has compassed The country of Moab: All the way to Eglaim her wailing, Even at Beer-elim her wailing!

ח כִּי־הִקִּיפָה הַזְּעָקָה אֶת־גְּבוּל מוֹאָב עַד־ אֶגְלַיִם יִלְלָתָהּ וּבְאֵר אֵילִים יִלְלָתָהּ:

9 Ah, the waters of Dimon are full of blood For I pour added [water] on Dimon; I drench it – for Moab's refugees – With soil for its remnant.

ט כִּי מֵי דִימוֹן מָלְאוּ דָם כִּי־אָשִׁית עַל־ דִּימוֹן נוֹסָפוֹת לִפְלֵיטַת מוֹאָב אַרְיֵה וְלִשְׁאֵרִית אֲדָמָה:

16 1 Dispatch as messenger The ruler of the land, From Sela in the wilderness To the mount of Fair *Tzion*:

טז א שִׁלְחוּ־כַר מֹשֵׁל־אֶרֶץ מִסֶּלַע מִדְבָּרָה אֶל־הַר בַּת־צִיּוֹן:

2 "Like fugitive birds, Like nestlings driven away, Moab's villagers linger By the fords of the Arnon.

ב וְהָיָה כְעוֹף־נוֹדֵד קֵן מְשֻׁלָּח תִּהְיֶינָה בְּנוֹת מוֹאָב מַעְבָּרֹת לְאַרְנוֹן:

3 Give advice, Offer counsel. At high noon make Your shadow like night: Conceal the outcasts, Betray not the fugitives.

ג הָבִיאוּ [הָבִיאִי] עֵצָה עֲשׂוּ פְלִילָה שִׁיתִי כַלַּיִל צִלֵּךְ בְּתוֹךְ צָהֳרַיִם סַתְּרִי נִדָּחִים נֹדֵד אַל־תְּגַלִּי:

Israeli soldiers praying at the Western Wall

15:5 My heart cries out for Moab Having taunted Babylon, Assyria, and the Philistines, *Yeshayahu* now turns to *Yehuda's* southeastern neighbor, Moab. As the previous prophecies describe, the upcoming destruction and desolation of Moab will be total. What is noteworthy, however, is the prophet's refusal to rejoice over Moab's downfall. Though Moab is one of Israel's ancient enemies, *Yeshayahu* cannot restrain himself from sympathizing over their plight. This is reminiscent of the verse in Proverbs (24:17) "If your enemy falls, do not exult; If he trips, let your heart not rejoice."

⁴ Let Moab's outcasts Find asylum in you; Be a shelter for them Against the despoiler." For violence has vanished, Rapine is ended, And marauders have perished from this land.

ד יָגוּרוּ בָךְ נִדָּחַי מוֹאָב הֱוִי־סֵתֶר לָמוֹ מִפְּנֵי שׁוֹדֵד כִּי־אָפֵס הַמֵּץ כָּלָה שֹׁד תַּמּוּ רֹמֵס מִן־הָאָרֶץ:

⁵ And a throne shall be established in goodness In the tent of *David*, And on it shall sit in faithfulness A ruler devoted to justice And zealous for equity.

ה וְהוּכַן בַּחֶסֶד כִּסֵּא וְיָשַׁב עָלָיו בֶּאֱמֶת בְּאֹהֶל דָּוִד שֹׁפֵט וְדֹרֵשׁ מִשְׁפָּט וּמְהִר צֶדֶק:

v'-hu-KHAN ba-KHE-sed ki-SAY v'-ya-SHAV a-LAV be-e-MET b'-O-hel
da-VID sho-FAYT v'-do-RAYSH mish-PAT um-HEER TZE-dek

⁶ "We have heard of Moab's pride – Most haughty is he – Of his pride and haughtiness and arrogance, And of the iniquity in him."

ו שָׁמַעְנוּ גְאוֹן־מוֹאָב גֵּא מְאֹד גַּאֲוָתוֹ וּגְאוֹנוֹ וְעֶבְרָתוֹ לֹא־כֵן בַּדָּיו:

⁷ Ah, let Moab howl; Let all in Moab howl! For the raisin-cakes of Kir-hareseth You shall moan most pitifully.

ז לָכֵן יְיֵלִיל מוֹאָב לְמוֹאָב כֻּלֹּה יְיֵלִיל לַאֲשִׁישֵׁי קִיר־חֲרֶשֶׂת תֶּהְגּוּ אַךְ־נְכָאִים:

⁸ The vineyards of Heshbon are withered, And the vines of Sibmah; Their tendrils spread To Baale-goiim, And reached to Jazer, And strayed to the desert; Their shoots spread out And crossed the sea.

ח כִּי שַׁדְמוֹת חֶשְׁבּוֹן אֻמְלָל גֶּפֶן שִׂבְמָה בַּעֲלֵי גוֹיִם הָלְמוּ שְׂרוּקֶיהָ עַד־יַעְזֵר נָגָעוּ תָּעוּ מִדְבָּר שְׁלֻחוֹתֶיהָ נִטְּשׁוּ עָבְרוּ יָם:

⁹ Therefore, As I weep for Jazer, So I weep for Sibmah's vines; O Heshbon and Elealeh, I drench you with my tears. Ended are the shouts Over your fig and grain harvests.

ט עַל־כֵּן אֶבְכֶּה בִּבְכִי יַעְזֵר גֶּפֶן שִׂבְמָה אֲרַיָּוֶךְ דִּמְעָתִי חֶשְׁבּוֹן וְאֶלְעָלֵה כִּי עַל־ קֵיצֵךְ וְעַל־קְצִירֵךְ הֵידָד נָפָל:

¹⁰ Rejoicing and gladness Are gone from the farm land; In the vineyards no shouting Or cheering is heard. No more does the treader Tread wine in the presses – The shouts have been silenced.

י וְנֶאֱסַף שִׂמְחָה וָגִיל מִן־הַכַּרְמֶל וּבַכְּרָמִים לֹא־יְרֻנָּן לֹא יְרֹעָע יַיִן בַּיְקָבִים לֹא־יִדְרֹךְ הַדֹּרֵךְ הֵידָד הִשְׁבַּתִּי:

¹¹ Therefore, Like a lyre my heart moans for Moab, And my very soul for Kir-heres.

יא עַל־כֵּן מֵעַי לְמוֹאָב כַּכִּנּוֹר יֶהֱמוּ וְקִרְבִּי לְקִיר חָרֶשׂ:

¹² And when it has become apparent that Moab has gained nothing in the outdoor shrine, he shall come to pray in his temple – but to no avail.

יב וְהָיָה כִי־נִרְאָה כִּי־נִלְאָה מוֹאָב עַל־ הַבָּמָה וּבָא אֶל־מִקְדָּשׁוֹ לְהִתְפַּלֵּל וְלֹא יוּכָל:

¹³ That is the word that *Hashem* spoke concerning Moab long ago.

יג זֶה הַדָּבָר אֲשֶׁר דִּבֶּר יְהוָה אֶל־מוֹאָב מֵאָז:

16:5 A ruler devoted to justice, and zealous for equity In the time of King *David*, Moab paid tribute to *Yisrael* and *Yehuda* (II Samuel 8:2). *Yeshayahu* foresees a time when the remnant of Moab that survives the calamities will once again send tribute to *Yehuda* and live with Israel in friendship and brotherhood. However, for that to happen, the king that sits on *David*'s throne will have to be a worthy one, who promotes justice for the poor and needy; instead of delaying justice, he hastens to execute it quickly throughout *Eretz Yisrael*.

A modern court house in *Be'er Sheva*

Isaiah

14 And now *Hashem* has spoken: In three years, fixed like the years of a hired laborer, Moab's population, with all its huge multitude, shall shrink. Only a remnant shall be left, of no consequence.

יד וְעַתָּה דִּבֶּר יְהֹוָה לֵאמֹר בְּשָׁלֹשׁ שָׁנִים כִּשְׁנֵי שָׂכִיר וְנִקְלָה כְּבוֹד מוֹאָב בְּכֹל הֶהָמוֹן הָרָב וּשְׁאָר מְעַט מִזְעָר לוֹא כַבִּיר:

17 **1** The "Damascus" Pronouncement. Behold, Damascus shall cease to be a city; It shall become a heap of ruins.

יז א מַשָּׂא דַּמָּשֶׂק הִנֵּה דַמֶּשֶׂק מוּסָר מֵעִיר וְהָיְתָה מְעִי מַפָּלָה:

2 The towns of Aroer shall be deserted; They shall be a place for flocks To lie down, with none disturbing.

ב עֲזֻבוֹת עָרֵי עֲרֹעֵר לַעֲדָרִים תִּהְיֶינָה וְרָבְצוּ וְאֵין מַחֲרִיד:

3 Fortresses shall cease from *Efraim*, And sovereignty from Damascus; The remnant of Aram shall become Like the mass of Israelites – declares the LORD of Hosts.

ג וְנִשְׁבַּת מִבְצָר מֵאֶפְרַיִם וּמַמְלָכָה מִדַּמֶּשֶׂק וּשְׁאָר אֲרָם כִּכְבוֹד בְּנֵי־יִשְׂרָאֵל יִהְיוּ נְאֻם יְהֹוָה צְבָאוֹת:

4 In that day, The mass of *Yaakov* shall dwindle, And the fatness of his body become lean:

ד וְהָיָה בַּיּוֹם הַהוּא יִדַּל כְּבוֹד יַעֲקֹב וּמִשְׁמַן בְּשָׂרוֹ יֵרָזֶה:

5 After being like the standing grain Harvested by the reaper – Who reaps ears by the armful – He shall be like the ears that are gleaned In the Valley of Rephaim.

ה וְהָיָה כֶּאֱסֹף קָצִיר קָמָה וּזְרֹעוֹ שִׁבֳּלִים יִקְצוֹר וְהָיָה כִּמְלַקֵּט שִׁבֳּלִים בְּעֵמֶק רְפָאִים:

6 Only gleanings shall be left of him, As when one beats an olive tree: Two berries or three on the topmost branch, Four or five on the boughs of the crown – declares *Hashem*, the God of *Yisrael*.

ו וְנִשְׁאַר־בּוֹ עוֹלֵלֹת כְּנֹקֶף זַיִת שְׁנַיִם שְׁלֹשָׁה גַּרְגְּרִים בְּרֹאשׁ אָמִיר אַרְבָּעָה חֲמִשָּׁה בִּסְעִפֶיהָ פֹּרִיָּה נְאֻם־יְהֹוָה אֱלֹהֵי יִשְׂרָאֵל:

7 In that day, men shall turn to their Maker, their eyes look to the Holy One of *Yisrael*;

ז בַּיּוֹם הַהוּא יִשְׁעֶה הָאָדָם עַל־עֹשֵׂהוּ וְעֵינָיו אֶל־קְדוֹשׁ יִשְׂרָאֵל תִּרְאֶינָה:

ba-YOM ha-HU yish-EH ha-a-DAM al o-SAY-hu
v'-ay-NAV el k'-DOSH yis-ra-AYL tir-E-nah

8 they shall not turn to the altars that their own hands made, or look to the sacred posts and incense stands that their own fingers wrought.

ח וְלֹא יִשְׁעֶה אֶל־הַמִּזְבְּחוֹת מַעֲשֵׂה יָדָיו וַאֲשֶׁר עָשׂוּ אֶצְבְּעֹתָיו לֹא יִרְאֶה וְהָאֲשֵׁרִים וְהָחַמָּנִים:

Members of the *B'nei Menashe*, descendants of the lost tribe of *Menashe*, arrive at Ben Gurion airport

17:7 In that day, men shall turn to their Maker *Yeshayahu* prophesies about Damascus, the capital city of Aram. Once Israel's vicious enemy to the north, Aram had allied itself with Israel in a futile attempt to stave off destruction at the hands of the invading Assyrians. *Yeshayahu* describes the totality of the destruction of both Aram and *Yisrael*, but then notes that a few of the Israelites are to be saved, as a remnant made holy, awakened to return to God. This remnant appears in the time of King *Yoshiyahu*, about whom the Bible recounts that offerings of money were made for the Temple service by men of "*Menashe* and *Ephraim*, and from all the remnant of *Yisrael*," which the *Leviim* collected and brought to *Yerushalayim* (II Chronicles 34:9). Similarly, in the times of *Mashiach*, the entire kingdom of *Yisrael*, the remnants of all ten of its "lost tribes," will return to the Lord and their land.

9 In that day, their fortress cities shall be like the deserted sites which the Horesh and the Amir abandoned because of the Israelites; and there shall be desolation.

ט בַּיּוֹם הַהוּא יִהְיוּ עָרֵי מָעֻזּוֹ כַּעֲזוּבַת הַחֹרֶשׁ וְהָאָמִיר אֲשֶׁר עָזְבוּ מִפְּנֵי בְּנֵי יִשְׂרָאֵל וְהָיְתָה שְׁמָמָה:

10 Truly, you have forgotten the God who saves you And have not remembered the Rock who shelters you; That is why, though you plant a delightful sapling, What you sow proves a disappointing slip.

י כִּי שָׁכַחַתְּ אֱלֹהֵי יִשְׁעֵךְ וְצוּר מָעֻזֵּךְ לֹא זָכָרְתְּ עַל־כֵּן תִּטְּעִי נִטְעֵי נַעֲמָנִים וּזְמֹרַת זָר תִּזְרָעֶנּוּ:

11 On the day that you plant, you see it grow; On the morning you sow, you see it bud – But the branches wither away On a day of sickness and mortal agony.

יא בְּיוֹם נִטְעֵךְ תְּשַׂגְשֵׂגִי וּבַבֹּקֶר זַרְעֵךְ תַּפְרִיחִי נֵד קָצִיר בְּיוֹם נַחֲלָה וּכְאֵב אָנוּשׁ:

12 Ah, the roar of many peoples That roar as roars the sea, The rage of nations that rage As rage the mighty waters –

יב הוֹי הֲמוֹן עַמִּים רַבִּים כַּהֲמוֹת יַמִּים יֶהֱמָיוּן וּשְׁאוֹן לְאֻמִּים כִּשְׁאוֹן מַיִם כַּבִּירִים יִשָּׁאוּן:

13 Nations raging like massive waters! But He shouts at them, and they flee far away, Driven like chaff before winds in the hills, And like tumbleweed before a gale.

יג לְאֻמִּים כִּשְׁאוֹן מַיִם רַבִּים יִשָּׁאוּן וְגָעַר בּוֹ וְנָס מִמֶּרְחָק וְרֻדַּף כְּמֹץ הָרִים לִפְנֵי־רוּחַ וּכְגַלְגַּל לִפְנֵי סוּפָה:

14 At eventide, lo, terror! By morning, it is no more. Such is the lot of our despoilers, The portion of them that plunder us.

יד לְעֵת עֶרֶב וְהִנֵּה בַלָּהָה בְּטֶרֶם בֹּקֶר אֵינֶנּוּ זֶה חֵלֶק שׁוֹסֵינוּ וְגוֹרָל לְבֹזְזֵינוּ:

18 1 Ah, land in the deep shadow of wings, Beyond the rivers of Nubia!

יח א הוֹי אֶרֶץ צִלְצַל כְּנָפָיִם אֲשֶׁר מֵעֵבֶר לְנַהֲרֵי־כוּשׁ:

2 Go, swift messengers, To a nation far and remote, To a people thrust forth and away – A nation of gibber and chatter – Whose land is cut off by streams; Which sends out envoys by sea, In papyrus vessels upon the water!*

ב הַשֹּׁלֵחַ בַּיָּם צִירִים וּבִכְלֵי־גֹמֶא עַל־פְּנֵי־מַיִם לְכוּ מַלְאָכִים קַלִּים אֶל־גּוֹי מְמֻשָּׁךְ וּמוֹרָט אֶל־עַם נוֹרָא מִן־הוּא וָהָלְאָה גּוֹי קַו־קָו וּמְבוּסָה אֲשֶׁר־בָּזְאוּ נְהָרִים אַרְצוֹ:

3 [Say this:] "All you who live in the world And inhabit the earth, When a flag is raised in the hills, take note! When a *shofar* is blown, give heed!"

ג כָּל־יֹשְׁבֵי תֵבֵל וְשֹׁכְנֵי אָרֶץ כִּנְשֹׂא־נֵס הָרִים תִּרְאוּ וְכִתְקֹעַ שׁוֹפָר תִּשְׁמָעוּ:

*kol yo-sh'-VAY tay-VAYL v'-sho-kh'-NAY A-retz kin-so NAYS
ha-REEM tir-U v'-khit-KO-a sho-FAR tish-MA-u*

4 For thus *Hashem* said to me: "I rest calm and confident in My habitation – Like a scorching heat upon sprouts, Like a rain-cloud in the heat of reaping time."

ד כִּי כֹה אָמַר יְהוָה אֵלַי אֶשְׁקוֹטָה [אֶשְׁקֳטָה] וְאַבִּיטָה בִמְכוֹנִי כְּחֹם צַח עֲלֵי־אוֹר כְּעָב טַל בְּחֹם קָצִיר:

---

* "Which sends out envoys by sea, In papyrus vessels upon the water!" brought down from the beginning of the verse for clarity

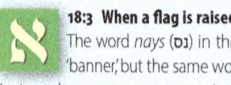

18:3 When a flag is raised in the hills, take note
The word *nays* (נס) in this verse means 'flag' or 'banner,' but the same word also means 'miracle.' Just as a banner serves as a reminder to onlookers, a mir- acle is also meant to remind "all inhabitants of the world" that *Hashem* directs all events from behind the scenes.

A young boy holding the Israeli flag

5 For before the harvest, yet after the budding, When the blossom has hardened into berries, He will trim away the twigs with pruning hooks, And lop off the trailing branches.

ה כִּי־לִפְנֵי קָצִיר כִּתָם־פֶּרַח וּבֹסֶר גֹּמֵל יִהְיֶה נִצָּה וְכָרַת הַזַּלְזַלִּים בַּמַּזְמֵרוֹת וְאֶת־הַנְּטִישׁוֹת הֵסִיר הֵתַז:

6 They shall all be left To the kites of the hills And to the beasts of the earth; The kites shall summer on them And all the beasts of the earth shall winter on them.

ו יֵעָזְבוּ יַחְדָּו לְעֵיט הָרִים וּלְבֶהֱמַת הָאָרֶץ וְקָץ עָלָיו הָעַיִט וְכָל־בֶּהֱמַת הָאָרֶץ עָלָיו תֶּחֱרָף:

7 In that time, Tribute shall be brought to the LORD of Hosts [From] a people far and remote, From a people thrust forth and away – A nation of gibber and chatter, Whose land is cut off by streams – At the place where the name of the LORD of Hosts abides, At Mount *Tzion*.

ז בָּעֵת הַהִיא יוּבַל־שַׁי לַיהֹוָה צְבָאוֹת עַם מְמֻשָּׁךְ וּמוֹרָט וּמֵעַם נוֹרָא מִן־הוּא וָהָלְאָה גּוֹי קַו־קָו וּמְבוּסָה אֲשֶׁר בָּזְאוּ נְהָרִים אַרְצוֹ אֶל־מְקוֹם שֵׁם־יְהֹוָה צְבָאוֹת הַר־צִיּוֹן:

19 1 The "Egypt" Pronouncement. Mounted on a swift cloud, *Hashem* will come to Egypt; Egypt's idols shall tremble before Him, And the heart of the Egyptians shall sink within them.

יט א מַשָּׂא מִצְרָיִם הִנֵּה יְהֹוָה רֹכֵב עַל־עָב קַל וּבָא מִצְרַיִם וְנָעוּ אֱלִילֵי מִצְרַיִם מִפָּנָיו וּלְבַב מִצְרַיִם יִמַּס בְּקִרְבּוֹ:

2 "I will incite Egyptian against Egyptian: They shall war with each other, Every man with his fellow, City with city And kingdom with kingdom.

ב וְסִכְסַכְתִּי מִצְרַיִם בְּמִצְרַיִם וְנִלְחֲמוּ אִישׁ־בְּאָחִיו וְאִישׁ בְּרֵעֵהוּ עִיר בְּעִיר מַמְלָכָה בְּמַמְלָכָה:

3 Egypt shall be drained of spirit, And I will confound its plans; So they will consult the idols and the shades And the ghosts and the familiar spirits.

ג וְנָבְקָה רוּחַ־מִצְרַיִם בְּקִרְבּוֹ וַעֲצָתוֹ אֲבַלֵּעַ וְדָרְשׁוּ אֶל־הָאֱלִילִים וְאֶל־הָאִטִּים וְאֶל־הָאֹבוֹת וְאֶל־הַיִּדְּעֹנִים:

4 And I will place the Egyptians At the mercy of a harsh master, And a ruthless king shall rule them" – declares the Sovereign, the LORD of Hosts.

ד וְסִכַּרְתִּי אֶת־מִצְרַיִם בְּיַד אֲדֹנִים קָשֶׁה וּמֶלֶךְ עַז יִמְשָׁל־בָּם נְאֻם הָאָדוֹן יְהֹוָה צְבָאוֹת:

5 Water shall fail from the seas, Rivers dry up and be parched,

ה וְנִשְּׁתוּ־מַיִם מֵהַיָּם וְנָהָר יֶחֱרַב וְיָבֵשׁ:

6 Channels turn foul as they ebb, And Egypt's canals run dry. Reed and rush shall decay,

ו וְהֶאֶזְנִיחוּ נְהָרוֹת דָּלְלוּ וְחָרְבוּ יְאֹרֵי מָצוֹר קָנֶה וָסוּף קָמֵלוּ:

7 And the Nile papyrus by the Nile-side And everything sown by the Nile Shall wither, blow away, and vanish.

ז עָרוֹת עַל־יְאוֹר עַל־פִּי יְאוֹר וְכֹל מִזְרַע יְאוֹר יִיבַשׁ נִדַּף וְאֵינֶנּוּ:

8 The fishermen shall lament; All who cast lines in the Nile shall mourn, And those who spread nets on the water shall languish.

ח וְאָנוּ הַדַּיָּגִים וְאָבְלוּ כָּל־מַשְׁלִיכֵי בַיְאוֹר חַכָּה וּפֹרְשֵׂי מִכְמֹרֶת עַל־פְּנֵי־מַיִם אֻמְלָלוּ:

9 The flax workers, too, shall be dismayed, Both carders and weavers chagrined.

ט וּבֹשׁוּ עֹבְדֵי פִשְׁתִּים שְׂרִיקוֹת וְאֹרְגִים חוֹרָי:

10 Her foundations shall be crushed, And all who make dams shall be despondent.

י וְהָיוּ שָׁתֹתֶיהָ מְדֻכָּאִים כָּל־עֹשֵׂי שֶׂכֶר אַגְמֵי־נָפֶשׁ:

Isaiah

11 Utter fools are the nobles of Tanis; The sagest of Pharaoh's advisers [Have made] absurd predictions. How can you say to Pharaoh, "I am a scion of sages, A scion of Kedemite kings"?

יא אַךְ־אֱוִלִים שָׂרֵי צֹעַן חַכְמֵי יֹעֲצֵי פַרְעֹה עֵצָה נִבְעָרָה אֵיךְ תֹּאמְרוּ אֶל־פַּרְעֹה בֶּן־חֲכָמִים אֲנִי בֶּן־מַלְכֵי־קֶדֶם:

12 Where, indeed, are your sages? Let them tell you, let them discover What the Lord of Hosts has planned against Egypt.

יב אַיָּם אֵפוֹא חֲכָמֶיךָ וְיַגִּידוּ נָא לָךְ וְיֵדְעוּ מַה־יָּעַץ יְהֹוָה צְבָאוֹת עַל־מִצְרָיִם:

13 The nobles of Tanis have been fools, The nobles of Memphis deluded; Egypt has been led astray By the chiefs of her tribes.

יג נוֹאֲלוּ שָׂרֵי צֹעַן נִשְׁאוּ שָׂרֵי נֹף הִתְעוּ אֶת־מִצְרַיִם פִּנַּת שְׁבָטֶיהָ:

14 *Hashem* has mixed within her A spirit of distortion, Which shall lead Egypt astray I all her undertakings As a vomiting drunkard goes astray;

יד יְהֹוָה מָסַךְ בְּקִרְבָּהּ רוּחַ עִוְעִים וְהִתְעוּ אֶת־מִצְרַיִם בְּכָל־מַעֲשֵׂהוּ כְּהִתָּעוֹת שִׁכּוֹר בְּקִיאוֹ:

15 Nothing shall be achieved in Egypt By either head or tail, Palm branch or reed.

טו וְלֹא־יִהְיֶה לְמִצְרַיִם מַעֲשֶׂה אֲשֶׁר יַעֲשֶׂה רֹאשׁ וְזָנָב כִּפָּה וְאַגְמוֹן:

16 In that day, the Egyptians shall be like women, trembling and terrified because the Lord of Hosts will raise His hand against them.

טז בַּיּוֹם הַהוּא יִהְיֶה מִצְרַיִם כַּנָּשִׁים וְחָרַד וּפָחַד מִפְּנֵי תְּנוּפַת יַד־יְהֹוָה צְבָאוֹת אֲשֶׁר־הוּא מֵנִיף עָלָיו:

17 And the land of *Yehuda* shall also be the dread of the Egyptians; they shall quake whenever anybody mentions it to them, because of what the Lord of Hosts is planning against them.

יז וְהָיְתָה אַדְמַת יְהוּדָה לְמִצְרַיִם לְחָגָּא כֹּל אֲשֶׁר יַזְכִּיר אֹתָהּ אֵלָיו יִפְחָד מִפְּנֵי עֲצַת יְהֹוָה צְבָאוֹת אֲשֶׁר־הוּא יוֹעֵץ עָלָיו:

18 In that day, there shall be several towns in the land of Egypt speaking the language of Canaan and swearing loyalty to the Lord of Hosts; one shall be called Town of Heres.

יח בַּיּוֹם הַהוּא יִהְיוּ חָמֵשׁ עָרִים בְּאֶרֶץ מִצְרַיִם מְדַבְּרוֹת שְׂפַת כְּנַעַן וְנִשְׁבָּעוֹת לַיהֹוָה צְבָאוֹת עִיר הַהֶרֶס יֵאָמֵר לְאֶחָת:

ba-YOM ha-HU yih-YU kha-MAYSH a-REEM b'-E-retz mitz-RA-yim m'-da-b'-ROT s'-FAT k'-NA-an v'-nish-ba-OT la-do-NAI tz'-va-OT eer ha-HE-res yay-a-MAYR l'-e-KHAT

19 In that day, there shall be a altar to *Hashem* inside the land of Egypt and a pillar to *Hashem* at its border.

יט בַּיּוֹם הַהוּא יִהְיֶה מִזְבֵּחַ לַיהֹוָה בְּתוֹךְ אֶרֶץ מִצְרָיִם וּמַצֵּבָה אֵצֶל־גְּבוּלָהּ לַיהֹוָה:

Torah scroll, written in Lashon HaKodesh

19:18 Speaking the language of Canaan *Yeshayahu* prophesies that there will be five Egyptian cities that speak the language of Canaan and swear by *Hashem*'s name. According to *Ramban* (Exodus 30:13), the term "language of Canaan" refers to the Hebrew language, known in Jewish literature as *Lashon HaKodesh* (לשון הקודש), 'the Holy Tongue,' because it is the language with which God speaks to His prophets and His nation. After the Egyptians in these cities experience *Hashem*'s strength, they will be so moved to worship Him that they will learn the holy language and erect an altar on which to serve God. This will also represent a partial fulfillment of another of *Yeshayahu*'s prophecies, that in the future the whole world will be filled with knowledge of God (11:9).

20 They shall serve as a symbol and reminder of the LORD of Hosts in the land of Egypt, so that when [the Egyptians] cry out to *Hashem* against oppressors, He will send them a savior and champion to deliver them.

כ וְהָיָה לְאוֹת וּלְעֵד לַיהוָה צְבָאוֹת בְּאֶרֶץ מִצְרָיִם כִּי־יִצְעֲקוּ אֶל־יְהוָה מִפְּנֵי לֹחֲצִים וְיִשְׁלַח לָהֶם מוֹשִׁיעַ וָרָב וְהִצִּילָם:

21 For *Hashem* will make Himself known to the Egyptians, and the Egyptians shall acknowledge *Hashem* in that day, and they shall serve [Him] with sacrifice and oblation and shall make vows to *Hashem* and fulfill them.

כא וְנוֹדַע יְהוָה לְמִצְרַיִם וְיָדְעוּ מִצְרַיִם אֶת־יְהוָה בַּיּוֹם הַהוּא וְעָבְדוּ זֶבַח וּמִנְחָה וְנָדְרוּ־נֵדֶר לַיהוָה וְשִׁלֵּמוּ:

22 *Hashem* will first afflict and then heal the Egyptians; when they turn back to *Hashem*, He will respond to their entreaties and heal them.

כב וְנָגַף יְהוָה אֶת־מִצְרַיִם נָגֹף וְרָפוֹא וְשָׁבוּ עַד־יְהוָה וְנֶעְתַּר לָהֶם וּרְפָאָם:

23 In that day, there shall be a highway from Egypt to Assyria. The Assyrians shall join with the Egyptians and Egyptians with the Assyrians, and then the Egyptians together with the Assyrians shall serve [*Hashem*].

כג בַּיּוֹם הַהוּא תִּהְיֶה מְסִלָּה מִמִּצְרַיִם אַשּׁוּרָה וּבָא־אַשּׁוּר בְּמִצְרַיִם וּמִצְרַיִם בְּאַשּׁוּר וְעָבְדוּ מִצְרַיִם אֶת־אַשּׁוּר:

24 In that day, *Yisrael* shall be a third partner with Egypt and Assyria as a blessing on earth;

כד בַּיּוֹם הַהוּא יִהְיֶה יִשְׂרָאֵל שְׁלִישִׁיָּה לְמִצְרַיִם וּלְאַשּׁוּר בְּרָכָה בְּקֶרֶב הָאָרֶץ:

25 for the LORD of Hosts will bless them, saying, "Blessed be My people Egypt, My handiwork Assyria, and My very own *Yisrael*."

כה אֲשֶׁר בֵּרֲכוֹ יְהוָה צְבָאוֹת לֵאמֹר בָּרוּךְ עַמִּי מִצְרַיִם וּמַעֲשֵׂה יָדַי אַשּׁוּר וְנַחֲלָתִי יִשְׂרָאֵל:

20 1 It was the year that the Tartan came to *Ashdod* – being sent by King Sargon of Assyria – and attacked *Ashdod* and took it.

כ א בִּשְׁנַת בֹּא תַרְתָּן אַשְׁדּוֹדָה בִּשְׁלֹחַ אֹתוֹ סַרְגוֹן מֶלֶךְ אַשּׁוּר וַיִּלָּחֶם בְּאַשְׁדּוֹד וַיִּלְכְּדָהּ:

2 Previously, *Hashem* had spoken to *Yeshayahu* son of *Amotz*, saying, "Go, untie the sackcloth from your loins and take your sandals off your feet," which he had done, going naked and barefoot.

ב בָּעֵת הַהִיא דִּבֶּר יְהוָה בְּיַד יְשַׁעְיָהוּ בֶן־אָמוֹץ לֵאמֹר לֵךְ וּפִתַּחְתָּ הַשַּׂק מֵעַל מָתְנֶיךָ וְנַעַלְךָ תַחֲלֹץ מֵעַל רַגְלֶיךָ וַיַּעַשׂ כֵּן הָלֹךְ עָרוֹם וְיָחֵף:

ba-AYT ha-HEE di-BER a-do-NAI b'-YAD y'-sha-YA-hu ven a-MOTZ lay-MOR
LAYKH u-fi-takh-TA ha-SAK may-AL mot-NE-kha v'-na-al-KHA ta-kha-LOTZ
may-AL rag-LE-kha va-YA-as KAYN ha-LOKH a-ROM v'-ya-KHAYF

Man lifting up his hands to Heaven in prayer

20:2 Go, untie the sackcloth from your loins Egypt encouraged the Philistines to revolt against Assyria, and supported the rebellion for three years (713–711 BCE), only to then cowardly hand the Philistine king of *Ashdod* over to the Assyrians. In an attempt to dissuade *Yehuda* from similarly relying on Egypt for protection against the Assyrian army, *Yeshayahu* becomes a living sign to the people. He is to loosen his clothes at his loins, wear no upper garments, and go barefoot. This behavior is designed to signify that the Egyptians and Ethiopians will be led away as captives by the king of Assyria, and to remind the people not to rebel against *Hashem*'s message or try to rely on Egypt for salvation. Though it is tempting to rely on people or material wealth for success, *Yeshayahu*'s message is that God is the only true source of success and salvation.

3 And now *Hashem* said, "It is a sign and a portent for Egypt and Nubia. Just as My servant *Yeshayahu* has gone naked and barefoot for three years,

ג וַיֹּאמֶר יְהֹוָה כַּאֲשֶׁר הָלַךְ עַבְדִּי יְשַׁעְיָהוּ עָרוֹם וְיָחֵף שָׁלֹשׁ שָׁנִים אוֹת וּמוֹפֵת עַל־מִצְרַיִם וְעַל־כּוּשׁ:

4 so shall the king of Assyria drive off the captives of Egypt and the exiles of Nubia, young and old, naked and barefoot and with bared buttocks – to the shame of Egypt!

ד כֵּן יִנְהַג מֶלֶךְ־אַשּׁוּר אֶת־שְׁבִי מִצְרַיִם וְאֶת־גָּלוּת כּוּשׁ נְעָרִים וּזְקֵנִים עָרוֹם וְיָחֵף וַחֲשׂוּפַי שֵׁת עֶרְוַת מִצְרָיִם:

5 And they shall be dismayed and chagrined because of Nubia their hope and Egypt their boast.

ה וְחַתּוּ וָבֹשׁוּ מִכּוּשׁ מַבָּטָם וּמִן־מִצְרַיִם תִּפְאַרְתָּם:

6 In that day, the dwellers of this coastland shall say, 'If this could happen to those we looked to, to whom we fled for help and rescue from the king of Assyria, how can we ourselves escape?'"

ו וְאָמַר יֹשֵׁב הָאִי הַזֶּה בַּיּוֹם הַהוּא הִנֵּה־כֹה מַבָּטֵנוּ אֲשֶׁר־נַסְנוּ שָׁם לְעֶזְרָה לְהִנָּצֵל מִפְּנֵי מֶלֶךְ אַשּׁוּר וְאֵיךְ נִמָּלֵט אֲנָחְנוּ:

21 1 The "Desert of the Sea" Pronouncement. Like the gales That race through the *Negev*, It comes from the desert, The terrible land.

כא א מַשָּׂא מִדְבַּר־יָם כְּסוּפוֹת בַּנֶּגֶב לַחֲלֹף מִמִּדְבָּר בָּא מֵאֶרֶץ נוֹרָאָה:

2 A harsh prophecy Has been announced to me: "The betrayer is betraying, The ravager ravaging. Advance, Elam! Lay siege, Media! I have put an end To all her sighing."

ב חָזוּת קָשָׁה הֻגַּד־לִי הַבּוֹגֵד בּוֹגֵד וְהַשּׁוֹדֵד שׁוֹדֵד עֲלִי עֵילָם צוּרִי מָדַי כָּל־אַנְחָתָה הִשְׁבַּתִּי:

3 Therefore my loins Are seized with trembling; I am gripped by pangs Like a woman in travail, Too anguished to hear, Too frightened to see.

ג עַל־כֵּן מָלְאוּ מָתְנַי חַלְחָלָה צִירִים אֲחָזוּנִי כְּצִירֵי יוֹלֵדָה נַעֲוֵיתִי מִשְּׁמֹעַ נִבְהַלְתִּי מֵרְאוֹת:

4 My mind is confused, I shudder in panic. My night of pleasure He has turned to terror:

ד תָּעָה לְבָבִי פַּלָּצוּת בִּעֲתָתְנִי אֵת נֶשֶׁף חִשְׁקִי שָׂם לִי לַחֲרָדָה:

5 "Set the table!" To "Let the watchman watch!" "Eat and drink!" To "Up, officers! Grease the shields!"

ה עָרֹךְ הַשֻּׁלְחָן צָפֹה הַצָּפִית אָכוֹל שָׁתֹה קוּמוּ הַשָּׂרִים מִשְׁחוּ מָגֵן:

*a-ROKH ha-shul-KHAN tza-FOH ha-tza-FEET a-KHOL
sha-TOH KU-mu ha-sa-REEM mish-KHU ma-GAYN*

6 For thus my Lord said to me: "Go, set up a sentry; Let him announce what he sees.

ו כִּי כֹה אָמַר אֵלַי אֲדֹנָי לֵךְ הַעֲמֵד הַמְצַפֶּה אֲשֶׁר יִרְאֶה יַגִּיד:

7 He will see mounted men, Horsemen in pairs – Riders on asses, Riders on camels – And he will listen closely, Most attentively."

ז וְרָאָה רֶכֶב צֶמֶד פָּרָשִׁים רֶכֶב חֲמוֹר רֶכֶב גָּמָל וְהִקְשִׁיב קֶשֶׁב רַב־קָשֶׁב:

21:5 Eat and drink *Yeshayahu* relays another prophecy directed towards Babylon. Since their country is protected by watchmen, its nobles eat, oblivious to the danger that approaches. Their dining, however, is interrupted with the call to battle. The fulfillment of *Yeshayahu*'s prophecy is described in *Sefer Daniel* 5, which depicts the capture of Babylon as its inhabitants are engaged in revelry at Belshazzar's feast. To *Yehuda*, which looks for allies against the Assyrian threat, *Yeshayahu* reiterates that Babylon's time is also limited. The surest guarantee of safety is trust in *Hashem* alone.

Middle-Eastern feast

Isaiah

8 And [like] a lion he called out: "On my Lord's lookout I stand Ever by day, And at my post I watch Every night.

ח וַיִּקְרָא אַרְיֵה עַל־מִצְפֶּה אֲדֹנָי אָנֹכִי עֹמֵד תָּמִיד יוֹמָם וְעַל־מִשְׁמַרְתִּי אָנֹכִי נִצָּב כָּל־הַלֵּילוֹת:

9 And there they come, mounted men – Horsemen in pairs!" Then he spoke up and said, "Fallen, fallen is Babylon, And all the images of her gods Have crashed to the ground!"

ט וְהִנֵּה־זֶה בָא רֶכֶב אִישׁ צֶמֶד פָּרָשִׁים וַיַּעַן וַיֹּאמֶר נָפְלָה נָפְלָה בָבֶל וְכָל־פְּסִילֵי אֱלֹהֶיהָ שִׁבַּר לָאָרֶץ:

10 My threshing, the product of my threshing floor: What I have heard from the Lᴏʀᴅ of Hosts, The God of *Yisrael* – That I have told to you.

י מְדֻשָׁתִי וּבֶן־גָּרְנִי אֲשֶׁר שָׁמַעְתִּי מֵאֵת יְהוָה צְבָאוֹת אֱלֹהֵי יִשְׂרָאֵל הִגַּדְתִּי לָכֶם:

11 The "Dumah" Pronouncement. A call comes to me from Seir: "Watchman, what of the night? Watchman, what of the night?"

יא מַשָּׂא דּוּמָה אֵלַי קֹרֵא מִשֵּׂעִיר שֹׁמֵר מַה־מִּלַּיְלָה שֹׁמֵר מַה־מִּלֵּיל:

12 The watchman replied, "Morning came, and so did night. If you would inquire, inquire. Come back again."

יב אָמַר שֹׁמֵר אָתָה בֹקֶר וְגַם־לָיְלָה אִם־ תִּבְעָיוּן בְּעָיוּ שֻׁבוּ אֵתָיוּ:

13 The "In the Steppe" Pronouncement. In the scrub, in the steppe, you will lodge, O caravans of the Dedanites!

יג מַשָּׂא בַּעְרָב בַּיַּעַר בַּעְרַב תָּלִינוּ אֹרְחוֹת דְּדָנִים:

14 Meet the thirsty with water, You who dwell in the land of Tema; Greet the fugitive with bread.

יד לִקְרַאת צָמֵא הֵתָיוּ מָיִם יֹשְׁבֵי אֶרֶץ תֵּימָא בְּלַחְמוֹ קִדְּמוּ נֹדֵד:

15 For they have fled before swords: Before the whetted sword, Before the bow that was drawn, Before the stress of war.

טו כִּי־מִפְּנֵי חֲרָבוֹת נָדָדוּ מִפְּנֵי חֶרֶב נְטוּשָׁה וּמִפְּנֵי קֶשֶׁת דְּרוּכָה וּמִפְּנֵי כֹּבֶד מִלְחָמָה:

16 For thus my Lord has said to me: "In another year, fixed like the years of a hired laborer, all the multitude of Kedar shall vanish;

טז כִּי־כֹה אָמַר אֲדֹנָי אֵלָי בְּעוֹד שָׁנָה כִּשְׁנֵי שָׂכִיר וְכָלָה כָּל־כְּבוֹד קֵדָר:

17 the remaining bows of Kedar's warriors shall be few in number; for *Hashem*, the God of *Yisrael*, has spoken.

יז וּשְׁאָר מִסְפַּר־קֶשֶׁת גִּבּוֹרֵי בְנֵי־קֵדָר יִמְעָטוּ כִּי יְהוָה אֱלֹהֵי־יִשְׂרָאֵל דִּבֵּר:

22 1 The "Valley of Vision" Pronouncement. What can have happened to you That you have gone, all of you, up on the roofs,

כב א מַשָּׂא גֵּיא חִזָּיוֹן מַה־לָּךְ אֵפוֹא כִּי־עָלִית כֻּלָּךְ לַגַּגּוֹת:

2 O you who were full of tumult, You clamorous town, You city so gay? Your slain are not the slain of the sword Nor the dead of battle.

ב תְּשֻׁאוֹת מְלֵאָה עִיר הוֹמִיָּה קִרְיָה עַלִּיזָה חֲלָלַיִךְ לֹא חַלְלֵי־חֶרֶב וְלֹא מֵתֵי מִלְחָמָה:

3 Your officers have all departed, They fled far away; Your survivors were all taken captive, Taken captive without their bows.

ג כָּל־קְצִינַיִךְ נָדְדוּ־יַחַד מִקֶּשֶׁת אֻסָּרוּ כָּל־ נִמְצָאַיִךְ אֻסְּרוּ יַחְדָּו מֵרָחוֹק בָּרָחוּ:

4 That is why I say, "Let me be, I will weep bitterly. Press not to comfort me For the ruin of my poor people."

ד עַל־כֵּן אָמַרְתִּי שְׁעוּ מִנִּי אֲמָרֵר בַּבֶּכִי אַל־תָּאִיצוּ לְנַחֲמֵנִי עַל־שֹׁד בַּת־עַמִּי:

⁵ For my Lord God of Hosts had a day Of tumult and din and confusion – Kir raged in the Valley of Vision, And Shoa on the hill;

ה כִּי יוֹם מְהוּמָה וּמְבוּסָה וּמְבוּכָה לַאדֹנָי יְהֹוִה צְבָאוֹת בְּגֵיא חִזָּיוֹן מְקַרְקַר קִר וְשׁוֹעַ אֶל־הָהָר:

⁶ While Elam bore the quiver In troops of mounted men, And Kir bared the shield –

ו וְעֵילָם נָשָׂא אַשְׁפָּה בְּרֶכֶב אָדָם פָּרָשִׁים וְקִיר עֵרָה מָגֵן:

⁷ And your choicest lowlands Were filled with chariots and horsemen: They stormed at *Yehuda*'s* gateway

ז וַיְהִי מִבְחַר־עֲמָקַיִךְ מָלְאוּ רָכֶב וְהַפָּרָשִׁים שֹׁת שָׁתוּ הַשָּׁעְרָה:

⁸ And pressed beyond its screen. You gave thought on that day To the arms in the Forest House,

ח וַיְגַל אֵת מָסַךְ יְהוּדָה וַתַּבֵּט בַּיּוֹם הַהוּא אֶל־נֶשֶׁק בֵּית הַיָּעַר:

⁹ And you took note of the many breaches In the City of *David*. And you collected the water of the Lower Pool;

ט וְאֵת בְּקִיעֵי עִיר־דָּוִד רְאִיתֶם כִּי־רָבּוּ וַתְּקַבְּצוּ אֶת־מֵי הַבְּרֵכָה הַתַּחְתּוֹנָה:

¹⁰ and you counted the houses of *Yerushalayim* and pulled houses down to fortify the wall;

י וְאֶת־בָּתֵּי יְרוּשָׁלַ͏ִם סְפַרְתֶּם וַתִּתְצוּ הַבָּתִּים לְבַצֵּר הַחוֹמָה:

¹¹ and you constructed a basin between the two walls for the water of the old pool. But you gave no thought to Him who planned it, You took no note of Him who designed it long before.

יא וּמִקְוָה עֲשִׂיתֶם בֵּין הַחֹמֹתַיִם לְמֵי הַבְּרֵכָה הַיְשָׁנָה וְלֹא הִבַּטְתֶּם אֶל־עֹשֶׂיהָ וְיֹצְרָהּ מֵרָחוֹק לֹא רְאִיתֶם:

u-mik-VAH a-see-TEM BAYN ha-kho-mo-TA-yim l'-MAY ha-b'-ray-KHAH hai-sha-NAH v'-LO hi-bat-TEM el o-SE-ha v'-yo-tz'-RAH may-ra-KHOK LO r'-ee-TEM

¹² My Lord God of Hosts summoned on that day To weeping and lamenting, To tonsuring and girding with sackcloth.

יב וַיִּקְרָא אֲדֹנָי יְהֹוִה צְבָאוֹת בַּיּוֹם הַהוּא לִבְכִי וּלְמִסְפֵּד וּלְקָרְחָה וְלַחֲגֹר שָׂק:

¹³ Instead, there was rejoicing and merriment, Killing of cattle and slaughtering of sheep, Eating of meat and drinking of wine: "Eat and drink, for tomorrow we die!"

יג וְהִנֵּה שָׂשׂוֹן וְשִׂמְחָה הָרֹג בָּקָר וְשָׁחֹט צֹאן אָכֹל בָּשָׂר וְשָׁתוֹת יַיִן אָכוֹל וְשָׁתוֹ כִּי מָחָר נָמוּת:

¹⁴ Then the Lᴏʀᴅ of Hosts revealed Himself to my ears: "This iniquity shall never be forgiven you Until you die," said my Lord God of Hosts.

יד וְנִגְלָה בְאָזְנָי יְהֹוָה צְבָאוֹת אִם־יְכֻפַּר הֶעָוֹן הַזֶּה לָכֶם עַד־תְּמֻתוּן אָמַר אֲדֹנָי יְהֹוִה צְבָאוֹת:

---

* The word "Yehuda" brought up from verse 8 for clarity

22:11 And you constructed a basin between the two walls Verses 8–11 describe the serious military preparations made to fend off the upcoming Assyrian assault. *Yeshayahu* does not oppose this *per se* – he simply asks that they combine their trust in themselves with faith in *Hashem*. The "basin between the two walls" refers to *Chizkiyahu's* tunnel, which he dug in order to provide a source of water for the besieged city of *Yerushalayim* (II Chronicles 32). The tunnel was re-discovered in 1867 by the British explorer Captain Charles Warren. Near the exit from the tunnel, an ancient Hebrew inscription describing its amazing construction was discovered. A team of diggers started at each end of the 1,500 foot-long tunnel. They eventually met in the middle by listening for the sounds of each other's pickaxes. The marks of the ancient pickaxes are visible on the walls of the tunnel, going first in one direction and switching in the middle to go in the other direction. Today, wading through the water of *Chizkiyahu's* tunnel is a popular attraction among visitors to the city of *Yerushalayim*.

The ancient inscription outside *Chizkiyahu's* water tunnel

15 Thus said my Lord God of Hosts: Go in to see that steward, that Shebna, in charge of the palace:

טו כֹּה אָמַר אֲדֹנָי יֱהֹוִה צְבָאֹות לֶךְ־בֹּא אֶל־הַסֹּכֵן הַזֶּה עַל־שֶׁבְנָא אֲשֶׁר עַל־הַבָּיִת:

16 What have you here, and whom have you here, That you have hewn out a tomb for yourself here? – O you who have hewn your tomb on high; O you who have hollowed out for yourself an abode in the cliff!

טז מַה־לְּךָ פֹה וּמִי לְךָ פֹה כִּי־חָצַבְתָּ לְּךָ פֹּה קָבֶר חֹצְבִי מָרֹום קִבְרֹו חֹקְקִי בַסֶּלַע מִשְׁכָּן לֹו:

17 *Hashem* is about to shake you Severely, fellow, and then wrap you around Himself.

יז הִנֵּה יְהֹוָה מְטַלְטֶלְךָ טַלְטֵלָה גָּבֶר וְעֹטְךָ עָטֹה:

18 Indeed, He will wind you about Him as a headdress, a turban. Off to a broad land! There shall you die, and there shall be the chariots bearing your body, O shame of your master's house!

יח צָנֹוף יִצְנָפְךָ צְנֵפָה כַּדּוּר אֶל־אֶרֶץ רַחֲבַת יָדָיִם שָׁמָּה תָמוּת וְשָׁמָּה מַרְכְּבֹות כְּבֹודֶךָ קְלֹון בֵּית אֲדֹנֶיךָ:

19 For I will hurl you from your station And you shall be torn down from your stand.

יט וַהֲדַפְתִּיךָ מִמַּצָּבֶךָ וּמִמַּעֲמָדְךָ יֶהֶרְסֶךָ:

20 And in that day, I will summon My servant Eliakim son of *Chilkiyahu,*

כ וְהָיָה בַּיֹּום הַהוּא וְקָרָאתִי לְעַבְדִּי לְאֶלְיָקִים בֶּן־חִלְקִיָּהוּ:

21 and I will invest him with your tunic, gird him with your sash, and deliver your authority into his hand; and he shall be a father to the inhabitants of *Yerushalayim* and the men of *Yehuda.*

כא וְהִלְבַּשְׁתִּיו כֻּתָּנְתֶּךָ וְאַבְנֵטְךָ אֲחַזְּקֶנּוּ וּמֶמְשַׁלְתְּךָ אֶתֵּן בְּיָדֹו וְהָיָה לְאָב לְיֹושֵׁב יְרוּשָׁלַםִ וּלְבֵית יְהוּדָה:

22 I will place the keys of *David*'s palace on his shoulders; and what he unlocks none may shut, and what he locks none may open.

כב וְנָתַתִּי מַפְתֵּחַ בֵּית־דָּוִד עַל־שִׁכְמֹו וּפָתַח וְאֵין סֹגֵר וְסָגַר וְאֵין פֹּתֵחַ:

23 He shall be a seat of honor to his father's household. I will fix him as a peg in a firm place,

כג וּתְקַעְתִּיו יָתֵד בְּמָקֹום נֶאֱמָן וְהָיָה לְכִסֵּא כָבֹוד לְבֵית אָבִיו:

24 on which all the substance of his father's household shall be hung: the sprouts and the leaves – all the small vessels, from bowls to all sorts of jars.

כד וְתָלוּ עָלָיו כֹּל כְּבֹוד בֵּית־אָבִיו הַצֶּאֱצָאִים וְהַצְּפִעֹות כֹּל כְּלֵי הַקָּטָן מִכְּלֵי הָאַגָּנֹות וְעַד כָּל־כְּלֵי הַנְּבָלִים:

25 In that day – declares the Lord of Hosts – the peg fixed in a firm place shall give way: it shall be cut down and shall fall, and the weight it supports shall be destroyed. For it is *Hashem* who has spoken.

כה בַּיֹּום הַהוּא נְאֻם יְהֹוָה צְבָאֹות תָּמוּשׁ הַיָּתֵד הַתְּקוּעָה בְּמָקֹום נֶאֱמָן וְנִגְדְּעָה וְנָפְלָה וְנִכְרַת הַמַּשָּׂא אֲשֶׁר־עָלֶיהָ כִּי יְהֹוָה דִּבֵּר:

23 ¹ The "Tyre" Pronouncement. Howl, you ships of Tarshish! For havoc has been wrought, not a house is left; As they came from the land of Kittim, This was revealed to them.

כג א מַשָּׂא צֹר הֵילִילוּ אֳנִיֹּות תַּרְשִׁישׁ כִּי־שֻׁדַּד מִבַּיִת מִבֹּוא מֵאֶרֶץ כִּתִּים נִגְלָה־לָמֹו:

2 Moan, you coastland dwellers, You traders of Sidon, Once thronged by seafarers,

ב דֹּמּוּ יֹשְׁבֵי אִי סֹחֵר צִידֹון עֹבֵר יָם מִלְאוּךְ:

3 Over many waters Your revenue came: From the trade of nations, From the grain of Shihor, The harvest of the Nile.

ג וּבְמַיִם רַבִּים זֶרַע שִׁחֹר קְצִיר יְאֹור תְּבוּאָתָהּ וַתְּהִי סְחַר גֹּויִם:

Isaiah

⁴ Be ashamed, O Sidon! For the sea – this stronghold of the sea – declares, "I am as one who has never labored, Never given birth, Never raised youths Or reared maidens!"

ד בּוֹשִׁי צִידוֹן כִּי־אָמַר יָם מָעוֹז הַיָּם לֵאמֹר לֹא־חַלְתִּי וְלֹא־יָלַדְתִּי וְלֹא גִדַּלְתִּי בַּחוּרִים רוֹמַמְתִּי בְתוּלוֹת:

⁵ When the Egyptians heard it, they quailed As when they heard about Tyre.

ה כַּאֲשֶׁר־שֵׁמַע לְמִצְרָיִם יָחִילוּ כְּשֵׁמַע צֹר:

⁶ Pass on to Tarshish – Howl, you coastland dwellers!

ו עִבְרוּ תַּרְשִׁישָׁה הֵילִילוּ יֹשְׁבֵי אִי:

⁷ Was such your merry city In former times, of yore? Did her feet carry her off To sojourn far away?

ז הֲזֹאת לָכֶם עַלִּיזָה מִימֵי־קֶדֶם קַדְמָתָהּ יֹבִלוּהָ רַגְלֶיהָ מֵרָחוֹק לָגוּר:

⁸ Who was it that planned this For crown-wearing Tyre, Whose merchants were nobles, Whose traders the world honored?

ח מִי יָעַץ זֹאת עַל־צֹר הַמַּעֲטִירָה אֲשֶׁר סֹחֲרֶיהָ שָׂרִים כִּנְעָנֶיהָ נִכְבַּדֵּי־אָרֶץ:

⁹ The Lᴏʀᴅ of Hosts planned it – To defile all glorious beauty, To shame all the honored of the world.

ט יְהֹוָה צְבָאוֹת יְעָצָהּ לְחַלֵּל גְּאוֹן כָּל־צְבִי לְהָקֵל כָּל־נִכְבַּדֵּי־אָרֶץ:

a-do-NAI tz'-va-OT y'-a-TZAH l'-kha-LAYL g'-ON kol
tz'-VEE l'-ha-KAYL kol nikh-ba-day A-retz

¹⁰ Traverse your land like the Nile, Fair Tarshish; This is a harbor no more.

י עִבְרִי אַרְצֵךְ כַּיְאֹר בַּת־תַּרְשִׁישׁ אֵין מֵזַח עוֹד:

¹¹ *Hashem* poised His arm o'er the sea And made kingdoms quake; It was He decreed destruction For Phoenicia's strongholds,

יא יָדוֹ נָטָה עַל־הַיָּם הִרְגִּיז מַמְלָכוֹת יְהֹוָה צִוָּה אֶל־כְּנַעַן לַשְׁמִד מָעֻזְנֶיהָ:

¹² And said, "You shall be gay no more, O plundered one, Fair Maiden Sidon. Up, cross over to Kittim – Even there you shall have no rest."

יב וַיֹּאמֶר לֹא־תוֹסִיפִי עוֹד לַעְלוֹז הַמְעֻשָּׁקָה בְּתוּלַת בַּת־צִידוֹן כִּתִּיִּם [כִּתִּים] קוּמִי עֲבֹרִי גַּם־שָׁם לֹא־יָנוּחַ לָךְ:

¹³ Behold the land of Chaldea – This is the people that has ceased to be. Assyria, which founded it for ships, Which raised its watchtowers, Erected its ramparts, Has turned it into a ruin.

יג הֵן אֶרֶץ כַּשְׂדִּים זֶה הָעָם לֹא הָיָה אַשּׁוּר יְסָדָהּ לְצִיִּים הֵקִימוּ בחיניו [בַחוּנָיו] עֹרְרוּ אַרְמְנוֹתֶיהָ שָׂמָהּ לְמַפֵּלָה:

¹⁴ Howl, O ships of Tarshish, For your stronghold is destroyed!

יד הֵילִילוּ אֳנִיּוֹת תַּרְשִׁישׁ כִּי שֻׁדַּד מָעֻזְכֶן:

The Mediterranean coast at Rosh Hanikra near the Lebanon border

23:9 To defile all glorious beauty *Yeshayahu* concludes his prophecies against the nations with a description of the impending downfall of Tyre. Just as Babylon and Assyria represented the pinnacle of military might in the ancient world, Tyre represented the height of commercial power and riches. Based on the coast of what is today Lebanon, Tyre established trading colonies throughout the Mediterranean Sea, as far away as Spain. Verses 1–7 describe how the shocking news of Tyre's downfall would reverberate throughout the ancient world. *Yeshayahu* places the blame for the downfall on Tyre's sense of pride; rather than being thankful to *Hashem* who granted them riches, they viewed themselves as a great power. This idea of pride is a common theme throughout the prophecies of *Yeshayahu*. In chapter 2, he describes the pride of Israel as being the source of their sins which ultimately lead to their exile. When humanity abandons its arrogance and recognizes God's goodness, He will again reveal Himself to the world.

15 In that day, Tyre shall remain forgotten for seventy years, equaling the lifetime of one king. After a lapse of seventy years, it shall go with Tyre as with the harlot in the ditty:

16 Take a lyre, go about the town, Harlot long forgotten; Sweetly play, make much music, To bring you back to mind.

17 For after a lapse of seventy years, *Hashem* will take note of Tyre, and she shall resume her "fee-taking" and "play the harlot" with all the kingdoms of the world, on the face of the earth.

18 But her profits and "hire" shall be consecrated to *Hashem*. They shall not be treasured or stored; rather shall her profits go to those who abide before *Hashem*, that they may eat their fill and clothe themselves elegantly.

24 1 Behold, *Hashem* will strip the earth bare, And lay it waste, And twist its surface, And scatter its inhabitants.

2 Layman and *Kohen* shall fare alike, Slave and master, Handmaid and mistress, Buyer and seller, Lender and borrower, Creditor and debtor.

3 The earth shall be bare, bare; It shall be plundered, plundered; For it is *Hashem* who spoke this word.

4 The earth is withered, sear; The world languishes, it is sear; The most exalted people of the earth languish.

5 For the earth was defiled Under its inhabitants; Because they transgressed teachings, Violated laws, Broke the ancient covenant.

טו וְהָיָה בַיּוֹם הַהוּא וְנִשְׁכַּחַת צֹר שִׁבְעִים שָׁנָה כִּימֵי מֶלֶךְ אֶחָד מִקֵּץ שִׁבְעִים שָׁנָה יִהְיֶה לְצֹר כְּשִׁירַת הַזּוֹנָה:

טז קְחִי כִנּוֹר סֹבִּי עִיר זוֹנָה נִשְׁכָּחָה הֵיטִיבִי נַגֵּן הַרְבִּי־שִׁיר לְמַעַן תִּזָּכֵרִי:

יז וְהָיָה מִקֵּץ שִׁבְעִים שָׁנָה יִפְקֹד יְהֹוָה אֶת־צֹר וְשָׁבָה לְאֶתְנַנָּה וְזָנְתָה אֶת־כָּל־מַמְלְכוֹת הָאָרֶץ עַל־פְּנֵי הָאֲדָמָה:

יח וְהָיָה סַחְרָהּ וְאֶתְנַנָּהּ קֹדֶשׁ לַיהֹוָה לֹא יֵאָצֵר וְלֹא יֵחָסֵן כִּי לַיֹּשְׁבִים לִפְנֵי יְהֹוָה יִהְיֶה סַחְרָהּ לֶאֱכֹל לְשָׂבְעָה וְלִמְכַסֶּה עָתִיק:

כד א הִנֵּה יְהֹוָה בּוֹקֵק הָאָרֶץ וּבוֹלְקָהּ וְעִוָּה פָנֶיהָ וְהֵפִיץ יֹשְׁבֶיהָ:

ב וְהָיָה כָעָם כַּכֹּהֵן כַּעֶבֶד כַּאדֹנָיו כַּשִּׁפְחָה כַּגְבִרְתָּהּ כַּקּוֹנֶה כַּמּוֹכֵר כַּמַּלְוֶה כַּלֹּוֶה כַּנֹּשֶׁה כַּאֲשֶׁר נֹשֵׁא בוֹ:

ג הִבּוֹק תִּבּוֹק הָאָרֶץ וְהִבּוֹז תִּבּוֹז כִּי יְהֹוָה דִּבֶּר אֶת־הַדָּבָר הַזֶּה:

ד אָבְלָה נָבְלָה הָאָרֶץ אֻמְלְלָה נָבְלָה תֵּבֵל אֻמְלָלוּ מְרוֹם עַם־הָאָרֶץ:

ה וְהָאָרֶץ חָנְפָה תַּחַת יֹשְׁבֶיהָ כִּי־עָבְרוּ תוֹרֹת חָלְפוּ חֹק הֵפֵרוּ בְּרִית עוֹלָם:

v'-ha-A-retz kha-n'-FAH TA-khat yo-sh'-VE-ha kee a-v'-RU
to-ROT kha-l'-FU KHOK hay-FAY-ru b'-REET o-LAM

24:5 For the earth was defiled under its inhabitants Chapter 24 begins four chapters which describe the total destruction of the earth, for it to then be replaced by a more righteous and just world. *Yeshayahu* explains why this will occur – it is the same reason that led God to bring about the flood in the times of *Noach*. Due to man's wicked behavior, the earth is "defiled" or "polluted" by sin (see Leviticus 18:25, Numbers 35:33), and must be purged. The eternal covenant between *Hashem* and man was made after the flood between God and *Noach* (Genesis 9:16). According to Jewish tradition, the Seven Noahide Laws, universal laws applying to all of mankind, were given by God at that time. These laws serve as the foundation of all ethics and morality, and, if followed appropriately, will ensure that the world is filled with justice and righteousness. (For a list of the seven laws, see the commentary to II Kings 10:27).

A rainbow, symbol that *Hashem* will never again destroy the world by flood, in the desert

⁶ That is why a curse consumes the earth, And its inhabitants pay the penalty; That is why earth's dwellers have dwindled, And but few men are left.

ו עַל־כֵּן אָלָה אָכְלָה אֶרֶץ וַיֶּאְשְׁמוּ יֹשְׁבֵי בָהּ עַל־כֵּן חָרוּ יֹשְׁבֵי אֶרֶץ וְנִשְׁאַר אֱנוֹשׁ מִזְעָר:

⁷ The new wine fails, The vine languishes; And all the merry-hearted sigh.

ז אָבַל תִּירוֹשׁ אֻמְלְלָה־גָּפֶן נֶאֶנְחוּ כָּל־שִׂמְחֵי־לֵב:

⁸ Stilled is the merriment of timbrels, Ended the clamor of revelers, Stilled the merriment of lyres.

ח שָׁבַת מְשׂוֹשׂ תֻּפִּים חָדַל שְׁאוֹן עַלִּיזִים שָׁבַת מְשׂוֹשׂ כִּנּוֹר:

⁹ They drink their wine without song; Liquor tastes bitter to the drinker.

ט בַּשִּׁיר לֹא יִשְׁתּוּ־יָיִן יֵמַר שֵׁכָר לְשֹׁתָיו:

¹⁰ Towns are broken, empty; Every house is shut, none enters;

י נִשְׁבְּרָה קִרְיַת־תֹּהוּ סֻגַּר כָּל־בַּיִת מִבּוֹא:

¹¹ Even over wine, a cry goes up in the streets: The sun has set on all joy, The gladness of the earth is banished.

יא צְוָחָה עַל־הַיַּיִן בַּחוּצוֹת עָרְבָה כָּל־שִׂמְחָה גָּלָה מְשׂוֹשׂ הָאָרֶץ:

¹² Desolation is left in the town And the gate is battered to ruins.

יב נִשְׁאַר בָּעִיר שַׁמָּה וּשְׁאִיָּה יֻכַּת־שָׁעַר:

¹³ For thus shall it be among the peoples In the midst of the earth: As when the olive tree is beaten out, Like gleanings when the vintage is over.

יג כִּי כֹה יִהְיֶה בְּקֶרֶב הָאָרֶץ בְּתוֹךְ הָעַמִּים כְּנֹקֶף זַיִת כְּעוֹלֵלֹת אִם־כָּלָה בָצִיר:

¹⁴ These shall lift up their voices, Exult in the majesty of *Hashem*. They shall shout from the sea:

יד הֵמָּה יִשְׂאוּ קוֹלָם יָרֹנּוּ בִּגְאוֹן יְהֹוָה צָהֲלוּ מִיָּם:

¹⁵ Therefore, honor *Hashem* with lights In the coastlands of the sea – The name of *Hashem*, the God of *Yisrael*.

טו עַל־כֵּן בָּאֻרִים כַּבְּדוּ יְהֹוָה בְּאִיֵּי הַיָּם שֵׁם יְהֹוָה אֱלֹהֵי יִשְׂרָאֵל:

¹⁶ From the end of the earth We hear singing: Glory to the righteous! And I said: I waste away! I waste away! Woe is me! The faithless have acted faithlessly; The faithless have broken faith!

טז מִכְּנַף הָאָרֶץ זְמִרֹת שָׁמַעְנוּ צְבִי לַצַּדִּיק וָאֹמַר רָזִי־לִי רָזִי־לִי אוֹי לִי בֹּגְדִים בָּגָדוּ וּבֶגֶד בּוֹגְדִים בָּגָדוּ:

¹⁷ Terror, and pit, and trap Upon you who dwell on earth!

יז פַּחַד וָפַחַת וָפָח עָלֶיךָ יוֹשֵׁב הָאָרֶץ:

¹⁸ He who flees at the report of the terror Shall fall into the pit; And he who climbs out of the pit Shall be caught in the trap. For sluices are opened on high, And earth's foundations tremble.

יח וְהָיָה הַנָּס מִקּוֹל הַפַּחַד יִפֹּל אֶל־הַפַּחַת וְהָעוֹלֶה מִתּוֹךְ הַפַּחַת יִלָּכֵד בַּפָּח כִּי־אֲרֻבּוֹת מִמָּרוֹם נִפְתָּחוּ וַיִּרְעֲשׁוּ מוֹסְדֵי אָרֶץ:

¹⁹ The earth is breaking, breaking; The earth is crumbling, crumbling. The earth is tottering, tottering;

יט רֹעָה הִתְרֹעֲעָה הָאָרֶץ פּוֹר הִתְפּוֹרְרָה אֶרֶץ מוֹט הִתְמוֹטְטָה אָרֶץ:

²⁰ The earth is swaying like a drunkard; It is rocking to and fro like a hut. Its iniquity shall weigh it down, And it shall fall, to rise no more.

כ נוֹעַ תָּנוּעַ אֶרֶץ כַּשִּׁכּוֹר וְהִתְנוֹדְדָה כַּמְּלוּנָה וְכָבַד עָלֶיהָ פִּשְׁעָהּ וְנָפְלָה וְלֹא־תֹסִיף קוּם:

²¹ In that day, *Hashem* will punish The host of heaven in heaven And the kings of the earth on earth.

כא וְהָיָה בַּיּוֹם הַהוּא יִפְקֹד יְהֹוָה עַל־צְבָא הַמָּרוֹם בַּמָּרוֹם וְעַל־מַלְכֵי הָאֲדָמָה עַל־הָאֲדָמָה:

Isaiah

22 They shall be gathered in a dungeon As captives are gathered; And shall be locked up in a prison. But after many days they shall be remembered.

כב וְאֻסְּפוּ אֲסֵפָה אַסִּיר עַל־בּוֹר וְסֻגְּרוּ עַל־מַסְגֵּר וּמֵרֹב יָמִים יִפָּקֵדוּ:

23 Then the moon shall be ashamed, And the sun shall be abashed. For the Lord of Hosts will reign On Mount *Tzion* and in *Yerushalayim*, And the Presence will be revealed to His elders.

כג וְחָפְרָה הַלְּבָנָה וּבוֹשָׁה הַחַמָּה כִּי־מָלַךְ יְהֹוָה צְבָאוֹת בְּהַר צִיּוֹן וּבִירוּשָׁלַם וְנֶגֶד זְקֵנָיו כָּבוֹד:

25

1 *Hashem*, You are my God; I will extol You, I will praise Your name. For You planned graciousness of old, Counsels of steadfast faithfulness.

א יְהֹוָה אֱלֹהַי אַתָּה אֲרוֹמִמְךָ אוֹדֶה שִׁמְךָ כִּי עָשִׂיתָ פֶּלֶא עֵצוֹת מֵרָחוֹק אֱמוּנָה אֹמֶן:

2 For You have turned a city into a stone heap, A walled town into a ruin, The citadel of strangers into rubble, Never to be rebuilt.

ב כִּי שַׂמְתָּ מֵעִיר לַגָּל קִרְיָה בְצוּרָה לְמַפֵּלָה אַרְמוֹן זָרִים מֵעִיר לְעוֹלָם לֹא יִבָּנֶה:

3 Therefore a fierce people must honor You, A city of cruel nations must fear You.

ג עַל־כֵּן יְכַבְּדוּךָ עַם־עָז קִרְיַת גּוֹיִם עָרִיצִים יִירָאוּךָ:

4 For You have been a refuge for the poor man, A shelter for the needy man in his distress – Shelter from rainstorm, shade from heat. When the fury of tyrants was like a winter rainstorm,

ד כִּי־הָיִיתָ מָעוֹז לַדָּל מָעוֹז לָאֶבְיוֹן בַּצַּר־לוֹ מַחְסֶה מִזֶּרֶם צֵל מֵחֹרֶב כִּי רוּחַ עָרִיצִים כְּזֶרֶם קִיר:

5 The rage of strangers like heat in the desert, You subdued the heat with the shade of clouds, The singing of the tyrants was vanquished.

ה כְּחֹרֶב בְּצָיוֹן שְׁאוֹן זָרִים תַּכְנִיעַ חֹרֶב בְּצֵל עָב זְמִיר עָרִיצִים יַעֲנֶה:

6 The Lord of Hosts will make on this mount For all the peoples A banquet of rich viands, A banquet of choice wines – Of rich viands seasoned with marrow, Of choice wines well refined.

ו וְעָשָׂה יְהֹוָה צְבָאוֹת לְכָל־הָעַמִּים בָּהָר הַזֶּה מִשְׁתֵּה שְׁמָנִים מִשְׁתֵּה שְׁמָרִים שְׁמָנִים מְמֻחָיִים שְׁמָרִים מְזֻקָּקִים:

7 And He will destroy on this mount the shroud That is drawn over the faces of all the peoples And the covering that is spread Over all the nations:

ז וּבִלַּע בָּהָר הַזֶּה פְּנֵי־הַלּוֹט הַלּוֹט עַל־כָּל־הָעַמִּים וְהַמַּסֵּכָה הַנְּסוּכָה עַל־כָּל־הַגּוֹיִם:

8 He will destroy death forever. My *Hashem* will wipe the tears away From all faces And will put an end to the reproach of His people Over all the earth – For it is *Hashem* who has spoken.

ח בִּלַּע הַמָּוֶת לָנֶצַח וּמָחָה אֲדֹנָי יְהֹוָה דִּמְעָה מֵעַל כָּל־פָּנִים וְחֶרְפַּת עַמּוֹ יָסִיר מֵעַל כָּל־הָאָרֶץ כִּי יְהֹוָה דִּבֵּר:

bi-LA ha-MA-vet la-NE-tzakh u-ma-KHAH a-do-NAI e-lo-HEEM dim-AH may-AL kol pa-NEEM v'-kher-PAT a-MO ya-SEER may-AL kol ha-A-retz KEE a-do-NAI di-BAYR

Praying at *Rachel*'s tomb in *Beit Lechem*

25:8 He will destroy death forever Celebrating the ultimate defeat of evil, *Hashem* will hold a banquet at His mountain (*Tzion*), and all those who celebrate will witness the undoing of *Adam's* punishment; the removal of death from the world. This idea also appears in the prophecies of *Hoshea* – "From Sheol itself I will save them, Redeem them from very Death. Where, O Death, are your plagues? Your pestilence where, O Sheol?" (Hosea 13:14). The wiping away of tears in this verse refers to *Rachel*'s tears in *Yirmiyahu's* prophecy of the ingathering of the exiles (31:15), as the verse states, "Restrain your voice from weeping, your eyes from shedding tears; for there is a reward for your labor, declares *Hashem*. They shall return from the enemy's land." God's consolation from the pains of death and exile will be an important part of the redemption and complete return to Israel, for which His nation prays every day.

⁹ In that day they shall say: This is our God; We trusted in Him, and He delivered us. This is *Hashem*, in whom we trusted; Let us rejoice and exult in His deliverance!

ט וְאָמַר בַּיּוֹם הַהוּא הִנֵּה אֱלֹהֵינוּ זֶה קִוִּינוּ לוֹ וְיוֹשִׁיעֵנוּ זֶה יְהוָה קִוִּינוּ לוֹ נָגִילָה וְנִשְׂמְחָה בִּישׁוּעָתוֹ:

¹⁰ For the hand of *Hashem* shall descend Upon this mount, And Moab shall be trampled under Him As straw is threshed to bits at Madmenah.

י כִּי־תָנוּחַ יַד־יְהוָה בָּהָר הַזֶּה וְנָדוֹשׁ מוֹאָב תַּחְתָּיו כְּהִדּוּשׁ מַתְבֵּן בְּמֵי [בְּמוֹ] מַדְמֵנָה:

¹¹ Then He will spread out His hands in their homeland, As a swimmer spreads his hands out to swim, And He will humble their pride Along with the emblems of their power.

יא וּפֵרַשׂ יָדָיו בְּקִרְבּוֹ כַּאֲשֶׁר יְפָרֵשׂ הַשֹּׂחֶה לִשְׂחוֹת וְהִשְׁפִּיל גַּאֲוָתוֹ עִם אָרְבּוֹת יָדָיו:

¹² Yea, the secure fortification of their walls He will lay low and humble, Will raze to the ground, to the very dust.

יב וּמִבְצַר מִשְׂגַּב חוֹמֹתֶיךָ הֵשַׁח הִשְׁפִּיל הִגִּיעַ לָאָרֶץ עַד־עָפָר:

26 ¹ In that day, this song shall be sung In the land of *Yehuda*: Ours is a mighty city; He makes victory our inner and outer wall.

כו א בַּיּוֹם הַהוּא יוּשַׁר הַשִּׁיר־הַזֶּה בְּאֶרֶץ יְהוּדָה עִיר עָז־לָנוּ יְשׁוּעָה יָשִׁית חוֹמוֹת וָחֵל:

² Open the gates, and let A righteous nation enter, [A nation] that keeps faith.

ב פִּתְחוּ שְׁעָרִים וְיָבֹא גוֹי־צַדִּיק שֹׁמֵר אֱמֻנִים:

pit-KHU sh'-a-REEM v'-ya-VO goy tza-DEEK sho-MAYR e-mu-NEEM

³ The confident mind You guard in safety, In safety because it trusts in You.

ג יֵצֶר סָמוּךְ תִּצֹּר שָׁלוֹם שָׁלוֹם כִּי בְךָ בָּטוּחַ:

⁴ Trust in *Hashem* for ever and ever, For in Yah *Hashem* you have an everlasting Rock.

ד בִּטְחוּ בַיהוָה עֲדֵי־עַד כִּי בְּיָהּ יְהוָה צוּר עוֹלָמִים:

⁵ For He has brought low those who dwelt high up, Has humbled the secure city, Humbled it to the ground, Leveled it with the dust –

ה כִּי הֵשַׁח יֹשְׁבֵי מָרוֹם קִרְיָה נִשְׂגָּבָה יַשְׁפִּילֶנָּה יַשְׁפִּילָהּ עַד־אֶרֶץ יַגִּיעֶנָּה עַד־עָפָר:

⁶ To be trampled underfoot, By the feet of the needy, By the soles of the poor.

ו תִּרְמְסֶנָּה רָגֶל רַגְלֵי עָנִי פַּעֲמֵי דַלִּים:

⁷ The path is level for the righteous man; O Just One, You make smooth the course of the righteous.

ז אֹרַח לַצַּדִּיק מֵישָׁרִים יָשָׁר מַעְגַּל צַדִּיק תְּפַלֵּס:

26:2 A righteous nation Israel's first Chief Rabbi, Abraham Isaac Kook, expounds upon the nature of righteousness, described in beautiful poetry in this verse. "The purely righteous do not complain about evil, but increase justice. They do not complain about godlessness, but increase faith. They do not complain about ignorance, but increase wisdom." Let us strive to become "purely righteous" by increasing justice, faith and wisdom in this world.

Rabbi Abraham Issac Kook (1865–1935)

8 For Your just ways, *Hashem*, we look to You; We long for the name by which You are called.

ח אַף אֹרַח מִשְׁפָּטֶיךָ יְהוָה קִוִּינוּךָ לְשִׁמְךָ וּלְזִכְרְךָ תַּאֲוַת־נָפֶשׁ:

9 At night I yearn for You with all my being, I seek You with all the spirit within me. For when Your judgments are wrought on earth, The inhabitants of the world learn righteousness.

ט נַפְשִׁי אִוִּיתִיךָ בַּלַּיְלָה אַף־רוּחִי בְקִרְבִּי אֲשַׁחֲרֶךָּ כִּי כַּאֲשֶׁר מִשְׁפָּטֶיךָ לָאָרֶץ צֶדֶק לָמְדוּ יֹשְׁבֵי תֵבֵל:

10 But when the scoundrel is spared, he learns not righteousness; In a place of integrity, he does wrong – He ignores the majesty of *Hashem*.

י יֻחַן רָשָׁע בַּל־לָמַד צֶדֶק בְּאֶרֶץ נְכֹחוֹת יְעַוֵּל וּבַל־יִרְאֶה גֵּאוּת יְהוָה:

11 *Hashem*! They see not Your hand exalted. Let them be shamed as they behold Your zeal for Your people And fire consuming Your adversaries.

יא יְהוָה רָמָה יָדְךָ בַּל־יֶחֱזָיוּן יֶחֱזוּ וְיֵבֹשׁוּ קִנְאַת־עָם אַף־אֵשׁ צָרֶיךָ תֹאכְלֵם:

12 *Hashem*! May You appoint well-being for us, Since You have also requited all our misdeeds.

יב יְהוָה תִּשְׁפֹּת שָׁלוֹם לָנוּ כִּי גַּם כָּל־מַעֲשֵׂינוּ פָּעַלְתָּ לָנוּ:

13 *Hashem* our God! Lords other than You possessed us, But only Your name shall we utter.

יג יְהוָה אֱלֹהֵינוּ בְּעָלוּנוּ אֲדֹנִים זוּלָתֶךָ לְבַד־בְּךָ נַזְכִּיר שְׁמֶךָ:

14 They are dead, they can never live; Shades, they can never rise; Of a truth, You have dealt with them and wiped them out, Have put an end to all mention of them.

יד מֵתִים בַּל־יִחְיוּ רְפָאִים בַּל־יָקֻמוּ לָכֵן פָּקַדְתָּ וַתַּשְׁמִידֵם וַתְּאַבֵּד כָּל־זֵכֶר לָמוֹ:

15 When You added to the nation, *Hashem*, When You added to the nation, Extending all the boundaries of the land, You were honored.

טו יָסַפְתָּ לַגּוֹי יְהוָה יָסַפְתָּ לַגּוֹי נִכְבָּדְתָּ רִחַקְתָּ כָּל־קַצְוֵי־אָרֶץ:

16 *Hashem*! In their distress, they sought You; Your chastisement reduced them To anguished whispered prayer.

טז יְהוָה בַּצַּר פְּקָדוּךָ צָקוּן לַחַשׁ מוּסָרְךָ לָמוֹ:

17 Like a woman with child Approaching childbirth, Writhing and screaming in her pangs, So are we become because of You, *Hashem*.

יז כְּמוֹ הָרָה תַּקְרִיב לָלֶדֶת תָּחִיל תִּזְעַק בַּחֲבָלֶיהָ כֵּן הָיִינוּ מִפָּנֶיךָ יְהוָה:

18 We were with child, we writhed – It is as though we had given birth to wind; We have won no victory on earth; The inhabitants of the world have not come to life!

יח הָרִינוּ חַלְנוּ כְּמוֹ יָלַדְנוּ רוּחַ יְשׁוּעֹת בַּל־נַעֲשֶׂה אֶרֶץ וּבַל־יִפְּלוּ יֹשְׁבֵי תֵבֵל:

19 Oh, let Your dead revive! Let corpses arise! Awake and shout for joy, You who dwell in the dust! – For Your dew is like the dew on fresh growth; You make the land of the shades come to life.

יט יִחְיוּ מֵתֶיךָ נְבֵלָתִי יְקוּמוּן הָקִיצוּ וְרַנְּנוּ שֹׁכְנֵי עָפָר כִּי טַל אוֹרֹת טַלֶּךָ וָאָרֶץ רְפָאִים תַּפִּיל:

20 Go, my people, enter your chambers, And lock your doors behind you. Hide but a little moment, Until the indignation passes.

כ לֵךְ עַמִּי בֹּא בַחֲדָרֶיךָ וּסְגֹר דְּלָתֶיךָ [דְּלָתְךָ] בַּעֲדֶךָ חֲבִי כִמְעַט־רֶגַע עַד־יַעֲבָר־[יַעֲבָר־] זָעַם:

²¹ For lo! *Hashem* shall come forth from His place To punish the dwellers of the earth For their iniquity; And the earth shall disclose its bloodshed And shall no longer conceal its slain.

כא כִּי־הִנֵּה יְהוָה יֹצֵא מִמְּקוֹמוֹ לִפְקֹד עֲוֹן יֹשֵׁב־הָאָרֶץ עָלָיו וְגִלְּתָה הָאָרֶץ אֶת־דָּמֶיהָ וְלֹא־תְכַסֶּה עוֹד עַל־הֲרוּגֶיהָ:

27 ¹ In that day *Hashem* will punish, With His great, cruel, mighty sword Leviathan the Elusive Serpent – Leviathan the Twisting Serpent; He will slay the Dragon of the sea.

כז א בַּיּוֹם הַהוּא יִפְקֹד יְהוָה בְּחַרְבוֹ הַקָּשָׁה וְהַגְּדוֹלָה וְהַחֲזָקָה עַל לִוְיָתָן נָחָשׁ בָּרִחַ וְעַל לִוְיָתָן נָחָשׁ עֲקַלָּתוֹן וְהָרַג אֶת־הַתַּנִּין אֲשֶׁר בַּיָּם:

² In that day, They shall sing of it: "Vineyard of Delight."

ב בַּיּוֹם הַהוּא כֶּרֶם חֶמֶד עַנּוּ־לָהּ:

³ I *Hashem* keep watch over it, I water it every moment; That no harm may befall it, I watch it night and day.

ג אֲנִי יְהוָה נֹצְרָהּ לִרְגָעִים אַשְׁקֶנָּה פֶּן יִפְקֹד עָלֶיהָ לַיְלָה וָיוֹם אֶצֳּרֶנָּה:

⁴ There is no anger in Me: If one offers Me thorns and thistles, I will march to battle against him, And set all of them on fire.

ד חֵמָה אֵין לִי מִי־יִתְּנֵנִי שָׁמִיר שַׁיִת בַּמִּלְחָמָה אֶפְשְׂעָה בָהּ אֲצִיתֶנָּה יָחַד:

⁵ But if he holds fast to My refuge, He makes Me his friend; He makes Me his friend.

ה אוֹ יַחֲזֵק בְּמָעוּזִּי יַעֲשֶׂה שָׁלוֹם לִי שָׁלוֹם יַעֲשֶׂה־לִּי:

⁶ [In days] to come *Yaakov* shall strike root, *Yisrael* shall sprout and blossom, And the face of the world Shall be covered with fruit.

ו הַבָּאִים יַשְׁרֵשׁ יַעֲקֹב יָצִיץ וּפָרַח יִשְׂרָאֵל וּמָלְאוּ פְנֵי־תֵבֵל תְּנוּבָה:

ha-ba-EEM yash-RAYSH ya-a-KOV ya-TZEETZ u-fa-RAKH
yis-ra-AYL u-ma-l'-U f'-nay tay-VAYL t'-nu-VAH

⁷ Was he beaten as his beater has been? Did he suffer such slaughter as his slayers?

ז הַכְּמַכַּת מַכֵּהוּ הִכָּהוּ אִם־כְּהֶרֶג הֲרֻגָיו הֹרָג:

⁸ Assailing them with fury unchained, His pitiless blast bore them off On a day of gale.

ח בְּסַאסְּאָה בְּשַׁלְחָהּ תְּרִיבֶנָּה הָגָה בְּרוּחוֹ הַקָּשָׁה בְּיוֹם קָדִים:

⁹ Assuredly, by this alone Shall *Yaakov*'s sin be purged away; This is the only price For removing his guilt: That he make all the altar-stones Like shattered blocks of chalk – With no sacred post left standing, Nor any incense *Mizbayach*.

ט לָכֵן בְּזֹאת יְכֻפַּר עֲוֹן־יַעֲקֹב וְזֶה כָּל־פְּרִי הָסִר חַטָּאתוֹ בְּשׂוּמוֹ כָּל־אַבְנֵי מִזְבֵּחַ כְּאַבְנֵי־גִר מְנֻפָּצוֹת לֹא־יָקֻמוּ אֲשֵׁרִים וְחַמָּנִים:

Isaiah

27:6 *Yaakov* **shall strike root** In chapter 5, Yeshayahu describes Israel as a rebellious vine that produces inferior fruits. Here is the happy conclusion to *Hashem*'s song to His vineyard. While God may punish, it is not out of anger or fury (verse 4), but the hope that it will lead to harmony between Israel and *Hashem*. In this chapter, Israel is attached to its land with an unbreakable connection, like a deeply rooted vineyard. As a result, "*Yaakov* shall strike root, *Yisrael* shall sprout and blossom, and the face of the world shall be covered with fruit." Indeed, with the contemporary return of the Jews to *Eretz Yisrael*, the former desert land has begun to blossom and bud, a sure sign of divine favor.

A vineyard in the Judean hills

10 Thus fortified cities lie desolate, Homesteads deserted, forsaken like a wilderness; There calves graze, there they lie down And consume its boughs.

י כִּי עִיר בְּצוּרָה בָּדָד נָוֶה מְשֻׁלָּח וְנֶעֱזָב כַּמִּדְבָּר שָׁם יִרְעֶה עֵגֶל וְשָׁם יִרְבָּץ וְכִלָּה סְעִפֶיהָ:

11 When its crown is withered, they break; Women come and make fires with them. For they are a people without understanding; That is why Their Maker will show them no mercy, Their Creator will deny them grace.

יא בִּיבֹשׁ קְצִירָהּ תִּשָּׁבַרְנָה נָשִׁים בָּאוֹת מְאִירוֹת אוֹתָהּ כִּי לֹא עַם־בִּינוֹת הוּא עַל־כֵּן לֹא־יְרַחֲמֶנּוּ עֹשֵׂהוּ וְיֹצְרוֹ לֹא יְחֻנֶּנּוּ:

12 And in that day, *Hashem* will beat out [the peoples like grain] from the channel of the Euphrates to the Wadi of Egypt; and you shall be picked up one by one, O children of *Yisrael*!

יב וְהָיָה בַּיּוֹם הַהוּא יַחְבֹּט יְהוָה מִשִּׁבֹּלֶת הַנָּהָר עַד־נַחַל מִצְרַיִם וְאַתֶּם תְּלֻקְּטוּ לְאַחַד אֶחָד בְּנֵי יִשְׂרָאֵל:

13 And in that day, a great *shofar* shall be sounded; and the strayed who are in the land of Assyria and the expelled who are in the land of Egypt shall come and worship *Hashem* on the holy mount, in *Yerushalayim*.

יג וְהָיָה בַּיּוֹם הַהוּא יִתָּקַע בְּשׁוֹפָר גָּדוֹל וּבָאוּ הָאֹבְדִים בְּאֶרֶץ אַשּׁוּר וְהַנִּדָּחִים בְּאֶרֶץ מִצְרָיִם וְהִשְׁתַּחֲווּ לַיהוָה בְּהַר הַקֹּדֶשׁ בִּירוּשָׁלָ͏ִם:

28 ¹ Ah, the proud crowns of the drunkards of *Efraim*, Whose glorious beauty is but wilted flowers On the heads of men bloated with rich food, Who are overcome by wine!

כח א הוֹי עֲטֶרֶת גֵּאוּת שִׁכֹּרֵי אֶפְרַיִם וְצִיץ נֹבֵל צְבִי תִפְאַרְתּוֹ אֲשֶׁר עַל־רֹאשׁ גֵּיא־שְׁמָנִים הֲלוּמֵי יָיִן:

² Lo, my Lord has something strong and mighty, Like a storm of hail, A shower of pestilence. Something like a storm of massive, torrential rain Shall be hurled with force to the ground.

ב הִנֵּה חָזָק וְאַמִּץ לַאדֹנָי כְּזֶרֶם בָּרָד שַׂעַר קָטֶב כְּזֶרֶם מַיִם כַּבִּירִים שֹׁטְפִים הִנִּיחַ לָאָרֶץ בְּיָד:

³ Trampled underfoot shall be The proud crowns of the drunkards of *Efraim*,

ג בְּרַגְלַיִם תֵּרָמַסְנָה עֲטֶרֶת גֵּאוּת שִׁכּוֹרֵי אֶפְרָיִם:

⁴ The wilted flowers – On the heads of men bloated with rich food – That are his glorious beauty. They shall be like an early fig Before the fruit harvest; Whoever sees it devours it While it is still in his hand.

ד וְהָיְתָה צִיצַת נֹבֵל צְבִי תִפְאַרְתּוֹ אֲשֶׁר עַל־רֹאשׁ גֵּיא שְׁמָנִים כְּבִכּוּרָהּ בְּטֶרֶם קַיִץ אֲשֶׁר יִרְאֶה הָרֹאֶה אוֹתָהּ בְּעוֹדָהּ בְּכַפּוֹ יִבְלָעֶנָּה:

⁵ In that day, the Lᴏʀᴅ of Hosts shall become a crown of beauty and a diadem of glory for the remnant of His people,

ה בַּיּוֹם הַהוּא יִהְיֶה יְהוָה צְבָאוֹת לַעֲטֶרֶת צְבִי וְלִצְפִירַת תִּפְאָרָה לִשְׁאָר עַמּוֹ:

⁶ and a spirit of judgment for him who sits in judgment and of valor for those who repel attacks at the gate.

ו וּלְרוּחַ מִשְׁפָּט לַיּוֹשֵׁב עַל־הַמִּשְׁפָּט וְלִגְבוּרָה מְשִׁיבֵי מִלְחָמָה שָׁעְרָה:

⁷ But these are also muddled by wine And dazed by liquor: *Kohen* and *Navi* Are muddled by liquor; They are confused by wine, They are dazed by liquor; They are muddled in their visions, They stumble in judgment.

ז וְגַם־אֵלֶּה בַּיַּיִן שָׁגוּ וּבַשֵּׁכָר תָּעוּ כֹּהֵן וְנָבִיא שָׁגוּ בַשֵּׁכָר נִבְלְעוּ מִן־הַיַּיִן תָּעוּ מִן־הַשֵּׁכָר שָׁגוּ בָרֹאֶה פָּקוּ פְּלִילִיָּה:

8 Yea, all tables are covered With vomit and filth, So that no space is left.

ח כִּי כָּל־שֻׁלְחָנוֹת מָלְאוּ קִיא צֹאָה בְּלִי מָקוֹם:

9 "To whom would he give instruction? To whom expound a message? To those newly weaned from milk, Just taken away from the breast?

ט אֶת־מִי יוֹרֶה דֵעָה וְאֶת־מִי יָבִין שְׁמוּעָה גְּמוּלֵי מֵחָלָב עַתִּיקֵי מִשָּׁדָיִם:

10 That same mutter upon mutter, Murmur upon murmur, Now here, now there!"

י כִּי צַו לָצָו צַו לָצָו קַו לָקָו קַו לָקָו זְעֵיר שָׁם זְעֵיר שָׁם:

11 Truly, as one who speaks to that people in a stammering jargon and an alien tongue

יא כִּי בְּלַעֲגֵי שָׂפָה וּבְלָשׁוֹן אַחֶרֶת יְדַבֵּר אֶל־הָעָם הַזֶּה:

12 is he who declares to them, "This is the resting place, let the weary rest; this is the place of re pose." They refuse to listen.

יב אֲשֶׁר אָמַר אֲלֵיהֶם זֹאת הַמְּנוּחָה הָנִיחוּ לֶעָיֵף וְזֹאת הַמַּרְגֵּעָה וְלֹא אָבוּא שְׁמוֹעַ:

13 To them the word of *Hashem* is: "Mutter upon mutter, Murmur upon murmur, Now here, now there." And so they will march, But they shall fall backward, And be injured and snared and captured.

יג וְהָיָה לָהֶם דְּבַר־יְהֹוָה צַו לָצָו צַו לָצָו קַו לָקָו קַו לָקָו זְעֵיר שָׁם זְעֵיר שָׁם לְמַעַן יֵלְכוּ וְכָשְׁלוּ אָחוֹר וְנִשְׁבָּרוּ וְנוֹקְשׁוּ וְנִלְכָּדוּ:

14 Hear now the word of *Hashem*, You men of mockery, Who govern that people In *Yerushalayim*!

יד לָכֵן שִׁמְעוּ דְבַר־יְהֹוָה אַנְשֵׁי לָצוֹן מֹשְׁלֵי הָעָם הַזֶּה אֲשֶׁר בִּירוּשָׁלָם:

15 For you have said, "We have made a covenant with Death, Concluded a pact with Sheol. When the sweeping flood passes through, It shall not reach us; For we have made falsehood our refuge, Taken shelter in treachery."

טו כִּי אֲמַרְתֶּם כָּרַתְנוּ בְרִית אֶת־מָוֶת וְעִם־שְׁאוֹל עָשִׂינוּ חֹזֶה שִׁיט [שׁוֹט] שׁוֹטֵף כִּי־עָבַר [יַעֲבֹר] לֹא יְבוֹאֵנוּ כִּי שַׂמְנוּ כָזָב מַחְסֵנוּ וּבַשֶּׁקֶר נִסְתָּרְנוּ:

16 Assuredly, Thus said *Hashem*: "Behold, I will found in *Tzion*, Stone by stone, A tower of precious cornerstones, Exceedingly firm; He who trusts need not fear.

טז לָכֵן כֹּה אָמַר אֲדֹנָי יֱהֹוִה הִנְנִי יִסַּד בְּצִיּוֹן אָבֶן אֶבֶן בֹּחַן פִּנַּת יִקְרַת מוּסָד מוּסָד הַמַּאֲמִין לֹא יָחִישׁ:

la-KHAYN KO a-MAR a-do-NAI e-lo-HEEM hi-n'-NEE
yi-SAD b'-tzi-YON A-ven E-ven BO-khan pi-NAT yik-RAT
mu-SAD mu-SAD ha-ma-a-MEEN LO ya-KHEESH

17 But I will apply judgment as a measuring line And retribution as weights; Hail shall sweep away the refuge of falsehood, And flood-waters engulf your shelter.

יז וְשַׂמְתִּי מִשְׁפָּט לְקָו וּצְדָקָה לְמִשְׁקָלֶת וְיָעָה בָרָד מַחְסֵה כָזָב וְסֵתֶר מַיִם יִשְׁטֹפוּ:

18 Your covenant with Death shall be annulled, Your pact with Sheol shall not endure; When the sweeping flood passes through, You shall be its victims.

יח וְכֻפַּר בְּרִיתְכֶם אֶת־מָוֶת וְחָזוּתְכֶם אֶת־שְׁאוֹל לֹא תָקוּם שׁוֹט שׁוֹטֵף כִּי יַעֲבֹר וִהְיִיתֶם לוֹ לְמִרְמָס:

אבן

28:16 I will found in *Tzion*, stone by stone The Hebrew word for 'stone' is *even* (אבן). What is interesting about this word is that it contains within it the Hebrew words for 'father,' *av* (אב), and 'son,' *ben* (בן). Once again, the Hebrew root of a simple word teaches a profound lesson, by alluding to the fact that the bond between a father and his son is as strong as a rock, and as precious as a fine stone.

A stone pyramid at the Ramon Crater

Isaiah

Isaiah

19 It shall catch you Every time it passes through; It shall pass through every morning, Every day and every night. And it shall be sheer horror To grasp the message."

יט מִדֵּי עָבְרוֹ יִקַּח אֶתְכֶם כִּי־בַבֹּקֶר בַּבֹּקֶר יַעֲבֹר בַּיּוֹם וּבַלָּיְלָה וְהָיָה רַק־זְוָעָה הָבִין שְׁמוּעָה:

20 The couch is too short for stretching out, And the cover too narrow for curling up!

כ כִּי־קָצַר הַמַּצָּע מֵהִשְׂתָּרֵעַ וְהַמַּסֵּכָה צָרָה כְּהִתְכַּנֵּס:

21 For *Hashem* will arise As on the hill of Perazim, He will rouse Himself As in the vale of *Givon*, To do His work – Strange is His work! And to perform His task – Astounding is His task!

כא כִּי כְהַר־פְּרָצִים יָקוּם יְהֹוָה כְּעֵמֶק בְּגִבְעוֹן יִרְגָּז לַעֲשׂוֹת מַעֲשֵׂהוּ זָר מַעֲשֵׂהוּ וְלַעֲבֹד עֲבֹדָתוֹ נָכְרִיָּה עֲבֹדָתוֹ:

22 Therefore, refrain from mockery, Lest your bonds be tightened. For I have heard a decree of destruction From my Lord God of Hosts Against all the land.

כב וְעַתָּה אַל־תִּתְלוֹצָצוּ פֶּן־יֶחְזְקוּ מוֹסְרֵיכֶם כִּי־כָלָה וְנֶחֱרָצָה שָׁמַעְתִּי מֵאֵת אֲדֹנָי יֱהֹוִה צְבָאוֹת עַל־כָּל־הָאָרֶץ:

23 Give diligent ear to my words, Attend carefully to what I say.

כג הַאֲזִינוּ וְשִׁמְעוּ קוֹלִי הַקְשִׁיבוּ וְשִׁמְעוּ אִמְרָתִי:

24 Does he who plows to sow Plow all the time, Breaking up and furrowing his land?

כד הֲכֹל הַיּוֹם יַחֲרֹשׁ הַחֹרֵשׁ לִזְרֹעַ יְפַתַּח וִישַׂדֵּד אַדְמָתוֹ:

25 When he has smoothed its surface, Does he not rather broadcast black cumin And scatter cumin, Or set wheat in a row, Barley in a strip, And emmer in a patch?

ha-LO im shi-VAH fa-NE-ha v'-hay-FEETZ KE-tzakh v'-kha-MON yiz-ROK v'-SAM khi-TAH so-RAH us-o-RAH nis-MAN v'-khu-SE-met g'-vu-la-TO

כה הֲלוֹא אִם־שִׁוָּה פָנֶיהָ וְהֵפִיץ קֶצַח וְכַמֹּן יִזְרֹק וְשָׂם חִטָּה שׂוֹרָה וּשְׂעֹרָה נִסְמָן וְכֻסֶּמֶת גְּבֻלָתוֹ:

26 For He teaches him the right manner, His *Hashem* instructs him.

כו וְיִסְּרוֹ לַמִּשְׁפָּט אֱלֹהָיו יוֹרֶנּוּ:

27 So, too, black cumin is not threshed with a threshing board, Nor is the wheel of a threshing sledge rolled over cumin; But black cumin is beaten out with a stick And cumin with a rod.

כז כִּי לֹא בֶחָרוּץ יוּדַשׁ קֶצַח וְאוֹפַן עֲגָלָה עַל־כַּמֹּן יוּסָּב כִּי בַמַּטֶּה יֵחָבֶט קֶצַח וְכַמֹּן בַּשָּׁבֶט:

28 It is cereal that is crushed. For even if he threshes it thoroughly, And the wheel of his sledge and his horses overwhelm it, He does not crush it.

כח לֶחֶם יוּדָק כִּי לֹא לָנֶצַח אָדוֹשׁ יְדוּשֶׁנּוּ וְהָמַם גִּלְגַּל עֶגְלָתוֹ וּפָרָשָׁיו לֹא־יְדֻקֶּנּוּ:

A wheat field in the Elah Valley

28:25 Or set wheat in a row Wheat, the first of the seven special agricultural products of *Eretz Yisrael* (Deuteronomy 8:8), has been one of the world's major crops since biblical times. The first mention of wheat in the Bible is found in *Sefer Bereishit* (30:14): "Once, at the time of the wheat harvest, Re-

uven came upon some mandrakes in the field…" So important is wheat flour that the Rabbis taught: "Where there is no flour, there is no *Torah*; and where there is no *Torah*, there is no flour" (*Ethics of the Fathers*), emphasizing the mutual dependency of the physical world and spiritual pursuits.

29 That, too, is ordered by the LORD of Hosts; His counsel is unfathomable, His wisdom marvelous.

כט גַּם־זֹאת מֵעִם יְהֹוָה צְבָאוֹת יָצָאָה הִפְלִיא עֵצָה הִגְדִּיל תּוּשִׁיָּה:

29 1 "Ah, Ariel, Ariel, City where *David* camped! Add year to year, Let festivals come in their cycles!

כט א הוֹי אֲרִיאֵל אֲרִיאֵל קִרְיַת חָנָה דָוִד סְפוּ שָׁנָה עַל־שָׁנָה חַגִּים יִנְקֹפוּ:

2 And I will harass Ariel, And there shall be sorrow and sighing. She shall be to Me like Ariel.

ב וַהֲצִיקוֹתִי לַאֲרִיאֵל וְהָיְתָה תַאֲנִיָּה וַאֲנִיָּה וְהָיְתָה לִּי כַּאֲרִיאֵל:

3 And I will camp against you round about; I will lay siege to you with a mound, And I will set up siegeworks against you.

ג וְחָנִיתִי כַדּוּר עָלָיִךְ וְצַרְתִּי עָלַיִךְ מֻצָּב וַהֲקִימֹתִי עָלַיִךְ מְצֻרֹת:

4 And you shall speak from lower than the ground, Your speech shall be humbler than the sod; Your speech shall sound like a ghost's from the ground, Your voice shall chirp from the sod.

ד וְשָׁפַלְתְּ מֵאֶרֶץ תְּדַבֵּרִי וּמֵעָפָר תִּשַּׁח אִמְרָתֵךְ וְהָיָה כְּאוֹב מֵאֶרֶץ קוֹלֵךְ וּמֵעָפָר אִמְרָתֵךְ תְּצַפְצֵף:

5 And like fine dust shall be The multitude of your strangers; And like flying chaff, The multitude of tyrants." And suddenly, in an instant,

ה וְהָיָה כְּאָבָק דַּק הֲמוֹן זָרָיִךְ וּכְמֹץ עֹבֵר הֲמוֹן עָרִיצִים וְהָיָה לְפֶתַע פִּתְאֹם:

6 She shall be remembered of the LORD of Hosts With roaring, and shaking, and deafening noise, Storm, and tempest, and blaze of consuming fire.

ו מֵעִם יְהֹוָה צְבָאוֹת תִּפָּקֵד בְּרַעַם וּבְרַעַשׁ וְקוֹל גָּדוֹל סוּפָה וּסְעָרָה וְלַהַב אֵשׁ אוֹכֵלָה:

7 Then, like a dream, a vision of the night, Shall be the multitude of nations That war upon Ariel, And all her besiegers, and the siegeworks against her, And those who harass her.

ז וְהָיָה כַּחֲלוֹם חֲזוֹן לַיְלָה הֲמוֹן כָּל־הַגּוֹיִם הַצֹּבְאִים עַל־אֲרִיאֵל וְכָל־צֹבֶיהָ וּמְצֹדָתָהּ וְהַמְּצִיקִים לָהּ:

8 Like one who is hungry And dreams he is eating, But wakes to find himself empty; And like one who is thirsty And dreams he is drinking, But wakes to find himself faint And utterly parched – So shall be all the multitude of nations That war upon Mount *Tzion*.

ח וְהָיָה כַּאֲשֶׁר יַחֲלֹם הָרָעֵב וְהִנֵּה אוֹכֵל וְהֵקִיץ וְרֵיקָה נַפְשׁוֹ וְכַאֲשֶׁר יַחֲלֹם הַצָּמֵא וְהִנֵּה שֹׁתֶה וְהֵקִיץ וְהִנֵּה עָיֵף וְנַפְשׁוֹ שׁוֹקֵקָה כֵּן יִהְיֶה הֲמוֹן כָּל־הַגּוֹיִם הַצֹּבְאִים עַל־הַר צִיּוֹן:

9 Act stupid and be stupefied! Act blind and be blinded! (They are drunk, but not from wine, They stagger, but not from liquor.)

ט הִתְמַהְמְהוּ וּתְמָהוּ הִשְׁתַּעַשְׁעוּ וָשֹׁעוּ שָׁכְרוּ וְלֹא־יַיִן נָעוּ וְלֹא שֵׁכָר:

10 For *Hashem* has spread over you A spirit of deep sleep, And has shut your eyes, the *Neviim*, And covered your heads, the seers;

י כִּי־נָסַךְ עֲלֵיכֶם יְהֹוָה רוּחַ תַּרְדֵּמָה וַיְעַצֵּם אֶת־עֵינֵיכֶם אֶת־הַנְּבִיאִים וְאֶת־רָאשֵׁיכֶם הַחֹזִים כִּסָּה:

11 So that all prophecy has been to you Like the words of a sealed document. If it is handed to one who can read and he is asked to read it, he will say, "I can't, because it is sealed";

יא וַתְּהִי לָכֶם חָזוּת הַכֹּל כְּדִבְרֵי הַסֵּפֶר הֶחָתוּם אֲשֶׁר־יִתְּנוּ אֹתוֹ אֶל־יוֹדֵעַ הַסֵּפֶר [סֵפֶר] לֵאמֹר קְרָא נָא־זֶה וְאָמַר לֹא אוּכַל כִּי חָתוּם הוּא:

12 and if the document is handed to one who cannot read and he is asked to read it, he will say, "I can't read."

יב וְנִתַּן הַסֵּפֶר עַל אֲשֶׁר לֹא־יָדַע סֵפֶר לֵאמֹר קְרָא נָא־זֶה וְאָמַר לֹא יָדַעְתִּי סֵפֶר:

13 My Lord said: Because that people has approached [Me] with its mouth And honored Me with its lips, But has kept its heart far from Me, And its worship of Me has been A commandment of men, learned by rote –

וַיֹּאמֶר אֲדֹנָי יַעַן כִּי נִגַּשׁ הָעָם הַזֶּה בְּפִיו וּבִשְׂפָתָיו כִּבְּדוּנִי וְלִבּוֹ רִחַק מִמֶּנִּי וַתְּהִי יִרְאָתָם אֹתִי מִצְוַת אֲנָשִׁים מְלֻמָּדָה: יג

*va-YO-mer a-do-NAI YA-an KEE ni-GASH ha-AM ha-ZEH b'-FEEV
u-vis-fa-TAV ki-b'-DU-nee v'-li-BO ri-KHAK mi-ME-nee va-t'-HEE
yir-a-TAM o-TEE mitz-VAT a-na-SHEEM m'-lu-ma-DAH*

14 Truly, I shall further baffle that people With bafflement upon bafflement; And the wisdom of its wise shall fail, And the prudence of its prudent shall vanish.

לָכֵן הִנְנִי יוֹסִף לְהַפְלִיא אֶת־הָעָם־הַזֶּה הַפְלֵא וָפֶלֶא וְאָבְדָה חָכְמַת חֲכָמָיו וּבִינַת נְבֹנָיו תִּסְתַּתָּר: יד

15 Ha! Those who would hide their plans Deep from *Hashem*! Who do their work in dark places And say, "Who sees us, who takes note of us?"

הוֹי הַמַּעֲמִיקִים מֵיהוָֹה לַסְתִּר עֵצָה וְהָיָה בְמַחְשָׁךְ מַעֲשֵׂיהֶם וַיֹּאמְרוּ מִי רֹאֵנוּ וּמִי יֹדְעֵנוּ: טו

16 How perverse of you! Should the potter be accounted as the clay? Should what is made say of its Maker, "He did not make me," And what is formed say of Him who formed it, "He did not understand"?

הַפְכְּכֶם אִם־כְּחֹמֶר הַיֹּצֵר יֵחָשֵׁב כִּי־יֹאמַר מַעֲשֶׂה לְעֹשֵׂהוּ לֹא עָשָׂנִי וְיֵצֶר אָמַר לְיוֹצְרוֹ לֹא הֵבִין: טז

17 Surely, in a little while, Lebanon will be transformed into farm land, And farm land accounted as mere brush.

הֲלוֹא־עוֹד מְעַט מִזְעָר וְשָׁב לְבָנוֹן לַכַּרְמֶל וְהַכַּרְמֶל לַיַּעַר יֵחָשֵׁב: יז

18 In that day, the deaf shall hear even written words, And the eyes of the blind shall see Even in darkness and obscurity.

וְשָׁמְעוּ בַיּוֹם־הַהוּא הַחֵרְשִׁים דִּבְרֵי־סֵפֶר וּמֵאֹפֶל וּמֵחֹשֶׁךְ עֵינֵי עִוְרִים תִּרְאֶינָה: יח

19 Then the humble shall have increasing joy through *Hashem*, And the neediest of men shall exult In the Holy One of *Yisrael*.

וְיָסְפוּ עֲנָוִים בַּיהוָֹה שִׂמְחָה וְאֶבְיוֹנֵי אָדָם בִּקְדוֹשׁ יִשְׂרָאֵל יָגִילוּ: יט

20 For the tyrant shall be no more, The scoffer shall cease to be; And those diligent for evil shall be wiped out,

כִּי־אָפֵס עָרִיץ וְכָלָה לֵץ וְנִכְרְתוּ כָּל־שֹׁקְדֵי אָוֶן: כ

21 Who cause men to lose their lawsuits, Laying a snare for the arbiter at the gate, And wronging by falsehood Him who was in the right.

מַחֲטִיאֵי אָדָם בְּדָבָר וְלַמּוֹכִיחַ בַּשַּׁעַר יְקֹשׁוּן וַיַּטּוּ בַתֹּהוּ צַדִּיק: כא

29:13 And its worship of Me has been a commandment of men, learned by rote For what sin did God punish *Yehuda*? Compared to *Shomron*, the northern kingdom, with all its idolatries and immoralities, *Yehuda* seemed positively pious. In fact, they had purified their country under *Chizkiyahu*. *Yeshayahu* answers with one sentence. Though the people prayed and performed the ritual commandments, their service was not genuine, but only lip-service. Some commentators understood this as hypocrisy; however others interpret *Yeshayahu's* description in a more literal sense – unfeeling, robotic observance that has no value. *Hashem* wants both our consistent external actions with corresponding internal feelings united in His service.

A young boy praying at the Western Wall

²² Assuredly, thus said *Hashem* to the House of *Yaakov*, Who redeemed *Avraham*: No more shall *Yaakov* be shamed, No longer his face grow pale.

לָכֵן כֹּה־אָמַר יְהוָה אֶל־בֵּית יַעֲקֹב אֲשֶׁר פָּדָה אֶת־אַבְרָהָם לֹא־עַתָּה יֵבוֹשׁ יַעֲקֹב וְלֹא עַתָּה פָּנָיו יֶחֱוָרוּ:

²³ For when he – that is, his children – behold what My hands have wrought in his midst, they will hallow My name. Men will hallow the Holy One of *Yaakov* And stand in awe of the God of *Yisrael*.

כִּי בִרְאֹתוֹ יְלָדָיו מַעֲשֵׂה יָדַי בְּקִרְבּוֹ יַקְדִּישׁוּ שְׁמִי וְהִקְדִּישׁוּ אֶת־קְדוֹשׁ יַעֲקֹב וְאֶת־אֱלֹהֵי יִשְׂרָאֵל יַעֲרִיצוּ:

²⁴ And the confused shall acquire insight And grumblers accept instruction.

וְיָדְעוּ תֹעֵי־רוּחַ בִּינָה וְרוֹגְנִים יִלְמְדוּ־לֶקַח:

30 ¹ Oh, disloyal sons! – declares *Hashem* – Making plans Against My wishes, Weaving schemes Against My will, Thereby piling Guilt on guilt –

ל א הוֹי בָּנִים סוֹרְרִים נְאֻם־יְהוָה לַעֲשׂוֹת עֵצָה וְלֹא מִנִּי וְלִנְסֹךְ מַסֵּכָה וְלֹא רוּחִי לְמַעַן סְפוֹת חַטָּאת עַל־חַטָּאת:

² Who set out to go down to Egypt Without asking Me, To seek refuge with Pharaoh, To seek shelter under the protection of Egypt.

ב הַהֹלְכִים לָרֶדֶת מִצְרַיִם וּפִי לֹא שָׁאָלוּ לָעוֹז בְּמָעוֹז פַּרְעֹה וְלַחְסוֹת בְּצֵל מִצְרָיִם:

³ The refuge with Pharaoh shall result in your shame; The shelter under Egypt's protection, in your chagrin.

ג וְהָיָה לָכֶם מָעוֹז פַּרְעֹה לְבֹשֶׁת וְהֶחָסוּת בְּצֵל־מִצְרַיִם לִכְלִמָּה:

⁴ Though his officers are present in Zoan, And his messengers reach as far as Hanes,

ד כִּי־הָיוּ בְצֹעַן שָׂרָיו וּמַלְאָכָיו חָנֵס יַגִּיעוּ:

⁵ They all shall come to shame Because of a people that does not avail them, That is of no help or avail, But [brings] only chagrin and disgrace.

ה כֹּל הִבְאִישׁ [הֹבִישׁ] עַל־עַם לֹא־יוֹעִילוּ לָמוֹ לֹא לְעֵזֶר וְלֹא לְהוֹעִיל כִּי לְבֹשֶׁת וְגַם־לְחֶרְפָּה:

⁶ The "Beasts of the *Negev*" Pronouncement. Through a land of distress and hardship, Of lion and roaring king-beast, Of viper and flying seraph, They convey their wealth on the backs of asses, Their treasures on camels' humps, To a people of no avail.

ו מַשָּׂא בַּהֲמוֹת נֶגֶב בְּאֶרֶץ צָרָה וְצוּקָה לָבִיא וָלַיִשׁ מֵהֶם אֶפְעֶה וְשָׂרָף מְעוֹפֵף יִשְׂאוּ עַל־כֶּתֶף עֲיָרִים חֵילֵהֶם וְעַל־דַּבֶּשֶׁת גְּמַלִּים אוֹצְרֹתָם עַל־עַם לֹא יוֹעִילוּ:

⁷ For the help of Egypt Shall be vain and empty. Truly, I call this, "They are a threat that has ceased."

ז וּמִצְרַיִם הֶבֶל וָרִיק יַעְזֹרוּ לָכֵן קָרָאתִי לָזֹאת רַהַב הֵם שָׁבֶת:

⁸ Now, Go, write it down on a tablet And inscribe it in a record, That it may be with them for future days, A witness forever.

ח עַתָּה בּוֹא כָתְבָהּ עַל־לוּחַ אִתָּם וְעַל־סֵפֶר חֻקָּהּ וּתְהִי לְיוֹם אַחֲרוֹן לָעַד עַד־עוֹלָם:

⁹ For it is a rebellious people, Faithless children, Children who refused to heed The instruction of *Hashem*;

ט כִּי עַם מְרִי הוּא בָּנִים כֶּחָשִׁים בָּנִים לֹא־אָבוּ שְׁמוֹעַ תּוֹרַת יְהוָה:

¹⁰ Who said to the seers, "Do not see," To the *Neviim*, "Do not prophesy truth to us; Speak to us falsehoods, Prophesy delusions.

י אֲשֶׁר אָמְרוּ לָרֹאִים לֹא תִרְאוּ וְלַחֹזִים לֹא תֶחֱזוּ־לָנוּ נְכֹחוֹת דַּבְּרוּ־לָנוּ חֲלָקוֹת חֲזוּ מַהֲתַלּוֹת:

¹¹ Leave the way! Get off the path! Let us hear no more About the Holy One of *Yisrael*!"

יא סוּרוּ מִנֵּי־דֶרֶךְ הַטּוּ מִנֵּי־אֹרַח הַשְׁבִּיתוּ מִפָּנֵינוּ אֶת־קְדוֹשׁ יִשְׂרָאֵל:

Isaiah

12 Assuredly, Thus said the Holy One of *Yisrael*: Because you have rejected this word, And have put your trust and reliance In that which is fraudulent and tortuous –

יב לָכֵן כֹּה אָמַר קְדוֹשׁ יִשְׂרָאֵל יַעַן מָאָסְכֶם בַּדָּבָר הַזֶּה וַתִּבְטְחוּ בְּעֹשֶׁק וְנָלוֹז וַתִּשָּׁעֲנוּ עָלָיו:

13 Of a surety, This iniquity shall work on you Like a spreading breach that occurs in a lofty wall, Whose crash comes sudden and swift.

יג לָכֵן יִהְיֶה לָכֶם הֶעָוֹן הַזֶּה כְּפֶרֶץ נֹפֵל נִבְעָה בְּחוֹמָה נִשְׂגָּבָה אֲשֶׁר־פִּתְאֹם לְפֶתַע יָבוֹא שִׁבְרָהּ:

14 It is smashed as one smashes an earthen jug, Ruthlessly shattered So that no shard is left in its breakage To scoop coals from a brazier, Or ladle water from a puddle.

יד וּשְׁבָרָהּ כְּשֵׁבֶר נֵבֶל יוֹצְרִים כָּתוּת לֹא יַחְמֹל וְלֹא־יִמָּצֵא בִמְכִתָּתוֹ חֶרֶשׂ לַחְתּוֹת אֵשׁ מִיָּקוּד וְלַחְשֹׂף מַיִם מִגֶּבֶא:

15 For thus said my God, The Holy One of *Yisrael*, "You shall triumph by stillness and quiet; Your victory shall come about Through calm and confidence." But you refused.

טו כִּי כֹה־אָמַר אֲדֹנָי יֱהֹוִה קְדוֹשׁ יִשְׂרָאֵל בְּשׁוּבָה וָנַחַת תִּוָּשֵׁעוּן בְּהַשְׁקֵט וּבְבִטְחָה תִּהְיֶה גְּבוּרַתְכֶם וְלֹא אֲבִיתֶם:

16 "No," you declared. "We shall flee on steeds" – Therefore you shall flee! "We shall ride on swift mounts" – Therefore your pursuers shall prove swift!

טז וַתֹּאמְרוּ לֹא־כִי עַל־סוּס נָנוּס עַל־כֵּן תְּנוּסוּן וְעַל־קַל נִרְכָּב עַל־כֵּן יִקַּלּוּ רֹדְפֵיכֶם:

17 One thousand before the shout of one – You shall flee at the shout of five; Till what is left of you Is like a mast on a hilltop, Like a pole upon a mountain.

יז אֶלֶף אֶחָד מִפְּנֵי גַּעֲרַת אֶחָד מִפְּנֵי גַּעֲרַת חֲמִשָּׁה תָּנֻסוּ עַד אִם־נוֹתַרְתֶּם כַּתֹּרֶן עַל־רֹאשׁ הָהָר וְכַנֵּס עַל־הַגִּבְעָה:

18 Truly, *Hashem* is waiting to show you grace, Truly, He will arise to pardon you. For *Hashem* is a God of justice; Happy are all who wait for Him.

יח וְלָכֵן יְחַכֶּה יְהֹוָה לַחֲנַנְכֶם וְלָכֵן יָרוּם לְרַחֶמְכֶם כִּי־אֱלֹהֵי מִשְׁפָּט יְהֹוָה אַשְׁרֵי כָּל־חוֹכֵי לוֹ:

v'-la-KHAYN y'-kha-KEH a-do-NAI la-kha-nan-KHEM v'-la-KHAYN ya-RUM
l'-ra-khem-KHEM kee e-lo-HAY mish-PAT a-do-NAI ash-RAY kol kho-KHAY LO

19 Indeed, O people in *Tzion*, dwellers of *Yerushalayim*, you shall not have cause to weep. He will grant you His favor at the sound of your cry; He will respond as soon as He hears it.

יט כִּי־עַם בְּצִיּוֹן יֵשֵׁב בִּירוּשָׁלָ͏ִם בָּכוֹ לֹא־תִבְכֶּה חָנוֹן יָחְנְךָ לְקוֹל זַעֲקֶךָ כְּשָׁמְעָתוֹ עָנָךְ:

30:18 Truly, *Hashem* is waiting Despite the fate of *Ashdod* ten years earlier, abandoned by Egypt to destruction by Assyria, there were still those in *Yehuda* who felt that an alliance with Pharaoh would be the best defense against the Assyrians. *Yeshayahu* describes a delegation that traveled southwards through the *Negev* desert with donkeys bearing treasures, in hopes of buying Egyptian loyalty. *Hashem* expresses His frustration with Israel for continuing their rebellious practices, placing their trust in others and not in Him. However, *Yeshayahu* states, divine patience was not yet exhausted. If they would cry out to *Hashem* (verse 19) and abolish idolatry entirely (verse 22), He would be gracious to his people. This is an important message for mankind. *Hashem* is a God of patience and forgiveness. Though people sin

A donkey in the *Negev* desert

and turn their backs on Him, He is always waiting for them to correct their ways, so that He can be gracious to them and have compassion on them.

²⁰ My Lord will provide for you meager bread and scant water. Then your Guide will no more be ignored, but your eyes will watch your Guide;

כ וְנָתַן לָכֶם אֲדֹנָי לֶחֶם צָר וּמַיִם לָחַץ וְלֹא־יִכָּנֵף עוֹד מוֹרֶיךָ וְהָיוּ עֵינֶיךָ רֹאוֹת אֶת־מוֹרֶיךָ:

²¹ and, whenever you deviate to the right or to the left, your ears will heed the command from behind you: "This is the road; follow it!"

כא וְאָזְנֶיךָ תִּשְׁמַעְנָה דָבָר מֵאַחֲרֶיךָ לֵאמֹר זֶה הַדֶּרֶךְ לְכוּ בוֹ כִּי תַאֲמִינוּ וְכִי תַשְׂמְאִילוּ:

²² And you will treat as unclean the silver overlay of your images and the golden plating of your idols. You will cast them away like a menstruous woman. "Out!" you will call to them.

כב וְטִמֵּאתֶם אֶת־צִפּוּי פְּסִילֵי כַסְפֶּךָ וְאֶת־אֲפֻדַּת מַסֵּכַת זְהָבֶךָ תִּזְרֵם כְּמוֹ דָוָה צֵא תֹּאמַר לוֹ:

²³ So rain shall be provided for the seed with which you sow the ground, and the bread that the ground brings forth shall be rich and fat. Your livestock, in that day, shall graze in broad pastures;

כג וְנָתַן מְטַר זַרְעֲךָ אֲשֶׁר־תִּזְרַע אֶת־הָאֲדָמָה וְלֶחֶם תְּבוּאַת הָאֲדָמָה וְהָיָה דָשֵׁן וְשָׁמֵן יִרְעֶה מִקְנֶיךָ בַּיּוֹם הַהוּא כַּר נִרְחָב:

²⁴ as for the cattle and the asses that till the soil, they shall partake of salted fodder that has been winnowed with shovel and fan.

כד וְהָאֲלָפִים וְהָעֲיָרִים עֹבְדֵי הָאֲדָמָה בְּלִיל חָמִיץ יֹאכֵלוּ אֲשֶׁר־זֹרֶה בָרַחַת וּבַמִּזְרֶה:

²⁵ And on every high mountain and on every lofty hill, there shall appear brooks and watercourses – on a day of heavy slaughter, when towers topple.

כה וְהָיָה עַל־כָּל־הַר גָּבֹהַּ וְעַל כָּל־גִּבְעָה נִשָּׂאָה פְּלָגִים יִבְלֵי־מָיִם בְּיוֹם הֶרֶג רָב בִּנְפֹל מִגְדָּלִים:

²⁶ And the light of the moon shall become like the light of the sun, and the light of the sun shall become sevenfold, like the light of the seven days, when *Hashem* binds up His people's wounds and heals the injuries it has suffered.

כו וְהָיָה אוֹר־הַלְּבָנָה כְּאוֹר הַחַמָּה וְאוֹר הַחַמָּה יִהְיֶה שִׁבְעָתַיִם כְּאוֹר שִׁבְעַת הַיָּמִים בְּיוֹם חֲבֹשׁ יְהוָה אֶת־שֶׁבֶר עַמּוֹ וּמַחַץ מַכָּתוֹ יִרְפָּא:

²⁷ Behold *Hashem* Himself Comes from afar In blazing wrath, With a heavy burden – His lips full of fury, His tongue like devouring fire,

כז הִנֵּה שֵׁם־יְהוָה בָּא מִמֶּרְחָק בֹּעֵר אַפּוֹ וְכֹבֶד מַשָּׂאָה שְׂפָתָיו מָלְאוּ זַעַם וּלְשׁוֹנוֹ כְּאֵשׁ אֹכָלֶת:

²⁸ And his breath like a raging torrent Reaching halfway up the neck – To set a misguiding yoke upon nations And a misleading bridle upon the jaws of peoples,

כח וְרוּחוֹ כְּנַחַל שׁוֹטֵף עַד־צַוָּאר יֶחֱצֶה לַהֲנָפָה גוֹיִם בְּנָפַת שָׁוְא וְרֶסֶן מַתְעֶה עַל לְחָיֵי עַמִּים:

²⁹ For you, there shall be singing As on a night when a festival is hallowed; There shall be rejoicing as when they march With flute, with timbrels, and with lyres* To the Rock of *Yisrael* on the Mount of *Hashem*.

כט הַשִּׁיר יִהְיֶה לָכֶם כְּלֵיל הִתְקַדֶּשׁ־חָג וְשִׂמְחַת לֵבָב כַּהוֹלֵךְ בֶּחָלִיל לָבוֹא בְהַר־יְהוָה אֶל־צוּר יִשְׂרָאֵל:

³⁰ For *Hashem* will make His majestic voice heard And display the sweep of His arm In raging wrath, In a devouring blaze of fire, In tempest, and rainstorm, and hailstones.

ל וְהִשְׁמִיעַ יְהוָה אֶת־הוֹד קוֹלוֹ וְנַחַת זְרוֹעוֹ יַרְאֶה בְּזַעַף אַף וְלַהַב אֵשׁ אוֹכֵלָה נֶפֶץ וָזֶרֶם וְאֶבֶן בָּרָד:

---

* "with timbrels, and with lyres" brought up from verse 32 for clarity

לא כִּי־מִקּוֹל יְהֹוָה יֵחַת אַשּׁוּר בַּשֵּׁבֶט יַכֶּה:

31 Truly, Assyria, who beats with the rod, Shall be cowed by the voice of *Hashem*;

לב וְהָיָה כֹּל מַעֲבַר מַטֵּה מֽוּסָדָה אֲשֶׁר יָנִיחַ יְהֹוָה עָלָיו בְּתֻפִּים וּבְכִנֹּרוֹת וּבְמִלְחֲמוֹת תְּנוּפָה נִלְחַם־בָּהּ [בָּם:]

32 And each time the appointed staff passes by, *Hashem* will bring down [His arm] upon him And will do battle with him as he waves it.

לג כִּי־עָרוּךְ מֵאֶתְמוּל תׇּפְתֶּה גַּם־הוּא [הִיא] לַמֶּלֶךְ הוּכָן הֶעֱמִיק הִרְחִב מְדֻרָתָהּ אֵשׁ וְעֵצִים הַרְבֵּה נִשְׁמַת יְהֹוָה כְּנַחַל גׇּפְרִית בֹּעֲרָה בָּהּ:

33 The Topheth has long been ready for him; He too is destined for Melech – His firepit has been made both wide and deep, With plenty of fire and firewood, And with the breath of *Hashem* Burning in it like a stream of sulfur.

א הוֹי הַיֹּרְדִים מִצְרַיִם לְעֶזְרָה עַל־סוּסִים יִשָּׁעֵנוּ וַיִּבְטְחוּ עַל־רֶכֶב כִּי רָב וְעַל פָּרָשִׁים כִּי־עָצְמוּ מְאֹד וְלֹא שָׁעוּ עַל־קְדוֹשׁ יִשְׂרָאֵל וְאֶת־יְהֹוָה לֹא דָרָשׁוּ:

31 1 Ha! Those who go down to Egypt for help And rely upon horses! They have put their trust in abundance of chariots, In vast numbers of riders, And they have not turned to the Holy One of *Yisrael*, They have not sought *Hashem*.

ב וְגַם־הוּא חָכָם וַיָּבֵא רָע וְאֶת־דְּבָרָיו לֹא הֵסִיר וְקָם עַל־בֵּית מְרֵעִים וְעַל־עֶזְרַת פֹּעֲלֵי אָוֶן:

2 But He too is wise! He has brought on misfortune, And has not canceled His word. So He shall rise against the house of evildoers, And the allies of the workers of iniquity.

ג וּמִצְרַיִם אָדָם וְלֹא־אֵל וְסוּסֵיהֶם בָּשָׂר וְלֹא־רוּחַ וַיהֹוָה יַטֶּה יָדוֹ וְכָשַׁל עוֹזֵר וְנָפַל עָזֻר וְיַחְדָּו כֻּלָּם יִכְלָיוּן:

3 For the Egyptians are man, not *Hashem*, And their horses are flesh, not spirit; And when *Hashem* stretches out His arm, The helper shall trip And the helped one shall fall, And both shall perish together.

ד כִּי כֹה אָמַר־יְהֹוָה אֵלַי כַּאֲשֶׁר יֶהְגֶּה הָאַרְיֵה וְהַכְּפִיר עַל־טַרְפּוֹ אֲשֶׁר יִקָּרֵא עָלָיו מְלֹא רֹעִים מִקּוֹלָם לֹא יֵחָת וּמֵהֲמוֹנָם לֹא יַעֲנֶה כֵּן יֵרֵד יְהֹוָה צְבָאוֹת לִצְבֹּא עַל־הַר־צִיּוֹן וְעַל־גִּבְעָתָהּ:

4 For thus *Hashem* has said to me: As a lion – a great beast – Growls over its prey And, when the shepherds gather In force against him, Is not dismayed by their cries Nor cowed by their noise – So the Lᴏʀᴅ of Hosts will descend to make war Against the mount and the hill of *Tzion*.

ה כְּצִפֳּרִים עָפוֹת כֵּן יָגֵן יְהֹוָה צְבָאוֹת עַל־יְרוּשָׁלַ͏ִם גָּנוֹן וְהִצִּיל פָּסֹחַ וְהִמְלִיט:

5 Like the birds that fly, even so will the Lᴏʀᴅ of Hosts shield *Yerushalayim*, shielding and saving, protecting and rescuing.

ו שׁוּבוּ לַאֲשֶׁר הֶעְמִיקוּ סָרָה בְּנֵי יִשְׂרָאֵל:

6 Return, O children of *Yisrael*, to Him to whom they have been so shamefully false;

ז כִּי בַּיּוֹם הַהוּא יִמְאָסוּן אִישׁ אֱלִילֵי כַסְפּוֹ וֶאֱלִילֵי זְהָבוֹ אֲשֶׁר עָשׂוּ לָכֶם יְדֵיכֶם חֵטְא:

7 for in that day everyone will reject his idols of silver and idols of gold, which your hands have made for your guilt.

ח וְנָפַל אַשּׁוּר בְּחֶרֶב לֹא־אִישׁ וְחֶרֶב לֹא־אָדָם תֹּאכְלֶנּוּ וְנָס לוֹ מִפְּנֵי־חֶרֶב וּבַחוּרָיו לָמַס יִהְיוּ:

8 Then Assyria shall fall, Not by the sword of man; A sword not of humans shall devour him. He shall shrivel before the sword, And his young men pine away.

9 His rock shall melt with terror, And his officers shall collapse from weakness – Declares *Hashem*, who has a fire in *Tzion*, Who has an oven in *Yerushalayim*.

ט וְסַלְעוֹ מִמָּגוֹר יַעֲבוֹר וְחַתּוּ מִנֵּס שָׂרָיו נְאֻם־יְהֹוָה אֲשֶׁר־אוּר לוֹ בְּצִיּוֹן וְתַנּוּר לוֹ בִּירוּשָׁלָ͏ִם:

*v'-sal-O mi-ma-GOR ya-a-VOR v'-kha-TU mi-NAYS sa-RAV n'-um
a-do-NAI a-sher UR LO b'-tzi-YON v'-ta-NUR LO bee-ru-sha-LA-im*

32 1 Behold, a king shall reign in righteousness, And ministers shall govern with justice;

לב א הֵן לְצֶדֶק יִמְלָךְ־מֶלֶךְ וּלְשָׂרִים לְמִשְׁפָּט יָשֹׂרוּ:

2 Every one of them shall be Like a refuge from gales, A shelter from rainstorms; Like brooks of water in a desert, Like the shade of a massive rock In a languishing land.

ב וְהָיָה־אִישׁ כְּמַחֲבֵא־רוּחַ וְסֵתֶר זָרֶם כְּפַלְגֵי־מַיִם בְּצָיוֹן כְּצֵל סֶלַע־כָּבֵד בְּאֶרֶץ עֲיֵפָה:

3 Then the eyes of those who have sight shall not be sealed, And the ears of those who have hearing shall listen;

ג וְלֹא תִשְׁעֶינָה עֵינֵי רֹאִים וְאָזְנֵי שֹׁמְעִים תִּקְשַׁבְנָה:

4 And the minds of the thoughtless shall attend and note, And the tongues of mumblers shall speak with fluent eloquence.

ד וּלְבַב נִמְהָרִים יָבִין לָדָעַת וּלְשׁוֹן עִלְּגִים תְּמַהֵר לְדַבֵּר צָחוֹת:

5 No more shall a villain be called noble, Nor shall "gentleman" be said of a knave.

ה לֹא־יִקָּרֵא עוֹד לְנָבָל נָדִיב וּלְכִילַי לֹא יֵאָמֵר שׁוֹעַ:

6 For the villain speaks villainy And plots treachery; To act impiously And to preach disloyalty against *Hashem*; To leave the hungry unsatisfied And deprive the thirsty of drink.

ו כִּי נָבָל נְבָלָה יְדַבֵּר וְלִבּוֹ יַעֲשֶׂה־אָוֶן לַעֲשׂוֹת חֹנֶף וּלְדַבֵּר אֶל־יְהֹוָה תּוֹעָה לְהָרִיק נֶפֶשׁ רָעֵב וּמַשְׁקֶה צָמֵא יַחְסִיר:

7 As for the knave, his tools are knavish. He forges plots To destroy the poor with falsehoods And the needy when they plead their cause.

ז וְכֵלַי כֵּלָיו רָעִים הוּא זִמּוֹת יָעָץ לְחַבֵּל עֲנָוִים [עֲנִיִּים] בְּאִמְרֵי־שֶׁקֶר וּבְדַבֵּר אֶבְיוֹן מִשְׁפָּט:

8 But the noble has noble intentions And is constant in noble acts.

ח וְנָדִיב נְדִיבוֹת יָעָץ וְהוּא עַל־נְדִיבוֹת יָקוּם:

9 You carefree women, Attend, hear my words! You confident ladies, Give ear to my speech!

ט נָשִׁים שַׁאֲנַנּוֹת קֹמְנָה שְׁמַעְנָה קוֹלִי בָּנוֹת בֹּטְחוֹת הַאְזֵנָּה אִמְרָתִי:

10 In little more than a year, You shall be troubled, O confident ones, When the vintage is over And no ingathering takes place.

י יָמִים עַל־שָׁנָה תִּרְגַּזְנָה בֹּטְחוֹת כִּי כָּלָה בָצִיר אֹסֶף בְּלִי יָבוֹא:

אוֹר
תַּנּוּר

31:9 Who has a fire in *Tzion*, who has an oven in *Yerushalayim* In Hebrew, the word *shuv* (שוב) means both 'repent,' and 'return.' *Yeshayahu* begs the people to repent and return to *Hashem*. If they do so, he promises, Assyria will fall before God, whom the prophet describes as both a 'fire,' in Hebrew *ur* (אור), and an 'oven,' *tanur* (תנור). While both metaphors involve fire, there is an importance difference between a fire and an oven. The metaphor of fire describes *Hashem* burning and destroying the Assyrian enemy. But in the metaphor of the oven, the same fire is a source of heat and comfort, thus reminding us that our actions determine whether *Hashem* relates to us as fire of destruction or a helpful oven.

A pita bread oven in the Old City of *Yerushalayim*

54

Isaiah

11 Tremble, you carefree ones! Quake, O confident ones! Strip yourselves naked, Put the cloth about your loins!

יא חִרְדוּ שַׁאֲנַנּוֹת רְגָזָה בֹּטְחוֹת פְּשֹׁטָה וְעֹרָה וַחֲגוֹרָה עַל־חֲלָצָיִם:

12 Lament upon the breasts, For the pleasant fields, For the spreading grapevines,

יב עַל־שָׁדַיִם סֹפְדִים עַל־שְׂדֵי־חֶמֶד עַל־גֶּפֶן פֹּרִיָּה:

13 For my people's soil – It shall be overgrown with briers and thistles – Aye, and for all the houses of delight, For the city of mirth.

יג עַל אַדְמַת עַמִּי קוֹץ שָׁמִיר תַּעֲלֶה כִּי עַל־כָּל־בָּתֵּי מָשׂוֹשׂ קִרְיָה עַלִּיזָה:

14 For the castle shall be abandoned, The noisy city forsaken; Citadel and tower shall become Bare places forever, A stamping ground for wild asses, A pasture for flocks –

יד כִּי־אַרְמוֹן נֻטָּשׁ הֲמוֹן עִיר עֻזָּב עֹפֶל וָבַחַן הָיָה בְעַד מְעָרוֹת עַד־עוֹלָם מְשׂוֹשׂ פְּרָאִים מִרְעֵה עֲדָרִים:

15 Till a spirit from on high is poured out on us, And wilderness is transformed into farm land, While farm land rates as mere brush.

טו עַד־יֵעָרֶה עָלֵינוּ רוּחַ מִמָּרוֹם וְהָיָה מִדְבָּר לַכַּרְמֶל וכרמל [וְהַכַּרְמֶל] לַיַּעַר יֵחָשֵׁב:

16 Then justice shall abide in the wilderness And righteousness shall dwell on the farm land.

טז וְשָׁכַן בַּמִּדְבָּר מִשְׁפָּט וּצְדָקָה בַּכַּרְמֶל תֵּשֵׁב:

17 For the work of righteousness shall be peace, And the effect of righteousness, calm and confidence forever.

יז וְהָיָה מַעֲשֵׂה הַצְּדָקָה שָׁלוֹם וַעֲבֹדַת הַצְּדָקָה הַשְׁקֵט וָבֶטַח עַד־עוֹלָם:

18 Then my people shall dwell in peaceful homes, In secure dwellings, In untroubled places of rest.

יח וְיָשַׁב עַמִּי בִּנְוֵה שָׁלוֹם וּבְמִשְׁכְּנוֹת מִבְטַחִים וּבִמְנוּחֹת שַׁאֲנַנּוֹת:

v'-ya-SHAV a-MEE bin-VAY sha-LOM uv-mish-k'-NOT
miv-ta-KHEEM u-vim-nu-KHOT sha-a-na-NOT

19 And the brush shall sink and vanish, Even as the city is laid low.

יט וּבָרַד בְּרֶדֶת הַיָּעַר וּבַשִּׁפְלָה תִּשְׁפַּל הָעִיר:

20 Happy shall you be who sow by all waters, Who send out cattle and asses to pasture.

כ אַשְׁרֵיכֶם זֹרְעֵי עַל־כָּל־מָיִם מְשַׁלְּחֵי רֶגֶל־הַשּׁוֹר וְהַחֲמוֹר:

33 1 Ha, you ravager who are not ravaged, You betrayer who have not been betrayed! When you have done ravaging, you shall be ravaged; When you have finished betraying, you shall be betrayed.

לג א הוֹי שׁוֹדֵד וְאַתָּה לֹא שָׁדוּד וּבוֹגֵד וְלֹא־בָגְדוּ בוֹ כַּהֲתִמְךָ שׁוֹדֵד תּוּשַּׁד כַּנְּלֹתְךָ לִבְגֹּד יִבְגְּדוּ־בָךְ:

32:18 Then my people shall dwell in peaceful homes The ultimate hope that *Yeshayahu* holds for his people is that they can dwell calmly in the Land of Israel. His supplications are the prayers of all the prophets. For example, *Hoshea* writes, "In that day I will make a covenant for them with the beasts of the field; the birds of the air and the creeping things of the ground; I will also banish bow, sword and war from the land. Thus I will let them lie down in safety" (2:20). *Rambam* similarly concludes the *Mishneh Torah*, his monumental work summarizing Jewish law, with the declaration that the reason the Jewish people want the *Mashiach* to come is not because they want to rule over other nations, but rather out of desire to dwell in

Sunrise over Peace Valley in northern Israel

quiet and peace in their land so they can pursue righteousness. This remains the hope and dream of the Jewish people today: that the *Mashiach* will come quickly and bring peace to the entire world.

² *Hashem*, be gracious to us! It is to You we have looked; Be their arm every morning, Also our deliverance in time of stress.

ב יְהֹוָה חָנֵּנוּ לְךָ קִוִּינוּ הֱיֵה זְרֹעָם לַבְּקָרִים אַף־יְשׁוּעָתֵנוּ בְּעֵת צָרָה:

³ At [Your] roaring, peoples have fled, Before Your majesty nations have scattered;

ג מִקּוֹל הָמוֹן נָדְדוּ עַמִּים מֵרוֹמְמֻתֶךָ נָפְצוּ גּוֹיִם:

⁴ And spoil was gathered as locusts are gathered, It was amassed as grasshoppers are amassed.

ד וְאֻסַּף שְׁלַלְכֶם אֹסֶף הֶחָסִיל כְּמַשַּׁק גֵּבִים שׁוֹקֵק בּוֹ:

⁵ *Hashem* is exalted, He dwells on high! [Of old] He filled *Tzion* With justice and righteousness.

ה נִשְׂגָּב יְהֹוָה כִּי שֹׁכֵן מָרוֹם מִלֵּא צִיּוֹן מִשְׁפָּט וּצְדָקָה:

nis-GAV a-do-NAI KEE sho-KHAYN ma-ROM
mi-LAY tzi-YON mish-PAT utz-da-KAH

⁶ Faithfulness to Your charge was [her] wealth, Wisdom and devotion [her] triumph, Reverence for *Hashem* – that was her treasure.

ו וְהָיָה אֱמוּנַת עִתֶּיךָ חֹסֶן יְשׁוּעֹת חָכְמַת וָדָעַת יִרְאַת יְהֹוָה הִיא אוֹצָרוֹ:

⁷ Hark! The Arielites cry aloud; Shalom's messengers weep bitterly.

ז הֵן אֶרְאֶלָּם צָעֲקוּ חֻצָה מַלְאֲכֵי שָׁלוֹם מַר יִבְכָּיוּן:

⁸ Highways are desolate, Wayfarers have ceased. A covenant has been renounced, Cities rejected Mortal man despised.

ח נָשַׁמּוּ מְסִלּוֹת שָׁבַת עֹבֵר אֹרַח הֵפֵר בְּרִית מָאַס עָרִים לֹא חָשַׁב אֱנוֹשׁ:

⁹ The land is wilted and withered; Lebanon disgraced and moldering, *Sharon* is become like a desert, And Bashan and *Carmel* are stripped bare.

ט אָבַל אֻמְלְלָה אָרֶץ הֶחְפִּיר לְבָנוֹן קָמַל הָיָה הַשָּׁרוֹן כָּעֲרָבָה וְנֹעֵר בָּשָׁן וְכַרְמֶל:

¹⁰ "Now I will arise," says *Hashem*, "Now I will exalt Myself, now raise Myself high.

י עַתָּה אָקוּם יֹאמַר יְהֹוָה עַתָּה אֵרוֹמָם עַתָּה אֶנָּשֵׂא:

¹¹ You shall conceive hay, Give birth to straw; My breath will devour you like fire.

יא תַּהֲרוּ חֲשַׁשׁ תֵּלְדוּ קַשׁ רוּחֲכֶם אֵשׁ תֹּאכַלְכֶם:

¹² Peoples shall be burnings of lime, Thorns cut down that are set on fire.

יב וְהָיוּ עַמִּים מִשְׂרְפוֹת שִׂיד קוֹצִים כְּסוּחִים בָּאֵשׁ יִצַּתּוּ:

¹³ Hear, you who are far, what I have done; You who are near, note My might."

יג שִׁמְעוּ רְחוֹקִים אֲשֶׁר עָשִׂיתִי וּדְעוּ קְרוֹבִים גְּבֻרָתִי:

¹⁴ Sinners in *Tzion* are frightened, The godless are seized with trembling: "Who of us can dwell with the devouring fire: Who of us can dwell with the never-dying blaze?"

יד פָּחֲדוּ בְצִיּוֹן חַטָּאִים אָחֲזָה רְעָדָה חֲנֵפִים מִי יָגוּר לָנוּ אֵשׁ אוֹכֵלָה מִי־יָגוּר לָנוּ מוֹקְדֵי עוֹלָם:

Rabbi Tuly Weisz delivering food to Israel's poor

א **33:5** **he filled *tzion* with justice and righteousness** the last word of this verse is *tzedaka* (צדקה). in hebrew, this word is used to mean both 'charity' and 'justice.' while in english these concepts are very different, the hebrew word teaches that the act of giving to those who are less fortunate is not to be seen primarily as benevolence or kindness. Rather, it is an act of justice and righteousness, which fulfills a duty expected of everyone, both rich and poor.

צדקה

Isaiah

15 He who walks in righteousness, Speaks uprightly, Spurns profit from fraudulent dealings, Waves away a bribe instead of grasping it, Stops his ears against listening to infamy, Shuts his eyes against looking at evil –

טו הֹלֵךְ צְדָקוֹת וְדֹבֵר מֵישָׁרִים מֹאֵס בְּבֶצַע מַעֲשַׁקּוֹת נֹעֵר כַּפָּיו מִתְּמֹךְ בַּשֹּׁחַד אֹטֵם אָזְנוֹ מִשְּׁמֹעַ דָּמִים וְעֹצֵם עֵינָיו מֵרְאוֹת בְּרָע:

16 Such a one shall dwell in lofty security, With inaccessible cliffs for his stronghold, With his food supplied And his drink assured.

טז הוּא מְרוֹמִים יִשְׁכֹּן מְצָדוֹת סְלָעִים מִשְׂגַּבּוֹ לַחְמוֹ נִתָּן מֵימָיו נֶאֱמָנִים:

17 When your eyes behold a king in his beauty, When they contemplate the land round about,

יז מֶלֶךְ בְּיָפְיוֹ תֶּחֱזֶינָה עֵינֶיךָ תִּרְאֶינָה אֶרֶץ מַרְחַקִּים:

18 Your throat shall murmur in awe, "Where is one who could count? Where is one who could weigh? Where is one who could count [all these] towers?"

יח לִבְּךָ יֶהְגֶּה אֵימָה אַיֵּה סֹפֵר אַיֵּה שֹׁקֵל אַיֵּה סֹפֵר אֶת־הַמִּגְדָּלִים:

19 No more shall you see the barbarian folk, The people of speech too obscure to comprehend, So stammering of tongue that they are not understood.

יט אֶת־עַם נוֹעָז לֹא תִרְאֶה עַם עִמְקֵי שָׂפָה מִשְּׁמוֹעַ נִלְעַג לָשׁוֹן אֵין בִּינָה:

20 When you gaze upon *Tzion*, our city of assembly, Your eyes shall behold *Yerushalayim* As a secure homestead, A tent not to be transported, Whose pegs shall never be pulled up, And none of whose ropes shall break.

כ חֲזֵה צִיּוֹן קִרְיַת מוֹעֲדֵנוּ עֵינֶיךָ תִרְאֶינָה יְרוּשָׁלַ͏ִם נָוֶה שַׁאֲנָן אֹהֶל בַּל־יִצְעָן בַּל־יִסַּע יְתֵדֹתָיו לָנֶצַח וְכָל־חֲבָלָיו בַּל־יִנָּתֵקוּ:

21 For there *Hashem* in His greatness shall be for us Like a region of rivers, of broad streams, Where no floating vessels can sail And no mighty craft can travel – Their ropes are slack, They cannot steady the sockets of their masts, They cannot spread a sail.*

כא כִּי אִם־שָׁם אַדִּיר יְהֹוָה לָנוּ מְקוֹם־נְהָרִים יְאֹרִים רַחֲבֵי יָדָיִם בַּל־תֵּלֶךְ בּוֹ אֳנִי־שַׁיִט וְצִי אַדִּיר לֹא יַעַבְרֶנּוּ:

22 For *Hashem* shall be our ruler, *Hashem* shall be our prince, *Hashem* shall be our king: He shall deliver us.

כב כִּי יְהֹוָה שֹׁפְטֵנוּ יְהֹוָה מְחֹקְקֵנוּ יְהֹוָה מַלְכֵּנוּ הוּא יוֹשִׁיעֵנוּ:

23 Then shall indeed much spoil be divided, Even the lame shall seize booty.

כג נִטְּשׁוּ חֲבָלָיִךְ בַּל־יְחַזְּקוּ כֵן־תָּרְנָם בַּל־פָּרְשׂוּ נֵס אָז חֻלַּק עַד־שָׁלָל מַרְבֶּה פִּסְחִים בָּזְזוּ בַז:

24 And none who lives there shall say, "I am sick"; It shall be inhabited by folk whose sin has been forgiven.

כד וּבַל־יֹאמַר שָׁכֵן חָלִיתִי הָעָם הַיֹּשֵׁב בָּהּ נְשֻׂא עָוֹן:

34 1 Approach, O nations, and listen, Give heed, O peoples! Let the earth and those in it hear; The world, and what it brings forth.

לד א קִרְבוּ גוֹיִם לִשְׁמֹעַ וּלְאֻמִּים הַקְשִׁיבוּ תִּשְׁמַע הָאָרֶץ וּמְלֹאָהּ תֵּבֵל וְכָל־צֶאֱצָאֶיהָ:

2 For *Hashem* is angry at all the nations, Furious at all their host; He has doomed them, consigned them to slaughter.

ב כִּי קֶצֶף לַיהֹוָה עַל־כָּל־הַגּוֹיִם וְחֵמָה עַל־כָּל־צְבָאָם הֶחֱרִימָם נְתָנָם לַטָּבַח:

---

* "Their ropes are slack, They cannot steady the sockets of their masts, They cannot spread a sail" brought up from verse 23 for clarity

3 Their slain shall be left lying, And the stench of their corpses shall mount; And the hills shall be drenched with their blood,

ג וְחַלְלֵיהֶם יֻשְׁלָכוּ וּפִגְרֵיהֶם יַעֲלֶה בָאְשָׁם וְנָמַסּוּ הָרִים מִדָּמָם:

4 All the host of heaven shall molder. The heavens shall be rolled up like a scroll, And all their host shall wither Like a leaf withering on the vine, Or shriveled fruit on a fig tree.

ד וְנָמַקּוּ כָּל־צְבָא הַשָּׁמַיִם וְנָגֹלּוּ כַסֵּפֶר הַשָּׁמָיִם וְכָל־צְבָאָם יִבּוֹל כִּנְבֹל עָלֶה מִגֶּפֶן וּכְנֹבֶלֶת מִתְּאֵנָה:

5 For My sword shall be drunk in the sky; Lo, it shall come down upon Edom, Upon the people I have doomed, To wreak judgment.

ה כִּי־רִוְּתָה בַשָּׁמַיִם חַרְבִּי הִנֵּה עַל־אֱדוֹם תֵּרֵד וְעַל־עַם חֶרְמִי לְמִשְׁפָּט:

6 *Hashem* has a sword; it is sated with blood, It is gorged with fat – The blood of lambs and he-goats, The kidney fat of rams. For *Hashem* holds a sacrifice in Bozrah, A great slaughter in the land of Edom.

ו חֶרֶב לַיהוָה מָלְאָה דָם הֻדַּשְׁנָה מֵחֵלֶב מִדַּם כָּרִים וְעַתּוּדִים מֵחֵלֶב כִּלְיוֹת אֵילִים כִּי זֶבַח לַיהוָה בְּבָצְרָה וְטֶבַח גָּדוֹל בְּאֶרֶץ אֱדוֹם:

7 Wild oxen shall fall with them, Young bulls with mighty steers; And their land shall be drunk with blood, Their soil shall be saturated with fat.

ז וְיָרְדוּ רְאֵמִים עִמָּם וּפָרִים עִם־אַבִּירִים וְרִוְּתָה אַרְצָם מִדָּם וַעֲפָרָם מֵחֵלֶב יְדֻשָּׁן:

8 For it is *Hashem*'s day of retribution, The year of vindication for *Tzion*'s cause.

ח כִּי יוֹם נָקָם לַיהוָה שְׁנַת שִׁלּוּמִים לְרִיב צִיּוֹן:

9 Its streams shall be turned to pitch And its soil to sulfur. Its land shall become burning pitch,

ט וְנֶהֶפְכוּ נְחָלֶיהָ לְזֶפֶת וַעֲפָרָהּ לְגָפְרִית וְהָיְתָה אַרְצָהּ לְזֶפֶת בֹּעֵרָה:

10 Night and day it shall never go out; Its smoke shall rise for all time. Through the ages it shall lie in ruins; Through the aeons none shall traverse it.

י לַיְלָה וְיוֹמָם לֹא תִכְבֶּה לְעוֹלָם יַעֲלֶה עֲשָׁנָהּ מִדּוֹר לָדוֹר תֶּחֱרָב לְנֵצַח נְצָחִים אֵין עֹבֵר בָּהּ:

11 Jackdaws and owls shall possess it; Great owls and ravens shall dwell there. He shall measure it with a line of chaos And with weights of emptiness.

יא וִירֵשׁוּהָ קָאַת וְקִפּוֹד וְיַנְשׁוֹף וְעֹרֵב יִשְׁכְּנוּ־בָהּ וְנָטָה עָלֶיהָ קַו־תֹהוּ וְאַבְנֵי־בֹהוּ:

12 It shall be called, "No kingdom is there," Its nobles and all its lords shall be nothing.

יב חֹרֶיהָ וְאֵין־שָׁם מְלוּכָה יִקְרָאוּ וְכָל־שָׂרֶיהָ יִהְיוּ אָפֶס:

13 Thorns shall grow up in its palaces, Nettles and briers in its strongholds. It shall be a home of jackals, An abode of ostriches.

יג וְעָלְתָה אַרְמְנֹתֶיהָ סִירִים קִמּוֹשׂ וָחוֹחַ בְּמִבְצָרֶיהָ וְהָיְתָה נְוֵה תַנִּים חָצִיר לִבְנוֹת יַעֲנָה:

14 Wildcats shall meet hyenas, Goat-demons shall greet each other; There too the lilith shall repose And find herself a resting place.

יד וּפָגְשׁוּ צִיִּים אֶת־אִיִּים וְשָׂעִיר עַל־רֵעֵהוּ יִקְרָא אַךְ־שָׁם הִרְגִּיעָה לִּילִית וּמָצְאָה לָהּ מָנוֹחַ:

15 There the arrow-snake shall nest and lay eggs, And shall brood and hatch in its shade. There too the buzzards shall gather With one another.

טו שָׁמָּה קִנְּנָה קִפּוֹז וַתְּמַלֵּט וּבָקְעָה וְדָגְרָה בְצִלָּהּ אַךְ־שָׁם נִקְבְּצוּ דַיּוֹת אִשָּׁה רְעוּתָהּ:

16 Search and read it in the scroll of *Hashem*: Not one of these shall be absent, Not one shall miss its fellow. For His mouth has spoken, It is His spirit that has assembled them,

טז דִּרְשׁוּ מֵעַל־סֵפֶר יְהֹוָה וּקְרָאוּ אַחַת מֵהֵנָּה לֹא נֶעְדָּרָה אִשָּׁה רְעוּתָהּ לֹא פָקָדוּ כִּי־פִי הוּא צִוָּה וְרוּחוֹ הוּא קִבְּצָן:

dir-SHU may-al SAY-fer a-do-NAI uk-RA-u a-KHAT may-HAY-nah LO ne-DA-rah
i-SHAH r'-u-TAH LO fa-KA-du kee FEE HU tzi-VAH v'-ru-KHO HU ki-b'-TZAN

17 And it is He who apportioned it to them by lot, Whose hand divided it for them with the line. They shall possess it for all time, They shall dwell there through the ages.

יז וְהוּא־הִפִּיל לָהֶן גּוֹרָל וְיָדוֹ חִלְּקַתָּה לָהֶם בַּקָּו עַד־עוֹלָם יִירָשׁוּהָ לְדוֹר וָדוֹר יִשְׁכְּנוּ־בָהּ:

35 1 The arid desert shall be glad, The wilderness shall rejoice And shall blossom like a rose.

ה א יְשֻׂשׂוּם מִדְבָּר וְצִיָּה וְתָגֵל עֲרָבָה וְתִפְרַח כַּחֲבַצָּלֶת:

2 It shall blossom abundantly, It shall also exult and shout. It shall receive the glory of Lebanon, The splendor of *Carmel* and *Sharon*. They shall behold the glory of *Hashem*, The splendor of our God.

ב פָּרֹחַ תִּפְרַח וְתָגֵל אַף גִּילַת וְרַנֵּן כְּבוֹד הַלְּבָנוֹן נִתַּן־לָהּ הֲדַר הַכַּרְמֶל וְהַשָּׁרוֹן הֵמָּה יִרְאוּ כְבוֹד־יְהֹוָה הֲדַר אֱלֹהֵינוּ:

3 Strengthen the hands that are slack; Make firm the tottering knees!

ג חַזְּקוּ יָדַיִם רָפוֹת וּבִרְכַּיִם כֹּשְׁלוֹת אַמֵּצוּ:

4 Say to the anxious of heart, "Be strong, fear not; Behold your God! Requital is coming, The recompense of *Hashem* – He Himself is coming to give you triumph."

ד אִמְרוּ לְנִמְהֲרֵי־לֵב חִזְקוּ אַל־תִּירָאוּ הִנֵּה אֱלֹהֵיכֶם נָקָם יָבוֹא גְּמוּל אֱלֹהִים הוּא יָבוֹא וְיֹשַׁעֲכֶם:

5 Then the eyes of the blind shall be opened, And the ears of the deaf shall be unstopped.

ה אָז תִּפָּקַחְנָה עֵינֵי עִוְרִים וְאָזְנֵי חֵרְשִׁים תִּפָּתַחְנָה:

6 Then the lame shall leap like a deer, And the tongue of the dumb shall shout aloud; For waters shall burst forth in the desert, Streams in the wilderness.

ו אָז יְדַלֵּג כָּאַיָּל פִּסֵּחַ וְתָרֹן לְשׁוֹן אִלֵּם כִּי־נִבְקְעוּ בַמִּדְבָּר מַיִם וּנְחָלִים בָּעֲרָבָה:

7 Torrid earth shall become a pool; Parched land, fountains of water; The home of jackals, a pasture; The abode [of ostriches], reeds and rushes.

ז וְהָיָה הַשָּׁרָב לַאֲגַם וְצִמָּאוֹן לְמַבּוּעֵי מָיִם בִּנְוֵה תַנִּים רִבְצָהּ חָצִיר לְקָנֶה וָגֹמֶא:

8 And a highway shall appear there, Which shall be called the Sacred Way. No one unclean shall pass along it, But it shall be for them. No traveler, not even fools, shall go astray.

ח וְהָיָה־שָׁם מַסְלוּל וָדֶרֶךְ וְדֶרֶךְ הַקֹּדֶשׁ יִקָּרֵא לָהּ לֹא־יַעַבְרֶנּוּ טָמֵא וְהוּא־לָמוֹ הֹלֵךְ דֶּרֶךְ וֶאֱוִילִים לֹא יִתְעוּ:

34:16 Search and read it in the scroll of *Hashem*
Yeshayahu states that a reading of "the scroll of *Hashem*" will reveal that none of the animals "shall be absent." *Rashi* suggests that this "scroll of *Hashem*" refers to *Sefer Bereishit*, which describes how every creature and its mate was gathered to *Noach* in the ark at the time of the flood. Since these animals heeded *Hashem's* command to come to the ark, not one of them went missing. The message, then, is clear. If even animals are capable of obeying divine decrees and thereby rewarded with protection, then how much more so should humanity be willing to listen to *Hashem's* word.

Replica of Noah's Ark at the Biblical Zoo in *Yerushalayim*

9 No lion shall be there, No ferocious beast shall set foot on it – These shall not be found there. But the redeemed shall walk it;

ט לֹא־יִהְיֶה שָׁם אַרְיֵה וּפְרִיץ חַיּוֹת בַּל־
יַעֲלֶנָּה לֹא תִמָּצֵא שָׁם וְהָלְכוּ גְּאוּלִים:

10 And the ransomed of *Hashem* shall return, And come with shouting to *Tzion*, Crowned with joy everlasting. They shall attain joy and gladness, While sorrow and sighing flee.

י וּפְדוּיֵי יְהֹוָה יְשֻׁבוּן וּבָאוּ צִיּוֹן בְּרִנָּה
וְשִׂמְחַת עוֹלָם עַל־רֹאשָׁם שָׂשׂוֹן
וְשִׂמְחָה יַשִּׂיגוּ וְנָסוּ יָגוֹן וַאֲנָחָה:

uf-du-YAY a-do-NAI y'-shu-VUN u-VA-u tzi-YON b'-ri-NAH v'-sim-KHAT o-LAM al ro-SHAM sa-SON v'-sim-KHAH ya-SEE-gu v'-NA-su ya-GON va-a-na-KHAH

36 1 In the fourteenth year of King *Chizkiyahu*, King Sennacherib of Assyria marched against all the fortified towns of *Yehuda* and seized them.

לו א וַיְהִי בְּאַרְבַּע עֶשְׂרֵה שָׁנָה לַמֶּלֶךְ חִזְקִיָּהוּ
עָלָה סַנְחֵרִיב מֶלֶךְ־אַשּׁוּר עַל כָּל־עָרֵי
יְהוּדָה הַבְּצֻרוֹת וַיִּתְפְּשֵׂם:

2 From Lachish, the king of Assyria sent the Rabshakeh, with a large force, to King *Chizkiyahu* in *Yerushalayim*. [The Rabshakeh] took up a position near the conduit of the Upper Pool, by the road of the Fuller's Field;

ב וַיִּשְׁלַח מֶלֶךְ־אַשּׁוּר אֶת־רַב־שָׁקֵה
מִלָּכִישׁ יְרוּשָׁלַמָה אֶל־הַמֶּלֶךְ חִזְקִיָּהוּ
בְּחֵיל כָּבֵד וַיַּעֲמֹד בִּתְעָלַת הַבְּרֵכָה
הָעֶלְיוֹנָה בִּמְסִלַּת שְׂדֵה כוֹבֵס:

3 and Eliakim son of *Chilkiyahu* who was in charge of the palace, Shebna the scribe, and Joah son of *Asaf* the recorder went out to him.

ג וַיֵּצֵא אֵלָיו אֶלְיָקִים בֶּן־חִלְקִיָּהוּ אֲשֶׁר
עַל־הַבָּיִת וְשֶׁבְנָא הַסֹּפֵר וְיוֹאָח בֶּן־אָסָף
הַמַּזְכִּיר:

4 The Rabshakeh said to them, "You tell *Chizkiyahu*: Thus said the Great King, the king of Assyria: What makes you so confident?

ד וַיֹּאמֶר אֲלֵיהֶם רַב־שָׁקֵה אִמְרוּ־נָא אֶל־
חִזְקִיָּהוּ כֹּה־אָמַר הַמֶּלֶךְ הַגָּדוֹל מֶלֶךְ
אַשּׁוּר מָה הַבִּטָּחוֹן הַזֶּה אֲשֶׁר בָּטָחְתָּ:

5 I suppose mere talk makes counsel and valor for war! Look, on whom are you relying, that you have rebelled against me?

ה אָמַרְתִּי אַךְ־דְּבַר־שְׂפָתַיִם עֵצָה וּגְבוּרָה
לַמִּלְחָמָה עַתָּה עַל־מִי בָטַחְתָּ כִּי מָרַדְתָּ
בִּי:

6 You are relying on Egypt, that splintered reed of a staff, which enters and punctures the palm of anyone who leans on it. That's what Pharaoh king of Egypt is like to all who rely on him.

ו הִנֵּה בָטַחְתָּ עַל־מִשְׁעֶנֶת הַקָּנֶה הָרָצוּץ
הַזֶּה עַל־מִצְרַיִם אֲשֶׁר יִסָּמֵךְ אִישׁ עָלָיו
וּבָא בְכַפּוֹ וּנְקָבָהּ כֵּן פַּרְעֹה מֶלֶךְ־מִצְרַיִם
לְכָל־הַבֹּטְחִים עָלָיו:

א **35:10 Crowned with joy everlasting** The Hebrew language includes many words used to describe various forms of happiness. According to former British Chief Rabbi Jonathan Sacks, the term *osher* (אושר) refers to a type of personal happiness that one experiences when engaging in an activity such as listening to music or observing something spectacular in nature. *Simcha* (שמחה), on the other hand, is a type of happiness that is created in the company of others, such as when celebrating a wedding or laughing as a family. In this verse, *Yeshayahu* promises that the ransomed of *Hashem* will return with 'everlasting joy,' *simchat olam* (שמחת עולם), upon their heads. The *simcha*, the shared joy of the redemption of the nation returning to *Hashem* and to the Holy Land, will last forever.

Rabbi Lord Jonathan Sacks (1948–2020)

אושר
שמחה

7 And if you tell me that you are relying on *Hashem* your God, He is the very one whose shrines and altars *Chizkiyahu* did away with, telling *Yehuda* and *Yerushalayim*, 'You must worship only at this *Mizbayach*!'

ז וְכִי־תֹאמַר אֵלַי אֶל־יְהֹוָה אֱלֹהֵינוּ בָּטָחְנוּ הֲלוֹא־הוּא אֲשֶׁר הֵסִיר חִזְקִיָּהוּ אֶת־בָּמֹתָיו וְאֶת־מִזְבְּחֹתָיו וַיֹּאמֶר לִיהוּדָה וְלִירוּשָׁלַ͏ִם לִפְנֵי הַמִּזְבֵּחַ הַזֶּה תִּשְׁתַּחֲווּ׃

v'-khee to-MAR ay-LAI el a-do-NAI e-lo-HAY-nu ba-TAKH-nu ha-LO HU a-SHER hay-SEER khiz-ki-YA-hu et ba-mo-TAV v'-et miz-b'-kho-TAV va-YO-mer lee-hu-DAH v'-lee-ru-sha-LA-im lif-NAY ha-miz-BAY-akh ha-ZEH tish-ta-kha-VU

8 Come now, make this wager with my master, the king of Assyria: I'll give you two thousand horses, if you can produce riders to mount them.

ח וְעַתָּה הִתְעָרֶב נָא אֶת־אֲדֹנִי הַמֶּלֶךְ אַשּׁוּר וְאֶתְּנָה לְךָ אַלְפַּיִם סוּסִים אִם־תּוּכַל לָתֶת לְךָ רֹכְבִים עֲלֵיהֶם׃

9 So how could you refuse anything, even to the deputy of one of my master's lesser servants, relying on Egypt for chariots and horsemen?

ט וְאֵיךְ תָּשִׁיב אֵת פְּנֵי פַחַת אַחַד עַבְדֵי אֲדֹנִי הַקְּטַנִּים וַתִּבְטַח לְךָ עַל־מִצְרַיִם לְרֶכֶב וּלְפָרָשִׁים׃

10 And do you think I have marched against this land to destroy it without *Hashem*? *Hashem* Himself told me: Go up against that land and destroy it."

י וְעַתָּה הֲמִבַּלְעֲדֵי יְהֹוָה עָלִיתִי עַל־הָאָרֶץ הַזֹּאת לְהַשְׁחִיתָהּ יְהֹוָה אָמַר אֵלַי עֲלֵה אֶל־הָאָרֶץ הַזֹּאת וְהַשְׁחִיתָהּ׃

11 Eliakim, Shebna, and Joah replied to the Rabshakeh, "Please, speak to your servants in Aramaic, since we understand it; do not speak to us in Judean in the hearing of the people on the wall."

יא וַיֹּאמֶר אֶלְיָקִים וְשֶׁבְנָא וְיוֹאָח אֶל־רַב־שָׁקֵה דַּבֶּר־נָא אֶל־עֲבָדֶיךָ אֲרָמִית כִּי שֹׁמְעִים אֲנָחְנוּ וְאַל־תְּדַבֵּר אֵלֵינוּ יְהוּדִית בְּאָזְנֵי הָעָם אֲשֶׁר עַל־הַחוֹמָה׃

12 But the Rabshakeh replied, "Was it to your master and to you that my master sent me to speak those words? It was precisely to the men who are sitting on the wall – who will have to eat their dung and drink their urine with you."

יב וַיֹּאמֶר רַב־שָׁקֵה הַאֶל אֲדֹנֶיךָ וְאֵלֶיךָ שְׁלָחַנִי אֲדֹנִי לְדַבֵּר אֶת־הַדְּבָרִים הָאֵלֶּה הֲלֹא עַל־הָאֲנָשִׁים הַיֹּשְׁבִים עַל־הַחוֹמָה לֶאֱכֹל אֶת־חרייהם [צוֹאָתָם] וְלִשְׁתּוֹת אֶת־שיניהם [מֵימֵי] רגליהם [רַגְלֵיהֶם] עִמָּכֶם׃

13 And the Rabshakeh stood and called out in a loud voice in Judean:

יג וַיַּעֲמֹד רַב־שָׁקֵה וַיִּקְרָא בְקוֹל־גָּדוֹל יְהוּדִית וַיֹּאמֶר שִׁמְעוּ אֶת־דִּבְרֵי הַמֶּלֶךְ הַגָּדוֹל מֶלֶךְ אַשּׁוּר׃

14 "Hear the words of the Great King, the king of Assyria! Thus said the king: Don't let *Chizkiyahu* deceive you, for he will not be able to save you.

יד כֹּה אָמַר הַמֶּלֶךְ אַל־יַשִּׁא לָכֶם חִזְקִיָּהוּ כִּי לֹא־יוּכַל לְהַצִּיל אֶתְכֶם׃

A four-horned altar at Tel *Be'er Sheva*

36:7 Whose shrines and altars *Chizkiyahu* did away with Chapters 36–39 describe the most important event of *Yeshayahu*'s career – the Assyrian invasion of *Yehuda* and siege on *Yerushalayim* in 701 BCE. Chapter 36 describes how the Assyrian envoy Rabshakeh taunts the trust that *Chizki-* *yahu* and the people place in *Hashem*. He points to the seeming contradiction between their trust in God and *Chizkiyahu*'s recent religious reforms, in which the king had removed the shrines and broken down the altars outside the *Beit Hamikdash*, at which the people had improperly worshipped *Hashem* for centuries. What he did not understand, though, is that God does not require a multitude of sacrifices to please Him. Instead, He desires a just and righteous society centered around the Temple.

Isaiah

¹⁵ Don't let *Chizkiyahu* make you rely on *Hashem*, saying, '*Hashem* will surely save us; this city will not fall into the hands of Assyria!'

טו וְאַל־יַבְטַח אֶתְכֶם חִזְקִיָּהוּ אֶל־יְהוָה לֵאמֹר הַצֵּל יַצִּילֵנוּ יְהוָה לֹא תִנָּתֵן הָעִיר הַזֹּאת בְּיַד מֶלֶךְ אַשּׁוּר:

¹⁶ Don't listen to *Chizkiyahu*. For thus said the king of Assyria: Make your peace with me and come out to me, so that you may all eat from your vines and your fig trees and drink water from your cisterns,

טז אַל־תִּשְׁמְעוּ אֶל־חִזְקִיָּהוּ כִּי כֹה אָמַר הַמֶּלֶךְ אַשּׁוּר עֲשׂוּ־אִתִּי בְרָכָה וּצְאוּ אֵלַי וְאִכְלוּ אִישׁ־גַּפְנוֹ וְאִישׁ תְּאֵנָתוֹ וּשְׁתוּ אִישׁ מֵי־בוֹרוֹ:

¹⁷ until I come and take you away to a land like your own, a land of bread and wine, of grain [fields] and vineyards.

יז עַד־בֹּאִי וְלָקַחְתִּי אֶתְכֶם אֶל־אֶרֶץ כְּאַרְצְכֶם אֶרֶץ דָּגָן וְתִירוֹשׁ אֶרֶץ לֶחֶם וּכְרָמִים:

¹⁸ Beware of letting *Chizkiyahu* mislead you by saying, '*Hashem* will save us.' Did any of the gods of the other nations save his land from the king of Assyria?

יח פֶּן־יַסִּית אֶתְכֶם חִזְקִיָּהוּ לֵאמֹר יְהוָה יַצִּילֵנוּ הַהִצִּילוּ אֱלֹהֵי הַגּוֹיִם אִישׁ אֶת־אַרְצוֹ מִיַּד מֶלֶךְ אַשּׁוּר:

¹⁹ Where were the gods of Hamath and Arpad? Where were the gods of Sepharvaim? And did they save *Shomron* from me?

יט אַיֵּה אֱלֹהֵי חֲמָת וְאַרְפָּד אַיֵּה אֱלֹהֵי סְפַרְוָיִם וְכִי־הִצִּילוּ אֶת־שֹׁמְרוֹן מִיָּדִי:

²⁰ Which among all the gods of those countries saved their countries from me, that *Hashem* should save *Yerushalayim* from me?"

כ מִי בְּכָל־אֱלֹהֵי הָאֲרָצוֹת הָאֵלֶּה אֲשֶׁר־הִצִּילוּ אֶת־אַרְצָם מִיָּדִי כִּי־יַצִּיל יְהוָה אֶת־יְרוּשָׁלַם מִיָּדִי:

²¹ But they were silent and did not answer him with a single word; for the king's order was: "Do not answer him."

כא וַיַּחֲרִישׁוּ וְלֹא־עָנוּ אֹתוֹ דָּבָר כִּי־מִצְוַת הַמֶּלֶךְ הִיא לֵאמֹר לֹא תַעֲנֻהוּ:

²² And so Eliakim son of *Chilkiyahu* who was in charge of the palace, Shebna the scribe, and Joah son of *Asaf* the recorder came to *Chizkiyahu* with their clothes rent, and they reported to him what the Rabshakeh had said.

כב וַיָּבֹא אֶלְיָקִים בֶּן־חִלְקִיָּהוּ אֲשֶׁר־עַל־הַבַּיִת וְשֶׁבְנָא הַסּוֹפֵר וְיוֹאָח בֶּן־אָסָף הַמַּזְכִּיר אֶל־חִזְקִיָּהוּ קְרוּעֵי בְגָדִים וַיַּגִּידוּ לוֹ אֵת דִּבְרֵי רַב־שָׁקֵה:

37 ¹ When King *Chizkiyahu* heard this, he rent his clothes and covered himself with sackcloth and went into the House of *Hashem*.

לז א וַיְהִי כִּשְׁמֹעַ הַמֶּלֶךְ חִזְקִיָּהוּ וַיִּקְרַע אֶת־בְּגָדָיו וַיִּתְכַּס בַּשָּׂק וַיָּבֹא בֵּית יְהוָה:

² He also sent Eliakim, who was in charge of the palace, Shebna, the scribe, and the senior *Kohanim*, covered with sackcloth, to the *Navi Yeshayahu* son of *Amotz*.

ב וַיִּשְׁלַח אֶת־אֶלְיָקִים אֲשֶׁר־עַל־הַבַּיִת וְאֵת שֶׁבְנָא הַסּוֹפֵר וְאֵת זִקְנֵי הַכֹּהֲנִים מִתְכַּסִּים בַּשַּׂקִּים אֶל־יְשַׁעְיָהוּ בֶן־אָמוֹץ הַנָּבִיא:

³ They said to him, "Thus said *Chizkiyahu*: This day is a day of distress, of chastisement, and of disgrace. The babes have reached the birthstool, but the strength to give birth is lacking.

ג וַיֹּאמְרוּ אֵלָיו כֹּה אָמַר חִזְקִיָּהוּ יוֹם־צָרָה וְתוֹכֵחָה וּנְאָצָה הַיּוֹם הַזֶּה כִּי בָאוּ בָנִים עַד־מַשְׁבֵּר וְכֹחַ אַיִן לְלֵדָה:

4 Perhaps *Hashem* your God will take note of the words of the Rabshakeh, whom his master the king of Assyria has sent to blaspheme the living *Hashem*, and will mete out judgment for the words that *Hashem* your God has heard – if you will offer up prayer for the surviving remnant."

ד אוּלַי יִשְׁמַע יְהֹוָה אֱלֹהֶיךָ אֵת דִּבְרֵי־רַב־שָׁקֵה אֲשֶׁר שְׁלָחוֹ מֶלֶךְ־אַשּׁוּר אֲדֹנָיו לְחָרֵף אֱלֹהִים חַי וְהוֹכִיחַ בַּדְּבָרִים אֲשֶׁר שָׁמַע יְהֹוָה אֱלֹהֶיךָ וְנָשָׂאתָ תְפִלָּה בְּעַד הַשְּׁאֵרִית הַנִּמְצָאָה:

5 When King *Chizkiyahu*'s ministers came to *Yeshayahu*,

ה וַיָּבֹאוּ עַבְדֵי הַמֶּלֶךְ חִזְקִיָּהוּ אֶל־יְשַׁעְיָהוּ:

6 *Yeshayahu* said to them, "Tell your master as follows: Thus said *Hashem*: Do not be frightened by the words of blasphemy against Me that you have heard from the minions of the king of Assyria.

ו וַיֹּאמֶר אֲלֵיהֶם יְשַׁעְיָהוּ כֹּה תֹאמְרוּן אֶל־אֲדֹנֵיכֶם כֹּה אָמַר יְהֹוָה אַל־תִּירָא מִפְּנֵי הַדְּבָרִים אֲשֶׁר שָׁמַעְתָּ אֲשֶׁר גִּדְּפוּ נַעֲרֵי מֶלֶךְ־אַשּׁוּר אוֹתִי:

7 I will delude him: He will hear a rumor and return to his land, and I will make him fall by the sword in his land."

ז הִנְנִי נוֹתֵן בּוֹ רוּחַ וְשָׁמַע שְׁמוּעָה וְשָׁב אֶל־אַרְצוֹ וְהִפַּלְתִּיו בַּחֶרֶב בְּאַרְצוֹ:

8 The Rabshakeh, meanwhile, heard that [the King] had left Lachish; he turned back and found the king of Assyria attacking Libnah.

ח וַיָּשָׁב רַב־שָׁקֵה וַיִּמְצָא אֶת־מֶלֶךְ אַשּׁוּר נִלְחָם עַל־לִבְנָה כִּי שָׁמַע כִּי נָסַע מִלָּכִישׁ:

9 But [the king of Assyria] learned that King Tirhakah of Nubia had come out to fight him; and when he heard it, he sent messengers to *Chizkiyahu*, saying,

ט וַיִּשְׁמַע עַל־תִּרְהָקָה מֶלֶךְ־כּוּשׁ לֵאמֹר יָצָא לְהִלָּחֵם אִתָּךְ וַיִּשְׁמַע וַיִּשְׁלַח מַלְאָכִים אֶל־חִזְקִיָּהוּ לֵאמֹר:

10 "Tell this to King *Chizkiyahu* of *Yehuda*: Do not let your God, on whom you are relying, mislead you into thinking that *Yerushalayim* will not be delivered into the hands of the king of Assyria.

י כֹּה תֹאמְרוּן אֶל־חִזְקִיָּהוּ מֶלֶךְ־יְהוּדָה לֵאמֹר אַל־יַשִּׁאֲךָ אֱלֹהֶיךָ אֲשֶׁר אַתָּה בֹּטֵחַ בּוֹ לֵאמֹר לֹא תִנָּתֵן יְרוּשָׁלַם בְּיַד מֶלֶךְ אַשּׁוּר:

11 You yourself have heard what the kings of Assyria have done to all the lands, how they have annihilated them; and can you escape?

יא הִנֵּה אַתָּה שָׁמַעְתָּ אֲשֶׁר עָשׂוּ מַלְכֵי אַשּׁוּר לְכָל־הָאֲרָצוֹת לְהַחֲרִימָם וְאַתָּה תִּנָּצֵל:

12 Were the nations that my predecessors destroyed – Gozan, Haran, Rezeph, and the Bethedenites in Telassar – saved by their gods?

יב הַהִצִּילוּ אוֹתָם אֱלֹהֵי הַגּוֹיִם אֲשֶׁר הִשְׁחִיתוּ אֲבוֹתַי אֶת־גּוֹזָן וְאֶת־חָרָן וְרֶצֶף וּבְנֵי־עֶדֶן אֲשֶׁר בִּתְלַשָּׂר:

13 Where is the king of Hamath? and the king of Arpad? and the kings of Lair, Sepharvaim, Hena, and Ivvah?"

יג אַיֵּה מֶלֶךְ־חֲמָת וּמֶלֶךְ אַרְפָּד וּמֶלֶךְ לָעִיר סְפַרְוָיִם הֵנַע וְעִוָּה:

14 *Chizkiyahu* received the letter from the messengers and read it. *Chizkiyahu* then went up to the House of *Hashem* and spread it out before *Hashem*.

יד וַיִּקַּח חִזְקִיָּהוּ אֶת־הַסְּפָרִים מִיַּד הַמַּלְאָכִים וַיִּקְרָאֵהוּ וַיַּעַל בֵּית יְהֹוָה וַיִּפְרְשֵׂהוּ חִזְקִיָּהוּ לִפְנֵי יְהֹוָה:

15 And *Chizkiyahu* prayed to *Hashem*:

טו וַיִּתְפַּלֵּל חִזְקִיָּהוּ אֶל־יְהֹוָה לֵאמֹר:

16 "O LORD of Hosts, enthroned on the *Keruvim*! You alone are God of all the kingdoms of the earth. You made the heavens and the earth.

טז יְהֹוָה צְבָאוֹת אֱלֹהֵי יִשְׂרָאֵל יֹשֵׁב הַכְּרֻבִים אַתָּה־הוּא הָאֱלֹהִים לְבַדְּךָ לְכֹל מַמְלְכוֹת הָאָרֶץ אַתָּה עָשִׂיתָ אֶת־הַשָּׁמַיִם וְאֶת־הָאָרֶץ:

Isaiah

¹⁷ *Hashem*, incline Your ear and hear, open Your eye and see. Hear all the words that Sennacherib has sent to blaspheme the living *Hashem*!

יז הַטֵּה יְהֹוָה אׇזְנְךָ וּֽשֲׁמָע פְּקַח יְהֹוָה עֵינֶךָ וּרְאֵה וּשְׁמַע אֵת כׇּל־דִּבְרֵי סַנְחֵרִיב אֲשֶׁר שָׁלַח לְחָרֵף אֱלֹהִים חָֽי׃

¹⁸ True, *Hashem*, the kings of Assyria have annihilated all the nations and their lands

יח אׇמְנָם יְהֹוָה הֶחֱרִיבוּ מַלְכֵי אַשּׁוּר אֶת־ כׇּל־הָאֲרָצוֹת וְאֶת־אַרְצָֽם׃

¹⁹ and have committed their gods to the flames and have destroyed them; for they are not gods, but man's handwork of wood and stone.

יט וְנָתֹן אֶת־אֱלֹהֵיהֶם בָּאֵשׁ כִּי לֹא אֱלֹהִים הֵמָּה כִּי אִם־מַעֲשֵׂה יְדֵי־אָדָם עֵץ וָאֶבֶן וַֽיְאַבְּדֽוּם׃

²⁰ But now, *Hashem* our God, deliver us from his hands, and let all the kingdoms of the earth know that You, *Hashem*, alone [are *Hashem*]."

כ וְעַתָּה יְהֹוָה אֱלֹהֵינוּ הוֹשִׁיעֵנוּ מִיָּדוֹ וְיֵֽדְעוּ כׇּל־מַמְלְכוֹת הָאָרֶץ כִּֽי־אַתָּה יְהֹוָה לְבַדֶּֽךָ׃

v'-a-TAH a-do-NAI e-lo-HAY-nu ho-shee-AY-nu mi-ya-DO v'-yay-d'-U
kol mam-l'-KHOT ha-A-retz kee a-TAH a-do-NAI l'-va-DE-kha

²¹ Then *Yeshayahu* son of *Amotz* sent this message to *Chizkiyahu*: "Thus said *Hashem*, the God of *Yisrael*, to whom you have prayed, concerning King Sennacherib of Assyria

כא וַיִּשְׁלַח יְשַׁעְיָהוּ בֶן־אָמוֹץ אֶל־חִזְקִיָּהוּ לֵאמֹר כֹּֽה־אָמַר יְהֹוָה אֱלֹהֵי יִשְׂרָאֵל אֲשֶׁר הִתְפַּלַּלְתָּ אֵלַי אֶל־סַנְחֵרִיב מֶלֶךְ אַשּֽׁוּר׃

²² this is the word that *Hashem* has spoken concerning him: Fair Maiden *Tzion* despises you, She mocks at you; Fair *Yerushalayim* shakes Her head at you.

כב זֶה הַדָּבָר אֲשֶׁר־דִּבֶּר יְהֹוָה עָלָיו בָּזָה לְךָ לָעֲגָה לְךָ בְּתוּלַת בַּת־צִיּוֹן אַחֲרֶיךָ רֹאשׁ הֵנִיעָה בַּת יְרוּשָׁלָֽ͏ִם׃

²³ Whom have you blasphemed and reviled? Against whom made loud your voice And haughtily raised your eyes? Against the Holy One of *Yisrael*!

כג אֶת־מִי חֵרַפְתָּ וְגִדַּפְתָּ וְעַל־מִי הֲרִימוֹתָה קּוֹל וַתִּשָּׂא מָרוֹם עֵינֶיךָ אֶל־קְדוֹשׁ יִשְׂרָאֵֽל׃

²⁴ Through your servants you have blasphemed my Lord. Because you thought, 'Thanks to my vast chariotry, It is I who have climbed the highest mountains, To the remotest parts of the Lebanon, And have cut down its loftiest cedars, Its choicest cypresses, And have reached its highest peak, Its densest forest.

כד בְּיַד עֲבָדֶיךָ חֵרַפְתָּ אֲדֹנָי וַתֹּאמֶר בְּרֹב רִכְבִּי אֲנִי עָלִיתִי מְרוֹם הָרִים יַרְכְּתֵי לְבָנוֹן וְאֶכְרֹת קוֹמַת אֲרָזָיו מִבְחַר בְּרֹשָׁיו וְאָבוֹא מְרוֹם קִצּוֹ יַעַר כַּרְמִלּֽוֹ׃

37:20 Let all the kingdoms of the earth know that You, *Hashem*, alone [are *Hashem*] In his prayer at *Yerushalayim*'s most dire hour, *Chizkiyahu* re- veals himself to be a true *eved Hashem* (עבד השם), 'servant of God.' He prays not for the sake of his own honor, nor even for his country or his people, whose fate is bound up with his own, but for *Hashem*'s glory in front of the world at large. This is similar to *Moshe*'s song, sung after the Jews crossed the Sea of Reeds, joyfully declaring, "The peoples hear, they tremble; agony grips the dwellers in Philistia.

Now are the clans of Edom dismayed; the tribes of Moab – trembling grips them… *Hashem* will reign for ever and ever!" (Exodus 15:14–15, 18). *David* expressed this best – "May they know that Your name, Yours alone, is *Hashem*, supreme over all the earth" (Psalm 83:19). A true servant of God and leader of Israel recognizes that his ultimate purpose in this world is to spread knowledge of *Hashem* and His glory throughout the world.

Israeli flag at the beach in *Tel Aviv*

25 It is I who have drawn And drunk water. I have dried up with the soles of my feet All the streams of Egypt.'

כה אֲנִי קַרְתִּי וְשָׁתִיתִי מָיִם וְאַחְרִב בְּכַף־פְּעָמַי כֹּל יְאֹרֵי מָצוֹר:

26 Have you not heard? Of old I planned that very thing, I designed it long ago, And now have fulfilled it. And it has come to pass, Laying fortified towns waste in desolate heaps.

כו הֲלוֹא־שָׁמַעְתָּ לְמֵרָחוֹק אוֹתָהּ עָשִׂיתִי מִימֵי קֶדֶם וִיצַרְתִּיהָ עַתָּה הֲבֵאתִיהָ וּתְהִי לְהַשְׁאוֹת גַּלִּים נִצִּים עָרִים בְּצֻרוֹת:

27 Their inhabitants are helpless, Dismayed and shamed. They were but grass of the field And green herbage, Grass of the roofs that is blasted Before the east wind.

כז וְיֹשְׁבֵיהֶן קִצְרֵי־יָד חַתּוּ וָבֹשׁוּ הָיוּ עֵשֶׂב שָׂדֶה וִירַק דֶּשֶׁא חֲצִיר גַּגּוֹת וּשְׁדֵמָה לִפְנֵי קָמָה:

28 I know your stayings And your goings and comings, And how you have raged against Me,

כח וְשִׁבְתְּךָ וְצֵאתְךָ וּבוֹאֲךָ יָדָעְתִּי וְאֵת הִתְרַגֶּזְךָ אֵלָי:

29 Because you have raged against Me, And your tumult has reached My ears, I will place My hook in your nose And My bit between your jaws; And I will make you go back by the road By which you came.

כט יַעַן הִתְרַגֶּזְךָ אֵלַי וְשַׁאֲנַנְךָ עָלָה בְאָזְנָי וְשַׂמְתִּי חַחִי בְּאַפֶּךָ וּמִתְגִּי בִּשְׂפָתֶיךָ וַהֲשִׁיבֹתִיךָ בַּדֶּרֶךְ אֲשֶׁר־בָּאתָ בָּהּ:

30 "And this is the sign for you: This year you eat what grows of itself, and the next year what springs from that, and in the third year sow and reap and plant vineyards and eat their fruit.

ל וְזֶה־לְּךָ הָאוֹת אָכוֹל הַשָּׁנָה סָפִיחַ וּבַשָּׁנָה הַשֵּׁנִית שָׁחִיס וּבַשָּׁנָה הַשְּׁלִישִׁית זִרְעוּ וְקִצְרוּ וְנִטְעוּ כְרָמִים וְאִכוּל [וְאִכְלוּ] פִרְיָם:

31 And the survivors of the House of *Yehuda* that have escaped shall renew its trunk below and produce boughs above.

לא וְיָסְפָה פְּלֵיטַת בֵּית־יְהוּדָה הַנִּשְׁאָרָה שֹׁרֶשׁ לְמָטָּה וְעָשָׂה פְרִי לְמָעְלָה:

32 For a remnant shall come forth from *Yerushalayim*, Survivors from Mount *Tzion*. The zeal of the Lord of Hosts Shall bring this to pass.

לב כִּי מִירוּשָׁלִַם תֵּצֵא שְׁאֵרִית וּפְלֵיטָה מֵהַר צִיּוֹן קִנְאַת יְהוָה צְבָאוֹת תַּעֲשֶׂה־זֹּאת:

33 "Assuredly, thus said *Hashem* concerning the king of Assyria: He shall not enter this city; He shall not shoot an arrow at it, Or advance upon it with a shield, Or pile up a siegemound against it.

לג לָכֵן כֹּה־אָמַר יְהוָה אֶל־מֶלֶךְ אַשּׁוּר לֹא יָבוֹא אֶל־הָעִיר הַזֹּאת וְלֹא־יוֹרֶה שָׁם חֵץ וְלֹא־יְקַדְּמֶנָּה מָגֵן וְלֹא־יִשְׁפֹּךְ עָלֶיהָ סֹלְלָה:

34 He shall go back By the way he came, He shall not enter this city – declares *Hashem*;

לד בַּדֶּרֶךְ אֲשֶׁר־בָּא בָּהּ יָשׁוּב וְאֶל־הָעִיר הַזֹּאת לֹא יָבוֹא נְאֻם־יְהוָה:

35 I will protect and save this city for My sake And for the sake of My servant *David*."

לה וְגַנּוֹתִי עַל־הָעִיר הַזֹּאת לְהוֹשִׁיעָהּ לְמַעֲנִי וּלְמַעַן דָּוִד עַבְדִּי:

36 [That night] an angel of *Hashem* went out and struck down one hundred and eighty-five thousand in the Assyrian camp, and the following morning they were all dead corpses.

לו וַיֵּצֵא מַלְאַךְ יְהוָה וַיַּכֶּה בְּמַחֲנֵה אַשּׁוּר מֵאָה וּשְׁמֹנִים וַחֲמִשָּׁה אָלֶף וַיַּשְׁכִּימוּ בַבֹּקֶר וְהִנֵּה כֻלָּם פְּגָרִים מֵתִים:

37 So King Sennacherib of Assyria broke camp and retreated, and stayed in Nineveh.

לז וַיִּסַּע וַיֵּלֶךְ וַיָּשָׁב סַנְחֵרִיב מֶלֶךְ־אַשּׁוּר וַיֵּשֶׁב בְּנִינְוֵה:

³⁸ While he was worshiping in the temple of his god Nisroch, he was struck down with the sword by his sons Adrammelech and Sarezer. They fled to the land of Ararat, and his son Esarhaddon succeeded him as king.

לח וַיְהִי הוּא מִשְׁתַּחֲוֶה בֵּית נִסְרֹךְ אֱלֹהָיו וְאַדְרַמֶּלֶךְ וְשַׂרְאֶצֶר בָּנָיו הִכֻּהוּ בַחֶרֶב וְהֵמָּה נִמְלְטוּ אֶרֶץ אֲרָרָט וַיִּמְלֹךְ אֵסַר־חַדֹּן בְּנוֹ תַּחְתָּיו:

לח א

38 ¹ In those days *Chizkiyahu* fell dangerously ill. The *Navi Yeshayahu* son of *Amotz* came and said to him, "Thus said *Hashem*: Set your affairs in order, for you are going to die; you will not get well."

בַּיָּמִים הָהֵם חָלָה חִזְקִיָּהוּ לָמוּת וַיָּבוֹא אֵלָיו יְשַׁעְיָהוּ בֶן־אָמוֹץ הַנָּבִיא וַיֹּאמֶר אֵלָיו כֹּה־אָמַר יְהֹוָה צַו לְבֵיתֶךָ כִּי מֵת אַתָּה וְלֹא תִחְיֶה:

ba-ya-MEEM ha-HAYM kha-LAH khiz-ki-YA-hu la-MUT va-ya-VO ay-LAV y'-sha-ya-HU ven a-MOTZ ha-na-VEE va-YO-mer ay-LAV koh a-MAR a-do-NAI TZAV l'-vay-TE-kha KEE MAYT a-TAH v'-LO tikh-YEH

² Thereupon *Chizkiyahu* turned his face to the wall and prayed to *Hashem*.

ב וַיַּסֵּב חִזְקִיָּהוּ פָּנָיו אֶל־הַקִּיר וַיִּתְפַּלֵּל אֶל־יְהֹוָה:

³ "Please, *Hashem*," he said, "remember how I have walked before You sincerely and wholeheartedly, and have done what is pleasing to You." And *Chizkiyahu* wept profusely.

ג וַיֹּאמַר אָנָּה יְהֹוָה זְכָר־נָא אֵת אֲשֶׁר הִתְהַלַּכְתִּי לְפָנֶיךָ בֶּאֱמֶת וּבְלֵב שָׁלֵם וְהַטּוֹב בְּעֵינֶיךָ עָשִׂיתִי וַיֵּבְךְּ חִזְקִיָּהוּ בְּכִי גָדוֹל:

⁴ Then the word of *Hashem* came to *Yeshayahu*:

ד וַיְהִי דְּבַר־יְהֹוָה אֶל־יְשַׁעְיָהוּ לֵאמֹר:

⁵ "Go and tell *Chizkiyahu*: Thus said *Hashem*, the God of your father *David*: I have heard your prayer, I have seen your tears. I hereby add fifteen years to your life.

ה הָלוֹךְ וְאָמַרְתָּ אֶל־חִזְקִיָּהוּ כֹּה־אָמַר יְהֹוָה אֱלֹהֵי דָּוִד אָבִיךָ שָׁמַעְתִּי אֶת־תְּפִלָּתֶךָ רָאִיתִי אֶת־דִּמְעָתֶךָ הִנְנִי יוֹסִף עַל־יָמֶיךָ חֲמֵשׁ עֶשְׂרֵה שָׁנָה:

⁶ I will also rescue you and this city from the hands of the king of Assyria. I will protect this city.

ו וּמִכַּף מֶלֶךְ־אַשּׁוּר אַצִּילְךָ וְאֵת הָעִיר הַזֹּאת וְגַנּוֹתִי עַל־הָעִיר הַזֹּאת:

⁷ And this is the sign for you from *Hashem* that *Hashem* will do the thing that He has promised:

ז וְזֶה־לְּךָ הָאוֹת מֵאֵת יְהֹוָה אֲשֶׁר יַעֲשֶׂה יְהֹוָה אֶת־הַדָּבָר הַזֶּה אֲשֶׁר דִּבֵּר:

⁸ I am going to make the shadow on the steps, which has descended on the dial of *Achaz* because of the sun, recede ten steps." And the sun['s shadow] receded ten steps, the same steps as it had descended.

ח הִנְנִי מֵשִׁיב אֶת־צֵל הַמַּעֲלוֹת אֲשֶׁר יָרְדָה בְמַעֲלוֹת אָחָז בַּשֶּׁמֶשׁ אֲחֹרַנִּית עֶשֶׂר מַעֲלוֹת וַתָּשָׁב הַשֶּׁמֶשׁ עֶשֶׂר מַעֲלוֹת בַּמַּעֲלוֹת אֲשֶׁר יָרָדָה:

38:1 For you are going to die; you will not get well The Talmud (*Berachot* 10a) relates an ancient tradition regarding this exchange between *Yeshayahu* the prophet and King *Chizkiyahu*. When *Chizkiyahu* became sick, *Yeshayahu* came and said "You shall die and not live," meaning you shall die in this world and not live in the world to come either, because you did not try to have children. *Chizkiyahu* responded that he acted this way because he saw through prophecy that his children would be evil (referring to his son and successor,

Menashe). *Yeshayahu* said: "Why did you meddle with God's secrets? You should have done as you were commanded!" *Chizkiyahu* repented, and was granted additional years of life. The Talmud concludes with an important lesson: Even if a sharp sword rests upon a man's neck, he should not desist from prayer. It is never too late to return to *Hashem* and call out to Him in sincere prayer.

Woman deep in prayer at the Western Wall

9 A poem by King *Chizkiyahu* of *Yehuda* when he recovered from the illness he had suffered:

מִכְתָּב לְחִזְקִיָּהוּ מֶלֶךְ־יְהוּדָה בַּחֲלֹתוֹ וַיְחִי מֵחָלְיוֹ: ט

10 I had thought: I must depart in the middle of my days; I have been consigned to the gates of Sheol For the rest of my years.

אֲנִי אָמַרְתִּי בִּדְמִי יָמַי אֵלֵכָה בְּשַׁעֲרֵי שְׁאוֹל פֻּקַּדְתִּי יֶתֶר שְׁנוֹתָי: י

11 I thought, I shall never see Yah, Yah in the land of the living, Or ever behold men again Among those who inhabit the earth.

אָמַרְתִּי לֹא־אֶרְאֶה יָהּ יָהּ בְּאֶרֶץ הַחַיִּים לֹא־אַבִּיט אָדָם עוֹד עִם־יוֹשְׁבֵי חָדֶל: יא

12 My dwelling is pulled up and removed from me Like a tent of shepherds; My life is rolled up like a web And cut from the thrum. Only from daybreak to nightfall Was I kept whole,

דּוֹרִי נִסַּע וְנִגְלָה מִנִּי כְּאֹהֶל רֹעִי קִפַּדְתִּי כָאֹרֵג חַיַּי מִדַּלָּה יְבַצְּעֵנִי מִיּוֹם עַד־לַיְלָה תַּשְׁלִימֵנִי: יב

13 Then it was as though a lion Were breaking all my bones; I cried out until morning. (Only from daybreak to nightfall Was I kept whole.)

שִׁוִּיתִי עַד־בֹּקֶר כָּאֲרִי כֵּן יְשַׁבֵּר כָּל־עַצְמוֹתָי מִיּוֹם עַד־לַיְלָה תַּשְׁלִימֵנִי: יג

14 I piped like a swift or a swallow, I moaned like a dove, As my eyes, all worn, looked to heaven: "My Lord, I am in straits; Be my surety!"

כְּסוּס עָגוּר כֵּן אֲצַפְצֵף אֶהְגֶּה כַּיּוֹנָה דַּלּוּ עֵינַי לַמָּרוֹם אֲדֹנָי עָשְׁקָה־לִּי עָרְבֵנִי: יד

15 What can I say? He promised me, And He it is who has wrought it. All my sleep had fled Because of the bitterness of my soul.

מָה־אֲדַבֵּר וְאָמַר־לִי וְהוּא עָשָׂה אֶדַּדֶּה כָל־שְׁנוֹתַי עַל־מַר נַפְשִׁי: טו

16 My Lord, for all that and despite it My life-breath is revived; You have restored me to health and revived me.

אֲדֹנָי עֲלֵיהֶם יִחְיוּ וּלְכָל־בָּהֵן חַיֵּי רוּחִי וְתַחֲלִימֵנִי וְהַחֲיֵנִי: טז

17 Truly, it was for my own good That I had such great bitterness: You saved my life From the pit of destruction, For You have cast behind Your back All my offenses.

הִנֵּה לְשָׁלוֹם מַר־לִי מָר וְאַתָּה חָשַׁקְתָּ נַפְשִׁי מִשַּׁחַת בְּלִי כִּי הִשְׁלַכְתָּ אַחֲרֵי גֵוְךָ כָּל־חֲטָאָי: יז

18 For it is not Sheol that praises You, Not [the Land of] Death that extols You; Nor do they who descend into the Pit Hope for Your grace.

כִּי לֹא שְׁאוֹל תּוֹדֶךָּ מָוֶת יְהַלְלֶךָּ לֹא־יְשַׂבְּרוּ יוֹרְדֵי־בוֹר אֶל־אֲמִתֶּךָ: יח

19 The living, only the living Can give thanks to You As I do this day; Fathers relate to children Your acts of grace:

חַי חַי הוּא יוֹדֶךָ כָּמוֹנִי הַיּוֹם אָב לְבָנִים יוֹדִיעַ אֶל־אֲמִתֶּךָ: יט

20 "[It has pleased] *Hashem* to deliver us, That is why we offer up music All the days of our lives At the House of *Hashem*."

יְהֹוָה לְהוֹשִׁיעֵנִי וּנְגִנוֹתַי נְנַגֵּן כָּל־יְמֵי חַיֵּינוּ עַל־בֵּית יְהֹוָה: כ

21 When *Yeshayahu* said, "Let them take a cake of figs and apply it to the rash, and he will recover,"

וַיֹּאמֶר יְשַׁעְיָהוּ יִשְׂאוּ דְּבֶלֶת תְּאֵנִים וְיִמְרְחוּ עַל־הַשְּׁחִין וְיֶחִי: כא

22 *Chizkiyahu* asked, "What will be the sign that I shall go up to the House of *Hashem*?"

וַיֹּאמֶר חִזְקִיָּהוּ מָה אוֹת כִּי אֶעֱלֶה בֵּית יְהֹוָה: כב

39 ¹ At that time, Merodach-baladan son of Baladan, the king of Babylon, sent [envoys with] a letter and a gift to *Chizkiyahu*, for he had heard about his illness and recovery.

² *Chizkiyahu* was pleased by their coming, and he showed them his treasure house – the silver, the gold, the spices, and the fragrant oil – and all his armory, and everything that was to be found in his storehouses. There was nothing in his palace or in all his realm that *Chizkiyahu* did not show them.

³ Then the *Navi Yeshayahu* came to King *Chizkiyahu*. "What," he demanded of him, "did those men say to you? Where have they come to you from?" "They have come to me," replied *Chizkiyahu*, "from a far country, from Babylon."

⁴ Next he asked, "What have they seen in your palace?" And *Chizkiyahu* replied, "They have seen everything there is in my palace. There was nothing in my storehouses that I did not show them."

⁵ Then *Yeshayahu* said to *Chizkiyahu*, "Hear the word of the LORD of Hosts:

⁶ A time is coming when everything in your palace, which your ancestors have stored up to this day, will be carried off to Babylon; nothing will be left behind, said *Hashem*.

⁷ And some of your sons, your own issue, whom you will have fathered, will be taken to serve as eunuchs in the palace of the king of Babylon."

⁸ *Chizkiyahu* declared to *Yeshayahu*, "The word of *Hashem* that you have spoken is good." For he thought, "It means that safety is assured for my time."

לט א בְּעֵת הַהִוא שָׁלַח מְרֹדַךְ בַּלְאֲדָן בֶּן־בַּלְאֲדָן מֶלֶךְ־בָּבֶל סְפָרִים וּמִנְחָה אֶל־חִזְקִיָּהוּ וַיִּשְׁמַע כִּי חָלָה וַיֶּחֱזָק:

ב וַיִּשְׂמַח עֲלֵיהֶם חִזְקִיָּהוּ וַיַּרְאֵם אֶת־בֵּית נְכֹתֹה [נְכֹתוֹ] אֶת־הַכֶּסֶף וְאֶת־הַזָּהָב וְאֶת־הַבְּשָׂמִים וְאֵת הַשֶּׁמֶן הַטּוֹב וְאֵת כָּל־בֵּית כֵּלָיו וְאֵת כָּל־אֲשֶׁר נִמְצָא בְּאֹצְרֹתָיו לֹא־הָיָה דָבָר אֲשֶׁר לֹא־הֶרְאָם חִזְקִיָּהוּ בְּבֵיתוֹ וּבְכָל־מֶמְשַׁלְתּוֹ:

ג וַיָּבֹא יְשַׁעְיָהוּ הַנָּבִיא אֶל־הַמֶּלֶךְ חִזְקִיָּהוּ וַיֹּאמֶר אֵלָיו מָה אָמְרוּ הָאֲנָשִׁים הָאֵלֶּה וּמֵאַיִן יָבֹאוּ אֵלֶיךָ וַיֹּאמֶר חִזְקִיָּהוּ מֵאֶרֶץ רְחוֹקָה בָּאוּ אֵלַי מִבָּבֶל:

ד וַיֹּאמֶר מָה רָאוּ בְּבֵיתֶךָ וַיֹּאמֶר חִזְקִיָּהוּ אֵת כָּל־אֲשֶׁר בְּבֵיתִי רָאוּ לֹא־הָיָה דָבָר אֲשֶׁר לֹא־הִרְאִיתִים בְּאוֹצְרֹתָי:

ה וַיֹּאמֶר יְשַׁעְיָהוּ אֶל־חִזְקִיָּהוּ שְׁמַע דְּבַר־יְהֹוָה צְבָאוֹת:

ו הִנֵּה יָמִים בָּאִים וְנִשָּׂא כָּל־אֲשֶׁר בְּבֵיתֶךָ וַאֲשֶׁר אָצְרוּ אֲבֹתֶיךָ עַד־הַיּוֹם הַזֶּה בָּבֶל לֹא־יִוָּתֵר דָּבָר אָמַר יְהֹוָה:

ז וּמִבָּנֶיךָ אֲשֶׁר יֵצְאוּ מִמְּךָ אֲשֶׁר תּוֹלִיד יִקָּחוּ וְהָיוּ סָרִיסִים בְּהֵיכַל מֶלֶךְ בָּבֶל:

ח וַיֹּאמֶר חִזְקִיָּהוּ אֶל־יְשַׁעְיָהוּ טוֹב דְּבַר־יְהֹוָה אֲשֶׁר דִּבַּרְתָּ וַיֹּאמֶר כִּי יִהְיֶה שָׁלוֹם וֶאֱמֶת בְּיָמָי:

va-YO-mer khiz-ki-YA-hu el y'-sha-YA-hu TOV d'-var a-do-NAI a-SHER di-BAR-ta va-YO-mer KEE yih-YEH sha-LOM ve-e-MET b'-ya-MAI

39:8 The word of *Hashem* that you have spoken is good. King *Chizkiyahu's* response to *Yeshayahu's* prophecy, that future calamities that would befall his people do not matter as long as "safety is assured for my time," appears callous and out of character for the righteous king. However, it actually reflects *Chizkiyahu's* ability to see the good within the message delivered to him by *Yeshayahu*. It assured him of offspring, sons to sit upon his throne, and respite for his people. Most importantly, he understood that the period of peace would give the Children of Israel another chance to repent and erase the decree against them entirely. One should never underestimate the opportunity to make meaningful changes when given a second chance.

Father and sons praying at the Western Wall

40 ¹ Comfort, oh comfort My people, Says your God.

מ א נַחֲמוּ נַחֲמוּ עַמִּי יֹאמַר אֱלֹהֵיכֶם:

na-kha-MU na-kha-MU a-MEE yo-MAR e-lo-hay-KHEM

² Speak tenderly to *Yerushalayim*, And declare to her That her term of service is over, That her iniquity is expiated; For she has received at the hand of *Hashem* Double for all her sins.

ב דַּבְּרוּ עַל־לֵב יְרוּשָׁלַ͏ִם וְקִרְאוּ אֵלֶיהָ כִּי מָלְאָה צְבָאָהּ כִּי נִרְצָה עֲוֺנָהּ כִּי לָקְחָה מִיַּד יְהֹוָה כִּפְלַיִם בְּכָל־חַטֹּאתֶיהָ:

³ A voice rings out: "Clear in the desert A road for *Hashem*! Level in the wilderness A highway for our God!

ג קוֹל קוֹרֵא בַּמִּדְבָּר פַּנּוּ דֶּרֶךְ יְהֹוָה יַשְּׁרוּ בָּעֲרָבָה מְסִלָּה לֵאלֹהֵינוּ:

⁴ Let every valley be raised, Every hill and mount made low. Let the rugged ground become level And the ridges become a plain.

ד כָּל־גֶּיא יִנָּשֵׂא וְכָל־הַר וְגִבְעָה יִשְׁפָּלוּ וְהָיָה הֶעָקֹב לְמִישׁוֹר וְהָרְכָסִים לְבִקְעָה:

⁵ The Presence of *Hashem* shall appear And all flesh, as one, shall behold – For *Hashem* Himself has spoken."

ה וְנִגְלָה כְּבוֹד יְהֹוָה וְרָאוּ כָל־בָּשָׂר יַחְדָּו כִּי פִּי יְהֹוָה דִּבֵּר:

⁶ A voice rings out: "Proclaim!" Another asks, "What shall I proclaim?" "All flesh is grass, All its goodness like flowers of the field:

ו קוֹל אֹמֵר קְרָא וְאָמַר מָה אֶקְרָא כָּל־הַבָּשָׂר חָצִיר וְכָל־חַסְדּוֹ כְּצִיץ הַשָּׂדֶה:

⁷ Grass withers, flowers fade When the breath of *Hashem* blows on them. Indeed, man is but grass:

ז יָבֵשׁ חָצִיר נָבֵל צִיץ כִּי רוּחַ יְהֹוָה נָשְׁבָה בּוֹ אָכֵן חָצִיר הָעָם:

⁸ Grass withers, flowers fade – But the word of our God is always fulfilled!"

ח יָבֵשׁ חָצִיר נָבֵל צִיץ וּדְבַר־אֱלֹהֵינוּ יָקוּם לְעוֹלָם:

⁹ Ascend a lofty mountain, O herald of joy to *Tzion*; Raise your voice with power, O herald of joy to *Yerushalayim* – Raise it, have no fear; Announce to the cities of *Yehuda*: Behold your God!

ט עַל הַר־גָּבֹהַּ עֲלִי־לָךְ מְבַשֶּׂרֶת צִיּוֹן הָרִימִי בַכֹּחַ קוֹלֵךְ מְבַשֶּׂרֶת יְרוּשָׁלָ͏ִם הָרִימִי אַל־תִּירָאִי אִמְרִי לְעָרֵי יְהוּדָה הִנֵּה אֱלֹהֵיכֶם:

¹⁰ Behold, *Hashem* comes in might, And His arm wins triumph for Him; See, His reward is with Him, His recompense before Him.

י הִנֵּה אֲדֹנָי יְהֹוִה בְּחָזָק יָבוֹא וּזְרֹעוֹ מֹשְׁלָה לוֹ הִנֵּה שְׂכָרוֹ אִתּוֹ וּפְעֻלָּתוֹ לְפָנָיו:

¹¹ Like a shepherd He pastures His flock: He gathers the lambs in His arms And carries them in His bosom; Gently He drives the mother sheep.

יא כְּרֹעֶה עֶדְרוֹ יִרְעֶה בִּזְרֹעוֹ יְקַבֵּץ טְלָאִים וּבְחֵיקוֹ יִשָּׂא עָלוֹת יְנַהֵל:

 **40:1 Comfort, oh comfort My people** The *Torah* is always very careful to use words sparingly and not to repeat even a single word unnecessarily. If so, why is the word "comfort" repeated twice in this verse? The prophecy considers the future destructions of both the first and the second *Beit Hamikdash*. The loss of both Temples would constitute a double calamity for the Jewish people, and *Hashem* consequently promises that His consolation will also be double. This chapter is read annually on the *Shabbat* following the ninth day of the Hebrew month of *Av*, the national day of mourning for the destruction of the Temples. Each year, these words bring renewed hope that we will witness the double consolation promised in these verses, speedily in our days. May His comforting blessings be showered upon us all.

The southern wall of the Temple Mount from Second Temple times and the remains of Robinson's Arch

12 Who measured the waters with the hollow of His hand, And gauged the skies with a *zeret*, And meted earth's dust with a measure, And weighed the mountains with a scale And the hills with a balance?

יג מִי־מָדַד בְּשָׁעֳלוֹ מַיִם וְשָׁמַיִם בַּזֶּרֶת תִּכֵּן וְכָל בַּשָּׁלִשׁ עֲפַר הָאָרֶץ וְשָׁקַל בַּפֶּלֶס הָרִים וּגְבָעוֹת בְּמֹאזְנָיִם:

13 Who has plumbed the mind of *Hashem*, What man could tell Him His plan?

יג מִי־תִכֵּן אֶת־רוּחַ יְהֹוָה וְאִישׁ עֲצָתוֹ יוֹדִיעֶנּוּ:

14 Whom did He consult, and who taught Him, Guided Him in the way of right? Who guided Him in knowledge And showed Him the path of wisdom?

יד אֶת־מִי נוֹעָץ וַיְבִינֵהוּ וַיְלַמְּדֵהוּ בְּאֹרַח מִשְׁפָּט וַיְלַמְּדֵהוּ דַעַת וְדֶרֶךְ תְּבוּנוֹת יוֹדִיעֶנּוּ:

15 The nations are but a drop in a bucket, Reckoned as dust on a balance; The very coastlands He lifts like motes.

טו הֵן גּוֹיִם כְּמַר מִדְּלִי וּכְשַׁחַק מֹאזְנַיִם נֶחְשָׁבוּ הֵן אִיִּים כַּדַּק יִטּוֹל:

16 Lebanon is not fuel enough, Nor its beasts enough for sacrifice.

טז וּלְבָנוֹן אֵין דֵּי בָּעֵר וְחַיָּתוֹ אֵין דֵּי עוֹלָה:

17 All nations are as naught in His sight; He accounts them as less than nothing.

יז כָּל־הַגּוֹיִם כְּאַיִן נֶגְדּוֹ מֵאֶפֶס וָתֹהוּ נֶחְשְׁבוּ־לוֹ:

18 To whom, then, can you liken *Hashem*, What form compare to Him?

יח וְאֶל־מִי תְּדַמְּיוּן אֵל וּמַה־דְּמוּת תַּעַרְכוּ לוֹ:

19 The idol? A woodworker shaped it, And a smith overlaid it with gold, Forging links of silver.

יט הַפֶּסֶל נָסַךְ חָרָשׁ וְצֹרֵף בַּזָּהָב יְרַקְּעֶנּוּ וּרְתֻקוֹת כֶּסֶף צוֹרֵף:

20 As a gift, he chooses the mulberry – A wood that does not rot – Then seeks a skillful woodworker To make a firm idol, That will not topple.

כ הַמְסֻכָּן תְּרוּמָה עֵץ לֹא־יִרְקַב יִבְחָר חָרָשׁ חָכָם יְבַקֶּשׁ־לוֹ לְהָכִין פֶּסֶל לֹא יִמּוֹט:

21 Do you not know? Have you not heard? Have you not been told From the very first? Have you not discerned How the earth was founded?

כא הֲלוֹא תֵדְעוּ הֲלוֹא תִשְׁמָעוּ הֲלוֹא הֻגַּד מֵרֹאשׁ לָכֶם הֲלוֹא הֲבִינֹתֶם מוֹסְדוֹת הָאָרֶץ:

22 It is He who is enthroned above the vault of the earth, So that its inhabitants seem as grasshoppers; Who spread out the skies like gauze, Stretched them out like a tent to dwell in.

כב הַיֹּשֵׁב עַל־חוּג הָאָרֶץ וְיֹשְׁבֶיהָ כַּחֲגָבִים הַנּוֹטֶה כַדֹּק שָׁמַיִם וַיִּמְתָּחֵם כָּאֹהֶל לָשָׁבֶת:

23 He brings potentates to naught, Makes rulers of the earth as nothing.

כג הַנּוֹתֵן רוֹזְנִים לְאָיִן שֹׁפְטֵי אֶרֶץ כַּתֹּהוּ עָשָׂה:

24 Hardly are they planted, Hardly are they sown, Hardly has their stem Taken root in earth, When He blows upon them and they dry up, And the storm bears them off like straw.

כד אַף בַּל־נִטָּעוּ אַף בַּל־זֹרָעוּ אַף בַּל־שֹׁרֵשׁ בָּאָרֶץ גִּזְעָם וְגַם־נָשַׁף בָּהֶם וַיִּבָשׁוּ וּסְעָרָה כַּקַּשׁ תִּשָּׂאֵם:

25 To whom, then, can you liken Me, To whom can I be compared? – says the Holy One.

כה וְאֶל־מִי תְדַמְּיוּנִי וְאֶשְׁוֶה יֹאמַר קָדוֹשׁ:

26 Lift high your eyes and see: Who created these? He who sends out their host by count, Who calls them each by name: Because of His great might and vast power, Not one fails to appear.

כו שְׂאוּ־מָרוֹם עֵינֵיכֶם וּרְאוּ מִי־בָרָא אֵלֶּה הַמּוֹצִיא בְמִסְפָּר צְבָאָם לְכֻלָּם בְּשֵׁם יִקְרָא מֵרֹב אוֹנִים וְאַמִּיץ כֹּחַ אִישׁ לֹא נֶעְדָּר:

27 Why do you say, O *Yaakov*, Why declare, O *Yisrael*, "My way is hid from *Hashem*, My cause is ignored by my God"?

כז לָמָה תֹאמַר יַעֲקֹב וּתְדַבֵּר יִשְׂרָאֵל נִסְתְּרָה דַרְכִּי מֵיְהוָה וּמֵאֱלֹהַי מִשְׁפָּטִי יַעֲבוֹר:

28 Do you not know? Have you not heard? *Hashem* is God from of old, Creator of the earth from end to end He never grows faint or weary, His wisdom cannot be fathomed.

כח הֲלוֹא יָדַעְתָּ אִם־לֹא שָׁמַעְתָּ אֱלֹהֵי עוֹלָם יְהוָה בּוֹרֵא קְצוֹת הָאָרֶץ לֹא יִיעַף וְלֹא יִיגָע אֵין חֵקֶר לִתְבוּנָתוֹ:

29 He gives strength to the weary, Fresh vigor to the spent.

כט נֹתֵן לַיָּעֵף כֹּחַ וּלְאֵין אוֹנִים עָצְמָה יַרְבֶּה:

30 Youths may grow faint and weary, And young men stumble and fall;

ל וְיִעֲפוּ נְעָרִים וְיִגָעוּ וּבַחוּרִים כָּשׁוֹל יִכָּשֵׁלוּ:

31 But they who trust in *Hashem* shall renew their strength As eagles grow new plumes: They shall run and not grow weary, They shall march and not grow faint.

לא וְקוֹיֵ יְהוָה יַחֲלִיפוּ כֹחַ יַעֲלוּ אֵבֶר כַּנְּשָׁרִים יָרוּצוּ וְלֹא יִיגָעוּ יֵלְכוּ וְלֹא יִיעָפוּ:

41 1 Stand silent before Me, coastlands, And let nations renew their strength. Let them approach to state their case; Let us come forward together for argument.

א א הַחֲרִישׁוּ אֵלַי אִיִּים וּלְאֻמִּים יַחֲלִיפוּ כֹחַ יִגְּשׁוּ אָז יְדַבֵּרוּ יַחְדָּו לַמִּשְׁפָּט נִקְרָבָה:

2 Who has roused a victor from the East, Summoned him to His service? Has delivered up nations to him, And trodden sovereigns down? Has rendered their swords like dust, Their bows like wind-blown straw?

ב מִי הֵעִיר מִמִּזְרָח צֶדֶק יִקְרָאֵהוּ לְרַגְלוֹ יִתֵּן לְפָנָיו גּוֹיִם וּמְלָכִים יַרְדְּ יִתֵּן כֶּעָפָר חַרְבּוֹ כְּקַשׁ נִדָּף קַשְׁתּוֹ:

3 He pursues them, he goes on unscathed; No shackle is placed on his feet.

ג יִרְדְּפֵם יַעֲבוֹר שָׁלוֹם אֹרַח בְּרַגְלָיו לֹא יָבוֹא:

4 Who has wrought and achieved this? He who announced the generations from the start – I, *Hashem*, who was first And will be with the last as well.

ד מִי־פָעַל וְעָשָׂה קֹרֵא הַדֹּרוֹת מֵרֹאשׁ אֲנִי יְהוָה רִאשׁוֹן וְאֶת־אַחֲרֹנִים אֲנִי־הוּא:

5 The coastlands look on in fear, The ends of earth tremble. They draw near and come;

ה רָאוּ אִיִּים וְיִירָאוּ קְצוֹת הָאָרֶץ יֶחֱרָדוּ קָרְבוּ וַיֶּאֱתָיוּן:

6 Each one helps the other Saying to his fellow, "Take courage!"

ו אִישׁ אֶת־רֵעֵהוּ יַעְזֹרוּ וּלְאָחִיו יֹאמַר חֲזָק:

7 The woodworker encourages the smith; He who flattens with the hammer [Encourages] him who pounds the anvil. He says of the riveting, "It is good!" And he fixes it with nails, That it may not topple.

ז וַיְחַזֵּק חָרָשׁ אֶת־צֹרֵף מַחֲלִיק פַּטִּישׁ אֶת־הוֹלֶם פָּעַם אֹמֵר לַדֶּבֶק טוֹב הוּא וַיְחַזְּקֵהוּ בְמַסְמְרִים לֹא יִמּוֹט:

8 But you, *Yisrael*, My servant, *Yaakov*, whom I have
chosen, Seed of *Avraham* My friend –

ח וְאַתָּה יִשְׂרָאֵל עַבְדִּי יַעֲקֹב אֲשֶׁר
בְּחַרְתִּיךָ זֶרַע אַבְרָהָם אֹהֲבִי:

v'-a-TAH yis-ra-AYL av-DEE ya-a-KOV a-SHER
b'-khar-TEE-kha ZE-ra av-ra-HAM o-ha-VEE

9 You whom I drew from the ends of the earth And
called from its far corners, To whom I said: You are
My servant; I chose you, I have not rejected you –

ט אֲשֶׁר הֶחֱזַקְתִּיךָ מִקְצוֹת הָאָרֶץ
וּמֵאֲצִילֶיהָ קְרָאתִיךָ וָאֹמַר לְךָ עַבְדִּי־
אַתָּה בְּחַרְתִּיךָ וְלֹא מְאַסְתִּיךָ:

10 Fear not, for I am with you, Be not frightened, for
I am your God; I strengthen you and I help you, I
uphold you with My victorious right hand.

י אַל־תִּירָא כִּי עִמְּךָ־אָנִי אַל־תִּשְׁתָּע כִּי־
אֲנִי אֱלֹהֶיךָ אִמַּצְתִּיךָ אַף־עֲזַרְתִּיךָ אַף־
תְּמַכְתִּיךָ בִּימִין צִדְקִי:

11 Shamed and chagrined shall be All who contend
with you; They who strive with you Shall become
as naught and shall perish.

יא הֵן יֵבֹשׁוּ וְיִכָּלְמוּ כֹּל הַנֶּחֱרִים בָּךְ יִהְיוּ
כְאַיִן וְיֹאבְדוּ אַנְשֵׁי רִיבֶךָ:

12 You may seek, but shall not find Those who
struggle with you; Less than nothing shall be The
men who battle against you.

יב תְּבַקְשֵׁם וְלֹא תִמְצָאֵם אַנְשֵׁי מַצֻּתֶךָ
יִהְיוּ כְאַיִן וּכְאֶפֶס אַנְשֵׁי מִלְחַמְתֶּךָ:

13 For I *Hashem* am your God, Who grasped your
right hand, Who say to you: Have no fear; I will be
your help.

יג כִּי אֲנִי יְהֹוָה אֱלֹהֶיךָ מַחֲזִיק יְמִינֶךָ
הָאֹמֵר לְךָ אַל־תִּירָא אֲנִי עֲזַרְתִּיךָ:

14 Fear not, O worm *Yaakov*, O men of *Yisrael*: I will
help you – declares *Hashem* – I your Redeemer, the
Holy One of *Yisrael*.

יד אַל־תִּירְאִי תּוֹלַעַת יַעֲקֹב מְתֵי יִשְׂרָאֵל
אֲנִי עֲזַרְתִּיךְ נְאֻם־יְהֹוָה וְגֹאֲלֵךְ קְדוֹשׁ
יִשְׂרָאֵל:

15 I will make of you a threshing board, A new
thresher, with many spikes; You shall thresh
mountains to dust, And make hills like chaff.

טו הִנֵּה שַׂמְתִּיךְ לְמוֹרַג חָרוּץ חָדָשׁ בַּעַל
פִּיפִיּוֹת תָּדוּשׁ הָרִים וְתָדֹק וּגְבָעוֹת
כַּמֹּץ תָּשִׂים:

16 You shall winnow them And the wind shall carry
them off; The whirlwind shall scatter them. But you
shall rejoice in *Hashem*, And glory in the Holy One
of *Yisrael*.

טז תִּזְרֵם וְרוּחַ תִּשָּׂאֵם וּסְעָרָה תָּפִיץ
אוֹתָם וְאַתָּה תָּגִיל בַּיהֹוָה בִּקְדוֹשׁ
יִשְׂרָאֵל תִּתְהַלָּל:

17 The poor and the needy Seek water, and there is
none; Their tongue is parched with thirst. I *Hashem*
will respond to them. I, the God of *Yisrael*, will not
forsake them.

יז הָעֲנִיִּים וְהָאֶבְיוֹנִים מְבַקְשִׁים מַיִם וָאַיִן
לְשׁוֹנָם בַּצָּמָא נָשָׁתָּה אֲנִי יְהֹוָה אֶעֱנֵם
אֱלֹהֵי יִשְׂרָאֵל לֹא אֶעֶזְבֵם:

18 I will open up streams on the bare hills And
fountains amid the valleys; I will turn the desert
into ponds, The arid land into springs of water.

יח אֶפְתַּח עַל־שְׁפָיִים נְהָרוֹת וּבְתוֹךְ
בְּקָעוֹת מַעְיָנוֹת אָשִׂים מִדְבָּר לַאֲגַם־
מַיִם וְאֶרֶץ צִיָּה לְמוֹצָאֵי מָיִם:

**41:8 Seed of *Avraham* My
friend** Out of all of Israel's
ancestors, *Avraham* is singled
out as *ohavee* (אֹהֲבִי), which means 'my
friend,' or more literally, 'my lover.' *Rashi*
explains that unlike everyone else who

Pair of migratory birds in the spring

followed *Hashem*, *Avraham* did not
serve God out of familial obligation or
fear, but sought after Him like a lover
searches for his beloved. We, too, should
strive to emulate *Avraham*, to serve
Hashem out of love and not fear.

אֹהֲבִי

Isaiah

19 I will plant cedars in the wilderness, Acacias and myrtles and oleasters; I will set cypresses in the desert, Box trees and elms as well –

יט אֶתֵּן בַּמִּדְבָּר אֶרֶז שִׁטָּה וַהֲדַס וְעֵץ שָׁמֶן אָשִׂים בָּעֲרָבָה בְּרוֹשׁ תִּדְהָר וּתְאַשּׁוּר יַחְדָּו:

20 That men may see and know, Consider and comprehend That *Hashem*'s hand has done this, That the Holy One of *Yisrael* has wrought it.

כ לְמַעַן יִרְאוּ וְיֵדְעוּ וְיָשִׂימוּ וְיַשְׂכִּילוּ יַחְדָּו כִּי יַד־יְהֹוָה עָשְׂתָה זֹּאת וּקְדוֹשׁ יִשְׂרָאֵל בְּרָאָהּ:

21 Submit your case, says *Hashem*; Offer your pleas, says the King of *Yaakov*.

כא קָרְבוּ רִיבְכֶם יֹאמַר יְהֹוָה הַגִּישׁוּ עֲצֻמוֹתֵיכֶם יֹאמַר מֶלֶךְ יַעֲקֹב:

22 Let them approach and tell us what will happen. Tell us what has occurred, And we will take note of it; Or announce to us what will occur, That we may know the outcome.

כב יַגִּישׁוּ וְיַגִּידוּ לָנוּ אֵת אֲשֶׁר תִּקְרֶינָה הָרִאשֹׁנוֹת מָה הֵנָּה הַגִּידוּ וְנָשִׂימָה לִבֵּנוּ וְנֵדְעָה אַחֲרִיתָן אוֹ הַבָּאוֹת הַשְׁמִיעֻנוּ:

23 Foretell what is yet to happen, That we may know that you are gods! Do anything, good or bad, That we may be awed and see.

כג הַגִּידוּ הָאֹתִיּוֹת לְאָחוֹר וְנֵדְעָה כִּי אֱלֹהִים אַתֶּם אַף־תֵּיטִיבוּ וְתָרֵעוּ וְנִשְׁתָּעָה ונרא [וְנִרְאֶה] יַחְדָּו:

24 Why, you are less than nothing, Your effect is less than nullity; One who chooses you is an abomination.

כד הֵן־אַתֶּם מֵאַיִן וּפָעָלְכֶם מֵאָפַע תּוֹעֵבָה יִבְחַר בָּכֶם:

25 I have roused him from the north, and he has come, From the sunrise, one who invokes My name; And he has trampled rulers like mud, Like a potter treading clay.

כה הַעִירוֹתִי מִצָּפוֹן וַיַּאת מִמִּזְרַח־שֶׁמֶשׁ יִקְרָא בִשְׁמִי וְיָבֹא סְגָנִים כְּמוֹ־חֹמֶר וּכְמוֹ יוֹצֵר יִרְמָס־טִיט:

26 Who foretold this from the start, that we may note it; From aforetime, that we might say, "He is right"? Not one foretold, not one announced; No one has heard your utterance!

כו מִי־הִגִּיד מֵרֹאשׁ וְנֵדָעָה וּמִלְּפָנִים וְנֹאמַר צַדִּיק אַף אֵין־מַגִּיד אַף אֵין מַשְׁמִיעַ אַף אֵין־שֹׁמֵעַ אִמְרֵיכֶם:

27 The things once predicted to *Tzion* – Behold, here they are! And again I send a herald to *Yerushalayim*.

כז רִאשׁוֹן לְצִיּוֹן הִנֵּה הִנָּם וְלִירוּשָׁלַ͏ִם מְבַשֵּׂר אֶתֵּן:

28 But I look and there is not a man; Not one of them can predict Or can respond when I question him.

כח וְאֵרֶא וְאֵין אִישׁ וּמֵאֵלֶּה וְאֵין יוֹעֵץ וְאֶשְׁאָלֵם וְיָשִׁיבוּ דָבָר:

29 See, they are all nothingness, Their works are nullity, Their statues are naught and nil.

כט הֵן כֻּלָּם אָוֶן אֶפֶס מַעֲשֵׂיהֶם רוּחַ וָתֹהוּ נִסְכֵּיהֶם:

42 1 This is My servant, whom I uphold, My chosen one, in whom I delight. I have put My spirit upon him, He shall teach the true way to the nations.

מב א הֵן עַבְדִּי אֶתְמָךְ־בּוֹ בְּחִירִי רָצְתָה נַפְשִׁי נָתַתִּי רוּחִי עָלָיו מִשְׁפָּט לַגּוֹיִם יוֹצִיא:

2 He shall not cry out or shout aloud, Or make his voice heard in the streets.

ב לֹא יִצְעַק וְלֹא יִשָּׂא וְלֹא־יַשְׁמִיעַ בַּחוּץ קוֹלוֹ:

3 He shall not break even a bruised reed, Or snuff out even a dim wick. He shall bring forth the true way.

ג קָנֶה רָצוּץ לֹא יִשְׁבּוֹר וּפִשְׁתָּה כֵהָה לֹא יְכַבֶּנָּה לֶאֱמֶת יוֹצִיא מִשְׁפָּט:

4 He shall not grow dim or be bruised Till he has established the true way on earth; And the coastlands shall await his teaching.

ד לֹא יִכְהֶה וְלֹא יָרוּץ עַד־יָשִׂים בָּאָרֶץ מִשְׁפָּט וּלְתוֹרָתוֹ אִיִּים יְיַחֵילוּ:

5 Thus said *Hashem* the LORD, Who created the heavens and stretched them out, Who spread out the earth and what it brings forth, Who gave breath to the people upon it And life to those who walk thereon:

ה כֹּה־אָמַר הָאֵל יְהֹוָה בּוֹרֵא הַשָּׁמַיִם וְנוֹטֵיהֶם רֹקַע הָאָרֶץ וְצֶאֱצָאֶיהָ נֹתֵן נְשָׁמָה לָעָם עָלֶיהָ וְרוּחַ לַהֹלְכִים בָּהּ:

6 I *Hashem*, in My grace, have summoned you, And I have grasped you by the hand. I created you, and appointed you A covenant people, a light of nations –

ו אֲנִי יְהֹוָה קְרָאתִיךָ בְצֶדֶק וְאַחְזֵק בְּיָדֶךָ וְאֶצׇּרְךָ וְאֶתֶּנְךָ לִבְרִית עָם לְאוֹר גּוֹיִם:

*a-NEE a-do-NAI k'-ra-TEE-kha v'-TZE-dek v'-akh-ZAYK b'-ya-DE-kha
v'-e-tzor-KHA v'-e-ten-KHA liv-REET AM l'-OR go-YIM*

7 Opening eyes deprived of light, Rescuing prisoners from confinement, From the dungeon those who sit in darkness.

ז לִפְקֹחַ עֵינַיִם עִוְרוֹת לְהוֹצִיא מִמַּסְגֵּר אַסִּיר מִבֵּית כֶּלֶא יֹשְׁבֵי חֹשֶׁךְ:

8 I am *Hashem*, that is My name; I will not yield My glory to another, Nor My renown to idols.

ח אֲנִי יְהֹוָה הוּא שְׁמִי וּכְבוֹדִי לְאַחֵר לֹא־אֶתֵּן וּתְהִלָּתִי לַפְּסִילִים:

9 See, the things once predicted have come, And now I foretell new things, Announce to you ere they sprout up.

ט הָרִאשֹׁנוֹת הִנֵּה־בָאוּ וַחֲדָשׁוֹת אֲנִי מַגִּיד בְּטֶרֶם תִּצְמַחְנָה אַשְׁמִיע אֶתְכֶם:

10 Sing to *Hashem* a new song, His praise from the ends of the earth – You who sail the sea and you creatures in it, You coastlands and their inhabitants!

י שִׁירוּ לַיהֹוָה שִׁיר חָדָשׁ תְּהִלָּתוֹ מִקְצֵה הָאָרֶץ יוֹרְדֵי הַיָּם וּמְלֹאוֹ אִיִּים וְיֹשְׁבֵיהֶם:

11 Let the desert and its towns cry aloud, The villages where Kedar dwells; Let Sela's inhabitants shout, Call out from the peaks of the mountains.

יא יִשְׂאוּ מִדְבָּר וְעָרָיו חֲצֵרִים תֵּשֵׁב קֵדָר יָרֹנּוּ יֹשְׁבֵי סֶלַע מֵרֹאשׁ הָרִים יִצְוָחוּ:

12 Let them do honor to *Hashem*, And tell His glory in the coastlands.

יב יָשִׂימוּ לַיהֹוָה כָּבוֹד וּתְהִלָּתוֹ בָּאִיִּים יַגִּידוּ:

Isaiah

42:6 A light of nations This famous phrase captures the mission statement of the People of Israel. For most of Jewish history, the role of "light unto the nations" has been understood primarily as a private call to have a positive influence on the world by living an ethical life and setting a personal example of righteous behavior. Rarely was anyone on the outside ever interested in what the Jews as a nation had to say, and so the concept of *'ohr goyim'* was an ideal that individual Jews strived for. However, *Yeshayahu* is calling

Emblem of the State of Israel

for so much more. The "light" in his stirring description is capable of opening the eyes of the blind and leading the imprisoned out of darkness. The establishment of the State of Israel and its role on the international stage calls for a transformation of the "light unto the nations" metaphor from a passive, individual candle, to a powerful blaze, firing up the nations and igniting the world with righteousness. The State of Israel represents the historic opportunity for the People of Israel to fulfil their religious destiny as a nation.

13 *Hashem* goes forth like a warrior, Like a fighter He whips up His rage. He yells, He roars aloud, He charges upon His enemies.

יג יְהֹוָה כַּגִּבּוֹר יֵצֵא כְּאִישׁ מִלְחָמוֹת יָעִיר קִנְאָה יָרִיעַ אַף־יַצְרִיחַ עַל־אֹיְבָיו יִתְגַּבָּר:

14 "I have kept silent far too long, Kept still and restrained Myself; Now I will scream like a woman in labor, I will pant and I will gasp.

יד הֶחֱשֵׁיתִי מֵעוֹלָם אַחֲרִישׁ אֶתְאַפָּק כַּיּוֹלֵדָה אֶפְעֶה אֶשֹּׁם וְאֶשְׁאַף יָחַד:

15 Hills and heights will I scorch, Cause all their green to wither; I will turn rivers into isles, And dry the marshes up.

טו אַחֲרִיב הָרִים וּגְבָעוֹת וְכָל־עֶשְׂבָּם אוֹבִישׁ וְשַׂמְתִּי נְהָרוֹת לָאִיִּים וַאֲגַמִּים אוֹבִישׁ:

16 I will lead the blind By a road they did not know, And I will make them walk By paths they never knew. I will turn darkness before them to light, Rough places into level ground. These are the promises – I will keep them without fail.

טז וְהוֹלַכְתִּי עִוְרִים בְּדֶרֶךְ לֹא יָדָעוּ בִּנְתִיבוֹת לֹא־יָדְעוּ אַדְרִיכֵם אָשִׂים מַחְשָׁךְ לִפְנֵיהֶם לָאוֹר וּמַעֲקַשִּׁים לְמִישׁוֹר אֵלֶּה הַדְּבָרִים עֲשִׂיתִם וְלֹא עֲזַבְתִּים:

17 Driven back and utterly shamed Shall be those who trust in an image, Those who say to idols, 'You are our gods!'"

יז נָסֹגוּ אָחוֹר יֵבֹשׁוּ בֹשֶׁת הַבֹּטְחִים בַּפָּסֶל הָאֹמְרִים לְמַסֵּכָה אַתֶּם אֱלֹהֵינוּ:

18 Listen, you who are deaf; You blind ones, look up and see!

יח הַחֵרְשִׁים שְׁמָעוּ וְהַעִוְרִים הַבִּיטוּ לִרְאוֹת:

19 Who is so blind as My servant, So deaf as the messenger I send? Who is so blind as the chosen one, So blind as the servant of *Hashem*?

יט מִי עִוֵּר כִּי אִם־עַבְדִּי וְחֵרֵשׁ כְּמַלְאָכִי אֶשְׁלָח מִי עִוֵּר כִּמְשֻׁלָּם וְעִוֵּר כְּעֶבֶד יְהֹוָה:

20 Seeing many things, he gives no heed; With ears open, he hears nothing.

כ רָאִית [רָאוֹת] רַבּוֹת וְלֹא תִשְׁמֹר פָּקוֹחַ אָזְנַיִם וְלֹא יִשְׁמָע:

21 *Hashem* desires His [servant's] vindication, That he may magnify and glorify [His] Teaching.

כא יְהֹוָה חָפֵץ לְמַעַן צִדְקוֹ יַגְדִּיל תּוֹרָה וְיַאְדִּיר:

22 Yet it is a people plundered and despoiled: All of them are trapped in holes, Imprisoned in dungeons. They are given over to plunder, with none to rescue them; To despoilment, with none to say "Give back!"

כב וְהוּא עַם־בָּזוּז וְשָׁסוּי הָפֵחַ בַּחוּרִים כֻּלָּם וּבְבָתֵּי כְלָאִים הָחְבָּאוּ הָיוּ לָבַז וְאֵין מַצִּיל מְשִׁסָּה וְאֵין־אֹמֵר הָשַׁב:

23 If only you would listen to this, Attend and give heed from now on!

כג מִי בָכֶם יַאֲזִין זֹאת יַקְשֵׁב וְיִשְׁמַע לְאָחוֹר:

24 Who was it gave *Yaakov* over to despoilment And *Yisrael* to plunderers? Surely, *Hashem* against whom they sinned In whose ways they would not walk And whose Teaching they would not obey.

כד מִי־נָתַן לִמְשׁוֹסָה [לִמְשִׁסָּה] יַעֲקֹב וְיִשְׂרָאֵל לְבֹזְזִים הֲלוֹא יְהֹוָה זוּ חָטָאנוּ לוֹ וְלֹא־אָבוּ בִדְרָכָיו הָלוֹךְ וְלֹא שָׁמְעוּ בְּתוֹרָתוֹ:

25 So He poured out wrath upon them, His anger and the fury of war. It blazed upon them all about, but they heeded not; It burned among them, but they gave it no thought.

כה וַיִּשְׁפֹּךְ עָלָיו חֵמָה אַפּוֹ וֶעֱזוּז מִלְחָמָה וַתְּלַהֲטֵהוּ מִסָּבִיב וְלֹא יָדָע וַתִּבְעַר־בּוֹ וְלֹא־יָשִׂים עַל־לֵב:

Isaiah

43 ¹ But now thus said *Hashem* – Who created you, O *Yaakov*, Who formed you, O *Yisrael*: Fear not, for I will redeem you; I have singled you out by name, You are Mine.

מג א וְעַתָּה כֹּה־אָמַר יְהֹוָה בֹּרַאֲךָ יַעֲקֹב וְיֹצֶרְךָ יִשְׂרָאֵל אַל־תִּירָא כִּי גְאַלְתִּיךָ קָרָאתִי בְשִׁמְךָ לִי־אָתָּה:

v'-a-TAH koh a-MAR a-do-NAI bo-ra-a-KHA ya-a-KOV v'-yo-tzer-KHA yis-ra-AYL al tee-RA KEE g'-al-TEE-kha ka-RA-tee v'-shim-KHA lee A-tah

² When you pass through water, I will be with you; Through streams, They shall not overwhelm you. When you walk through fire, You shall not be scorched; Through flame, It shall not burn you.

ב כִּי־תַעֲבֹר בַּמַּיִם אִתְּךָ־אָנִי וּבַנְּהָרוֹת לֹא יִשְׁטְפוּךָ כִּי־תֵלֵךְ בְּמוֹ־אֵשׁ לֹא תִכָּוֶה וְלֶהָבָה לֹא תִבְעַר־בָּךְ:

³ For I *Hashem* am your God, The Holy One of *Yisrael*, your Savior. I give Egypt as a ransom for you, Ethiopia and Saba in exchange for you.

ג כִּי אֲנִי יְהֹוָה אֱלֹהֶיךָ קְדוֹשׁ יִשְׂרָאֵל מוֹשִׁיעֶךָ נָתַתִּי כָפְרְךָ מִצְרַיִם כּוּשׁ וּסְבָא תַּחְתֶּיךָ:

⁴ Because you are precious to Me, And honored, and I love you, I give men in exchange for you And peoples in your stead.

ד מֵאֲשֶׁר יָקַרְתָּ בְעֵינַי נִכְבַּדְתָּ וַאֲנִי אֲהַבְתִּיךָ וְאֶתֵּן אָדָם תַּחְתֶּיךָ וּלְאֻמִּים תַּחַת נַפְשֶׁךָ:

⁵ Fear not, for I am with you: I will bring your folk from the East, Will gather you out of the West;

ה אַל־תִּירָא כִּי אִתְּךָ־אָנִי מִמִּזְרָח אָבִיא זַרְעֶךָ וּמִמַּעֲרָב אֲקַבְּצֶךָּ:

⁶ I will say to the North, "Give back!" And to the South, "Do not withhold! Bring My sons from afar, And My daughters from the end of the earth –

ו אֹמַר לַצָּפוֹן תֵּנִי וּלְתֵימָן אַל־תִּכְלָאִי הָבִיאִי בָנַי מֵרָחוֹק וּבְנוֹתַי מִקְצֵה הָאָרֶץ:

⁷ All who are linked to My name, Whom I have created, Formed, and made for My glory –

ז כֹּל הַנִּקְרָא בִשְׁמִי וְלִכְבוֹדִי בְּרָאתִיו יְצַרְתִּיו אַף־עֲשִׂיתִיו:

⁸ Setting free that people, Blind though it has eyes And deaf though it has ears."

ח הוֹצִיא עַם־עִוֵּר וְעֵינַיִם יֵשׁ וְחֵרְשִׁים וְאָזְנַיִם לָמוֹ:

⁹ All the nations assemble as one, The peoples gather. Who among them declared this, Foretold to us the things that have happened? Let them produce their witnesses and be vindicated, That men, hearing them, may say, "It is true!"

ט כָּל־הַגּוֹיִם נִקְבְּצוּ יַחְדָּו וְיֵאָסְפוּ לְאֻמִּים מִי בָהֶם יַגִּיד זֹאת וְרִאשֹׁנוֹת יַשְׁמִיעֻנוּ יִתְּנוּ עֵדֵיהֶם וְיִצְדָּקוּ וְיִשְׁמְעוּ וְיֹאמְרוּ אֱמֶת:

¹⁰ My witnesses are you – declares *Hashem* – My servant, whom I have chosen. To the end that you may take thought, And believe in Me, And understand that I am He: Before Me no god was formed, And after Me none shall exist –

י אַתֶּם עֵדַי נְאֻם־יְהֹוָה וְעַבְדִּי אֲשֶׁר בָּחָרְתִּי לְמַעַן תֵּדְעוּ וְתַאֲמִינוּ לִי וְתָבִינוּ כִּי־אֲנִי הוּא לְפָנַי לֹא־נוֹצַר אֵל וְאַחֲרַי לֹא יִהְיֶה:

43:1 But now As he often does, *Yeshayahu* delivers severe rebuke (42:18–25) followed by comfort and consolation. He tells the people that *Hashem* has not cast Israel off. Rather, He will be present during the difficulties and will even bring a speedy return and restoration to Israel (verses 3–7). The opening words, "but now," mark the sharp contrast between the closing of chapter 42 and the opening of chapter 43. The prophet reassures that although Israel has undergone severe punishment and is still suffering, a dramatic change is approaching. The nation will return to its land in a remarkable expression of *Hashem*'s declaration, "You are Mine".

Jewish immigrants to the Land of Israel, 1947

Isaiah

¹¹ None but me, *Hashem*; Beside Me, none can grant triumph.

יא אָנֹכִי אָנֹכִי יְהֹוָה וְאֵין מִבַּלְעָדַי מוֹשִׁיעַ:

¹² I alone foretold the triumph And I brought it to pass; I announced it, And no strange god was among you. So you are My witnesses – declares *Hashem* – And I am *Hashem*.

יב אָנֹכִי הִגַּדְתִּי וְהוֹשַׁעְתִּי וְהִשְׁמַעְתִּי וְאֵין בָּכֶם זָר וְאַתֶּם עֵדַי נְאֻם־יְהֹוָה וַאֲנִי־אֵל:

¹³ Ever since day was, I am He; None can deliver from My hand. When I act, who can reverse it?

יג גַּם־מִיּוֹם אֲנִי הוּא וְאֵין מִיָּדִי מַצִּיל אֶפְעַל וּמִי יְשִׁיבֶנָּה:

¹⁴ Thus said *Hashem*, Your Redeemer, the Holy One of *Yisrael*: For your sake I send to Babylon; I will bring down all [her] bars, And the Chaldeans shall raise their voice in lamentation.

יד כֹּה־אָמַר יְהֹוָה גֹּאַלְכֶם קְדוֹשׁ יִשְׂרָאֵל לְמַעַנְכֶם שִׁלַּחְתִּי בָבֶלָה וְהוֹרַדְתִּי בָרִיחִים כֻּלָּם וְכַשְׂדִּים בָּאֳנִיּוֹת רִנָּתָם:

¹⁵ I am your Holy One, *Hashem*, Your King, the Creator of *Yisrael*.

טו אֲנִי יְהֹוָה קְדוֹשְׁכֶם בּוֹרֵא יִשְׂרָאֵל מַלְכְּכֶם:

¹⁶ Thus said *Hashem*, Who made a road through the sea And a path through mighty waters,

טז כֹּה אָמַר יְהֹוָה הַנּוֹתֵן בַּיָּם דָּרֶךְ וּבְמַיִם עַזִּים נְתִיבָה:

¹⁷ Who destroyed chariots and horses, And all the mighty host – They lay down to rise no more, They were extinguished, quenched like a wick:

יז הַמּוֹצִיא רֶכֶב־וָסוּס חַיִל וְעִזּוּז יַחְדָּו יִשְׁכְּבוּ בַּל־יָקוּמוּ דָּעֲכוּ כַּפִּשְׁתָּה כָבוּ:

¹⁸ Do not recall what happened of old, Or ponder what happened of yore!

יח אַל־תִּזְכְּרוּ רִאשֹׁנוֹת וְקַדְמֹנִיּוֹת אַל־תִּתְבֹּנָנוּ:

¹⁹ I am about to do something new; Even now it shall come to pass, Suddenly you shall perceive it: I will make a road through the wilderness And rivers in the desert.

יט הִנְנִי עֹשֶׂה חֲדָשָׁה עַתָּה תִצְמָח הֲלוֹא תֵדָעוּהָ אַף אָשִׂים בַּמִּדְבָּר דֶּרֶךְ בִּישִׁמוֹן נְהָרוֹת:

²⁰ The wild beasts shall honor Me, Jackals and ostriches, For I provide water in the wilderness, Rivers in the desert, To give drink to My chosen people,

כ תְּכַבְּדֵנִי חַיַּת הַשָּׂדֶה תַּנִּים וּבְנוֹת יַעֲנָה כִּי־נָתַתִּי בַמִּדְבָּר מַיִם נְהָרוֹת בִּישִׁימֹן לְהַשְׁקוֹת עַמִּי בְחִירִי:

²¹ The people I formed for Myself That they might declare My praise.

כא עַם־זוּ יָצַרְתִּי לִי תְּהִלָּתִי יְסַפֵּרוּ:

²² But you have not worshiped Me, O *Yaakov*, That you should be weary of Me, O *Yisrael*.

כב וְלֹא־אֹתִי קָרָאתָ יַעֲקֹב כִּי־יָגַעְתָּ בִּי יִשְׂרָאֵל:

²³ You have not brought Me your sheep for burnt offerings, Nor honored Me with your sacrifices. I have not burdened you with meal offerings, Nor wearied you about frankincense.

כג לֹא־הֵבֵיאתָ לִּי שֵׂה עֹלֹתֶיךָ וּזְבָחֶיךָ לֹא כִבַּדְתָּנִי לֹא הֶעֱבַדְתִּיךָ בְּמִנְחָה וְלֹא הוֹגַעְתִּיךָ בִּלְבוֹנָה:

²⁴ You have not bought Me fragrant reed with money, Nor sated Me with the fat of your sacrifices. Instead, you have burdened Me with your sins, You have wearied Me with your iniquities.

כד לֹא־קָנִיתָ לִּי בַכֶּסֶף קָנֶה וְחֵלֶב זְבָחֶיךָ לֹא הִרְוִיתָנִי אַךְ הֶעֱבַדְתַּנִי בְּחַטֹּאותֶיךָ הוֹגַעְתַּנִי בַּעֲוֹנֹתֶיךָ:

Isaiah

²⁵ It is I, I who – for My own sake – Wipe your transgressions away And remember your sins no more.

אָנֹכִי אָנֹכִי הוּא מֹחֶה פְשָׁעֶיךָ לְמַעֲנִי וְחַטֹּאתֶיךָ לֹא אֶזְכֹּר: כה

²⁶ Help me remember! Let us join in argument, Tell your version, That you may be vindicated.

הַזְכִּירֵנִי נִשָּׁפְטָה יָחַד סַפֵּר אַתָּה לְמַעַן תִּצְדָּק: כו

²⁷ Your earliest ancestor sinned, And your spokesmen transgressed against Me.

אָבִיךָ הָרִאשׁוֹן חָטָא וּמְלִיצֶיךָ פָּשְׁעוּ בִי: כז

²⁸ So I profaned the holy princes; I abandoned *Yaakov* to proscription And *Yisrael* to mockery.

וַאֲחַלֵּל שָׂרֵי קֹדֶשׁ וְאֶתְּנָה לַחֵרֶם יַעֲקֹב וְיִשְׂרָאֵל לְגִדּוּפִים: כח

^{44 1} But hear, now, O *Yaakov* My servant, *Yisrael* whom I have chosen!

וְעַתָּה שְׁמַע יַעֲקֹב עַבְדִּי וְיִשְׂרָאֵל בָּחַרְתִּי בוֹ: **מד** א

² Thus said *Hashem*, your Maker, Your Creator who has helped you since birth: Fear not, My servant *Yaakov*, Jeshurun whom I have chosen,

כֹּה־אָמַר יְהֹוָה עֹשֶׂךָ וְיֹצֶרְךָ מִבֶּטֶן יַעְזְרֶךָ אַל־תִּירָא עַבְדִּי יַעֲקֹב וִישֻׁרוּן בָּחַרְתִּי בוֹ: ב

³ Even as I pour water on thirsty soil, And rain upon dry ground, So will I pour My spirit on your offspring, My blessing upon your posterity.

כִּי אֶצָּק־מַיִם עַל־צָמֵא וְנֹזְלִים עַל־יַבָּשָׁה אֶצֹּק רוּחִי עַל־זַרְעֶךָ וּבִרְכָתִי עַל־צֶאֱצָאֶיךָ: ג

KEE e-tzak MA-yim al tza-MAY v'-no-z'-LEEM al ya-ba-SHAH e-TZOK ru-KHEE al zar-E-kha u-vir-kha-TEE al tze-e-tza-E-kha

⁴ And they shall sprout like grass, Like willows by watercourses.

וְצָמְחוּ בְּבֵין חָצִיר כַּעֲרָבִים עַל־יִבְלֵי־מָיִם: ד

⁵ One shall say, "I am *Hashem*'s," Another shall use the name of "*Yaakov*," Another shall mark his arm "of *Hashem*" And adopt the name of "*Yisrael*."

זֶה יֹאמַר לַיהֹוָה אָנִי וְזֶה יִקְרָא בְשֵׁם־יַעֲקֹב וְזֶה יִכְתֹּב יָדוֹ לַיהֹוָה וּבְשֵׁם יִשְׂרָאֵל יְכַנֶּה: ה

⁶ Thus said *Hashem*, the King of *Yisrael*, Their Redeemer, the LORD of Hosts: I am the first and I am the last, And there is no god but Me.

כֹּה־אָמַר יְהֹוָה מֶלֶךְ־יִשְׂרָאֵל וְגֹאֲלוֹ יְהֹוָה צְבָאוֹת אֲנִי רִאשׁוֹן וַאֲנִי אַחֲרוֹן וּמִבַּלְעָדַי אֵין אֱלֹהִים: ו

⁷ Who like Me can announce, Can foretell it – and match Me thereby? Even as I told the future to an ancient people, So let him foretell coming events to them.

וּמִי־כָמוֹנִי יִקְרָא וְיַגִּידֶהָ וְיַעְרְכֶהָ לִי מִשּׂוּמִי עַם־עוֹלָם וְאֹתִיּוֹת וַאֲשֶׁר תָּבֹאנָה יַגִּידוּ לָמוֹ: ז

⁸ Do not be frightened, do not be shaken! Have I not from of old predicted to you? I foretold, and you are My witnesses. Is there any god, then, but Me? "There is no other rock; I know none!"

אַל־תִּפְחֲדוּ וְאַל־תִּרְהוּ הֲלֹא מֵאָז הִשְׁמַעְתִּיךָ וְהִגַּדְתִּי וְאַתֶּם עֵדָי הֲיֵשׁ אֱלוֹהַּ מִבַּלְעָדַי וְאֵין צוּר בַּל־יָדָעְתִּי: ח

Isaiah

Rain water in the Judean desert

44:3 Even as I pour water on thirsty soil ... So will I pour My spirit on your offspring Water is often used as a metaphor for *Torah*. The Talmud (*Taanit* 7a) explains that "just as water leaves a high place and flows downward to a low place, so does *Torah* knowledge flow away from those who are arrogant and toward those who are humble." Furthermore, just as water nourishes and sustains the "thirsty soil" and "dry ground," the Bible is the source of our spiritual nourishment.

9 The makers of idols All work to no purpose; And the things they treasure Can do no good, As they themselves can testify. They neither look nor think, And so they shall be shamed.

ט יֹצְרֵי־פֶסֶל כֻּלָּם תֹּהוּ וַחֲמוּדֵיהֶם בַּל־יוֹעִילוּ וְעֵדֵיהֶם הֵמָּה בַּל־יִרְאוּ וּבַל־יֵדְעוּ לְמַעַן יֵבֹשׁוּ:

10 Who would fashion a god Or cast a statue That can do no good?

י מִי־יָצַר אֵל וּפֶסֶל נָסָךְ לְבִלְתִּי הוֹעִיל:

11 Lo, all its adherents shall be shamed; They are craftsmen, are merely human. Let them all assemble and stand up! They shall be cowed, and they shall be shamed.

יא הֵן כָּל־חֲבֵרָיו יֵבֹשׁוּ וְחָרָשִׁים הֵמָּה מֵאָדָם יִתְקַבְּצוּ כֻלָּם יַעֲמֹדוּ יִפְחֲדוּ יֵבֹשׁוּ יָחַד:

12 The craftsman in iron, with his tools, Works it over charcoal And fashions it by hammering, Working with the strength of his arm. Should he go hungry, his strength would ebb; Should he drink no water, he would grow faint.

יב חָרַשׁ בַּרְזֶל מַעֲצָד וּפָעַל בַּפֶּחָם וּבַמַּקָּבוֹת יִצְּרֵהוּ וַיִּפְעָלֵהוּ בִּזְרוֹעַ כֹּחוֹ גַּם־רָעֵב וְאֵין כֹּחַ לֹא־שָׁתָה מַיִם וַיִּיעָף:

13 The craftsman in wood measures with a line And marks out a shape with a stylus; He forms it with scraping tools, Marking it out with a compass. He gives it a human form, The beauty of a man, to dwell in a shrine.

יג חָרַשׁ עֵצִים נָטָה קָו יְתָאֲרֵהוּ בַשֶּׂרֶד יַעֲשֵׂהוּ בַּמַּקְצֻעוֹת וּבַמְּחוּגָה יְתָאֲרֵהוּ וַיַּעֲשֵׂהוּ כְּתַבְנִית אִישׁ כְּתִפְאֶרֶת אָדָם לָשֶׁבֶת בָּיִת:

14 For his use he cuts down cedars; He chooses plane trees and oaks. He sets aside trees of the forest; Or plants firs, and the rain makes them grow.

יד לִכְרָת־לוֹ אֲרָזִים וַיִּקַּח תִּרְזָה וְאַלּוֹן וַיְאַמֶּץ־לוֹ בַּעֲצֵי־יָעַר נָטַע אֹרֶן וְגֶשֶׁם יְגַדֵּל:

15 All this serves man for fuel: He takes some to warm himself, And he builds a fire and bakes bread. He also makes a god of it and worships it, Fashions an idol and bows down to it!

טו וְהָיָה לְאָדָם לְבָעֵר וַיִּקַּח מֵהֶם וַיָּחָם אַף־יַשִּׂיק וְאָפָה לָחֶם אַף־יִפְעַל־אֵל וַיִּשְׁתָּחוּ עָשָׂהוּ פֶסֶל וַיִּסְגָּד־לָמוֹ:

16 Part of it he burns in a fire: On that part he roasts* meat, He eats* the roast and is sated; He also warms himself and cries, "Ah, I am warm! I can feel the heat!"

טז חֶצְיוֹ שָׂרַף בְּמוֹ־אֵשׁ עַל־חֶצְיוֹ בָּשָׂר יֹאכֵל יִצְלֶה צָלִי וְיִשְׂבָּע אַף־יָחֹם וְיֹאמַר הֶאָח חַמּוֹתִי רָאִיתִי אוּר:

17 Of the rest he makes a god – his own carving! He bows down to it, worships it; He prays to it and cries, "Save me, for you are my god!"

יז וּשְׁאֵרִיתוֹ לְאֵל עָשָׂה לְפִסְלוֹ יִסְגּוֹד־ [יִסְגָּד־] לוֹ וְיִשְׁתַּחוּ וְיִתְפַּלֵּל אֵלָיו וְיֹאמַר הַצִּילֵנִי כִּי אֵלִי אָתָּה:

18 They have no wit or judgment: Their eyes are besmeared, and they see not; Their minds, and they cannot think.

יח לֹא יָדְעוּ וְלֹא יָבִינוּ כִּי טַח מֵרְאוֹת עֵינֵיהֶם מֵהַשְׂכִּיל לִבֹּתָם:

19 They do not give thought, They lack the wit and judgment to say: "Part of it burned in a fire; I also baked bread on the coals, I roasted meat and ate it – Should I make the rest an abhorrence? Should I bow to a block of wood?"

יט וְלֹא־יָשִׁיב אֶל־לִבּוֹ וְלֹא דַעַת וְלֹא־תְבוּנָה לֵאמֹר חֶצְיוֹ שָׂרַפְתִּי בְמוֹ־אֵשׁ וְאַף אָפִיתִי עַל־גֶּחָלָיו לֶחֶם אֶצְלֶה בָשָׂר וְאֹכֵל וְיִתְרוֹ לְתוֹעֵבָה אֶעֱשֶׂה לְבוּל עֵץ אֶסְגּוֹד:

---

* The words "roasts" and "eats" transposed for clarity

79

20 He pursues ashes! A deluded mind has led him astray, And he cannot save himself; He never says to himself, "The thing in my hand is a fraud!"

כ רֹעֶה אֵפֶר לֵב הוּתַל הִטָּהוּ וְלֹא־יַצִּיל אֶת־נַפְשׁוֹ וְלֹא יֹאמַר הֲלוֹא שֶׁקֶר בִּימִינִי:

21 Remember these things, O *Yaakov* For you, O *Yisrael*, are My servant: I fashioned you, you are My servant – O *Yisrael*, never forget Me.

כא זְכָר־אֵלֶּה יַעֲקֹב וְיִשְׂרָאֵל כִּי עַבְדִּי־אָתָּה יְצַרְתִּיךָ עֶבֶד־לִי אַתָּה יִשְׂרָאֵל לֹא תִנָּשֵׁנִי:

22 I wipe away your sins like a cloud, Your transgressions like mist – Come back to Me, for I redeem you.

כב מָחִיתִי כָעָב פְּשָׁעֶיךָ וְכֶעָנָן חַטֹּאותֶיךָ שׁוּבָה אֵלַי כִּי גְאַלְתִּיךָ:

23 Shout, O heavens, for *Hashem* has acted; Shout aloud, O depths of the earth! Shout for joy, O mountains, O forests with all your trees! For *Hashem* has redeemed *Yaakov*, Has glorified Himself through *Yisrael*.

כג רָנּוּ שָׁמַיִם כִּי־עָשָׂה יְהוָה הָרִיעוּ תַּחְתִּיּוֹת אָרֶץ פִּצְחוּ הָרִים רִנָּה יַעַר וְכָל־עֵץ בּוֹ כִּי־גָאַל יְהוָה יַעֲקֹב וּבְיִשְׂרָאֵל יִתְפָּאָר:

24 Thus said *Hashem*, your Redeemer, Who formed you in the womb: It is I, *Hashem*, who made everything, Who alone stretched out the heavens And unaided spread out the earth;

כד כֹּה־אָמַר יְהוָה גֹּאֲלֶךָ וְיֹצֶרְךָ מִבָּטֶן אָנֹכִי יְהוָה עֹשֶׂה כֹּל נֹטֶה שָׁמַיִם לְבַדִּי רֹקַע הָאָרֶץ מִי אִתִּי [מֵאִתִּי]:

25 Who annul the omens of diviners, And make fools of the augurs; Who turn sages back And make nonsense of their knowledge;

כה מֵפֵר אֹתוֹת בַּדִּים וְקֹסְמִים יְהוֹלֵל מֵשִׁיב חֲכָמִים אָחוֹר וְדַעְתָּם יְשַׂכֵּל:

26 But confirm the word of My servant And fulfill the prediction of My messengers. It is I who say of *Yerushalayim*, "It shall be inhabited," And of the towns of *Yehuda*, "They shall be rebuilt; And I will restore their ruined places."

כו מֵקִים דְּבַר עַבְדּוֹ וַעֲצַת מַלְאָכָיו יַשְׁלִים הָאֹמֵר לִירוּשָׁלַ͏ִם תּוּשָׁב וּלְעָרֵי יְהוּדָה תִּבָּנֶינָה וְחָרְבוֹתֶיהָ אֲקוֹמֵם:

27 [I,] who said to the deep, "Be dry; I will dry up your floods,"

כז הָאֹמֵר לַצּוּלָה חֳרָבִי וְנַהֲרֹתַיִךְ אוֹבִישׁ:

28 Am the same who says of Cyrus, "He is My shepherd; He shall fulfill all My purposes! He shall say of *Yerushalayim*, 'She shall be rebuilt,' And to the Temple: 'You shall be founded again.'"

כח הָאֹמֵר לְכוֹרֶשׁ רֹעִי וְכָל־חֶפְצִי יַשְׁלִם וְלֵאמֹר לִירוּשָׁלַ͏ִם תִּבָּנֶה וְהֵיכָל תִּוָּסֵד:

מה 45 1 Thus said *Hashem* to Cyrus, His anointed one – Whose right hand He has grasped, Treading down nations before him, Ungirding the loins of kings, Opening doors before him And letting no gate stay shut:

א כֹּה־אָמַר יְהוָה לִמְשִׁיחוֹ לְכוֹרֶשׁ אֲשֶׁר־ הֶחֱזַקְתִּי בִימִינוֹ לְרַד־לְפָנָיו גּוֹיִם וּמָתְנֵי מְלָכִים אֲפַתֵּחַ לִפְתֹּחַ לְפָנָיו דְּלָתַיִם וּשְׁעָרִים לֹא יִסָּגֵרוּ:

2 I will march before you And level the hills that loom up; I will shatter doors of bronze And cut down iron bars.

ב אֲנִי לְפָנֶיךָ אֵלֵךְ וַהֲדוּרִים אוֹשׁר [אֲיַשֵּׁר] דַּלְתוֹת נְחוּשָׁה אֲשַׁבֵּר וּבְרִיחֵי בַרְזֶל אֲגַדֵּעַ:

3 I will give you treasures concealed in the dark And secret hoards – So that you may know that it is I *Hashem*, The God of *Yisrael*, who call you by name.

ג וְנָתַתִּי לְךָ אוֹצְרוֹת חֹשֶׁךְ וּמַטְמֻנֵי מִסְתָּרִים לְמַעַן תֵּדַע כִּי־אֲנִי יְהוָה הַקּוֹרֵא בְשִׁמְךָ אֱלֹהֵי יִשְׂרָאֵל:

Isaiah

Isaiah

4 For the sake of My servant *Yaakov, Yisrael* My chosen one, I call you by name, I hail you by title, though you have not known Me.

ד לְמַעַן עַבְדִּי יַעֲקֹב וְיִשְׂרָאֵל בְּחִירִי
וָאֶקְרָא לְךָ בִּשְׁמֶךָ אֲכַנְּךָ וְלֹא יְדַעְתָּנִי:

l'-MA-an av-DEE ya-a-KOV v'-yis-ra-AYL b'-khee-REE va-ek-RA
l'-KHA bish-ME-kha a-kha-n'-KHA v'-LO y'-da-TA-nee

5 I am *Hashem* and there is none else; Beside Me, there is no god. I engird you, though you have not known Me,

ה אֲנִי יְהֹוָה וְאֵין עוֹד זוּלָתִי אֵין אֱלֹהִים
אֲאַזֶּרְךָ וְלֹא יְדַעְתָּנִי:

6 So that they may know, from east to west, That there is none but Me. I am *Hashem* and there is none else,

ו לְמַעַן יֵדְעוּ מִמִּזְרַח שֶׁמֶשׁ וּמִמַּעֲרָבָה
כִּי־אֶפֶס בִּלְעָדָי אֲנִי יְהֹוָה וְאֵין עוֹד:

7 I form light and create darkness, I make weal and create woe – I *Hashem* do all these things.

ז יוֹצֵר אוֹר וּבוֹרֵא חֹשֶׁךְ עֹשֶׂה שָׁלוֹם
וּבוֹרֵא רָע אֲנִי יְהֹוָה עֹשֶׂה כָל־אֵלֶּה:

8 Pour down, O skies, from above! Let the heavens rain down victory! Let the earth open up and triumph sprout Yes, let vindication spring up: I *Hashem* have created it.

ח הַרְעִיפוּ שָׁמַיִם מִמַּעַל וּשְׁחָקִים יִזְּלוּ־
צֶדֶק תִּפְתַּח־אֶרֶץ וְיִפְרוּ־יֶשַׁע וּצְדָקָה
תַצְמִיחַ יַחַד אֲנִי יְהֹוָה בְּרָאתִיו:

9 Shame on him who argues with his Maker, Though naught but a potsherd of earth! Shall the clay say to the potter, "What are you doing? Your work has no handles"?

ט הוֹי רָב אֶת־יֹצְרוֹ חֶרֶשׂ אֶת־חַרְשֵׂי
אֲדָמָה הֲיֹאמַר חֹמֶר לְיֹצְרוֹ מַה־תַּעֲשֶׂה
וּפָעָלְךָ אֵין־יָדַיִם לוֹ:

10 Shame on him who asks his father, "What are you begetting?" Or a woman, "What are you bearing?"

י הוֹי אֹמֵר לְאָב מַה־תּוֹלִיד וּלְאִשָּׁה מַה־
תְּחִילִין:

11 Thus said *Hashem, Yisrael*'s Holy One and Maker: Will you question Me on the destiny of My children, Will you instruct Me about the work of My hands?

יא כֹּה־אָמַר יְהֹוָה קְדוֹשׁ יִשְׂרָאֵל וְיֹצְרוֹ
הָאֹתִיּוֹת שְׁאָלוּנִי עַל־בָּנַי וְעַל־פֹּעַל יָדַי
תְּצַוֻּנִי:

12 It was I who made the earth And created man upon it; My own hands stretched out the heavens, And I marshaled all their host.

יב אָנֹכִי עָשִׂיתִי אֶרֶץ וְאָדָם עָלֶיהָ בָרָאתִי
אֲנִי יָדַי נָטוּ שָׁמַיִם וְכָל־צְבָאָם צִוֵּיתִי:

13 It was I who roused him for victory And who level all roads for him. He shall rebuild My city And let My exiled people go Without price and without payment – said the LORD of Hosts.

יג אָנֹכִי הַעִירֹתִהוּ בְצֶדֶק וְכָל־דְּרָכָיו
אֲיַשֵּׁר הוּא־יִבְנֶה עִירִי וְגָלוּתִי יְשַׁלֵּחַ לֹא
בִמְחִיר וְלֹא בְשֹׁחַד אָמַר יְהֹוָה צְבָאוֹת:

The Cyrus cylinder

45:4 For the sake of My servant *Yaakov, Yisrael* My chosen one The speed with which Cyrus rose to world dominion was nothing short of miraculous. At the beginning of the chapter, *Yeshayahu* predicts that on the night Cyrus will march his army into Babylonia, the gates of the city will be left open. In Cyrus's own chronicle of his conquest, he describes in amazement how the gates of the cities opened before his armies. According to the prophet, this will be a sign to the new king Cyrus that he was chosen for a larger, divine purpose – restoring the People of Israel to their natural home. Indeed, one of the first things Cyrus does as king is grant permission to the Jews to return to Israel and to rebuild the *Beit Hamikdash* (see Ezra 1), as predicted above (44:26–28).

14 Thus said *Hashem*: Egypt's wealth and Nubia's gains And Sabaites, long of limb, Shall pass over to you and be yours, Pass over and follow you in fetters, Bow low to you And reverently address you: "Only among you is *Hashem*, There is no other god at all!

יד כֹּה אָמַר יְהֹוָה יְגִיעַ מִצְרַיִם וּסְחַר־כּוּשׁ וּסְבָאִים אַנְשֵׁי מִדָּה עָלַיִךְ יַעֲבֹרוּ וְלָךְ יִהְיוּ אַחֲרַיִךְ יֵלֵכוּ בַּזִּקִּים יַעֲבֹרוּ וְאֵלַיִךְ יִשְׁתַּחֲווּ אֵלַיִךְ יִתְפַּלָּלוּ אַךְ בָּךְ אֵל וְאֵין עוֹד אֶפֶס אֱלֹהִים:

15 You are indeed a *Hashem* who concealed Himself, O God of *Yisrael*, who bring victory!

טו אָכֵן אַתָּה אֵל מִסְתַּתֵּר אֱלֹהֵי יִשְׂרָאֵל מוֹשִׁיעַ:

16 Those who fabricate idols, All are shamed and disgraced; To a man, they slink away in disgrace.

טז בּוֹשׁוּ וְגַם־נִכְלְמוּ כֻּלָּם יַחְדָּו הָלְכוּ בַכְּלִמָּה חָרָשֵׁי צִירִים:

17 But *Yisrael* has won through *Hashem* Triumph everlasting. You shall not be shamed or disgraced In all the ages to come!"

יז יִשְׂרָאֵל נוֹשַׁע בַּיהֹוָה תְּשׁוּעַת עוֹלָמִים לֹא־תֵבֹשׁוּ וְלֹא־תִכָּלְמוּ עַד־עוֹלְמֵי עַד:

18 For thus said *Hashem*, The Creator of heaven who alone is *Hashem*, Who formed the earth and made it, Who alone established it – He did not create it a waste, But formed it for habitation: I am *Hashem*, and there is none else.

יח כִּי כֹה אָמַר־יְהֹוָה בּוֹרֵא הַשָּׁמַיִם הוּא הָאֱלֹהִים יֹצֵר הָאָרֶץ וְעֹשָׂהּ הוּא כוֹנְנָהּ לֹא־תֹהוּ בְרָאָהּ לָשֶׁבֶת יְצָרָהּ אֲנִי יְהֹוָה וְאֵין עוֹד:

19 I did not speak in secret, At a site in a land of darkness; I did not say to the stock of *Yaakov*, "Seek Me out in a wasteland" – I *Hashem*, who foretell reliably, Who announce what is true.

יט לֹא בַסֵּתֶר דִּבַּרְתִּי בִּמְקוֹם אֶרֶץ חֹשֶׁךְ לֹא אָמַרְתִּי לְזֶרַע יַעֲקֹב תֹּהוּ בַקְּשׁוּנִי אֲנִי יְהֹוָה דֹּבֵר צֶדֶק מַגִּיד מֵישָׁרִים:

20 Come, gather together, Draw nigh, you remnants of the nations! No foreknowledge had they who carry their wooden images And pray to a god who cannot give success.

כ הִקָּבְצוּ וָבֹאוּ הִתְנַגְּשׁוּ יַחְדָּו פְּלִיטֵי הַגּוֹיִם לֹא יָדְעוּ הַנֹּשְׂאִים אֶת־עֵץ פִּסְלָם וּמִתְפַּלְלִים אֶל־אֵל לֹא יוֹשִׁיעַ:

21 Speak up, compare testimony – Let them even take counsel together! Who announced this aforetime, Foretold it of old? Was it not I *Hashem*? Then there is no god beside Me, No *Hashem* exists beside Me Who foretells truly and grants success.

כא הַגִּידוּ וְהַגִּישׁוּ אַף יִוָּעֲצוּ יַחְדָּו מִי הִשְׁמִיעַ זֹאת מִקֶּדֶם מֵאָז הִגִּידָהּ הֲלוֹא אֲנִי יְהֹוָה וְאֵין־עוֹד אֱלֹהִים מִבַּלְעָדַי אֵל־צַדִּיק וּמוֹשִׁיעַ אַיִן זוּלָתִי:

22 Turn to Me and gain success, All the ends of earth! For I am *Hashem*, and there is none else.

כב פְּנוּ־אֵלַי וְהִוָּשְׁעוּ כָּל־אַפְסֵי־אָרֶץ כִּי אֲנִי־אֵל וְאֵין עוֹד:

23 By Myself have I sworn, From My mouth has issued truth, A word that shall not turn back: To Me every knee shall bend, Every tongue swear loyalty.

כג בִּי נִשְׁבַּעְתִּי יָצָא מִפִּי צְדָקָה דָּבָר וְלֹא יָשׁוּב כִּי־לִי תִּכְרַע כָּל־בֶּרֶךְ תִּשָּׁבַע כָּל־לָשׁוֹן:

24 They shall say: "Only through *Hashem* Can I find victory and might. When people trust in Him, All their adversaries are put to shame.

כד אַךְ בַּיהֹוָה לִי אָמַר צְדָקוֹת וָעֹז עָדָיו יָבוֹא וְיֵבֹשׁוּ כֹּל הַנֶּחֱרִים בּוֹ:

25 It is through *Hashem* that all the offspring of *Yisrael* Have vindication and glory."

כה בַּיהֹוָה יִצְדְּקוּ וְיִתְהַלְלוּ כָּל־זֶרַע יִשְׂרָאֵל:

46 ¹ Bel is bowed, Nebo is cowering, Their images are a burden for beasts and cattle; The things you would carry [in procession] Are now piled as a burden On tired [beasts].

כָּרַע בֵּל קֹרֵס נְבוֹ הָיוּ עֲצַבֵּיהֶם לַחַיָּה וְלַבְּהֵמָה נְשֻׂאֹתֵיכֶם עֲמוּסוֹת מַשָּׂא לַעֲיֵפָה: א

² They cowered, they bowed as well, They could not rescue the burden, And they themselves went into captivity.

קָרְסוּ כָרְעוּ יַחְדָּו לֹא יָכְלוּ מַלֵּט מַשָּׂא וְנַפְשָׁם בַּשְּׁבִי הָלָכָה: ב

³ Listen to Me, O House of *Yaakov*, All that are left of the House of *Yisrael*, Who have been carried since birth, Supported since leaving the womb:

שִׁמְעוּ אֵלַי בֵּית יַעֲקֹב וְכָל־שְׁאֵרִית בֵּית יִשְׂרָאֵל הַעֲמֻסִים מִנִּי־בֶטֶן הַנְּשֻׂאִים מִנִּי־רָחַם: ג

⁴ Till you grow old, I will still be the same; When you turn gray, it is I who will carry; I was the Maker, and I will be the Bearer; And I will carry and rescue [you].

וְעַד־זִקְנָה אֲנִי הוּא וְעַד־שֵׂיבָה אֲנִי אֶסְבֹּל אֲנִי עָשִׂיתִי וַאֲנִי אֶשָּׂא וַאֲנִי אֶסְבֹּל וַאֲמַלֵּט: ד

⁵ To whom can you compare Me Or declare Me similar? To whom can you liken Me, So that we seem comparable?

לְמִי תְדַמְּיוּנִי וְתַשְׁווּ וְתַמְשִׁלוּנִי וְנִדְמֶה: ה

⁶ Those who squander gold from the purse And weigh out silver on the balance, They hire a metal worker to make it into a god, To which they bow down and prostrate themselves.

הַזָּלִים זָהָב מִכִּיס וְכֶסֶף בַּקָּנֶה יִשְׁקֹלוּ יִשְׂכְּרוּ צוֹרֵף וְיַעֲשֵׂהוּ אֵל יִסְגְּדוּ אַף־יִשְׁתַּחֲווּ: ו

⁷ They must carry it on their backs and transport it; When they put it down, it stands, It does not budge from its place. If they cry out to it, it does not answer; It cannot save them from their distress.

יִשָּׂאֻהוּ עַל־כָּתֵף יִסְבְּלֻהוּ וְיַנִּיחֻהוּ תַחְתָּיו וְיַעֲמֹד מִמְּקוֹמוֹ לֹא יָמִישׁ אַף־יִצְעַק אֵלָיו וְלֹא יַעֲנֶה מִצָּרָתוֹ לֹא יוֹשִׁיעֶנּוּ: ז

⁸ Keep this in mind, and stand firm! Take this to heart, you sinners!

זִכְרוּ־זֹאת וְהִתְאֹשָׁשׁוּ הָשִׁיבוּ פוֹשְׁעִים עַל־לֵב: ח

⁹ Bear in mind what happened of old; For I am *Hashem*, and there is none else, I am divine, and there is none like Me.

זִכְרוּ רִאשֹׁנוֹת מֵעוֹלָם כִּי אָנֹכִי אֵל וְאֵין עוֹד אֱלֹהִים וְאֶפֶס כָּמוֹנִי: ט

¹⁰ I foretell the end from the beginning, And from the start, things that had not occurred. I say: My plan shall be fulfilled; I will do all I have purposed.

מַגִּיד מֵרֵאשִׁית אַחֲרִית וּמִקֶּדֶם אֲשֶׁר לֹא־נַעֲשׂוּ אֹמֵר עֲצָתִי תָקוּם וְכָל־חֶפְצִי אֶעֱשֶׂה: י

¹¹ I summoned that swooping bird from the East; From a distant land, the man for My purpose. I have spoken, so I will bring it to pass; I have designed it, so I will complete it.

קֹרֵא מִמִּזְרָח עַיִט מֵאֶרֶץ מֶרְחָק אִישׁ עצתו [עֲצָתִי] אַף־דִּבַּרְתִּי אַף־אֲבִיאֶנָּה יְצַרְתִּי אַף־אֶעֱשֶׂנָּה: יא

¹² Listen to Me, you stubborn of heart, Who are far from victory:

שִׁמְעוּ אֵלַי אַבִּירֵי לֵב הָרְחוֹקִים מִצְּדָקָה: יב

13 I am bringing My victory close; It shall not be far,
And My triumph shall not be delayed. I will grant
triumph in *Tzion* To *Yisrael*, in whom I glory.

יג קֵרַ֤בְתִּי צִדְקָתִי֙ לֹ֣א תִרְחָ֔ק וּתְשׁוּעָתִ֖י
לֹ֣א תְאַחֵ֑ר וְנָתַתִּ֤י בְצִיּוֹן֙ תְּשׁוּעָ֔ה
לְיִשְׂרָאֵ֖ל תִּפְאַרְתִּֽי׃

*kay-RAV-tee tzid-ka-TEE LO tir-KHAK ut-shu-a-TEE LO t'-a-KHAYR
v'-na-ta-TEE v'-tzi-YON t'-shu-AH l'-yis-ra-AYL tif-ar-TEE*

47 1 Get down, sit in the dust, Fair Maiden Babylon;
Sit, dethroned, on the ground, O Fair Chaldea;
Nevermore shall they call you The tender and
dainty one.

מז א רְדִ֣י ׀ וּשְׁבִ֣י עַל־עָפָ֗ר בְּתוּלַת֙ בַּת־בָּבֶ֔ל
שְׁבִי־לָאָ֥רֶץ אֵין־כִּסֵּ֖א בַּת־כַּשְׂדִּ֑ים כִּ֣י לֹ֣א
תוֹסִ֔יפִי יִקְרְאוּ־לָ֖ךְ רַכָּ֥ה וַעֲנֻגָּֽה׃

2 Grasp the handmill and grind meal. Remove
your veil, Strip off your train, bare your leg, Wade
through the rivers.

ב קְחִ֧י רֵחַ֛יִם וְטַ֥חֲנִי קָ֑מַח גַּלִּ֤י צַמָּתֵךְ֙
חֶשְׂפִּי־שֹׁ֙בֶל֙ גַּלִּי־שׁ֔וֹק עִבְרִ֖י נְהָרֽוֹת׃

3 Your nakedness shall be uncovered, And your
shame shall be exposed. I will take vengeance, And
let no man intercede.

ג תִּגָּל֙ עֶרְוָתֵ֔ךְ גַּ֥ם תֵּרָאֶ֖ה חֶרְפָּתֵ֑ךְ נָקָ֣ם
אֶקָּ֔ח וְלֹ֥א אֶפְגַּ֖ע אָדָֽם׃

4 Our Redeemer – LORD of Hosts is His name – Is
the Holy One of *Yisrael*.

ד גֹּאֲלֵ֕נוּ יְהֹוָ֥ה צְבָא֖וֹת שְׁמ֑וֹ קְד֖וֹשׁ
יִשְׂרָאֵֽל׃

go-a-LAY-nu a-do-NAI tz'-va-OT sh'-MO k'-DOSH yis-ra-AYL

5 Sit silent; retire into darkness, O Fair Chaldea;
Nevermore shall they call you Mistress of
Kingdoms.

ה שְׁבִ֤י דוּמָם֙ וּבֹ֣אִי בַחֹ֔שֶׁךְ בַּת־כַּשְׂדִּ֑ים כִּ֣י
לֹ֣א תוֹסִ֔יפִי יִקְרְאוּ־לָ֖ךְ גְּבֶ֥רֶת מַמְלָכֽוֹת׃

6 I was angry at My people, I defiled My heritage; I
put them into your hands, But you showed them
no mercy. Even upon the aged you made Your yoke
exceedingly heavy.

ו קָצַ֤פְתִּי עַל־עַמִּי֙ חִלַּ֣לְתִּי נַחֲלָתִ֔י וָאֶתְּנֵ֖ם
בְּיָדֵ֑ךְ לֹא־שַׂ֤מְתְּ לָהֶם֙ רַחֲמִ֔ים עַל־זָקֵ֕ן
הִכְבַּ֥דְתְּ עֻלֵּ֖ךְ מְאֹֽד׃

7 You thought, "I shall always be The mistress still."
You did not take these things to heart, You gave no
thought to the end of it.

ז וַתֹּ֣אמְרִ֔י לְעוֹלָ֖ם אֶהְיֶ֣ה גְבָ֑רֶת עַ֣ד לֹא־
שַׂ֤מְתְּ אֵ֙לֶּה֙ עַל־לִבֵּ֔ךְ לֹ֥א זָכַ֖רְתְּ אַחֲרִיתָֽהּ׃

Yerushalayim

 46:13 I will grant triumph in *Tzion* to *Yisrael*, in whom I glory In the Bible, the word *Tzion* often refers to *Yerushalayim*. Reflecting upon the significance of the holy city, Holocaust survivor and Nobel prize winner Elie Wiesel said, "Jerusalem must remain the world's Jewish spiritual capital, not a symbol of anguish and bitterness, but a symbol of trust and hope. As the Hasidic master Rebbe Nahman of Bratslav said, 'Everything in this world has a heart; the heart itself has its own heart.' Jerusalem is the heart of our heart, the soul of our soul."

47:4 Our Redeemer – LORD of Hosts is His name *Yeshayahu* portrays Babylon in its humiliation as a female in deep distress, working at a wheel, exposed in the marketplace. Suddenly, Israel (or *Yeshayahu* himself) exclaims, "Our Redeemer – LORD of hosts is His name, the Holy One of *Yisrael*." This highlights the difference between Israel and Babylon. Though punished and exiled, *Hashem* is always present for the Israelites, offering hope and encouragement that they will be redeemed and returned to their land. Babylon, on the other hand, remains friendless and alone.

Isaiah

Isaiah

8 And now hear this, O pampered one – Who dwell in security, Who think to yourself, "I am, and there is none but me; I shall not become a widow Or know loss of children" –

ח וְעַתָּה שִׁמְעִי־זֹאת עֲדִינָה הַיּוֹשֶׁבֶת לָבֶטַח הָאֹמְרָה בִּלְבָבָהּ אֲנִי וְאַפְסִי עוֹד לֹא אֵשֵׁב אַלְמָנָה וְלֹא אֵדַע שְׁכוֹל:

9 These two things shall come upon you,Suddenly, in one day: Loss of children and widowhood Shall come upon you in full measure, Despite your many enchantments And all your countless spells.

ט וְתָבֹאנָה לָּךְ שְׁתֵּי־אֵלֶּה רֶגַע בְּיוֹם אֶחָד שְׁכוֹל וְאַלְמֹן כְּתֻמָּם בָּאוּ עָלַיִךְ בְּרֹב כְּשָׁפַיִךְ בְּעָצְמַת חֲבָרַיִךְ מְאֹד:

10 You were secure in your wickedness; You thought, "No one can see me." It was your skill and your science That led you astray. And you thought to yourself, "I am, and there is none but me."

י וַתִּבְטְחִי בְרָעָתֵךְ אָמַרְתְּ אֵין רֹאָנִי חָכְמָתֵךְ וְדַעְתֵּךְ הִיא שׁוֹבְבָתֶךְ וַתֹּאמְרִי בְלִבֵּךְ אֲנִי וְאַפְסִי עוֹד:

11 Evil is coming upon you Which you will not know how to charm away; Disaster is falling upon you Which you will not be able to appease; Coming upon you suddenly Is ruin of which you know nothing.

יא וּבָא עָלַיִךְ רָעָה לֹא תֵדְעִי שַׁחְרָהּ וְתִפֹּל עָלַיִךְ הֹוָה לֹא תוּכְלִי כַּפְּרָהּ וְתָבֹא עָלַיִךְ פִּתְאֹם שׁוֹאָה לֹא תֵדָעִי:

12 Stand up, with your spells and your many enchantments On which you labored since youth! Perhaps you'll be able to profit, Perhaps you will find strength.

יב עִמְדִי־נָא בַחֲבָרַיִךְ וּבְרֹב כְּשָׁפַיִךְ בַּאֲשֶׁר יָגַעַתְּ מִנְּעוּרָיִךְ אוּלַי תּוּכְלִי הוֹעִיל אוּלַי תַּעֲרוֹצִי:

13 You are helpless, despite all your art. Let them stand up and help you now, Th scanners of heaven, the star-gazers, Who announce, month by month, Whatever will come upon you.

יג נִלְאֵית בְּרֹב עֲצָתָיִךְ יַעַמְדוּ־נָא וְיוֹשִׁיעֻךְ הַברו [הֹבְרֵי] שָׁמַיִם הַחֹזִים בַּכּוֹכָבִים מוֹדִיעִם לֶחֳדָשִׁים מֵאֲשֶׁר יָבֹאוּ עָלָיִךְ:

14 See, they are become like straw, Fire consumes them; They cannot save themselves From the power of the flame; This is no coal for warming oneself, No fire to sit by!

יד הִנֵּה הָיוּ כְקַשׁ אֵשׁ שְׂרָפָתַם לֹא־יַצִּילוּ אֶת־נַפְשָׁם מִיַּד לֶהָבָה אֵין־גַּחֶלֶת לַחְמָם אוּר לָשֶׁבֶת נֶגְדּוֹ:

15 This is what they have profited you – The traders you dealt with since youth – Each has wandered off his own way, There is none to save you. ı

טו כֵּן הָיוּ־לָךְ אֲשֶׁר יָגָעַתְּ סֹחֲרַיִךְ מִנְּעוּרַיִךְ אִישׁ לְעֶבְרוֹ תָּעוּ אֵין מוֹשִׁיעֵךְ:

48 ¹ Listen to this, O House of *Yaakov*, Who bear the name *Yisrael* And have issued from the waters of *Yehuda*, Who swear by the name of *Hashem* And invoke the God of *Yisrael* – Though not in truth and sincerity –

ח א שִׁמְעוּ־זֹאת בֵּית־יַעֲקֹב הַנִּקְרָאִים בְּשֵׁם יִשְׂרָאֵל וּמִמֵּי יְהוּדָה יָצָאוּ הַנִּשְׁבָּעִים בְּשֵׁם יְהֹוָה וּבֵאלֹהֵי יִשְׂרָאֵל יַזְכִּירוּ לֹא בֶאֱמֶת וְלֹא בִצְדָקָה:

2 For you are called after the Holy City And you do lean on the God of *Yisrael*, Whose name is LORD of Hosts:

ב כִּי־מֵעִיר הַקֹּדֶשׁ נִקְרָאוּ וְעַל־אֱלֹהֵי יִשְׂרָאֵל נִסְמָכוּ יְהֹוָה צְבָאוֹת שְׁמוֹ:

3 Long ago, I foretold things that happened, From My mouth they issued, and I announced them; Suddenly I acted, and they came to pass.

ג הָרִאשֹׁנוֹת מֵאָז הִגַּדְתִּי וּמִפִּי יָצָאוּ וְאַשְׁמִיעֵם פִּתְאֹם עָשִׂיתִי וַתָּבֹאנָה:

⁴ Because I know how stubborn you are (Your neck is like an iron sinew And your forehead bronze),

ד מִדַּעְתִּי כִּי קָשֶׁה אָתָּה וְגִיד בַּרְזֶל עָרְפֶּךָ וּמִצְחֲךָ נְחוּשָׁה:

⁵ Therefore I told you long beforehand, Announced things to you ere they happened – That you might not say, "My idol caused them, My carved and molten images ordained them."

ה וָאַגִּיד לְךָ מֵאָז בְּטֶרֶם תָּבוֹא הִשְׁמַעְתִּיךָ פֶּן־תֹּאמַר עָצְבִּי עָשָׂם וּפִסְלִי וְנִסְכִּי צִוָּם:

⁶ You have heard all this; look, must you not acknowledge it? As of now, I announce to you new things, Well-guarded secrets you did not know.

ו שָׁמַעְתָּ חֲזֵה כֻּלָּהּ וְאַתֶּם הֲלוֹא תַגִּידוּ הִשְׁמַעְתִּיךָ חֲדָשׁוֹת מֵעַתָּה וּנְצֻרוֹת וְלֹא יְדַעְתָּם:

⁷ Only now are they created, and not of old; Before today you had not heard them; You cannot say, "I knew them already."

ז עַתָּה נִבְרְאוּ וְלֹא מֵאָז וְלִפְנֵי־יוֹם וְלֹא שְׁמַעְתָּם פֶּן־תֹּאמַר הִנֵּה יְדַעְתִּין:

⁸ You had never heard, you had never known, Your ears were not opened of old. Though I know that you are treacherous, That you were called a rebel from birth,

ח גַּם לֹא־שָׁמַעְתָּ גַּם לֹא יָדַעְתָּ גַּם מֵאָז לֹא־פִתְּחָה אָזְנֶךָ כִּי יָדַעְתִּי בָּגוֹד תִּבְגּוֹד וּפֹשֵׁעַ מִבֶּטֶן קֹרָא לָךְ:

⁹ For the sake of My name I control My wrath; To My own glory, I am patient with you, And I will not destroy you.

ט לְמַעַן שְׁמִי אַאֲרִיךְ אַפִּי וּתְהִלָּתִי אֶחֱטָם־לָךְ לְבִלְתִּי הַכְרִיתֶךָ:

¹⁰ See, I refine you, but not as silver; I test you in the furnace of affliction.

י הִנֵּה צְרַפְתִּיךָ וְלֹא בְכָסֶף בְּחַרְתִּיךָ בְּכוּר עֹנִי:

¹¹ For My sake, My own sake, do I act – Lest [My name] be dishonored! I will not give My glory to another.

יא לְמַעֲנִי לְמַעֲנִי אֶעֱשֶׂה כִּי אֵיךְ יֵחָל וּכְבוֹדִי לְאַחֵר לֹא־אֶתֵּן:

¹² Listen to Me, O *Yaakov, Yisrael*, whom I have called: I am He – I am the first, And I am the last as well.

יב שְׁמַע אֵלַי יַעֲקֹב וְיִשְׂרָאֵל מְקֹרָאִי אֲנִי־הוּא אֲנִי רִאשׁוֹן אַף אֲנִי אַחֲרוֹן:

¹³ My own hand founded the earth, My right hand spread out the skies. I call unto them, let them stand up.

יג אַף־יָדִי יָסְדָה אֶרֶץ וִימִינִי טִפְּחָה שָׁמָיִם קֹרֵא אֲנִי אֲלֵיהֶם יַעַמְדוּ יַחְדָּו:

¹⁴ Assemble, all of you, and listen! Who among you foretold these things: "He whom *Hashem* loves Shall work His will against Babylon, And, with His might, against Chaldea"?

יד הִקָּבְצוּ כֻלְּכֶם וּשְׁמָעוּ מִי בָהֶם הִגִּיד אֶת־אֵלֶּה יְהוָה אֲהֵבוֹ יַעֲשֶׂה חֶפְצוֹ בְּבָבֶל וּזְרֹעוֹ כַּשְׂדִּים:

¹⁵ I, I predicted, and I called him; I have brought him and he shall succeed in his mission.

טו אֲנִי אֲנִי דִּבַּרְתִּי אַף־קְרָאתִיו הֲבִיאֹתִיו וְהִצְלִיחַ דַּרְכּוֹ:

¹⁶ Draw near to Me and hear this: From the beginning, I did not speak in secret; From the time anything existed, I was there. "And now *Hashem* has sent me, endowed with His spirit."

טז קִרְבוּ אֵלַי שִׁמְעוּ־זֹאת לֹא מֵרֹאשׁ בַּסֵּתֶר דִּבַּרְתִּי מֵעֵת הֱיוֹתָהּ שָׁם אָנִי וְעַתָּה אֲדֹנָי יְהוִה שְׁלָחַנִי וְרוּחוֹ:

¹⁷ Thus said *Hashem* your Redeemer, The Holy One of *Yisrael*: I Ha3shem am your God, Instructing you for your own benefit. Guiding you in the way you should go.

יז כֹּה־אָמַר יְהוָה גֹּאַלְךָ קְדוֹשׁ יִשְׂרָאֵל אֲנִי יְהוָה אֱלֹהֶיךָ מְלַמֶּדְךָ לְהוֹעִיל מַדְרִיכֲךָ בְּדֶרֶךְ תֵּלֵךְ:

Isaiah

Isaiah

18 If only you would heed My commands! Then your prosperity would be like a river, Your triumph like the waves of the sea.

יח לוּא הִקְשַׁבְתָּ לְמִצְוֺתָי וַיְהִי כַנָּהָר שְׁלוֹמֶךָ וְצִדְקָתְךָ כְּגַלֵּי הַיָּם:

19 Your offspring would be as many as the sand, Their issue as many as its grains. Their name would never be cut off Or obliterated from before Me.

יט וַיְהִי כַחוֹל זַרְעֶךָ וְצֶאֱצָאֵי מֵעֶיךָ כִּמְעֹתָיו לֹא־יִכָּרֵת וְלֹא־יִשָּׁמֵד שְׁמוֹ מִלְּפָנָי:

20 Go forth from Babylon, Flee from Chaldea! Declare this with loud shouting, Announce this, Bring out the word to the ends of the earth! Say: "*Hashem* has redeemed His servant *Yaakov*!"

כ צְאוּ מִבָּבֶל בִּרְחוּ מִכַּשְׂדִּים בְּקוֹל רִנָּה הַגִּידוּ הַשְׁמִיעוּ זֹאת הוֹצִיאוּהָ עַד־קְצֵה הָאָרֶץ אִמְרוּ גָּאַל יְהוָה עַבְדּוֹ יַעֲקֹב:

21 They have known no thirst, Though He led them through parched places; He made water flow for them from the rock; He cleaved the rock and water gushed forth.

כא וְלֹא צָמְאוּ בָּחֳרָבוֹת הוֹלִיכָם מַיִם מִצּוּר הִזִּיל לָמוֹ וַיִּבְקַע־צוּר וַיָּזֻבוּ מָיִם:

22 There is no safety – said *Hashem* – for the wicked.

כב אֵין שָׁלוֹם אָמַר יְהוָה לָרְשָׁעִים:

AYN sha-LOM a-MAR a-do-NAI la-r'-sha-EEM

49 1 Listen, O coastlands, to me, And give heed, O nations afar: *Hashem* appointed me before I was born, He named me while I was in my mother's womb.

א שִׁמְעוּ אִיִּים אֵלַי וְהַקְשִׁיבוּ לְאֻמִּים מֵרָחוֹק יְהוָה מִבֶּטֶן קְרָאָנִי מִמְּעֵי אִמִּי הִזְכִּיר שְׁמִי:

2 He made my mouth like a sharpened blade, He hid me in the shadow of His hand, And He made me like a polished arrow; He concealed me in His quiver.

ב וַיָּשֶׂם פִּי כְּחֶרֶב חַדָּה בְּצֵל יָדוֹ הֶחְבִּיאָנִי וַיְשִׂימֵנִי לְחֵץ בָּרוּר בְּאַשְׁפָּתוֹ הִסְתִּירָנִי:

3 And He said to me, "You are My servant, *Yisrael* in whom I glory."

ג וַיֹּאמֶר לִי עַבְדִּי־אָתָּה יִשְׂרָאֵל אֲשֶׁר־בְּךָ אֶתְפָּאָר:

4 I thought, "I have labored in vain, I have spent my strength for empty breath." But my case rested with *Hashem*, My recompense was in the hands of my God.

ד וַאֲנִי אָמַרְתִּי לְרִיק יָגַעְתִּי לְתֹהוּ וְהֶבֶל כֹּחִי כִלֵּיתִי אָכֵן מִשְׁפָּטִי אֶת־יְהוָה וּפְעֻלָּתִי אֶת־אֱלֹהָי:

5 And now *Hashem* has resolved – He who formed me in the womb to be His servant – To bring back *Yaakov* to Himself, That *Yisrael* may be restored to Him. And I have been honored in the sight of *Hashem*, My *Hashem* has been my strength.

ה וְעַתָּה אָמַר יְהוָה יֹצְרִי מִבֶּטֶן לְעֶבֶד לוֹ לְשׁוֹבֵב יַעֲקֹב אֵלָיו וְיִשְׂרָאֵל לֹא [לוֹ] יֵאָסֵף וְאֶכָּבֵד בְּעֵינֵי יְהוָה וֵאלֹהַי הָיָה עֻזִּי:

 48:22 There is no safety *Yeshayahu* provides a triumphant account of the future journey out of Babylon and the return to Israel. In verse 21, he even includes allusions to the original journey through the desert to the Land of Israel. He concludes the section with the brief statement, "There is no safety – said *Hashem* – for the wicked." Most commentators suggest that this is a continuation of the above contrast between Israel and Babylon; while Israel is redeemed, the wicked Babylon will find no peace. The commentator *Ibn Ezra*, however, suggests that "the wicked" refers to the Jews who refuse to leave Babylon when they have the opportunity, choosing to live among an idolatrous people rather than return to the Holy Land.

New Jewish immigrants arriving at Ben Gurion airport

Isaiah

6 For He has said: "It is too little that you should be My servant In that I raise up the tribes of *Yaakov* And restore the survivors of *Yisrael*: I will also make you a light of nations, That My salvation may reach the ends of the earth."

ו וַיֹּאמֶר נָקֵל מִהְיוֹתְךָ לִי עֶבֶד לְהָקִים אֶת־שִׁבְטֵי יַעֲקֹב ונצירי [וּנְצוּרֵי] יִשְׂרָאֵל לְהָשִׁיב וּנְתַתִּיךָ לְאוֹר גּוֹיִם לִהְיוֹת יְשׁוּעָתִי עַד־קְצֵה הָאָרֶץ:

7 Thus said *Hashem*, The Redeemer of *Yisrael*, his Holy One, To the despised one, To the abhorred nations, To the slave of rulers: Kings shall see and stand up; Nobles, and they shall prostrate themselves – To the honor of *Hashem*, who is faithful, To the Holy One of *Yisrael* who chose you.

ז כֹּה אָמַר־יְהֹוָה גֹּאֵל יִשְׂרָאֵל קְדוֹשׁוֹ לִבְזֹה־נֶפֶשׁ לִמְתָעֵב גּוֹי לְעֶבֶד מֹשְׁלִים מְלָכִים יִרְאוּ וָקָמוּ שָׂרִים וְיִשְׁתַּחֲווּ לְמַעַן יְהֹוָה אֲשֶׁר נֶאֱמָן קְדֹשׁ יִשְׂרָאֵל וַיִּבְחָרֶךָ:

8 Thus said *Hashem*: In an hour of favor I answer you, And on a day of salvation I help you – I created you and appointed you a covenant people – Restoring the land, Allotting anew the desolate holdings,

ח כֹּה אָמַר יְהֹוָה בְּעֵת רָצוֹן עֲנִיתִיךָ וּבְיוֹם יְשׁוּעָה עֲזַרְתִּיךָ וְאֶצָּרְךָ וְאֶתֶּנְךָ לִבְרִית עָם לְהָקִים אֶרֶץ לְהַנְחִיל נְחָלוֹת שֹׁמֵמוֹת:

9 Saying to the prisoners, "Go free," To those who are in darkness, "Show yourselves." They shall pasture along the roads, On every bare height shall be their pasture.

ט לֵאמֹר לַאֲסוּרִים צֵאוּ לַאֲשֶׁר בַּחֹשֶׁךְ הִגָּלוּ עַל־דְּרָכִים יִרְעוּ וּבְכָל־שְׁפָיִים מַרְעִיתָם:

10 They shall not hunger or thirst, Hot wind and sun shall not strike them; For He who loves them will lead them, He will guide them to springs of water.

י לֹא יִרְעָבוּ וְלֹא יִצְמָאוּ וְלֹא־יַכֵּם שָׁרָב וָשָׁמֶשׁ כִּי־מְרַחֲמָם יְנַהֲגֵם וְעַל־מַבּוּעֵי מַיִם יְנַהֲלֵם:

11 I will make all My mountains a road, And My highways shall be built up.

יא וְשַׂמְתִּי כָל־הָרַי לַדָּרֶךְ וּמְסִלֹּתַי יְרֻמוּן:

12 Look! These are coming from afar, These from the north and the west, And these from the land of Sinim.

יב הִנֵּה־אֵלֶּה מֵרָחוֹק יָבֹאוּ וְהִנֵּה־אֵלֶּה מִצָּפוֹן וּמִיָּם וְאֵלֶּה מֵאֶרֶץ סִינִים:

13 Shout, O heavens, and rejoice, O earth! Break into shouting, O hills! For *Hashem* has comforted His people, And has taken back His afflicted ones in love.

יג רָנּוּ שָׁמַיִם וְגִילִי אָרֶץ יפצחו [וּפִצְחוּ] הָרִים רִנָּה כִּי־נִחַם יְהֹוָה עַמּוֹ וַעֲנִיָּו יְרַחֵם:

14 *Tzion* says, "*Hashem* has forsaken me, My Lord has forgotten me."

יד וַתֹּאמֶר צִיּוֹן עֲזָבַנִי יְהֹוָה וַאדֹנָי שְׁכֵחָנִי:

15 Can a woman forget her baby, Or disown the child of her womb? Though she might forget, I never could forget you.

טו הֲתִשְׁכַּח אִשָּׁה עוּלָהּ מֵרַחֵם בֶּן־בִּטְנָהּ גַּם־אֵלֶּה תִשְׁכַּחְנָה וְאָנֹכִי לֹא אֶשְׁכָּחֵךְ:

ha-tish-KAKH i-SHAH u-LAH may-ra-KHAYM ben bit-NAH gam AY-leh tish-KAKH-nah v'-a-no-KHEE lo esh-ka-KHAYKH

49:15 I never could forget you The relationship between *Hashem* and the Children of Israel is often compared to that of a husband and wife. There is, however, an additional element to the relationship; that of a parent and a child. While husbands and wives can fall out of love and the relationship can be formally ended, the mother who carries and gives birth to a child will always be that child's mother. In verse 14, Israel expresses its feelings of being abandoned and forgotten by *Hashem*. God responds in this verse by saying that His love for the Children of Israel is even deeper than a mother's love for her child, and promises that He could never forget His people.

Mother and daughter enjoying Israel's scenery

Isaiah

16 See, I have engraved you On the palms of My hands, Your walls are ever before Me.

טז הֵן עַל־כַּפַּיִם חַקֹּתִיךְ חוֹמֹתַיִךְ נֶגְדִּי תָּמִיד:

17 Swiftly your children are coming; Those who ravaged and ruined you shall leave you.

יז מִהֲרוּ בָּנָיִךְ מְהָרְסַיִךְ וּמַחֲרִבַיִךְ מִמֵּךְ יֵצֵאוּ:

18 Look up all around you and see: They are all assembled, are come to you! As I live – declares *Hashem* – You shall don them all like jewels, Deck yourself with them like a bride.

יח שְׂאִי־סָבִיב עֵינַיִךְ וּרְאִי כֻּלָּם נִקְבְּצוּ בָאוּ־לָךְ חַי־אָנִי נְאֻם־יְהוָה כִּי כֻלָּם כָּעֲדִי תִלְבָּשִׁי וּתְקַשְּׁרִים כַּכַּלָּה:

19 As for your ruins and desolate places And your land laid waste – You shall soon be crowded with settlers, While destroyers stay far from you.

יט כִּי חָרְבֹתַיִךְ וְשֹׁמְמֹתַיִךְ וְאֶרֶץ הֲרִסֻתֵיךְ כִּי עַתָּה תֵּצְרִי מִיּוֹשֵׁב וְרָחֲקוּ מְבַלְּעָיִךְ:

20 The children you thought you had lost Shall yet say in your hearing, "The place is too crowded for me; Make room for me to settle."

כ עוֹד יֹאמְרוּ בְאָזְנַיִךְ בְּנֵי שִׁכֻּלָיִךְ צַר־לִי הַמָּקוֹם גְּשָׁה־לִּי וְאֵשֵׁבָה:

21 And you will say to yourself, "Who bore these for me When I was bereaved and barren, Exiled and disdained – By whom, then, were these reared? I was left all alone – And where have these been?"

כא וְאָמַרְתְּ בִּלְבָבֵךְ מִי יָלַד־לִי אֶת־אֵלֶּה וַאֲנִי שְׁכוּלָה וְגַלְמוּדָה גֹּלָה וְסוּרָה וְאֵלֶּה מִי גִדֵּל הֵן אֲנִי נִשְׁאַרְתִּי לְבַדִּי אֵלֶּה אֵיפֹה הֵם:

22 Thus said *Hashem*: I will raise My hand to nations And lift up My ensign to peoples; And they shall bring your sons in their bosoms, And carry your daughters on their backs.

כב כֹּה־אָמַר אֲדֹנָי יְהוִה הִנֵּה אֶשָּׂא אֶל־גּוֹיִם יָדִי וְאֶל־עַמִּים אָרִים נִסִּי וְהֵבִיאוּ בָנַיִךְ בְּחֹצֶן וּבְנֹתַיִךְ עַל־כָּתֵף תִּנָּשֶׂאנָה:

*koh a-MAR a-do-NAI e-lo-HEEM hi-NAY e-SA el go-YIM
ya-DEE v'-el a-MEEM a-REEM ni-SEE v'-hay-VEE-u va-NA-yikh
b'-KHO-tzen uv-no-TA-yikh al ka-TAYF ti-na-SE-na*

23 Kings shall tend your children, Their queens shall serve you as nurses. They shall bow to you, face to the ground, And lick the dust of your feet. And you shall know that I am *Hashem* – Those who trust in Me shall not be shamed.

כג וְהָיוּ מְלָכִים אֹמְנַיִךְ וְשָׂרוֹתֵיהֶם מֵינִיקֹתַיִךְ אַפַּיִם אֶרֶץ יִשְׁתַּחֲווּ לָךְ וַעֲפַר רַגְלַיִךְ יְלַחֵכוּ וְיָדַעַתְּ כִּי־אֲנִי יְהוָה אֲשֶׁר לֹא־יֵבֹשׁוּ קֹוָי:

24 Can spoil be taken from a warrior, Or captives retrieved from a victor?

כד הֲיֻקַּח מִגִּבּוֹר מַלְקוֹחַ וְאִם־שְׁבִי צַדִּיק יִמָּלֵט:

Major-General
Orde Charles
Wingate
(1903–1944)

49:22 And they shall bring your sons in their bosoms *Yeshayahu* describes the great contributions that the nations and individual non-Jews will play in the resettlement of *Eretz Yisrael*. In modern times, this prophecy is being fulfilled by the unprecedented number of non-Jews who visit, support and pray for Israel. Great individual Christian warriors for *Tzion* have also emerged to fulfill *Yeshayahu's* prophecy. For example, Major-General Orde Charles Wingate

(1903–1944) was a British officer in Palestine during the Mandate, and trained many of the future leaders of the Israeli army. He drew on his love and knowledge of the Bible, and distilled strategies from the battles of *Yehoshua*, *Gidon* and King *David*. Known throughout Israel as "*ha-yedid*" (הידיד) or, 'the friend,' the Jewish people remember Orde Wingate and all the righteous non-Jews whose love for the Bible drove them to stand with Israel in her moment of need.

25 Yet thus said *Hashem*: Captives shall be taken from a warrior And spoil shall be retrieved from a tyrant; For I will contend with your adversaries, And I will deliver your children.

כה כִּי־כֹה אָמַר יְהֹוָה גַּם־שְׁבִי גִבּוֹר יֻקָּח וּמַלְקוֹחַ עָרִיץ יִמָּלֵט וְאֶת־יְרִיבֵךְ אָנֹכִי אָרִיב וְאֶת־בָּנַיִךְ אָנֹכִי אוֹשִׁיעַ:

26 I will make your oppressors eat their own flesh, They shall be drunk with their own blood as with wine. And all mankind shall know That I *Hashem* am your Savior, The Mighty One of *Yaakov*, your Redeemer.

כו וְהַאֲכַלְתִּי אֶת־מוֹנַיִךְ אֶת־בְּשָׂרָם וְכֶעָסִיס דָּמָם יִשְׁכָּרוּן וְיָדְעוּ כָל־בָּשָׂר כִּי אֲנִי יְהֹוָה מוֹשִׁיעֵךְ וְגֹאֲלֵךְ אֲבִיר יַעֲקֹב:

50 ¹ Thus said *Hashem*: Where is the bill of divorce Of your mother whom I dismissed? And which of My creditors was it To whom I sold you off? You were only sold off for your sins, And your mother dismissed for your crimes.

נ א כֹּה אָמַר יְהֹוָה אֵי זֶה סֵפֶר כְּרִיתוּת אִמְּכֶם אֲשֶׁר שִׁלַּחְתִּיהָ אוֹ מִי מִנּוֹשַׁי אֲשֶׁר־מָכַרְתִּי אֶתְכֶם לוֹ הֵן בַּעֲוֹנֹתֵיכֶם נִמְכַּרְתֶּם וּבְפִשְׁעֵיכֶם שֻׁלְּחָה אִמְּכֶם:

KOH a-MAR a-do-NAI AY ZEH SAY-fer k'-ree-TUT i-m'-KHEM a-SHER shi-lakh-TEE-ha O MEE mi-no-SHAI a-sher ma-KHAR-tee et-KHEM LO HAYN ba-a-vo-no-tay-KHEM nim-kar-TEM uv-fish-ay-KHEM shu-l'-KHAH i-m'-KHEM

² Why, when I came, was no one there, Why, when I called, would none respond? Is my arm, then, too short to rescue, Have I not the power to save? With a mere rebuke I dry up the sea, And turn rivers into desert. Their fish stink from lack of water; They lie dead of thirst.

ב מַדּוּעַ בָּאתִי וְאֵין אִישׁ קָרָאתִי וְאֵין עוֹנֶה הֲקָצוֹר קָצְרָה יָדִי מִפְּדוּת וְאִם־ אֵין־בִּי כֹחַ לְהַצִּיל הֵן בְּגַעֲרָתִי אַחֲרִיב יָם אָשִׂים נְהָרוֹת מִדְבָּר תִּבְאַשׁ דְּגָתָם מֵאֵין מַיִם וְתָמֹת בַּצָּמָא:

³ I clothe the skies in blackness And make their raiment sackcloth.

ג אַלְבִּישׁ שָׁמַיִם קַדְרוּת וְשַׂק אָשִׂים כְּסוּתָם:

⁴ *Hashem* gave me a skilled tongue, To know how to speak timely words to the weary. Morning by morning, He rouses, He rouses my ear To give heed like disciples.

ד אֲדֹנָי יְהֹוִה נָתַן לִי לְשׁוֹן לִמּוּדִים לָדַעַת לָעוּת אֶת־יָעֵף דָּבָר יָעִיר בַּבֹּקֶר בַּבֹּקֶר יָעִיר לִי אֹזֶן לִשְׁמֹעַ כַּלִּמּוּדִים:

⁵ *Hashem* opened my ears And I did not disobey, I did not run away.

ה אֲדֹנָי יְהֹוִה פָּתַח־לִי אֹזֶן וְאָנֹכִי לֹא מָרִיתִי אָחוֹר לֹא נְסוּגֹתִי:

⁶ I offered my back to the floggers, And my cheeks to those who tore out my hair. I did not hide my face From insult and spittle.

ו גֵּוִי נָתַתִּי לְמַכִּים וּלְחָיַי לְמֹרְטִים פָּנַי לֹא הִסְתַּרְתִּי מִכְּלִמּוֹת וָרֹק:

50:1 Where is the bill of divorce of your mother whom I dismissed? The prophets traditionally compare the relationship between *Hashem* and the Jewish people to that of a marriage, and to that of a parent and child. Having been exiled, Israel has good reason to fear that they have been divorced from God, or sold (see Psalms 44:13). However, *Hashem* assures His people that he has not written them a bill of divorce, nor has He sold them for any price. Despite everything, the People of Israel are still *Hashem*'s children and the objects of His affection. The bond between God and Israel is eternal, and their claim to *Eretz Yisrael*, which He gave them, will never be uprooted.

Smiling bride and groom

Isaiah

7 But *Hashem* will help me – Therefore I feel no disgrace; Therefore I have set my face like flint, And I know I shall not be shamed.

ז וַאדֹנָי יֱהוִֹה יַעֲזָר־לִי עַל־כֵּן לֹא נִכְלָמְתִּי עַל־כֵּן שַׂמְתִּי פָנַי כַּחַלָּמִישׁ וָאֵדַע כִּי־לֹא אֵבוֹשׁ:

8 My Vindicator is at hand – Who dares contend with me? Let us stand up together! Who would be my opponent? Let him approach me!

ח קָרוֹב מַצְדִּיקִי מִי־יָרִיב אִתִּי נַעַמְדָה יָּחַד מִי־בַעַל מִשְׁפָּטִי יִגַּשׁ אֵלָי:

9 Lo, *Hashem* will help me – Who can get a verdict against me? They shall all wear out like a garment, The moth shall consume them.

ט הֵן אֲדֹנָי יֱהוִֹה יַעֲזָר־לִי מִי־הוּא יַרְשִׁיעֵנִי הֵן כֻּלָּם כַּבֶּגֶד יִבְלוּ עָשׁ יֹאכְלֵם:

10 Who among you reveres *Hashem* And heeds the voice of His servant? – Though he walk in darkness And have no light, Let him trust in the name of *Hashem* And rely upon his God.

י מִי בָכֶם יְרֵא יֱהוָֹה שֹׁמֵעַ בְּקוֹל עַבְדּוֹ אֲשֶׁר הָלַךְ חֲשֵׁכִים וְאֵין נֹגַהּ לוֹ יִבְטַח בְּשֵׁם יְהוָֹה וְיִשָּׁעֵן בֵּאלֹהָיו:

11 But you are all kindlers of fire, Girding on firebrands. Walk by the blaze of your fire, By the brands that you have lit! This has come to you from My hand: You shall lie down in pain.

יא הֵן כֻּלְּכֶם קֹדְחֵי אֵשׁ מְאַזְּרֵי זִיקוֹת לְכוּ בְּאוֹר אֶשְׁכֶם וּבְזִיקוֹת בִּעַרְתֶּם מִיָּדִי הָיְתָה־זֹּאת לָכֶם לְמַעֲצֵבָה תִּשְׁכָּבוּן:

51 1 Listen to Me, you who pursue justice, You who seek *Hashem*: Look to the rock you were hewn from, To the quarry you were dug from.

א שִׁמְעוּ אֵלַי רֹדְפֵי צֶדֶק מְבַקְשֵׁי יְהוָֹה הַבִּיטוּ אֶל־צוּר חֻצַּבְתֶּם וְאֶל־מַקֶּבֶת בּוֹר נֻקַּרְתֶּם:

2 Look back to *Avraham* your father And to *Sara* who brought you forth. For he was only one when I called him, But I blessed him and made him many.

ב הַבִּיטוּ אֶל־אַבְרָהָם אֲבִיכֶם וְאֶל־שָׂרָה תְּחוֹלֶלְכֶם כִּי־אֶחָד קְרָאתִיו וַאֲבָרְכֵהוּ וְאַרְבֵּהוּ:

3 Truly *Hashem* has comforted *Tzion*, Comforted all her ruins; He has made her wilderness like Eden, Her desert like the Garden of *Hashem*. Gladness and joy shall abide there, Thanksgiving and the sound of music.

ג כִּי־נִחַם יְהוָֹה צִיּוֹן נִחַם כָּל־חָרְבֹתֶיהָ וַיָּשֶׂם מִדְבָּרָהּ כְּעֵדֶן וְעַרְבָתָהּ כְּגַן־יְהוָֹה שָׂשׂוֹן וְשִׂמְחָה יִמָּצֵא בָהּ תּוֹדָה וְקוֹל זִמְרָה:

*kee ni-KHAM a-do-NAI tzi-YON ni-KHAM kol kho-r'-vo-TE-ha
va-YA-sem mid-ba-RAH k'-AY-den v'-ar-va-TAH k'gan a-do-NAI
sa-SON v'-sim-KHA yi-ma-TZAY VAH to-DA v'-KOL zim-RAH*

4 Hearken to Me, My people, And give ear to Me, O My nation, For teaching shall go forth from Me, My way for the light of peoples. In a moment I will bring it:

ד הַקְשִׁיבוּ אֵלַי עַמִּי וּלְאוּמִּי אֵלַי הַאֲזִינוּ כִּי תוֹרָה מֵאִתִּי תֵצֵא וּמִשְׁפָּטִי לְאוֹר עַמִּים אַרְגִּיעַ:

51:3 Comforted all her ruins; he has made her wilderness like Eden The Land of Israel has a supernatural quality to it. While under foreign occupation, it resembles an arid desert. However, under Jewish sovereignty, it comes to life, flourishes, and yields great produce. Indeed, for nearly two millennia, as the land switched hands numerous times between various foreign powers, including the Romans, the Arabs and the Turks, the land lay utterly desolate. Amazingly, the modern rebirth of the Jewish state in 1948 has brought with it an astounding development of the land, to the point where once again the Jewish people can claim a flourishing country all their own. In agriculture, technology, and culture, Israel ranks among the most advanced countries of the world. Indeed, we are witnessing the Lord comfort "all her ruins."

The blooming Israeli desert

5 The triumph I grant is near, The success I give has gone forth. My arms shall provide for the peoples; The coastlands shall trust in Me, They shall look to My arm.

ה קָרוֹב צִדְקִי יָצָא יִשְׁעִי וּזְרֹעַי עַמִּים יִשְׁפֹּטוּ אֵלַי אִיִּים יְקַוּוּ וְאֶל־זְרֹעִי יְיַחֵלוּן:

6 Raise your eyes to the heavens, And look upon the earth beneath: Though the heavens should melt away like smoke, And the earth wear out like a garment, And its inhabitants die out as well, My victory shall stand forever, My triumph shall remain unbroken.

ו שְׂאוּ לַשָּׁמַיִם עֵינֵיכֶם וְהַבִּיטוּ אֶל־הָאָרֶץ מִתַּחַת כִּי־שָׁמַיִם כֶּעָשָׁן נִמְלָחוּ וְהָאָרֶץ כַּבֶּגֶד תִּבְלֶה וְיֹשְׁבֶיהָ כְּמוֹ־כֵן יְמוּתוּן וִישׁוּעָתִי לְעוֹלָם תִּהְיֶה וְצִדְקָתִי לֹא תֵחָת:

7 Listen to Me, you who care for the right, O people who lay My instruction to heart! Fear not the insults of men, And be not dismayed at their jeers;

ז שִׁמְעוּ אֵלַי יֹדְעֵי צֶדֶק עַם תּוֹרָתִי בְלִבָּם אַל־תִּירְאוּ חֶרְפַּת אֱנוֹשׁ וּמִגִּדֻּפֹתָם אַל־תֵּחָתּוּ:

8 For the moth shall eat them up like a garment, The worm shall eat them up like wool. But My triumph shall endure forever, My salvation through all the ages.

ח כִּי כַבֶּגֶד יֹאכְלֵם עָשׁ וְכַצֶּמֶר יֹאכְלֵם סָס וְצִדְקָתִי לְעוֹלָם תִּהְיֶה וִישׁוּעָתִי לְדוֹר דּוֹרִים:

9 Awake, awake, clothe yourself with splendor. O arm of *Hashem*! Awake as in days of old, As in former ages! It was you that hacked Rahab in pieces, That pierced the Dragon.

ט עוּרִי עוּרִי לִבְשִׁי־עֹז זְרוֹעַ יְהֹוָה עוּרִי כִּימֵי קֶדֶם דֹּרוֹת עוֹלָמִים הֲלוֹא אַתְּ־הִיא הַמַּחְצֶבֶת רַהַב מְחוֹלֶלֶת תַּנִּין:

10 It was you that dried up the Sea, The waters of the great deep; That made the abysses of the Sea A road the redeemed might walk.

י הֲלוֹא אַתְּ־הִיא הַמַּחֲרֶבֶת יָם מֵי תְּהוֹם רַבָּה הַשָּׂמָה מַעֲמַקֵּי־יָם דֶּרֶךְ לַעֲבֹר גְּאוּלִים:

11 So let the ransomed of *Hashem* return, And come with shouting to *Tzion*, Crowned with joy everlasting. Let them attain joy and gladness, While sorrow and sighing flee.

יא וּפְדוּיֵי יְהֹוָה יְשׁוּבוּן וּבָאוּ צִיּוֹן בְּרִנָּה וְשִׂמְחַת עוֹלָם עַל־רֹאשָׁם שָׂשׂוֹן וְשִׂמְחָה יַשִּׂיגוּן נָסוּ יָגוֹן וַאֲנָחָה:

12 I, I am He who comforts you! What ails you that you fear Man who must die, Mortals who fare like grass?

יב אָנֹכִי אָנֹכִי הוּא מְנַחֶמְכֶם מִי־אַתְּ וַתִּירְאִי מֵאֱנוֹשׁ יָמוּת וּמִבֶּן־אָדָם חָצִיר יִנָּתֵן:

13 You have forgotten *Hashem* your Maker, Who stretched out the skies and made firm the earth! And you live all day in constant dread Because of the rage of an oppressor Who is aiming to cut [you] down. Yet of what account is the rage of an oppressor?

יג וַתִּשְׁכַּח יְהֹוָה עֹשֶׂךָ נוֹטֶה שָׁמַיִם וְיֹסֵד אָרֶץ וַתְּפַחֵד תָּמִיד כָּל־הַיּוֹם מִפְּנֵי חֲמַת הַמֵּצִיק כַּאֲשֶׁר כּוֹנֵן לְהַשְׁחִית וְאַיֵּה חֲמַת הַמֵּצִיק:

14 Quickly the crouching one is freed; He is not cut down and slain, And he shall not want for food.

יד מִהַר צֹעֶה לְהִפָּתֵחַ וְלֹא־יָמוּת לַשַּׁחַת וְלֹא יֶחְסַר לַחְמוֹ:

15 For I *Hashem* your God – Who stir up the sea into roaring waves, Whose name is LORD of Hosts –

טו וְאָנֹכִי יְהֹוָה אֱלֹהֶיךָ רֹגַע הַיָּם וַיֶּהֱמוּ גַּלָּיו יְהֹוָה צְבָאוֹת שְׁמוֹ:

16 Have put My words in your mouth And sheltered you with My hand; I, who planted the skies and made firm the earth, Have said to *Tzion*: You are My people!

טז וָאָשִׂים דְּבָרַי בְּפִיךָ וּבְצֵל יָדִי כִּסִּיתִיךָ לִנְטֹעַ שָׁמַיִם וְלִיסֹד אָרֶץ וְלֵאמֹר לְצִיּוֹן עַמִּי־אָתָּה:

17 Rouse, rouse yourself! Arise, O *Yerushalayim*, You who from *Hashem*'s hand Have drunk the cup of His wrath, You who have drained to the dregs The bowl, the cup of reeling!

יז הִתְעוֹרְרִי הִתְעוֹרְרִי קוּמִי יְרוּשָׁלַםִ אֲשֶׁר שָׁתִית מִיַּד יְהֹוָה אֶת־כּוֹס חֲמָתוֹ אֶת־קֻבַּעַת כּוֹס הַתַּרְעֵלָה שָׁתִית מָצִית:

18 She has none to guide her Of all the sons she bore; None takes her by the hand, Of all the sons she reared.

יח אֵין־מְנַהֵל לָהּ מִכָּל־בָּנִים יָלָדָה וְאֵין מַחֲזִיק בְּיָדָהּ מִכָּל־בָּנִים גִּדֵּלָה:

19 These two things have befallen you: Wrack and ruin – who can console you? Famine and sword – how shall I comfort you?

יט שְׁתַּיִם הֵנָּה קֹרְאֹתַיִךְ מִי יָנוּד לָךְ הַשֹּׁד וְהַשֶּׁבֶר וְהָרָעָב וְהַחֶרֶב מִי אֲנַחֲמֵךְ:

20 Your sons lie in a swoon At the corner of every street – Like an antelope caught in a net – Drunk with the wrath of *Hashem*, With the rebuke of your God.

כ בָּנַיִךְ עֻלְּפוּ שָׁכְבוּ בְּרֹאשׁ כָּל־חוּצוֹת כְּתוֹא מִכְמָר הַמְלֵאִים חֲמַת־יְהֹוָה גַּעֲרַת אֱלֹהָיִךְ:

21 Therefore, Listen to this, unhappy one, Who are drunk, but not with wine!

כא לָכֵן שִׁמְעִי־נָא זֹאת עֲנִיָּה וּשְׁכֻרַת וְלֹא מִיָּיִן:

22 Thus said *Hashem*, your Lord, Your God who champions His people: Herewith I take from your hand The cup of reeling, The bowl, the cup of My wrath; You shall never drink it again.

כב כֹּה־אָמַר אֲדֹנַיִךְ יְהֹוָה וֵאלֹהַיִךְ יָרִיב עַמּוֹ הִנֵּה לָקַחְתִּי מִיָּדֵךְ אֶת־כּוֹס הַתַּרְעֵלָה אֶת־קֻבַּעַת כּוֹס חֲמָתִי לֹא־תוֹסִיפִי לִשְׁתּוֹתָהּ עוֹד:

23 I will put it in the hands of your tormentors, Who have commanded you, "Get down, that we may walk over you" – So that you made your back like the ground, Like a street for passersby.

כג וְשַׂמְתִּיהָ בְּיַד־מוֹגַיִךְ אֲשֶׁר־אָמְרוּ לְנַפְשֵׁךְ שְׁחִי וְנַעֲבֹרָה וַתָּשִׂימִי כָאָרֶץ גֵּוֵךְ וְכַחוּץ לַעֹבְרִים:

52 1 Awake, awake, O *Tzion*! Clothe yourself in splendor; Put on your robes of majesty, *Yerushalayim*, holy city! For the uncircumcised and the unclean Shall never enter you again.

נב א עוּרִי עוּרִי לִבְשִׁי עֻזֵּךְ צִיּוֹן לִבְשִׁי בִּגְדֵי תִפְאַרְתֵּךְ יְרוּשָׁלַםִ עִיר הַקֹּדֶשׁ כִּי לֹא יוֹסִיף יָבֹא־בָךְ עוֹד עָרֵל וְטָמֵא:

2 Arise, shake off the dust, Sit [on your throne], *Yerushalayim*! Loose the bonds from your neck, O captive one, Fair *Tzion*!

ב הִתְנַעֲרִי מֵעָפָר קוּמִי שְּׁבִי יְרוּשָׁלָםִ הִתְפַּתְּחוּ [הִתְפַּתְּחִי] מוֹסְרֵי צַוָּארֵךְ שְׁבִיָּה בַּת־צִיּוֹן:

3 For thus said *Hashem*: You were sold for no price, And shall be redeemed without money.

ג כִּי־כֹה אָמַר יְהֹוָה חִנָּם נִמְכַּרְתֶּם וְלֹא בְכֶסֶף תִּגָּאֵלוּ:

4 For thus said *Hashem*: Of old, My people went down To Egypt to sojourn there; But Assyria has robbed them, Giving nothing in return.

ד כִּי כֹה אָמַר אֲדֹנָי יְהֹוָה מִצְרַיִם יָרַד־עַמִּי בָרִאשֹׁנָה לָגוּר שָׁם וְאַשּׁוּר בְּאֶפֶס עֲשָׁקוֹ:

5 What therefore do I gain here? – declares *Hashem* – For My people has been carried off for nothing, Their mockers howl – declares *Hashem* – And constantly, unceasingly, My name is reviled.

ה וְעַתָּה מי־לי־[מַה־] [לִי־] פֹּה נְאֻם־יְהוָה כִּי־לֻקַּח עַמִּי חִנָּם משלו [מֹשְׁלָיו] יְהֵילִילוּ נְאֻם־יְהוָה וְתָמִיד כָּל־הַיּוֹם שְׁמִי מִנֹּאָץ:

6 Assuredly, My people shall learn My name, Assuredly [they shall learn] on that day That I, the One who promised, Am now at hand.

ו לָכֵן יֵדַע עַמִּי שְׁמִי לָכֵן בַּיּוֹם הַהוּא כִּי־אֲנִי־הוּא הַמְדַבֵּר הִנֵּנִי:

7 How welcome on the mountain Are the footsteps of the herald Announcing happiness, Heralding good fortune, Announcing victory, Telling *Tzion*, "Your God is King!"

ז מַה־נָּאווּ עַל־הֶהָרִים רַגְלֵי מְבַשֵּׂר מַשְׁמִיעַ שָׁלוֹם מְבַשֵּׂר טוֹב מַשְׁמִיעַ יְשׁוּעָה אֹמֵר לְצִיּוֹן מָלַךְ אֱלֹהָיִךְ:

8 Hark! Your watchmen raise their voices, As one they shout for joy; For every eye shall behold *Hashem*'s return to *Tzion*.

ח קוֹל צֹפַיִךְ נָשְׂאוּ קוֹל יַחְדָּו יְרַנֵּנוּ כִּי עַיִן בְּעַיִן יִרְאוּ בְּשׁוּב יְהוָה צִיּוֹן:

9 Raise a shout together, O ruins of *Yerushalayim*! For *Hashem* will comfort His people, Will redeem *Yerushalayim*.

ט פִּצְחוּ רַנְּנוּ יַחְדָּו חָרְבוֹת יְרוּשָׁלָ͏ִם כִּי־נִחַם יְהוָה עַמּוֹ גָּאַל יְרוּשָׁלָ͏ִם:

pitz-KHU ra-n'-NU yakh-DAV kho-r'-VOT y'-ru-sha-LA-im
kee ni-KHAM a-do-NAI a-MO ga-AL y'-ru-sha-LA-im

10 *Hashem* will bare His holy arm In the sight of all the nations, And the very ends of earth shall see The victory of our God.

י חָשַׂף יְהוָה אֶת־זְרוֹעַ קָדְשׁוֹ לְעֵינֵי כָּל־הַגּוֹיִם וְרָאוּ כָּל־אַפְסֵי־אָרֶץ אֵת יְשׁוּעַת אֱלֹהֵינוּ:

11 Turn, turn away, touch naught unclean As you depart from there; Keep pure, as you go forth from there, You who bear the vessels of *Hashem*!

יא סוּרוּ סוּרוּ צְאוּ מִשָּׁם טָמֵא אַל־תִּגָּעוּ צְאוּ מִתּוֹכָהּ הִבָּרוּ נֹשְׂאֵי כְּלֵי יְהוָה:

12 For you will not depart in haste, Nor will you leave in flight; For *Hashem* is marching before you, The God of *Yisrael* is your rear guard.

יב כִּי לֹא בְחִפָּזוֹן תֵּצֵאוּ וּבִמְנוּסָה לֹא תֵלֵכוּן כִּי־הֹלֵךְ לִפְנֵיכֶם יְהוָה וּמְאַסִּפְכֶם אֱלֹהֵי יִשְׂרָאֵל:

13 "Indeed, My servant shall prosper, Be exalted and raised to great heights.

יג הִנֵּה יַשְׂכִּיל עַבְדִּי יָרוּם וְנִשָּׂא וְגָבַהּ מְאֹד:

14 Just as the many were appalled at him – So marred was his appearance, unlike that of man, form, beyond human semblance –

יד כַּאֲשֶׁר שָׁמְמוּ עָלֶיךָ רַבִּים כֵּן־מִשְׁחַת מֵאִישׁ מַרְאֵהוּ וְתֹאֲרוֹ מִבְּנֵי אָדָם:

Yerushalayim at dusk

 52:9 Will redeem *Yerusha-layim* *Hashem* has many titles in the Bible, one of which is *go-ayl* (גואל), 'redeemer.' In Isaiah 49:7, He is referred to as the "Redeemer of Israel," and here He will "redeem *Yerushalayim*." The same word is used in the Bible in another context. *Sefer Vayikra* (25:25) states "his nearest redeemer shall come," referring to someone so deeply in debt that he is forced to sell his property until his closest relative comes to his aid. The *go-ayl* in this context is the person's closest relative. By referring to *Hashem* as the Redeemer of Israel, the prophet is expressing the idea that He is closer to them than any of their other close relations.

גואל

15 Just so he shall startle many nations. Kings shall be silenced because of him, For they shall see what has not been told them, Shall behold what they never have heard."

טו כֵּן יַזֶּה גּוֹיִם רַבִּים עָלָיו יִקְפְּצוּ מְלָכִים פִּיהֶם כִּי אֲשֶׁר לֹא־סֻפַּר לָהֶם רָאוּ וַאֲשֶׁר לֹא־שָׁמְעוּ הִתְבּוֹנָנוּ:

53 1 "Who can believe what we have heard? Upon whom has the arm of *Hashem*- been revealed?

נג א מִי הֶאֱמִין לִשְׁמֻעָתֵנוּ וּזְרוֹעַ יְהֹוָה עַל־מִי נִגְלָתָה:

2 For he has grown, by His favor, like a tree crown, Like a tree trunk out of arid ground. He had no form or beauty, that we should look at him: No charm, that we should find him pleasing.

ב וַיַּעַל כַּיּוֹנֵק לְפָנָיו וְכַשֹּׁרֶשׁ מֵאֶרֶץ צִיָּה לֹא־תֹאַר לוֹ וְלֹא הָדָר וְנִרְאֵהוּ וְלֹא־מַרְאֶה וְנֶחְמְדֵהוּ:

3 He was despised, shunned by men, A man of suffering, familiar with disease. As one who hid his face from us, He was despised, we held him of no account.

ג נִבְזֶה וַחֲדַל אִישִׁים אִישׁ מַכְאֹבוֹת וִידוּעַ חֹלִי וּכְמַסְתֵּר פָּנִים מִמֶּנּוּ נִבְזֶה וְלֹא חֲשַׁבְנֻהוּ:

4 Yet it was our sickness that he was bearing, Our suffering that he endured. We accounted him plagued, Smitten and afflicted by *Hashem*;

ד אָכֵן חֳלָיֵנוּ הוּא נָשָׂא וּמַכְאֹבֵינוּ סְבָלָם וַאֲנַחְנוּ חֲשַׁבְנֻהוּ נָגוּעַ מֻכֵּה אֱלֹהִים וּמְעֻנֶּה:

5 But he was wounded because of our sins, Crushed because of our iniquities. He bore the chastisement that made us whole, And by his bruises we were healed.

ה וְהוּא מְחֹלָל מִפְּשָׁעֵנוּ מְדֻכָּא מֵעֲוֺנֹתֵינוּ מוּסַר שְׁלוֹמֵנוּ עָלָיו וּבַחֲבֻרָתוֹ נִרְפָּא־לָנוּ:

6 We all went astray like sheep, Each going his own way; And *Hashem* visited upon him The guilt of all of us."

ו כֻּלָּנוּ כַּצֹּאן תָּעִינוּ אִישׁ לְדַרְכּוֹ פָּנִינוּ וַיהֹוָה הִפְגִּיעַ בּוֹ אֵת עֲוֺן כֻּלָּנוּ:

7 He was maltreated, yet he was submissive, He did not open his mouth; Like a sheep being led to slaughter, Like a ewe, dumb before those who shear her, He did not open his mouth.

ז נִגַּשׂ וְהוּא נַעֲנֶה וְלֹא יִפְתַּח־פִּיו כַּשֶּׂה לַטֶּבַח יוּבָל וּכְרָחֵל לִפְנֵי גֹזְזֶיהָ נֶאֱלָמָה וְלֹא יִפְתַּח פִּיו:

8 By oppressive judgment he was taken away, Who could describe his abode? For he was cut off from the land of the living Through the sin of my people, who deserved the punishment.

ח מֵעֹצֶר וּמִמִּשְׁפָּט לֻקָּח וְאֶת־דּוֹרוֹ מִי יְשׂוֹחֵחַ כִּי נִגְזַר מֵאֶרֶץ חַיִּים מִפֶּשַׁע עַמִּי נֶגַע לָמוֹ:

9 And his grave was set among the wicked, And with the rich, in his death – Though he had done no injustice And had spoken no falsehood.

ט וַיִּתֵּן אֶת־רְשָׁעִים קִבְרוֹ וְאֶת־עָשִׁיר בְּמֹתָיו עַל לֹא־חָמָס עָשָׂה וְלֹא מִרְמָה בְּפִיו:

10 But *Hashem* chose to crush him by disease, That, if he made himself an offering for guilt, He might see offspring and have long life, And that through him *Hashem*'s purpose might prosper.

י וַיהֹוָה חָפֵץ דַּכְּאוֹ הֶחֱלִי אִם־תָּשִׂים אָשָׁם נַפְשׁוֹ יִרְאֶה זֶרַע יַאֲרִיךְ יָמִים וְחֵפֶץ יְהֹוָה בְּיָדוֹ יִצְלָח:

11 Out of his anguish he shall see it; He shall enjoy it to the full through his devotion. "My righteous servant makes the many righteous, It is their punishment that he bears;

יא מֵעֲמַל נַפְשׁוֹ יִרְאֶה יִשְׂבָּע בְּדַעְתּוֹ יַצְדִּיק צַדִּיק עַבְדִּי לָרַבִּים וַעֲוֺנֹתָם הוּא יִסְבֹּל:

12 Assuredly, I will give him the many as his portion,
He shall receive the multitude as his spoil. For
he exposed himself to death And was numbered
among the sinners, Whereas he bore the guilt of
the many And made intercession for sinners."

לָכֵן אֲחַלֶּק־לוֹ בָרַבִּים וְאֶת־עֲצוּמִים יְחַלֵּק שָׁלָל תַּחַת אֲשֶׁר הֶעֱרָה לַמָּוֶת נַפְשׁוֹ וְאֶת־פֹּשְׁעִים נִמְנָה וְהוּא חֵטְא־רַבִּים נָשָׂא וְלַפֹּשְׁעִים יַפְגִּיעַ:

la-KHAYN a-kha-lek LO va-ra-BEEM v'-et a-tzu-MEEM y'-kha-LAYK
sha-LAL TA-khat a-SHER he-e-RAH la-MA-vet naf-SHO v'-et po-sh'-EEM
nim-NAH v'-HU khayt ra-BEEM na-SA v'-la-po-sh'-EEM yaf-GEE-a

54 1 Shout, O barren one, You who bore no child!
Shout aloud for joy, You who did not travail! For
the children of the wife forlorn Shall outnumber
those of the espoused – said *Hashem*.

רָנִּי עֲקָרָה לֹא יָלָדָה פִּצְחִי רִנָּה וְצַהֲלִי לֹא־חָלָה כִּי־רַבִּים בְּנֵי־שׁוֹמֵמָה מִבְּנֵי בְעוּלָה אָמַר יְהֹוָה:

2 Enlarge the site of your tent, Extend the size of
your dwelling, Do not stint! Lengthen the ropes,
and drive the pegs firm.

הַרְחִיבִי מְקוֹם אָהֳלֵךְ וִירִיעוֹת מִשְׁכְּנוֹתַיִךְ יַטּוּ אַל־תַּחְשֹׂכִי הַאֲרִיכִי מֵיתָרַיִךְ וִיתֵדֹתַיִךְ חַזֵּקִי:

har-KHEE-vee m'-KOM a-ho-LAYKH vee-ree-OT mish-k'-no-TA-yikh ya-TU al
takh-SO-khee ha-a-REE-khee may-ta-RA-yikh vee-tay-do-TA-yikh kha-ZAY-kee

3 For you shall spread out to the right and the left;
Your offspring shall dispossess nations And shall
people the desolate towns.

כִּי־יָמִין וּשְׂמֹאול תִּפְרֹצִי וְזַרְעֵךְ גּוֹיִם יִירָשׁ וְעָרִים נְשַׁמּוֹת יוֹשִׁיבוּ:

4 Fear not, you shall not be shamed; Do not cringe,
you shall not be disgraced. For you shall forget The
reproach of your youth, And remember no more
The shame of your widowhood.

אַל־תִּירְאִי כִּי־לֹא תֵבוֹשִׁי וְאַל־תִּכָּלְמִי כִּי לֹא תַחְפִּירִי כִּי בֹשֶׁת עֲלוּמַיִךְ תִּשְׁכָּחִי וְחֶרְפַּת אַלְמְנוּתַיִךְ לֹא תִזְכְּרִי־עוֹד:

5 For He who made you will espouse you – His
name is "LORD of Hosts." The Holy One of *Yisrael*
will redeem you – He is called "God of all the
Earth."

כִּי בֹעֲלַיִךְ עֹשַׂיִךְ יְהֹוָה צְבָאוֹת שְׁמוֹ וְגֹאֲלֵךְ קְדוֹשׁ יִשְׂרָאֵל אֱלֹהֵי כָל־הָאָרֶץ יִקָּרֵא:

53:12 Assuredly, I will give him the many as his portion Chapter 53 begins with a description of the suffering that Israel experiences. In this verse, however, *Yeshayahu* articulates the reward that awaits the nation. Because Israel, despite its suffering, placed the welfare of others above its own, it is promised that one day it too will be counted among the mighty, and that its portion, *Eretz Yisrael*, will be considered great. Today, the State of Israel is among the world's leaders in science, technology and medicine, and stands out in the region. In 2015, for example, the U.S. Patent Office reported 3,804 patents from Israel, as compared with 364 from Saudi Arabia, 56 from the United Arab Emirates, and 30 from Egypt. Truly, *Yeshayahu's* blessing is being realized and Israel's "portion" is growing.

54:2 Enlarge the site of your tent This verse contains a call to action for Jews everywhere to settle every corner of *Eretz Yisrael* and "en-large" their presence in the land. Based on this verse, the *Vilna Gaon* urged his students in the eighteenth century to move to Israel. "All the precious treasures included in the blessing of *harchava* ('enlargement') will come only when ac-tion is first taken by the People of Israel themselves in an awakening from below" said the *Vilna Gaon*. "Our task is to not sit passively and wait for redemption from exile, but rather to take action and bring it about." The Jewish people are not prisoners of fate, but partners with God in shaping their destiny. When they take action and settle the land, He will respond in kind and hasten the ingather-ing of the exiles.

Hydroponic containers with strawberry plants in an Israeli greenhouse

Isaiah

6 *Hashem* has called you back As a wife forlorn and forsaken. Can one cast off the wife of his youth? – said your God.

כִּי־כְאִשָּׁה עֲזוּבָה וַעֲצוּבַת רוּחַ קְרָאָךְ יְהוָה וְאֵשֶׁת נְעוּרִים כִּי תִמָּאֵס אָמַר אֱלֹהָיִךְ:

7 For a little while I forsook you, But with vast love I will bring you back.

בְּרֶגַע קָטֹן עֲזַבְתִּיךְ וּבְרַחֲמִים גְּדֹלִים אֲקַבְּצֵךְ:

8 In slight anger, for a moment, I hid My face from you; But with kindness everlasting I will take you back in love – said *Hashem* your Redeemer.

בְּשֶׁצֶף קֶצֶף הִסְתַּרְתִּי פָנַי רֶגַע מִמֵּךְ וּבְחֶסֶד עוֹלָם רִחַמְתִּיךְ אָמַר גֹּאֲלֵךְ יְהוָה:

9 For this to Me is like the waters of *Noach*: As I swore that the waters of *Noach* Nevermore would flood the earth, So I swear that I will not Be angry with you or rebuke you.

כִּי־מֵי נֹחַ זֹאת לִי אֲשֶׁר נִשְׁבַּעְתִּי מֵעֲבֹר מֵי־נֹחַ עוֹד עַל־הָאָרֶץ כֵּן נִשְׁבַּעְתִּי מִקְּצֹף עָלַיִךְ וּמִגְּעָר־בָּךְ:

10 For the mountains may move And the hills be shaken, But my loyalty shall never move from you, Nor My covenant of friendship be shaken – said *Hashem*, who takes you back in love.

כִּי הֶהָרִים יָמוּשׁוּ וְהַגְּבָעוֹת תְּמוּטֶנָה וְחַסְדִּי מֵאִתֵּךְ לֹא־יָמוּשׁ וּבְרִית שְׁלוֹמִי לֹא תָמוּט אָמַר מְרַחֲמֵךְ יְהוָה:

11 Unhappy, storm-tossed one, uncomforted! I will lay carbuncles as your building stones And make your foundations of sapphires.

עֲנִיָּה סֹעֲרָה לֹא נֻחָמָה הִנֵּה אָנֹכִי מַרְבִּיץ בַּפּוּךְ אֲבָנַיִךְ וִיסַדְתִּיךְ בַּסַּפִּירִים:

12 I will make your battlements of rubies, Your gates of precious stones, The whole encircling wall of gems.

וְשַׂמְתִּי כַּדְכֹד שִׁמְשֹׁתַיִךְ וּשְׁעָרַיִךְ לְאַבְנֵי אֶקְדָּח וְכָל־גְּבוּלֵךְ לְאַבְנֵי־חֵפֶץ:

13 And all your children shall be disciples of *Hashem*, And great shall be the happiness of your children;

וְכָל־בָּנַיִךְ לִמּוּדֵי יְהוָה וְרַב שְׁלוֹם בָּנָיִךְ:

14 You shall be established through righteousness. You shall be safe from oppression, And shall have no fear; From ruin, and it shall not come near you.

בִּצְדָקָה תִּכּוֹנָנִי רַחֲקִי מֵעֹשֶׁק כִּי־לֹא תִירָאִי וּמִמְּחִתָּה כִּי לֹא־תִקְרַב אֵלָיִךְ:

15 Surely no harm can be done Without My consent: Whoever would harm you Shall fall because of you.

הֵן גּוֹר יָגוּר אֶפֶס מֵאוֹתִי מִי־גָר אִתָּךְ עָלַיִךְ יִפּוֹל:

16 It is I who created the smith To fan the charcoal fire And produce the tools for his work; So it is I who create The instruments of havoc.

הן [הִנֵּה] אָנֹכִי בָּרָאתִי חָרָשׁ נֹפֵחַ בְּאֵשׁ פֶּחָם וּמוֹצִיא כְלִי לְמַעֲשֵׂהוּ וְאָנֹכִי בָּרָאתִי מַשְׁחִית לְחַבֵּל:

17 No weapon formed against you Shall succeed, And every tongue that contends with you at law You shall defeat. Such is the lot of the servants of *Hashem*, Such their triumph through Me – declares *Hashem*.

כָּל־כְּלִי יוּצַר עָלַיִךְ לֹא יִצְלָח וְכָל־לָשׁוֹן תָּקוּם־אִתָּךְ לַמִּשְׁפָּט תַּרְשִׁיעִי זֹאת נַחֲלַת עַבְדֵי יְהוָה וְצִדְקָתָם מֵאִתִּי נְאֻם־יְהוָה:

55 1 Ho, all who are thirsty, Come for water, Even if you have no money; Come, buy food and eat: Buy food without money, Wine and milk without cost.

נה א הוֹי כָּל־צָמֵא לְכוּ לַמַּיִם וַאֲשֶׁר אֵין־לוֹ כָּסֶף לְכוּ שִׁבְרוּ וֶאֱכֹלוּ וּלְכוּ שִׁבְרוּ בְּלוֹא־כֶסֶף וּבְלוֹא מְחִיר יַיִן וְחָלָב:

² Why do you spend money for what is not bread, Your earnings for what does not satisfy? Give heed to Me, And you shall eat choice food And enjoy the richest viands.

ב לָמָּה תִשְׁקְלוּ־כֶסֶף בְּלוֹא־לֶחֶם וִיגִיעֲכֶם בְּלוֹא לְשָׂבְעָה שִׁמְעוּ שָׁמוֹעַ אֵלַי וְאִכְלוּ־טוֹב וְתִתְעַנַּג בַּדֶּשֶׁן נַפְשְׁכֶם:

³ Incline your ear and come to Me; Hearken, and you shall be revived. And I will make with you an everlasting covenant, The enduring loyalty promised to *David*.

ג הַטּוּ אָזְנְכֶם וּלְכוּ אֵלַי שִׁמְעוּ וּתְחִי נַפְשְׁכֶם וְאֶכְרְתָה לָכֶם בְּרִית עוֹלָם חַסְדֵי דָוִד הַנֶּאֱמָנִים:

⁴ As I made him a leader of peoples, A prince and commander of peoples,

ד הֵן עֵד לְאוּמִּים נְתַתִּיו נָגִיד וּמְצַוֵּה לְאֻמִּים:

⁵ So you shall summon a nation you did not know, And a nation that did not know you Shall come running to you – For the sake of *Hashem* your God, The Holy One of *Yisrael* who has glorified you.

ה הֵן גּוֹי לֹא־תֵדַע תִּקְרָא וְגוֹי לֹא־יְדָעוּךָ אֵלֶיךָ יָרוּצוּ לְמַעַן יְהוָה אֱלֹהֶיךָ וְלִקְדוֹשׁ יִשְׂרָאֵל כִּי פֵאֲרָךְ:

⁶ Seek *Hashem* while He can be found, Call to Him while He is near.

ו דִּרְשׁוּ יְהוָה בְּהִמָּצְאוֹ קְרָאֻהוּ בִּהְיוֹתוֹ קָרוֹב:

dir-SHU a-do-NAI b'-hi-ma-tz'-O k'-ra-U-hu bih-yo-TO ka-ROV

⁷ Let the wicked give up his ways, The sinful man his plans; Let him turn back to *Hashem*, And He will pardon him; To our God, For he freely forgives.

ז יַעֲזֹב רָשָׁע דַּרְכּוֹ וְאִישׁ אָוֶן מַחְשְׁבֹתָיו וְיָשֹׁב אֶל־יְהוָה וִירַחֲמֵהוּ וְאֶל־אֱלֹהֵינוּ כִּי־יַרְבֶּה לִסְלוֹחַ:

⁸ For My plans are not your plans, Nor are My ways your ways – declares *Hashem*.

ח כִּי לֹא מַחְשְׁבוֹתַי מַחְשְׁבוֹתֵיכֶם וְלֹא דַרְכֵיכֶם דְּרָכָי נְאֻם יְהוָה:

⁹ But as the heavens are high above the earth, So are My ways high above your ways And My plans above your plans.

ט כִּי־גָבְהוּ שָׁמַיִם מֵאָרֶץ כֵּן גָּבְהוּ דְרָכַי מִדַּרְכֵיכֶם וּמַחְשְׁבֹתַי מִמַּחְשְׁבֹתֵיכֶם:

¹⁰ For as the rain or snow drops from heaven And returns not there, But soaks the earth And makes it bring forth vegetation, Yielding seed for sowing and bread for eating,

י כִּי כַּאֲשֶׁר יֵרֵד הַגֶּשֶׁם וְהַשֶּׁלֶג מִן־הַשָּׁמַיִם וְשָׁמָּה לֹא יָשׁוּב כִּי אִם־הִרְוָה אֶת־הָאָרֶץ וְהוֹלִידָהּ וְהִצְמִיחָהּ וְנָתַן זֶרַע לַזֹּרֵעַ וְלֶחֶם לָאֹכֵל:

¹¹ So is the word that issues from My mouth: It does not come back to Me unfulfilled, But performs what I purpose, Achieves what I sent it to do.

יא כֵּן יִהְיֶה דְבָרִי אֲשֶׁר יֵצֵא מִפִּי לֹא־יָשׁוּב אֵלַי רֵיקָם כִּי אִם־עָשָׂה אֶת־אֲשֶׁר חָפַצְתִּי וְהִצְלִיחַ אֲשֶׁר שְׁלַחְתִּיו:

¹² Yea, you shall leave in joy and be led home secure. Before you, mount and hill shall shout aloud, And all the trees of the field shall clap their hands.

יב כִּי־בְשִׂמְחָה תֵצֵאוּ וּבְשָׁלוֹם תּוּבָלוּן הֶהָרִים וְהַגְּבָעוֹת יִפְצְחוּ לִפְנֵיכֶם רִנָּה וְכָל־עֲצֵי הַשָּׂדֶה יִמְחֲאוּ־כָף:

55:6 Seek *Hashem* while He can be found The prophetic counsel "seek *Hashem* while He can be found; call to him while He is near" introduces a section offering hope and reward for those who sincerely desire to repent. This chapter is traditionally read publicly on fast days, days meant for introspection and inner reflection, and commentators provide many interpretations to its meaning. Some understand the phrase "seek *Hashem* while He can be found" as referring to the month before the Jewish New Year, *Rosh Hashana*, when prayer is especially desirable. The Jerusalem Talmud understands it in terms of location, "seek *Hashem* where He is found – in the synagogues, and in the study halls." The underlying message is the same: If you seek *Hashem* out in the right way, you will be able to find Him, and He is always there awaiting your return.

Inside the Hurva synagogue in the Old City of *Yerushalayim*

Isaiah

13 Instead of the brier, a cypress shall rise Instead of the nettle, a myrtle shall rise. These shall stand as a testimony to *Hashem*, As an everlasting sign that shall not perish.

יג תַּחַת הַנַּעֲצוּץ יַעֲלֶה בְרוֹשׁ תַּחַת [וְתַחַת] הַסִּרְפַּד יַעֲלֶה הֲדַס וְהָיָה לַיהוָה לְשֵׁם לְאוֹת עוֹלָם לֹא יִכָּרֵת:

56 ¹ Thus said *Hashem*: Observe what is right and do what is just; For soon My salvation shall come, And my deliverance be revealed.

נו א כֹּה אָמַר יְהוָה שִׁמְרוּ מִשְׁפָּט וַעֲשׂוּ צְדָקָה כִּי־קְרוֹבָה יְשׁוּעָתִי לָבוֹא וְצִדְקָתִי לְהִגָּלוֹת:

² Happy is the man who does this, The man who holds fast to it: Who keeps the *Shabbat* and does not profane it, And stays his hand from doing any evil.

ב אַשְׁרֵי אֱנוֹשׁ יַעֲשֶׂה־זֹּאת וּבֶן־אָדָם יַחֲזִיק בָּהּ שֹׁמֵר שַׁבָּת מֵחַלְּלוֹ וְשֹׁמֵר יָדוֹ מֵעֲשׂוֹת כָּל־רָע:

³ Let not the foreigner say, Who has attached himself to *Hashem*, "*Hashem* will keep me apart from His people"; And let not the eunuch say, "I am a withered tree."

ג וְאַל־יֹאמַר בֶּן־הַנֵּכָר הַנִּלְוָה אֶל־יְהוָה לֵאמֹר הַבְדֵּל יַבְדִּילַנִי יְהוָה מֵעַל עַמּוֹ וְאַל־יֹאמַר הַסָּרִיס הֵן אֲנִי עֵץ יָבֵשׁ:

⁴ For thus said *Hashem*: "As for the eunuchs who keep My *Shabbatot*, Who have chosen what I desire And hold fast to My covenant –

ד כִּי־כֹה אָמַר יְהוָה לַסָּרִיסִים אֲשֶׁר יִשְׁמְרוּ אֶת־שַׁבְּתוֹתַי וּבָחֲרוּ בַּאֲשֶׁר חָפָצְתִּי וּמַחֲזִיקִים בִּבְרִיתִי:

⁵ I will give them, in My House And within My walls, A monument and a name Better than sons or daughters. I will give them an everlasting name Which shall not perish.

ה וְנָתַתִּי לָהֶם בְּבֵיתִי וּבְחוֹמֹתַי יָד וָשֵׁם טוֹב מִבָּנִים וּמִבָּנוֹת שֵׁם עוֹלָם אֶתֶּן־לוֹ אֲשֶׁר לֹא יִכָּרֵת:

*v'-na-ta-TEE la-HEM b'-vay-TEE uv-kho-mo-TAI YAD va-SHAYM TOV
mi-ba-NEEM u-mi-ba-NOT SHAYM o-LAM e-ten LO a-SHER LO y'-ka-RAYT*

⁶ As for the foreigners Who attach themselves to *Hashem*, To minister to Him, And to love the name of *Hashem*, To be His servants – All who keep the *Shabbat* and do not profane it, And who hold fast to My covenant –

ו וּבְנֵי הַנֵּכָר הַנִּלְוִים עַל־יְהוָה לְשָׁרְתוֹ וּלְאַהֲבָה אֶת־שֵׁם יְהוָה לִהְיוֹת לוֹ לַעֲבָדִים כָּל־שֹׁמֵר שַׁבָּת מֵחַלְּלוֹ וּמַחֲזִיקִים בִּבְרִיתִי:

Hall of Names at Yad Vashem

56:5 A monument and a name Jerusalem's famous Holocaust museum, *Yad Vashem* ('a monument and a name'), takes its name from this biblical verse. *Yeshayahu* articulates *Hashem*'s promise that even those who are unable to have sons and daughters will be memorialized in *Yerushalayim* by their "everlasting name." According to its mission statement, the museum "safeguards the memory of the past and imparts its meaning for future generations." *Yad Vashem* has already collected and memorialized the names of over four million Jewish victims of Nazi persecution, and aims to persist until all 6,000,0000 names are recovered. The museum is often a first stop for visitors to the Jewish State, because in order to appreciate the State of Israel, one must understand the tragedy of the Holocaust.

7 I will bring them to My sacred mount And let them rejoice in My house of prayer. Their burnt offerings and sacrifices Shall be welcome on My *Mizbayach*; For My House shall be called A house of prayer for all peoples."

ז וַהֲבִיאוֹתִים אֶל־הַר קָדְשִׁי וְשִׂמַּחְתִּים בְּבֵית תְּפִלָּתִי עוֹלֹתֵיהֶם וְזִבְחֵיהֶם לְרָצוֹן עַל־מִזְבְּחִי כִּי בֵיתִי בֵּית־תְּפִלָּה יִקָּרֵא לְכׇל־הָעַמִּים:

8 Thus declares *Hashem*, Who gathers the dispersed of *Yisrael*: "I will gather still more to those already gathered."

ח נְאֻם אֲדֹנָי יֱהֹוִה מְקַבֵּץ נִדְחֵי יִשְׂרָאֵל עוֹד אֲקַבֵּץ עָלָיו לְנִקְבָּצָיו:

9 All you wild beasts, come and devour, All you beasts of the forest!

ט כֹּל חַיְתוֹ שָׂדָי אֵתָיוּ לֶאֱכֹל כׇּל־חַיְתוֹ בַיָּעַר:

10 The watchmen are blind, all of them, They perceive nothing. They are all dumb dogs That cannot bark; They lie sprawling, They love to drowse.

י צֹפוֹ [צֹפָיו] עִוְרִים כֻּלָּם לֹא יָדָעוּ כֻּלָּם כְּלָבִים אִלְּמִים לֹא יוּכְלוּ לִנְבֹּחַ הֹזִים שֹׁכְבִים אֹהֲבֵי לָנוּם:

11 Moreover, the dogs are greedy; They never know satiety. As for the shepherds, they know not What it is to give heed. Everyone has turned his own way, Every last one seeks his own advantage.

יא וְהַכְּלָבִים עַזֵּי־נֶפֶשׁ לֹא יָדְעוּ שׇׂבְעָה וְהֵמָּה רֹעִים לֹא יָדְעוּ הָבִין כֻּלָּם לְדַרְכָּם פָּנוּ אִישׁ לְבִצְעוֹ מִקָּצֵהוּ:

12 "Come, I'll get some wine Let us swill liquor. And tomorrow will be just the same, Or even much grander!"

יב אֵתָיוּ אֶקְחָה־יַיִן וְנִסְבְּאָה שֵׁכָר וְהָיָה כָזֶה יוֹם מָחָר גָּדוֹל יֶתֶר מְאֹד:

57 1 The righteous man perishes, And no one considers; Pious men are taken away, And no one gives thought That because of evil The righteous was taken away.

נז א הַצַּדִּיק אָבָד וְאֵין אִישׁ שָׂם עַל־לֵב וְאַנְשֵׁי־חֶסֶד נֶאֱסָפִים בְּאֵין מֵבִין כִּי־מִפְּנֵי הָרָעָה נֶאֱסַף הַצַּדִּיק:

2 Yet he shall come to peace, He shall have rest on his couch Who walked straightforward.

ב יָבוֹא שָׁלוֹם יָנוּחוּ עַל־מִשְׁכְּבוֹתָם הֹלֵךְ נְכֹחוֹ:

3 But as for you, come closer, You sons of a sorceress, You offspring of an adulterer and a harlot!

ג וְאַתֶּם קִרְבוּ־הֵנָּה בְּנֵי עֹנְנָה זֶרַע מְנָאֵף וַתִּזְנֶה:

4 With whom do you act so familiarly? At whom do you open your mouth And stick out your tongue? Why, you are children of iniquity, Offspring of treachery –

ד עַל־מִי תִּתְעַנְּגוּ עַל־מִי תַּרְחִיבוּ פֶה תַּאֲרִיכוּ לָשׁוֹן הֲלוֹא־אַתֶּם יִלְדֵי־פֶשַׁע זֶרַע שָׁקֶר:

5 You who inflame yourselves Among the terebinths, Under every verdant tree; Who slaughter children in the wadis, Among the clefts of the rocks.

ה הַנֵּחָמִים בָּאֵלִים תַּחַת כׇּל־עֵץ רַעֲנָן שֹׁחֲטֵי הַיְלָדִים בַּנְּחָלִים תַּחַת סְעִפֵי הַסְּלָעִים:

6 With such are your share and portion, They, they are your allotment; To them you have poured out libations, Presented offerings. Should I relent in the face of this?

ו בְּחַלְּקֵי־נַחַל חֶלְקֵךְ הֵם הֵם גּוֹרָלֵךְ גַּם־לָהֶם שָׁפַכְתְּ נֶסֶךְ הֶעֱלִית מִנְחָה הַעַל אֵלֶּה אֶנָּחֵם:

7 On a high and lofty hill You have set your couch; There, too, you have gone up To perform sacrifices.

ז עַל הַר־גָּבֹהַּ וְנִשָּׂא שַׂמְתְּ מִשְׁכָּבֵךְ גַּם־שָׁם עָלִית לִזְבֹּחַ זָבַח:

8 Behind the door and doorpost You have directed your thoughts; Abandoning Me, you have gone up On the couch you made so wide. You have made a covenant with them, You have loved bedding with them; You have chosen lust.

ח וְאַחַר הַדֶּלֶת וְהַמְּזוּזָה שַׂמְתְּ זִכְרוֹנֵךְ כִּי מֵאִתִּי גִּלִּית וַתַּעֲלִי הִרְחַבְתְּ מִשְׁכָּבֵךְ וַתִּכְרָת־לָךְ מֵהֶם אָהַבְתְּ מִשְׁכָּבָם יָד חָזִית:

9 You have approached the king with oil, You have provided many perfumes. And you have sent your envoys afar, Even down to the netherworld.

ט וַתָּשֻׁרִי לַמֶּלֶךְ בַּשֶּׁמֶן וַתַּרְבִּי רִקֻּחָיִךְ וַתְּשַׁלְּחִי צִירַיִךְ עַד־מֵרָחֹק וַתַּשְׁפִּילִי עַד־שְׁאוֹל:

10 Though wearied by much travel, You never said, "I give up!" You found gratification for your lust, And so you never cared.

י בְּרֹב דַּרְכֵּךְ יָגַעַתְּ לֹא אָמַרְתְּ נוֹאָשׁ חַיַּת יָדֵךְ מָצָאת עַל־כֵּן לֹא חָלִית:

11 Whom do you dread and fear, That you tell lies? But you gave no thought to Me, You paid no heed. It is because I have stood idly by so long That you have no fear of Me.

יא וְאֶת־מִי דָּאַגְתְּ וַתִּירְאִי כִּי תְכַזֵּבִי וְאוֹתִי לֹא זָכַרְתְּ לֹא־שַׂמְתְּ עַל־לִבֵּךְ הֲלֹא אֲנִי מַחְשֶׁה וּמֵעֹלָם וְאוֹתִי לֹא תִירָאִי:

12 I hereby pronounce judgment upon your deeds: Your assorted [idols]* shall not avail you,

יב אֲנִי אַגִּיד צִדְקָתֵךְ וְאֶת־מַעֲשַׂיִךְ וְלֹא יוֹעִילוּךְ:

13 Shall not save you when you cry out. They shall all be borne off by the wind, Snatched away by a breeze. But those who trust in Me shall inherit the land And possess My sacred mount.

יג בְּזַעֲקֵךְ יַצִּילֻךְ קִבּוּצַיִךְ וְאֶת־כֻּלָּם יִשָּׂא־רוּחַ יִקַּח־הָבֶל וְהַחוֹסֶה בִי יִנְחַל־אֶרֶץ וְיִירַשׁ הַר־קָדְשִׁי:

14 [The Lord] says: Build up, build up a highway! Clear a road! Remove all obstacles From the road of My people!

יד וְאָמַר סֹלּוּ־סֹלּוּ פַּנּוּ־דָרֶךְ הָרִימוּ מִכְשׁוֹל מִדֶּרֶךְ עַמִּי:

15 For thus said He who high aloft Forever dwells, whose name is holy: I dwell on high, in holiness; Yet with the contrite and the lowly in spirit – Reviving the spirits of the lowly, Reviving the hearts of the contrite.

טו כִּי כֹה אָמַר רָם וְנִשָּׂא שֹׁכֵן עַד וְקָדוֹשׁ שְׁמוֹ מָרוֹם וְקָדוֹשׁ אֶשְׁכּוֹן וְאֶת־דַּכָּא וּשְׁפַל־רוּחַ לְהַחֲיוֹת רוּחַ שְׁפָלִים וּלְהַחֲיוֹת לֵב נִדְכָּאִים:

16 For I will not always contend, I will not be angry forever: Nay, I who make spirits flag, Also create the breath of life.

טז כִּי לֹא לְעוֹלָם אָרִיב וְלֹא לָנֶצַח אֶקְצוֹף כִּי־רוּחַ מִלְּפָנַי יַעֲטוֹף וּנְשָׁמוֹת אֲנִי עָשִׂיתִי:

17 For their sinful greed I was angry; I struck them and turned away in My wrath. Though stubborn, they follow the way of their hearts,

יז בַּעֲוֹן בִּצְעוֹ קָצַפְתִּי וְאַכֵּהוּ הַסְתֵּר וְאֶקְצֹף וַיֵּלֶךְ שׁוֹבָב בְּדֶרֶךְ לִבּוֹ:

18 I note how they fare and will heal them: I will guide them and mete out solace to them, And to the mourners among them

יח דְּרָכָיו רָאִיתִי וְאֶרְפָּאֵהוּ וְאַנְחֵהוּ וַאֲשַׁלֵּם נִחֻמִים לוֹ וְלַאֲבֵלָיו:

---

* "Your assorted [idols]" brought up from verse 13 for clarity

19 heartening, comforting words It shall be well, Well with the far and the near – said *Hashem* – And I will heal them.

בּוֹרֵא נוב [נִיב] שְׂפָתָיִם שָׁלוֹם שָׁלוֹם לָרָחוֹק וְלַקָּרוֹב אָמַר יְהֹוָה וּרְפָאתִיו: יט

bo-RAY NEEV s'-fa-TA-yim sha-LOM sha-LOM la-ra-KHOK
v'-la-ka-ROV a-MAR a-do-NAI ur-fa-TEEV

20 But the wicked are like the troubled sea Which cannot rest, Whose waters toss up mire and mud.

וְהָרְשָׁעִים כַּיָּם נִגְרָשׁ כִּי הַשְׁקֵט לֹא יוּכָל וַיִּגְרְשׁוּ מֵימָיו רֶפֶשׁ וָטִיט: כ

21 There is no safety – said my God – For the wicked.

אֵין שָׁלוֹם אָמַר אֱלֹהַי לָרְשָׁעִים: כא

58 1 Cry with full throat, without restraint; Raise your voice like a *shofar*! Declare to My people their transgression, To the House of *Yaakov* their sin.

קְרָא בְגָרוֹן אַל תַּחְשֹׂךְ כַּשּׁוֹפָר הָרֵם קוֹלֶךָ וְהַגֵּד לְעַמִּי פִּשְׁעָם וּלְבֵית יַעֲקֹב חַטֹּאתָם: א נח

2 To be sure, they seek Me daily, Eager to learn My ways. Like a nation that does what is right, That has not abandoned the laws of its *Hashem*, They ask Me for the right way, They are eager for the nearness of *Hashem*:

וְאוֹתִי יוֹם יוֹם יִדְרֹשׁוּן וְדַעַת דְּרָכַי יֶחְפָּצוּן כְּגוֹי אֲשֶׁר־צְדָקָה עָשָׂה וּמִשְׁפַּט אֱלֹהָיו לֹא עָזָב יִשְׁאָלוּנִי מִשְׁפְּטֵי־צֶדֶק קִרְבַת אֱלֹהִים יֶחְפָּצוּן: ב

3 "Why, when we fasted, did You not see? When we starved our bodies, did You pay no heed?" Because on your fast day You see to your business And oppress all your laborers!

לָמָּה צַּמְנוּ וְלֹא רָאִיתָ עִנִּינוּ נַפְשֵׁנוּ וְלֹא תֵדָע הֵן בְּיוֹם צֹמְכֶם תִּמְצְאוּ־חֵפֶץ וְכָל־עַצְּבֵיכֶם תִּנְגֹּשׂוּ: ג

4 Because you fast in strife and contention, And you strike with a wicked fist! Your fasting today is not such As to make your voice heard on high.

הֵן לְרִיב וּמַצָּה תָּצוּמוּ וּלְהַכּוֹת בְּאֶגְרֹף רֶשַׁע לֹא־תָצוּמוּ כַיּוֹם לְהַשְׁמִיעַ בַּמָּרוֹם קוֹלְכֶם: ד

5 Is such the fast I desire, A day for men to starve their bodies? Is it bowing the head like a bulrush And lying in sackcloth and ashes? Do you call that a fast, A day when *Hashem* is favorable?

הֲכָזֶה יִהְיֶה צוֹם אֶבְחָרֵהוּ יוֹם עַנּוֹת אָדָם נַפְשׁוֹ הֲלָכֹף כְּאַגְמֹן רֹאשׁוֹ וְשַׂק וָאֵפֶר יַצִּיעַ הֲלָזֶה תִּקְרָא־צוֹם וְיוֹם רָצוֹן לַיהֹוָה: ה

6 No, this is the fast I desire: To unlock fetters of wickedness, And untie the cords of the yoke To let the oppressed go free; To break off every yoke.

הֲלוֹא זֶה צוֹם אֶבְחָרֵהוּ פַּתֵּחַ חַרְצֻבּוֹת רֶשַׁע הַתֵּר אֲגֻדּוֹת מוֹטָה וְשַׁלַּח רְצוּצִים חָפְשִׁים וְכָל־מוֹטָה תְּנַתֵּקוּ: ו

7 It is to share your bread with the hungry, And to take the wretched poor into your home; When you see the naked, to clothe him, And not to ignore your own kin.

הֲלוֹא פָרֹס לָרָעֵב לַחְמֶךָ וַעֲנִיִּים מְרוּדִים תָּבִיא בָיִת כִּי־תִרְאֶה עָרֹם וְכִסִּיתוֹ וּמִבְּשָׂרְךָ לֹא תִתְעַלָּם: ז

57:19 It shall be well, well with the far and the near *Yeshayahu* concludes the chapter with a promise that *Hashem* will provide the exiles who return with healing and comfort. The blessing of peace is proffered both to the far (those still in exile) and to the near (the exiles who already arrived in the Land of Israel). *Rashi* interprets the terms "far" and "near" as spiri-

tual markers – whether one has engaged in righteous behavior from birth, or only recently returned whole-heartedly to the right path, *Hashem*'s blessing of peace is upon them.

A white dove at the Western Wall

Isaiah

8 Then shall your light burst through like the dawn And your healing spring up quickly; Your Vindicator shall march before you, The Presence of *Hashem* shall be your rear guard.

9 Then, when you call, *Hashem* will answer; When you cry, He will say: Here I am. If you banish the yoke from your midst, The menacing hand, and evil speech,

10 And you offer your compassion to the hungry And satisfy the famished creature – Then shall your light shine in darkness, And your gloom shall be like noonday.

11 *Hashem* will guide you always; He will slake your thirst in parched places And give strength to your bones. You shall be like a watered garden, Like a spring whose waters do not fail.

12 Men from your midst shall rebuild ancient ruins, You shall restore foundations laid long ago. And you shall be called "Repairer of fallen walls, Restorer of lanes for habitation."

ח אָז יִבָּקַע כַּשַּׁחַר אוֹרֶךָ וַאֲרֻכָתְךָ מְהֵרָה תִצְמָח וְהָלַךְ לְפָנֶיךָ צִדְקֶךָ כְּבוֹד יְהוָה יַאַסְפֶךָ:

ט אָז תִּקְרָא וַיהוָה יַעֲנֶה תְּשַׁוַּע וְיֹאמַר הִנֵּנִי אִם־תָּסִיר מִתּוֹכְךָ מוֹטָה שְׁלַח אֶצְבַּע וְדַבֶּר־אָוֶן:

י וְתָפֵק לָרָעֵב נַפְשֶׁךָ וְנֶפֶשׁ נַעֲנָה תַּשְׂבִּיעַ וְזָרַח בַּחֹשֶׁךְ אוֹרֶךָ וַאֲפֵלָתְךָ כַּצָּהֳרָיִם:

יא וְנָחֲךָ יְהוָה תָּמִיד וְהִשְׂבִּיעַ בְּצַחְצָחוֹת נַפְשֶׁךָ וְעַצְמֹתֶיךָ יַחֲלִיץ וְהָיִיתָ כְּגַן רָוֶה וּכְמוֹצָא מַיִם אֲשֶׁר לֹא־יְכַזְּבוּ מֵימָיו:

יב וּבָנוּ מִמְּךָ חָרְבוֹת עוֹלָם מוֹסְדֵי דוֹר־ וָדוֹר תְּקוֹמֵם וְקֹרָא לְךָ גֹּדֵר פֶּרֶץ מְשֹׁבֵב נְתִיבוֹת לָשָׁבֶת:

u-va-NU mi-m'-KHA khor-VOT o-LAM mo-s'-DAY dor va-DOR t'-ko-MAYM v'-ko-RA l'-KHA go-DAYR PE-retz m'-sho-VAYV n'-tee-VOT la-SHA-vet

13 If you refrain from trampling the *Shabbat*, From pursuing your affairs on My holy day; If you call the *Shabbat* "delight," *Hashem*'s holy day "honored"; And if you honor it and go not your ways Nor look to your affairs, nor strike bargains –

יג אִם־תָּשִׁיב מִשַּׁבָּת רַגְלֶךָ עֲשׂוֹת חֲפָצֶיךָ בְּיוֹם קָדְשִׁי וְקָרָאתָ לַשַּׁבָּת עֹנֶג לִקְדוֹשׁ יְהוָה מְכֻבָּד וְכִבַּדְתּוֹ מֵעֲשׂוֹת דְּרָכֶיךָ מִמְּצוֹא חֶפְצְךָ וְדַבֵּר דָּבָר:

14 Then you can seek the favor of *Hashem*. I will set you astride the heights of the earth, And let you enjoy the heritage of your father *Yaakov* – For the mouth of *Hashem* has spoken.

יד אָז תִּתְעַנַּג עַל־יְהוָה וְהִרְכַּבְתִּיךָ עַל־ בָּמֳתֵי אָרֶץ וְהַאֲכַלְתִּיךָ נַחֲלַת יַעֲקֹב אָבִיךָ כִּי פִּי יְהוָה דִּבֵּר:

AZ tit-a-NAG al a-do-NAI v'-hir-kav-TEE-kha al BA-mo-tay A-retz v'-ha-a-khal-TEE-kha na-kha-LAT ya-a-KOV a-VEE-kha KEE PEE a-do-NAI di-BAYR

Naomi Shemer
(1930–2004)

58:12 You shall restore foundations laid long ago Although the Old City was lost in the 1948 War of Independence, it was liberated in the June 1967 Six-Day War. In May of 1967, Israeli songwriter, Naomi Shemer (1930–2004), composed the song *Yerushalayim Shel Zahav* (ירושלים של זהב), 'Jerusalem of Gold,' for the Israeli Song Festival. In it, she poetically describes the people's 2,000 year long, ongoing yearning for the city, "How the cisterns have dried, the market-place is empty, and no one frequents the Temple Mount, in the Old City. Jerusalem of gold, and of bronze, and of light, behold I am a lyre for all your songs." Not only an instant national hit, when war broke out a month later its lyrics and mel-

ody expressed the longing for ancient Jerusalem, which would be liberated in that war, in a way that mere words could not. Just after the war, Shemer added another stanza, "The cisterns are filled again with water, the square with joyous crowd, on the Temple Mount within the Old City, the *shofar* rings out loud." The ancient ruins were rebuilt and the foundations laid long ago restored. Fittingly, "Yerushalayim Shel Zahav" has become Israel's unofficial national anthem.

58:14 The heritage of your father Yaakov *Yeshayahu* describes the beautiful rewards for following *Hashem*'s commandments. Those

59 1 No, *Hashem*'s arm is not too short to save, Or His ear too dull to hear;

2 But your iniquities have been a barrier Between you and your God, Your sins have made Him turn His face away And refuse to hear you.

3 For your hands are defiled with crime And your fingers with iniquity. Your lips speak falsehood, Your tongue utters treachery.

4 No one sues justly Or pleads honestly; They rely on emptiness and speak falsehood, Conceiving wrong and begetting evil.

5 They hatch adder's eggs And weave spider webs; He who eats of those eggs will die, And if one is crushed, it hatches out a viper.

6 Their webs will not serve as a garment, What they make cannot serve as clothing; Their deeds are deeds of mischief, Their hands commit lawless acts,

7 Their feet run after evil, They hasten to shed the blood of the innocent. Their plans are plans of mischief, Destructiveness and injury are on their roads.

8 They do not care for the way of integrity, There is no justice on their paths. They make their courses crooked, No one who walks in them cares for integrity.

9 "That is why redress is far from us, And vindication does not reach us. We hope for light, and lo! there is darkness; For a gleam, and we must walk in gloom.

10 We grope, like blind men along a wall; Like those without eyes we grope. We stumble at noon, as if in darkness; Among the sturdy, we are like the dead.

11 We all growl like bears And moan like doves. We hope for redress, and there is none; For victory, and it is far from us.

12 For our many sins are before You, Our guilt testifies against us. We are aware of our sins, And we know well our iniquities:

נט א הֵן לֹא־קָצְרָה יַד־יְהֹוָה מֵהוֹשִׁיעַ וְלֹא־כָבְדָה אָזְנוֹ מִשְּׁמֽוֹעַ:

ב כִּי אִם־עֲוֺנֹֽתֵיכֶם הָיוּ מַבְדִּלִים בֵּינֵכֶם לְבֵין אֱלֹֽהֵיכֶם וְחַטֹּאותֵיכֶם הִסְתִּירוּ פָנִים מִכֶּם מִשְּׁמֽוֹעַ:

ג כִּי כַפֵּיכֶם נְגֹאֲלוּ בַדָּם וְאֶצְבְּעֽוֹתֵיכֶם בֶּֽעָוֺן שִׂפְתֽוֹתֵיכֶם דִּבְּרוּ־שֶׁקֶר לְשֽׁוֹנְכֶם עַוְלָה תֶהְגֶּֽה:

ד אֵין־קֹרֵא בְצֶדֶק וְאֵין נִשְׁפָּט בֶּאֱמוּנָה בָּטוֹחַ עַל־תֹּהוּ וְדַבֶּר־שָׁוְא הָרוֹ עָמָל וְהוֹלֵיד אָֽוֶן:

ה בֵּיצֵי צִפְעוֹנִי בִּקֵּעוּ וְקוּרֵי עַכָּבִישׁ יֶאֱרֹגוּ הָאֹכֵל מִבֵּֽיצֵיהֶם יָמוּת וְהַזּוּרֶה תִּבָּקַע אֶפְעֶֽה:

ו קֽוּרֵיהֶם לֹא־יִֽהְיוּ לְבֶגֶד וְלֹא יִתְכַּסּוּ בְּמַעֲשֵׂיהֶם מַעֲשֵׂיהֶם מַעֲשֵֽׂי־אָוֶן וּפֹעַל חָמָס בְּכַפֵּיהֶֽם:

ז רַגְלֵיהֶם לָרַע יָרֻצוּ וִֽימַהֲרוּ לִשְׁפֹּךְ דָּם נָקִי מַחְשְׁבֽוֹתֵיהֶם מַחְשְׁבוֹת אָוֶן שֹׁד וָשֶׁבֶר בִּמְסִלּוֹתָֽם:

ח דֶּרֶךְ שָׁלוֹם לֹא יָדָעוּ וְאֵין מִשְׁפָּט בְּמַעְגְּלוֹתָם נְתִֽיבֽוֹתֵיהֶם עִקְּשׁוּ לָהֶם כֹּל דֹּרֵךְ בָּהּ לֹא יָדַע שָׁלֽוֹם:

ט עַל־כֵּן רָחַק מִשְׁפָּט מִמֶּנּוּ וְלֹא תַשִּׂיגֵנוּ צְדָקָה נְקַוֶּה לָאוֹר וְהִנֵּה־חֹשֶׁךְ לִנְגֹהוֹת בָּאֲפֵלוֹת נְהַלֵּֽךְ:

י נְגַשְׁשָׁה כַֽעִוְרִים קִיר וּכְאֵין עֵינַיִם נְגַשֵּׁשָׁה כָּשַׁלְנוּ בַֽצׇּהֳרַיִם כַּנֶּשֶׁף בָּאַשְׁמַנִּים כַּמֵּתִֽים:

יא נֶהֱמֶה כַדֻּבִּים כֻּלָּנוּ וְכַיּוֹנִים הָגֹה נֶהְגֶּה נְקַוֶּה לַמִּשְׁפָּט וָאַיִן לִֽישׁוּעָה רָחֲקָה מִמֶּֽנּוּ:

יב כִּֽי־רַבּוּ פְשָׁעֵינוּ נֶגְדֶּךָ וְחַטֹּאותֵינוּ עָנְתָה בָּנוּ כִּֽי־פְשָׁעֵינוּ אִתָּנוּ וַעֲוֺנֹתֵינוּ יְדַעֲנֽוּם:

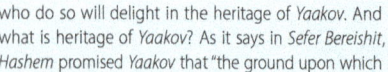
who do so will delight in the heritage of *Yaakov*. And what is heritage of *Yaakov*? As it says in *Sefer Bereishit*, *Hashem* promised *Yaakov* that "the ground upon which you are lying (i.e. the Land of Israel) I will assign to you and to your offspring" (Genesis 28:13).

Proposed site of *Yaakov*'s dream in *Beit El*

13 Rebellion, faithlessness to *Hashem*, And turning away from our God, Planning fraud and treachery, Conceiving lies and uttering them with the throat.

יג פָּשֹׁעַ וְכַחֵשׁ בַּיהוָה וְנָסוֹג מֵאַחַר אֱלֹהֵינוּ דַּבֶּר־עֹשֶׁק וְסָרָה הֹרוֹ וְהֹגוֹ מִלֵּב דִּבְרֵי־שָׁקֶר:

14 And so redress is turned back And vindication stays afar, Because honesty stumbles in the public square And uprightness cannot enter.

יד וְהֻסַּג אָחוֹר מִשְׁפָּט וּצְדָקָה מֵרָחוֹק תַּעֲמֹד כִּי־כָשְׁלָה בָרְחוֹב אֱמֶת וּנְכֹחָה לֹא־תוּכַל לָבוֹא:

15 Honesty has been lacking, He who turns away from evil is despoiled." *Hashem* saw and was displeased That there was no redress.

טו וַתְּהִי הָאֱמֶת נֶעְדֶּרֶת וְסָר מֵרָע מִשְׁתּוֹלֵל וַיַּרְא יְהוָה וַיֵּרַע בְּעֵינָיו כִּי־אֵין מִשְׁפָּט:

16 He saw that there was no man, He gazed long, but no one intervened. Then His own arm won Him triumph, His victorious right hand supported Him.

טז וַיַּרְא כִּי־אֵין אִישׁ וַיִּשְׁתּוֹמֵם כִּי אֵין מַפְגִּיעַ וַתּוֹשַׁע לוֹ זְרֹעוֹ וְצִדְקָתוֹ הִיא סְמָכָתְהוּ:

17 He donned victory like a coat of mail, With a helmet of triumph on His head; He clothed Himself with garments of retribution, Wrapped himself in zeal as in a robe.

יז וַיִּלְבַּשׁ צְדָקָה כַּשִּׁרְיָן וְכוֹבַע יְשׁוּעָה בְּרֹאשׁוֹ וַיִּלְבַּשׁ בִּגְדֵי נָקָם תִּלְבֹּשֶׁת וַיַּעַט כַּמְעִיל קִנְאָה:

18 According to their deserts, So shall He repay fury to His foes; He shall make requital to His enemies, Requital to the distant lands.

יח כְּעַל גְּמֻלוֹת כְּעַל יְשַׁלֵּם חֵמָה לְצָרָיו גְּמוּל לְאֹיְבָיו לָאִיִּים גְּמוּל יְשַׁלֵּם:

19 From the west, they shall revere the name of *Hashem*, And from the east, His Presence. For He shall come like a hemmed-in stream Which the wind of *Hashem* drives on;

יט וְיִרְאוּ מִמַּעֲרָב אֶת־שֵׁם יְהוָה וּמִמִּזְרַח־שֶׁמֶשׁ אֶת־כְּבוֹדוֹ כִּי־יָבוֹא כַנָּהָר צָר רוּחַ יְהוָה נֹסְסָה בוֹ:

20 He shall come as redeemer to *Tzion*, To those in *Yaakov* who turn back from sin – declares *Hashem*.

כ וּבָא לְצִיּוֹן גּוֹאֵל וּלְשָׁבֵי פֶשַׁע בְּיַעֲקֹב נְאֻם יְהוָה:

u-VA l'-tzi-YON go-AYL ul-sha-VAY FE-sha b'-ya-a-KOV n'-UM a-do-NAI

21 And this shall be My covenant with them, said *Hashem*: My spirit which is upon you, and the words which I have placed in your mouth, shall not be absent from your mouth, nor from the mouth of your children, nor from the mouth of your children's children – said *Hashem* – from now on, for all time.

כא וַאֲנִי זֹאת בְּרִיתִי אוֹתָם אָמַר יְהוָה רוּחִי אֲשֶׁר עָלֶיךָ וּדְבָרַי אֲשֶׁר־שַׂמְתִּי בְּפִיךָ לֹא־יָמוּשׁוּ מִפִּיךָ וּמִפִּי זַרְעֲךָ וּמִפִּי זֶרַע זַרְעֲךָ אָמַר יְהוָה מֵעַתָּה וְעַד־עוֹלָם:

Panoramic view of rebuilt *Yerushalayim*

59:20 He shall come as redeemer to *Tzion* After the climactic battle described above, *Yesha-yahu* promises that a redeemer will come to *Tzion*. *Rashi* observes, "As long as *Tzion* is in ruins, the redeemer has not yet come." On a simple level, *Rashi* is saying that once the redeemer comes, *Tzion* will be rebuilt. Hence, if *Tzion* remains in ruins then surely he has not yet come. On a deeper level, perhaps he is implying that for the redeemer to come, *Tzion* cannot be in a state of disrepair; instead, the city of *Yerushalayim* and the Land of Israel must first be built by the returnees to the land. Only then will God's spirit enter the people. Indeed, as the returnees of modern times have begun to rebuild and *Eretz Yisrael* flourishes, our generation eagerly awaits the redeemer to come.

Isaiah

60 ¹ Arise, shine, for your light has dawned; The Presence of *Hashem* has shone upon you!

KU-mee O-ree KEE VA o-RAYKH ukh-VOD a-do-NAI a-LA-yikh za-RAKH

ס א קוּמִי אוֹרִי כִּי בָא אוֹרֵךְ וּכְבוֹד יְהֹוָה עָלַיִךְ זָרָח:

² Behold! Darkness shall cover the earth, And thick clouds the peoples; But upon you *Hashem* will shine, And His Presence be seen over you.

ב כִּי־הִנֵּה הַחֹשֶׁךְ יְכַסֶּה־אֶרֶץ וַעֲרָפֶל לְאֻמִּים וְעָלַיִךְ יִזְרַח יְהֹוָה וּכְבוֹדוֹ עָלַיִךְ יֵרָאֶה:

³ And nations shall walk by your light, Kings, by your shining radiance.

ג וְהָלְכוּ גוֹיִם לְאוֹרֵךְ וּמְלָכִים לְנֹגַהּ זַרְחֵךְ:

⁴ Raise your eyes and look about: They have all gathered and come to you. Your sons shall be brought from afar, Your daughters like babes on shoulders.

ד שְׂאִי־סָבִיב עֵינַיִךְ וּרְאִי כֻּלָּם נִקְבְּצוּ בָאוּ־לָךְ בָּנַיִךְ מֵרָחוֹק יָבֹאוּ וּבְנֹתַיִךְ עַל־צַד תֵּאָמַנָה:

⁵ As you behold, you will glow; Your heart will throb and thrill – For the wealth of the sea shall pass on to you, The riches of nations shall flow to you.

ה אָז תִּרְאִי וְנָהַרְתְּ וּפָחַד וְרָחַב לְבָבֵךְ כִּי־יֵהָפֵךְ עָלַיִךְ הֲמוֹן יָם חֵיל גּוֹיִם יָבֹאוּ לָךְ:

⁶ Dust clouds of camels shall cover you, Dromedaries of Midian and Ephah. They all shall come from Sheba; They shall bear gold and frankincense, And shall herald the glories of *Hashem*.

ו שִׁפְעַת גְּמַלִּים תְּכַסֵּךְ בִּכְרֵי מִדְיָן וְעֵיפָה כֻּלָּם מִשְּׁבָא יָבֹאוּ זָהָב וּלְבוֹנָה יִשָּׂאוּ וּתְהִלֹּת יְהֹוָה יְבַשֵּׂרוּ:

⁷ All the flocks of Kedar shall be assembled for you, The rams of Nebaioth shall serve your needs; They shall be welcome offerings on My *Mizbayach*, And I will add glory to My glorious House.

ז כָּל־צֹאן קֵדָר יִקָּבְצוּ לָךְ אֵילֵי נְבָיוֹת יְשָׁרְתוּנֶךְ יַעֲלוּ עַל־רָצוֹן מִזְבְּחִי וּבֵית תִּפְאַרְתִּי אֲפָאֵר:

⁸ Who are these that float like a cloud, Like doves to their cotes?

ח מִי־אֵלֶּה כָּעָב תְּעוּפֶינָה וְכַיּוֹנִים אֶל־אֲרֻבֹּתֵיהֶם:

Isaiah

Yerushalayim

60:1 Arise, shine The prophet addresses *Yerushalayim*, calling upon the city to awaken and shine its light upon the world. Chaim Weizman (1874–1952) was a prominent scientist and Zionist leader who would have the honor of becoming the first President of the State of Israel. In 1948, Weizman eloquently explained the illumination that Jerusalem would provide the world as the new capital of the Jewish State: "Jerusalem holds a unique place in the heart of every Jew. Its restoration symbolizes the redemption of Israel. Rome was to the Italians the emblem of their military conquests and political organization. Athens embodies for the Greeks the noblest their genius had wrought in art and thought. To us Jerusalem has both a spiritual and a temporal significance. It is the City of God … it is also the capital of David and Solomon…. To the followers of the two other great monotheistic religions, Jerusalem is a site of sacred associations and holy memories. To us it is that and more than that. It is the centre of our ancient national glory. It was our lodestar in all our wanderings. It embodies all that is noblest in our hopes for the future. Jerusalem is the eternal mother of the Jewish people, precious and beloved even in its desolation. When David made Jerusalem the capital of Judea, on that day there began the Jewish Commonwealth. When Titus destroyed it on the 9th of Av, on that day there ended the Jewish Commonwealth. Nevertheless, even though our Commonwealth was destroyed, we never gave up Jerusalem…. It seems inconceivable that the establishment of a Jewish State should be accompanied by the detachment from it of its spiritual centre and historical capital."

9 Behold, the coastlands await me, With ships of Tarshish in the lead, To bring your sons from afar, And their silver and gold as well – For the name of *Hashem* your God, For the Holy One of *Yisrael*, who has glorified you.

ט כִּי־לִי אִיִּים יְקַוּוּ וָאֳנִיּוֹת תַּרְשִׁישׁ בָּרִאשֹׁנָה לְהָבִיא בָנַיִךְ מֵרָחוֹק כַּסְפָּם וּזְהָבָם אִתָּם לְשֵׁם יְהֹוָה אֱלֹהַיִךְ וְלִקְדוֹשׁ יִשְׂרָאֵל כִּי פֵאֲרָךְ:

10 Aliens shall rebuild your walls, Their kings shall wait upon you – For in anger I struck you down, But in favor I take you back.

י וּבָנוּ בְנֵי־נֵכָר חֹמֹתַיִךְ וּמַלְכֵיהֶם יְשָׁרְתוּנֶךְ כִּי בְקִצְפִּי הִכִּיתִיךְ וּבִרְצוֹנִי רִחַמְתִּיךְ:

11 Your gates shall always stay open – Day and night they shall never be shut – To let in the wealth of the nations, With their kings in procession.

יא וּפִתְּחוּ שְׁעָרַיִךְ תָּמִיד יוֹמָם וָלַיְלָה לֹא יִסָּגֵרוּ לְהָבִיא אֵלַיִךְ חֵיל גּוֹיִם וּמַלְכֵיהֶם נְהוּגִים:

12 For the nation or the kingdom That does not serve you shall perish; Such nations shall be destroyed.

יב כִּי־הַגּוֹי וְהַמַּמְלָכָה אֲשֶׁר לֹא־יַעַבְדוּךְ יֹאבֵדוּ וְהַגּוֹיִם חָרֹב יֶחֱרָבוּ:

13 The majesty of Lebanon shall come to you – Cypress and pine and box – To adorn the site of My Sanctuary, To glorify the place where My feet rest.

יג כְּבוֹד הַלְּבָנוֹן אֵלַיִךְ יָבוֹא בְּרוֹשׁ תִּדְהָר וּתְאַשּׁוּר יַחְדָּו לְפָאֵר מְקוֹם מִקְדָּשִׁי וּמְקוֹם רַגְלַי אֲכַבֵּד:

14 Bowing before you, shall come The children of those who tormented you; Prostrate at the soles of your feet Shall be all those who reviled you; And you shall be called "City of *Hashem*, *Tzion* of the Holy One of *Yisrael*."

יד וְהָלְכוּ אֵלַיִךְ שְׁחוֹחַ בְּנֵי מְעַנַּיִךְ וְהִשְׁתַּחֲווּ עַל־כַּפּוֹת רַגְלַיִךְ כָּל־מְנַאֲצָיִךְ וְקָרְאוּ לָךְ עִיר יְהֹוָה צִיּוֹן קְדוֹשׁ יִשְׂרָאֵל:

15 Whereas you have been forsaken, Rejected, with none passing through, I will mak you a pride everlasting, A joy for age after age.

טו תַּחַת הֱיוֹתֵךְ עֲזוּבָה וּשְׂנוּאָה וְאֵין עוֹבֵר וְשַׂמְתִּיךְ לִגְאוֹן עוֹלָם מְשׂוֹשׂ דּוֹר וָדוֹר:

16 You shall suck the milk of the nations, Suckle at royal breasts. And you shall know That I *Hashem* am your Savior, I, The Mighty One of *Yaakov*, am your Redeemer.

טז וְיָנַקְתְּ חֲלֵב גּוֹיִם וְשֹׁד מְלָכִים תִּינָקִי וְיָדַעַתְּ כִּי אֲנִי יְהֹוָה מוֹשִׁיעֵךְ וְגֹאֲלֵךְ אֲבִיר יַעֲקֹב:

17 Instead of copper I will bring gold, Instead of iron I will bring silver; Instead of wood, copper; And instead of stone, iron. And I will appoint Well-being as your government, Prosperity as your officials.

יז תַּחַת הַנְּחֹשֶׁת אָבִיא זָהָב וְתַחַת הַבַּרְזֶל אָבִיא כֶסֶף וְתַחַת הָעֵצִים נְחֹשֶׁת וְתַחַת הָאֲבָנִים בַּרְזֶל וְשַׂמְתִּי פְקֻדָּתֵךְ שָׁלוֹם וְנֹגְשַׂיִךְ צְדָקָה:

18 The cry "Violence!" Shall no more be heard in your land, Nor "Wrack and ruin!" Within your borders. And you shall name your walls "Victory" And your gates "Renown."

יח לֹא־יִשָּׁמַע עוֹד חָמָס בְּאַרְצֵךְ שֹׁד וָשֶׁבֶר בִּגְבוּלָיִךְ וְקָרָאת יְשׁוּעָה חוֹמֹתַיִךְ וּשְׁעָרַיִךְ תְּהִלָּה:

19 No longer shall you need the sun For light by day, Nor the shining of the moon For radiance [by night]; For *Hashem* shall be your light everlasting, Your God shall be your glory.

יט לֹא־יִהְיֶה־לָּךְ עוֹד הַשֶּׁמֶשׁ לְאוֹר יוֹמָם וּלְנֹגַהּ הַיָּרֵחַ לֹא־יָאִיר לָךְ וְהָיָה־לָךְ יְהֹוָה לְאוֹר עוֹלָם וֵאלֹהַיִךְ לְתִפְאַרְתֵּךְ:

107

20 Your sun shall set no more, Your moon no more withdraw; For *Hashem* shall be a light to you forever, And your days of mourning shall be ended.

כ לֹא־יָבוֹא עוֹד שִׁמְשֵׁךְ וִירֵחֵךְ לֹא יֵאָסֵף כִּי יְהוָה יִהְיֶה־לָּךְ לְאוֹר עוֹלָם וְשָׁלְמוּ יְמֵי אֶבְלֵךְ:

21 And your people, all of them righteous, Shall possess the land for all time; They are the shoot that I planted, My handiwork in which I glory.

כא וְעַמֵּךְ כֻּלָּם צַדִּיקִים לְעוֹלָם יִירְשׁוּ אָרֶץ נֵצֶר מַטָּעוֹ [מַטָּעַי] מַעֲשֵׂה יָדַי לְהִתְפָּאֵר:

22 The smallest shall become a clan; The least, a mighty nation. I *Hashem* will speed it in due time.

כב הַקָּטֹן יִהְיֶה לָאֶלֶף וְהַצָּעִיר לְגוֹי עָצוּם אֲנִי יְהוָה בְּעִתָּהּ אֲחִישֶׁנָּה:

61 ¹ The spirit of *Hashem* is upon me, Because *Hashem* has anointed me; He has sent me as a herald of joy to the humble, To bind up the wounded of heart, To proclaim release to the captives, Liberation to the imprisoned;

סא א רוּחַ אֲדֹנָי יֱהוִֹה עָלָי יַעַן מָשַׁח יְהוָה אֹתִי לְבַשֵּׂר עֲנָוִים שְׁלָחַנִי לַחֲבֹשׁ לְנִשְׁבְּרֵי־לֵב לִקְרֹא לִשְׁבוּיִם דְּרוֹר וְלַאֲסוּרִים פְּקַח־קוֹחַ:

² To proclaim a year of *Hashem*'s favor And a day of vindication by our God; To comfort all who mourn –

ב לִקְרֹא שְׁנַת־רָצוֹן לַיהוָה וְיוֹם נָקָם לֵאלֹהֵינוּ לְנַחֵם כָּל־אֲבֵלִים:

³ To provide for the mourners in *Tzion* – To give them a turban instead of ashes, The festive ointment instead of mourning, A garment of splendor instead of a drooping spirit. They shall be called terebinths of victory, Planted by *Hashem* for His glory.

ג לָשׂוּם לַאֲבֵלֵי צִיּוֹן לָתֵת לָהֶם פְּאֵר תַּחַת אֵפֶר שֶׁמֶן שָׂשׂוֹן תַּחַת אֵבֶל מַעֲטֵה תְהִלָּה תַּחַת רוּחַ כֵּהָה וְקֹרָא לָהֶם אֵילֵי הַצֶּדֶק מַטַּע יְהוָה לְהִתְפָּאֵר:

⁴ And they shall build the ancient ruins, Raise up the desolations of old, And renew the ruined cities, The desolations of many ages.

ד וּבָנוּ חָרְבוֹת עוֹלָם שֹׁמְמוֹת רִאשֹׁנִים יְקוֹמֵמוּ וְחִדְּשׁוּ עָרֵי חֹרֶב שֹׁמְמוֹת דּוֹר וָדוֹר:

⁵ Strangers shall stand and pasture your flocks, Aliens shall be your plowmen and vine-trimmers;

ה וְעָמְדוּ זָרִים וְרָעוּ צֹאנְכֶם וּבְנֵי נֵכָר אִכָּרֵיכֶם וְכֹרְמֵיכֶם:

v'-a-m'-DU za-REEM v'-ra-U tzo-n'-KHEM uv-NAY nay-KHAR i-ka-ray-HEM v'-kho-r'-may-KHEM

⁶ While you shall be called "*Kohanim* of *Hashem*," And termed "Servants of our God." You shall enjoy the wealth of nations And revel in their riches.

ו וְאַתֶּם כֹּהֲנֵי יְהוָה תִּקָּרֵאוּ מְשָׁרְתֵי אֱלֹהֵינוּ יֵאָמֵר לָכֶם חֵיל גּוֹיִם תֹּאכֵלוּ וּבִכְבוֹדָם תִּתְיַמָּרוּ:

61:5 Strangers shall stand and pasture your flocks During the Messianic age, non-Jews will play an essential role in helping the Jewish people settle the Land of Israel through agriculture, as this verse states, and they will also partner with the Jews in spiritual pursuits. Rabbi Israel Lipschitz (1782–1860), in his commentary *Tiferet Yisrael*, quotes this verse to prove that non-Jews will participate in the actual construction of the Holy Temple, similar to the assistance King *Shlomo* sought from King Hiram of Tyre who sent builders and artisans to help build the first *Beit Hamikdash*. In modern times, this verse serves as the inspiration for the hundreds of Christian volunteers who travel each year during the harvest season to assist Jewish farmers in Israel.

Rabbi Tuly Weisz and a Christian volunteer planting trees in the Land of Israel

Isaiah

Isaiah

7 Because your shame was double – Men cried, "Disgrace is their portion" – Assuredly, They shall have a double share in their land, Joy shall be theirs for all time.

ז תַּחַת בָּשְׁתְּכֶם מִשְׁנֶה וּכְלִמָּה יָרֹנּוּ חֶלְקָם לָכֵן בְּאַרְצָם מִשְׁנֶה יִירָשׁוּ שִׂמְחַת עוֹלָם תִּהְיֶה לָהֶם:

8 For I *Hashem* love justice, I hate robbery with a burnt offering. I will pay them their wages faithfully, And make a covenant with them for all time.

ח כִּי אֲנִי יְהוָה אֹהֵב מִשְׁפָּט שֹׂנֵא גָזֵל בְּעוֹלָה וְנָתַתִּי פְעֻלָּתָם בֶּאֱמֶת וּבְרִית עוֹלָם אֶכְרוֹת לָהֶם:

9 Their offspring shall be known among the nations, Their descendants in the midst of the peoples. All who see them shall recognize That they are a stock *Hashem* has blessed.

ט וְנוֹדַע בַּגּוֹיִם זַרְעָם וְצֶאֱצָאֵיהֶם בְּתוֹךְ הָעַמִּים כָּל־רֹאֵיהֶם יַכִּירוּם כִּי הֵם זֶרַע בֵּרַךְ יְהוָה:

10 I greatly rejoice in *Hashem*, My whole being exults in my God. For He has clothed me with garments of triumph, Wrapped me in a robe of victory, Like a bridegroom adorned with a turban, Like a bride bedecked with her finery.

י שׂוֹשׂ אָשִׂישׂ בַּיהוָה תָּגֵל נַפְשִׁי בֵּאלֹהַי כִּי הִלְבִּישַׁנִי בִּגְדֵי־יֶשַׁע מְעִיל צְדָקָה יְעָטָנִי כֶּחָתָן יְכַהֵן פְּאֵר וְכַכַּלָּה תַּעְדֶּה כֵלֶיהָ:

SOS a-SEES ba-do-NAI ta-GAYL naf-SHEE bay-lo-HAI KEE hil-bee-SHA-nee big-day YE-sha m'-EEL tz'-da-KAH y'-a-TA-nee ke-kha-TAN y'-kha-HAYN p'-AYR v'-kha-ka-LAH ta-DEH khay-LE-ha

11 For as the earth brings forth her growth And a garden makes the seed shoot up, So *Hashem* will make Victory and renown shoot up In the presence of all the nations.

יא כִּי כָאָרֶץ תּוֹצִיא צִמְחָהּ וּכְגַנָּה זֵרוּעֶיהָ תַצְמִיחַ כֵּן אֲדֹנָי יְהוִה יַצְמִיחַ צְדָקָה וּתְהִלָּה נֶגֶד כָּל־הַגּוֹיִם:

62 1 For the sake of *Tzion* I will not be silent, For the sake of *Yerushalayim* I will not be still, Till her victory emerge resplendent And her triumph like a flaming torch.

סב א לְמַעַן צִיּוֹן לֹא אֶחֱשֶׁה וּלְמַעַן יְרוּשָׁלַם לֹא אֶשְׁקוֹט עַד־יֵצֵא כַנֹּגַהּ צִדְקָהּ וִישׁוּעָתָהּ כְּלַפִּיד יִבְעָר:

2 Nations shall see your victory, And every king your majesty; And you shall be called by a new name Which *Hashem* Himself shall bestow.

ב וְרָאוּ גוֹיִם צִדְקֵךְ וְכָל־מְלָכִים כְּבוֹדֵךְ וְקֹרָא לָךְ שֵׁם חָדָשׁ אֲשֶׁר פִּי יְהוָה יִקֳּבֶנּוּ:

3 You shall be a glorious crown In the hand of *Hashem*, And a royal diadem In the palm of your God.

ג וְהָיִית עֲטֶרֶת תִּפְאֶרֶת בְּיַד־יְהוָה וּצְנִיף [וּצְנוֹף] מְלוּכָה בְּכַף־אֱלֹהָיִךְ:

61:10 I greatly rejoice in *Hashem* *Yeshayahu* speaks in his own voice, rejoicing in *Hashem's* goodness to His people. The salvation of the Jewish people, returned and dwelling safely in their own land, will be as visible as the fine jewels worn by a bridegroom and bride on their wedding day. In the meantime, while *Har Habayit* lies in ruin, the Jewish people observe a number of customs mourning the loss of the *Beit Hamikdash*. These include not wearing excessive amounts of jewelry and smashing a glass at Jewish wedding ceremonies, both as a reminder that the complete rebuilding of *Yerushalayim* and the *Beit Hamikdash* has yet to come.

Breaking the glass at a Jewish wedding

4 Nevermore shall you be called "Forsaken," Nor shall your land be called "Desolate"; But you shall be called "I delight in her," And your land "Espoused." For *Hashem* takes delight in you, And your land shall be espoused.

ד לֹא־יֵאָמֵר לָךְ עוֹד עֲזוּבָה וּלְאַרְצֵךְ לֹא־יֵאָמֵר עוֹד שְׁמָמָה כִּי לָךְ יִקָּרֵא חֶפְצִי־בָהּ וּלְאַרְצֵךְ בְּעוּלָה כִּי־חָפֵץ יְהֹוָה בָּךְ וְאַרְצֵךְ תִּבָּעֵל:

5 As a youth espouses a maiden, Your sons shall espouse you; And as a bridegroom rejoices over his bride, So will your God rejoice over you.

ה כִּי־יִבְעַל בָּחוּר בְּתוּלָה יִבְעָלוּךְ בָּנָיִךְ וּמְשׂוֹשׂ חָתָן עַל־כַּלָּה יָשִׂישׂ עָלַיִךְ אֱלֹהָיִךְ:

6 Upon your walls, O *Yerushalayim*, I have set watchmen, Who shall never be silent By day or by night. O you, *Hashem's* remembrancers Take no rest

ו עַל־חוֹמֹתַיִךְ יְרוּשָׁלַםִ הִפְקַדְתִּי שֹׁמְרִים כָּל־הַיּוֹם וְכָל־הַלַּיְלָה תָּמִיד לֹא יֶחֱשׁוּ הַמַּזְכִּרִים אֶת־יְהֹוָה אַל־דֳּמִי לָכֶם:

al kho-mo-TA-yikh y'-ru-sha-LA-im hif-KAD-tee sho-m'-REEM
kol ha-YOM v'-khol ha-LAI-lah ta-MEED lo ye-khe-SHU
ha-maz-ki-REEM et a-do-NAI al do-MEE la-KHEM

7 And give no rest to Him, Until He establish *Yerushalayim* And make her renowned on earth.

ז וְאַל־תִּתְּנוּ דֳמִי לוֹ עַד־יְכוֹנֵן וְעַד־יָשִׂים אֶת־יְרוּשָׁלַםִ תְּהִלָּה בָּאָרֶץ:

v'-al ti-t'-NU da-MEE LO ad y'-kho-NAYN v'-ad ya-SEEM
et y'-ru-sha-LA-im t'-hi-LAH ba-A-retz

8 *Hashem* has sworn by His right hand, By His mighty arm: Nevermore will I give your new grain To your enemies for food, Nor shall foreigners drink the new wine For which you have labored.

ח נִשְׁבַּע יְהֹוָה בִּימִינוֹ וּבִזְרוֹעַ עֻזּוֹ אִם־אֶתֵּן אֶת־דְּגָנֵךְ עוֹד מַאֲכָל לְאֹיְבַיִךְ וְאִם־יִשְׁתּוּ בְנֵי־נֵכָר תִּירוֹשֵׁךְ אֲשֶׁר יָגַעַתְּ בּוֹ:

9 But those who harvest it shall eat it And give praise to *Hashem*; And those who gather it shall drink it In My sacred courts.

ט כִּי מְאַסְפָיו יֹאכְלֻהוּ וְהִלְלוּ אֶת־יְהֹוָה וּמְקַבְּצָיו יִשְׁתֻּהוּ בְּחַצְרוֹת קָדְשִׁי:

10 Pass through, pass through the gates! Clear the road for the people; Build up, build up the highway, Remove the rocks! Raise an ensign over the peoples!

י עִבְרוּ עִבְרוּ בַּשְּׁעָרִים פַּנּוּ דֶּרֶךְ הָעָם סֹלּוּ סֹלּוּ הַמְסִלָּה סַקְּלוּ מֵאֶבֶן הָרִימוּ נֵס עַל־הָעַמִּים:

א **62:6 Who shall never be silent by day or by night** If the watchmen are upon the walls all day and all night, then why is the superfluous word *tamid* (תמיד) 'always,' included in this verse? 20th century American Rabbi David Stavsky explains in his book of sermons: "*Tamid,* 'always,' refers to speaking up about *Yerushalayim*. Never should we remain silent when *Yerushalayim* is threatened. We are not to remain quiet and passive. We are the guardians.... Therefore, *Yerushalayim* never can

become a bargaining chip in achieving peace. Not the Vatican, not Washington, not Hamas, not Hezbollah, not any Arab fundamentalist or terrorist can dictate terms. Threats of Jihad should not make us waiver. *Yerusha-*

The walls of *Yerushalayim* at sunset

layim is finally ours, and we are the watchmen *tamid*, always."

א **62:7 And give no rest to Him** The Hebrew word for rest in this verse is *damee* (דמי), which also means 'silence.' Interestingly, the same Hebrew word, *dam* (דם), means 'blood.' Commentators explain the connection in light of Ezekiel 16:6, "Live in spite of your blood." The hidden meaning behind the verse is, 'by your silence you shall live.' In relationships, the truism "silence is golden" can protect against an insensitive remark. So too when it comes to our relationship with *Hashem*. Oftentimes we cannot comprehend His ways, and we become frustrated and even angry with the suffering we see in this world. Nevertheless, we must try to emulate *Aharon's* example after losing two of his sons: *Vayidom Aharon* (וידם אהרן), '*Aharon* was silent' (Leviticus 10:3).

דם

11 See, *Hashem* has proclaimed To the end of the earth: Announce to Fair *Tzion*, Your Deliverer is coming! See, his reward is with Him, His recompense before Him.

הִנֵּה יְהֹוָה הִשְׁמִיעַ אֶל־קְצֵה הָאָרֶץ אִמְרוּ לְבַת־צִיּוֹן הִנֵּה יִשְׁעֵךְ בָּא הִנֵּה שְׂכָרוֹ אִתּוֹ וּפְעֻלָּתוֹ לְפָנָיו׃

12 And they shall be called, "The Holy People, The Redeemed of *Hashem*," And you shall be called, "Sought Out, A City Not Forsaken."

וְקָרְאוּ לָהֶם עַם־הַקֹּדֶשׁ גְּאוּלֵי יְהֹוָה וְלָךְ יִקָּרֵא דְרוּשָׁה עִיר לֹא נֶעֱזָבָה׃

63 1 Who is this coming from Edom, In crimsoned garments from Bozrah – Who is this, majestic in attire, Pressing forward in His great might? "It is I, who contend victoriously, Powerful to give triumph."

סג א מִי־זֶה בָּא מֵאֱדוֹם חֲמוּץ בְּגָדִים מִבָּצְרָה זֶה הָדוּר בִּלְבוּשׁוֹ צֹעֶה בְּרֹב כֹּחוֹ אֲנִי מְדַבֵּר בִּצְדָקָה רַב לְהוֹשִׁיעַ׃

2 Why is your clothing so red, Your garments like his who treads grapes?

ב מַדּוּעַ אָדֹם לִלְבוּשֶׁךָ וּבְגָדֶיךָ כְּדֹרֵךְ בְּגַת׃

3 "I trod out a vintage alone; Of the peoples no man was with Me. I trod them down in My anger, Trampled them in My rage; Their life-blood bespattered My garments, And all My clothing was stained.

ג פּוּרָה דָּרַכְתִּי לְבַדִּי וּמֵעַמִּים אֵין־אִישׁ אִתִּי וְאֶדְרְכֵם בְּאַפִּי וְאֶרְמְסֵם בַּחֲמָתִי וְיֵז נִצְחָם עַל־בְּגָדַי וְכָל־מַלְבּוּשַׁי אֶגְאָלְתִּי׃

4 For I had planned a day of vengeance, And My year of redemption arrived.

ד כִּי יוֹם נָקָם בְּלִבִּי וּשְׁנַת גְּאוּלַי בָּאָה׃

5 Then I looked, but there was none to help; I stared, but there was none to aid – So My own arm wrought the triumph, And My own rage was My aid.

ה וְאַבִּיט וְאֵין עֹזֵר וְאֶשְׁתּוֹמֵם וְאֵין סוֹמֵךְ וַתּוֹשַׁע לִי זְרֹעִי וַחֲמָתִי הִיא סְמָכָתְנִי׃

6 I trampled peoples in My anger, I made them drunk with My rage, And I hurled their glory to the ground."

ו וְאָבוּס עַמִּים בְּאַפִּי וַאֲשַׁכְּרֵם בַּחֲמָתִי וְאוֹרִיד לָאָרֶץ נִצְחָם׃

7 I will recount the kind acts of *Hashem*, The praises of *Hashem* – For all that *Hashem* has wrought for us, The vast bounty to the House of *Yisrael* That He bestowed upon them According to His mercy and His great kindness.

ז חַסְדֵי יְהֹוָה אַזְכִּיר תְּהִלֹּת יְהֹוָה כְּעַל כֹּל אֲשֶׁר־גְּמָלָנוּ יְהֹוָה וְרַב־טוּב לְבֵית יִשְׂרָאֵל אֲשֶׁר־גְּמָלָם כְּרַחֲמָיו וּכְרֹב חֲסָדָיו׃

8 He thought: Surely they are My people, Children who will not play false. So He was their Deliverer.

ח וַיֹּאמֶר אַךְ־עַמִּי הֵמָּה בָּנִים לֹא יְשַׁקֵּרוּ וַיְהִי לָהֶם לְמוֹשִׁיעַ׃

9 In all their troubles He was troubled, And the angel of His Presence delivered them. In His love and pity He Himself redeemed them, Raised them, and exalted them All the days of old.

ט בְּכָל־צָרָתָם לֹא [לוֹ] צָר וּמַלְאַךְ פָּנָיו הוֹשִׁיעָם בְּאַהֲבָתוֹ וּבְחֶמְלָתוֹ הוּא גְאָלָם וַיְנַטְּלֵם וַיְנַשְּׂאֵם כָּל־יְמֵי עוֹלָם׃

10 But they rebelled, and grieved His holy spirit; Then He became their enemy, And Himself made war against them.

י וְהֵמָּה מָרוּ וְעִצְּבוּ אֶת־רוּחַ קָדְשׁוֹ וַיֵּהָפֵךְ לָהֶם לְאוֹיֵב הוּא נִלְחַם־בָּם׃

¹¹ Then they remembered the ancient days, Him, who pulled His people out [of the water]: "Where is He who brought them up from the Sea Along with the shepherd of His flock? Where is He who put In their midst His holy spirit,

יא וַיִּזְכֹּר יְמֵי־עוֹלָם מֹשֶׁה עַמּוֹ אַיֵּה הַמַּעֲלֵם מִיָּם אֵת רֹעֵי צֹאנוֹ אַיֵּה הַשָּׂם בְּקִרְבּוֹ אֶת־רוּחַ קׇדְשׁוֹ:

¹² Who made His glorious arm March at the right hand of *Moshe*, Who divided the waters before them To make Himself a name for all time,

יב מוֹלִיךְ לִימִין מֹשֶׁה זְרוֹעַ תִּפְאַרְתּוֹ בּוֹקֵעַ מַיִם מִפְּנֵיהֶם לַעֲשׂוֹת לוֹ שֵׁם עוֹלָם:

¹³ Who led them through the deeps So that they did not stumble – As a horse in a desert,

יג מוֹלִיכָם בַּתְּהֹמוֹת כַּסּוּס בַּמִּדְבָּר לֹא יִכָּשֵׁלוּ:

¹⁴ Like a beast descending to the plain?" 'Twas the spirit of *Hashem* gave them rest; Thus did You shepherd Your people To win for Yourself a glorious name.

יד כַּבְּהֵמָה בַּבִּקְעָה תֵּרֵד רוּחַ יְהֹוָה תְּנִיחֶנּוּ כֵּן נִהַגְתָּ עַמְּךָ לַעֲשׂוֹת לְךָ שֵׁם תִּפְאָרֶת:

¹⁵ Look down from heaven and see, From Your holy and glorious height! Where is Your zeal, Your power? Your yearning and Your love Are being withheld from us!

טו הַבֵּט מִשָּׁמַיִם וּרְאֵה מִזְּבֻל קׇדְשְׁךָ וְתִפְאַרְתֶּךָ אַיֵּה קִנְאָתְךָ וּגְבוּרֹתֶךָ הֲמוֹן מֵעֶיךָ וְרַחֲמֶיךָ אֵלַי הִתְאַפָּקוּ:

¹⁶ Surely You are our Father: Though *Avraham* regard us not, And *Yisrael* recognize us not, You, *Hashem*, are our Father; From of old, Your name is "Our Redeemer."

טז כִּי־אַתָּה אָבִינוּ כִּי אַבְרָהָם לֹא יְדָעָנוּ וְיִשְׂרָאֵל לֹא יַכִּירָנוּ אַתָּה יְהֹוָה אָבִינוּ גֹּאֲלֵנוּ מֵעוֹלָם שְׁמֶךָ:

kee a-TAH a-VEE-nu KEE av-ra-HAM LO y'-da-A-nu v'-yis-ra-AYL LO ya-kee-RA-nu a-TAH a-do-NAI a-VEE-nu go-a-LAY-nu may-o-LAM sh'-ME-kha

¹⁷ Why, *Hashem*, do You make us stray from Your ways, And turn our hearts away from revering You? Relent for the sake of Your servants, The tribes that are Your very own!

יז לָמָּה תַתְעֵנוּ יְהֹוָה מִדְּרָכֶיךָ תַּקְשִׁיחַ לִבֵּנוּ מִיִּרְאָתֶךָ שׁוּב לְמַעַן עֲבָדֶיךָ שִׁבְטֵי נַחֲלָתֶךָ:

¹⁸ Our foes have trampled Your Sanctuary, Which Your holy people possessed but a little while.

יח לַמִּצְעָר יָרְשׁוּ עַם־קׇדְשֶׁךָ צָרֵינוּ בּוֹסְסוּ מִקְדָּשֶׁךָ:

¹⁹ We have become as a people You never ruled, To which Your name was never attached. If You would but tear open the heavens and come down, So that mountains would quake before

יט הָיִינוּ מֵעוֹלָם לֹא־מָשַׁלְתָּ בָּם לֹא־נִקְרָא שִׁמְךָ עֲלֵיהֶם לוּא־קָרַעְתָּ שָׁמַיִם יָרַדְתָּ מִפָּנֶיךָ הָרִים נָזֹלּוּ:

63:16 Though *Avraham* regard us not, and *Yisrael* recognize us not In this verse, the Jewish people turn to *Hashem* as their redeemer. At times, they feel that they are entitled to divine privilege on the mere basis of their descent from *Avraham* and *Yaakov*. However, they now renounce this with the realization that their forefathers, however righteous they were and through whom they were privileged to dwell in the land, could not intercede with *Hashem* when they sinned and were punished. They had to personally learn to trust in God alone as their Father. With this new understanding and trust in *Hashem*, they will merit to return to the land.

A father and son walk along the Yarkon River

112

64 ¹ You – As when fire kindles brushwood, And fire makes water boil – To make Your name known to Your adversaries So that nations will tremble at Your Presence,

א כִּקְדֹחַ אֵשׁ הֲמָסִים מַיִם תִּבְעֶה־אֵשׁ לְהוֹדִיעַ שִׁמְךָ לְצָרֶיךָ מִפָּנֶיךָ גּוֹיִם יִרְגָּזוּ:

² When You did wonders we dared not hope for, You came down And mountains quaked before You.

ב בַּעֲשׂוֹתְךָ נוֹרָאוֹת לֹא נְקַוֶּה יָרַדְתָּ מִפָּנֶיךָ הָרִים נָזֹלּוּ:

³ Such things had never been heard or noted. No eye has seen [them], O *Hashem*, but You, Who act for those who trust in You.

ג וּמֵעוֹלָם לֹא־שָׁמְעוּ לֹא הֶאֱזִינוּ עַיִן לֹא־רָאָתָה אֱלֹהִים זוּלָתְךָ יַעֲשֶׂה לִמְחַכֵּה־לוֹ:

⁴ Yet you have struck him who would gladly do justice, And remember You in Your ways. It is because You are angry that we have sinned; We have been steeped in them from of old, And can we be saved?

ד פָּגַעְתָּ אֶת־שָׂשׂ וְעֹשֵׂה צֶדֶק בִּדְרָכֶיךָ יִזְכְּרוּךָ הֵן־אַתָּה קָצַפְתָּ וַנֶּחֱטָא בָּהֶם עוֹלָם וְנִוָּשֵׁעַ:

⁵ We have all become like an unclean thing, And all our virtues like a filthy rag. We are all withering like leaves, And our iniquities, like a wind, carry us off.

ה וַנְּהִי כַטָּמֵא כֻּלָּנוּ וּכְבֶגֶד עִדִּים כָּל־צִדְקֹתֵינוּ וַנָּבֶל כֶּעָלֶה כֻּלָּנוּ וַעֲוֹנֵנוּ כָּרוּחַ יִשָּׂאֻנוּ:

⁶ Yet no one invokes Your name, Rouses himself to cling to You. For You have hidden Your face from us, MAnd made us melt because of our iniquities.

ו וְאֵין־קוֹרֵא בְשִׁמְךָ מִתְעוֹרֵר לְהַחֲזִיק בָּךְ כִּי־הִסְתַּרְתָּ פָנֶיךָ מִמֶּנּוּ וַתְּמוּגֵנוּ בְּיַד־עֲוֹנֵנוּ:

⁷ But now, *Hashem*, You are our Father; We are the clay, and You are the Potter, We are all the work of Your hands.

ז וְעַתָּה יְהֹוָה אָבִינוּ אָתָּה אֲנַחְנוּ הַחֹמֶר וְאַתָּה יֹצְרֵנוּ וּמַעֲשֵׂה יָדְךָ כֻּלָּנוּ:

v'-a-TAH a-do-NAI a-VEE-nu A-tah a-NAKH-nu ha-KHO-mer
v'-a-TAH yo-tz'-RAY-nu u-ma-a-SAY ya-d'-KHA ku-LA-nu

⁸ Be not implacably angry, *Hashem*, Do not remember iniquity forever. Oh, look down to Your people, to us all!

ח אַל־תִּקְצֹף יְהֹוָה עַד־מְאֹד וְאַל־לָעַד תִּזְכֹּר עָוֹן הֵן הַבֶּט־נָא עַמְּךָ כֻלָּנוּ:

⁹ Your holy cities have become a desert: *Tzion* has become a desert, *Yerushalayim* a desolation.

ט עָרֵי קָדְשְׁךָ הָיוּ מִדְבָּר צִיּוֹן מִדְבָּר הָיָתָה יְרוּשָׁלַ͏ִם שְׁמָמָה:

¹⁰ Our holy Temple, our pride, Where our fathers praised You, Has been consumed by fire: And all that was dear to us is ruined.

י בֵּית קָדְשֵׁנוּ וְתִפְאַרְתֵּנוּ אֲשֶׁר הִלְלוּךָ אֲבֹתֵינוּ הָיָה לִשְׂרֵפַת אֵשׁ וְכָל־מַחֲמַדֵּינוּ הָיָה לְחָרְבָּה:

Ancient pottery found in *Shilo*

64:7 We are the clay, and You are the Potter *Yeshayahu* presents the people's confession, that they are impure and unworthy of divine assistance, to *Hashem*. He then prays to God in their name not to be angry forever with them. They humbly acknowledge that they are like clay, and that *Hashem* is their potter. The people hope that since God formed Israel, He will not forsake the work of His hands (see Psalms 138:8). Rather, they hope for complete forgiveness, a return to their land and the rebuilding of the holy cities and the *Beit Hamikdash* which had become desolate (verses 9–10). This appeal was echoed throughout the generations, and has begun to be answered in our times.

11 At such things will You restrain Yourself, *Hashem*, Will You stand idly by and let us suffer so heavily?

יא הַעַל־אֵלֶּה תִתְאַפַּק יְהֹוָה תֶּחֱשֶׁה וּתְעַנֵּנוּ עַד־מְאֹד:

סה 1 I responded to those who did not ask, I was at hand to those who did not seek Me; I said, "Here I am, here I am," To a nation that did not invoke My name.

א נִדְרַשְׁתִּי לְלוֹא שָׁאָלוּ נִמְצֵאתִי לְלֹא בִקְשֻׁנִי אָמַרְתִּי הִנֵּנִי הִנֵּנִי אֶל־גּוֹי לֹא־קֹרָא בִשְׁמִי:

2 I constantly spread out My hands To a disloyal people, Who walk the way that is not good, Following their own designs;

ב פֵּרַשְׂתִּי יָדַי כָּל־הַיּוֹם אֶל־עַם סוֹרֵר הַהֹלְכִים הַדֶּרֶךְ לֹא־טוֹב אַחַר מַחְשְׁבֹתֵיהֶם:

3 The people who provoke My anger, Who continually, to My very face, Sacrifice in gardens and burn incense on tiles;

ג הָעָם הַמַּכְעִיסִים אוֹתִי עַל־פָּנַי תָּמִיד זֹבְחִים בַּגַּנּוֹת וּמְקַטְּרִים עַל־הַלְּבֵנִים:

4 Who sit inside tombs And pass the night in secret places; Who eat the flesh of swine, With broth of unclean things in their bowls;

ד הַיֹּשְׁבִים בַּקְּבָרִים וּבַנְּצוּרִים יָלִינוּ הָאֹכְלִים בְּשַׂר הַחֲזִיר וּפֶרֶק [וּמְרַק] פִּגֻּלִים כְּלֵיהֶם:

5 Who say, "Keep your distance! Don't come closer! For I would render you consecrated." Such things make My anger rage, Like fire blazing all day long.

ה הָאֹמְרִים קְרַב אֵלֶיךָ אַל־תִּגַּשׁ־בִּי כִּי קְדַשְׁתִּיךָ אֵלֶּה עָשָׁן בְּאַפִּי אֵשׁ יֹקֶדֶת כָּל־הַיּוֹם:

6 See, this is recorded before Me; I will not stand idly by, but will repay, Deliver their sins* into their bosom,

ו הִנֵּה כְתוּבָה לְפָנָי לֹא אֶחֱשֶׂה כִּי אִם־שִׁלַּמְתִּי וְשִׁלַּמְתִּי עַל־חֵיקָם:

7 And the sins of their fathers as well – said *Hashem* – For they made offerings upon the mountains And affronted Me upon the hills. I will count out their recompense in full, Into their bosoms.

ז עֲוֺנֹתֵיכֶם וַעֲוֺנֹת אֲבוֹתֵיכֶם יַחְדָּו אָמַר יְהֹוָה אֲשֶׁר קִטְּרוּ עַל־הֶהָרִים וְעַל־הַגְּבָעוֹת חֵרְפוּנִי וּמַדֹּתִי פְעֻלָּתָם רִאשֹׁנָה עַל־[אֶל־] חֵיקָם:

8 Thus said *Hashem*: As, when new wine is present in the cluster, One says, "Don't destroy it; there's good in it," So will I do for the sake of My servants, And not destroy everything.

ח כֹּה אָמַר יְהֹוָה כַּאֲשֶׁר יִמָּצֵא הַתִּירוֹשׁ בָּאֶשְׁכּוֹל וְאָמַר אַל־תַּשְׁחִיתֵהוּ כִּי בְרָכָה בּוֹ כֵּן אֶעֱשֶׂה לְמַעַן עֲבָדַי לְבִלְתִּי הַשְׁחִית הַכֹּל:

9 I will bring forth offspring from *Yaakov*, From *Yehuda* heirs to My mountains; My chosen ones shall take possession, My servants shall dwell thereon.

ט וְהוֹצֵאתִי מִיַּעֲקֹב זֶרַע וּמִיהוּדָה יוֹרֵשׁ הָרָי וִירֵשׁוּהָ בְחִירַי וַעֲבָדַי יִשְׁכְּנוּ־שָׁמָּה:

10 *Sharon* shall become a pasture for flocks, And the Valley of Achor a place for cattle to lie down, For My people who seek Me.

י וְהָיָה הַשָּׁרוֹן לִנְוֵה־צֹאן וְעֵמֶק עָכוֹר לְרֵבֶץ בָּקָר לְעַמִּי אֲשֶׁר דְּרָשׁוּנִי:

11 But as for you who forsake *Hashem*, Who ignore My holy mountain, Who set a table for Luck And fill a mixing bowl for Destiny:

יא וְאַתֶּם עֹזְבֵי יְהֹוָה הַשְּׁכֵחִים אֶת־הַר קָדְשִׁי הַעֹרְכִים לַגַּד שֻׁלְחָן וְהַמְמַלְאִים לַמְנִי מִמְסָךְ:

---

* "their sins" brought up from verse 7 for clarity

¹² I will destine you for the sword, You will all kneel down, to be slaughtered – Because, when I called, you did not answer, When I spoke, you would not listen. You did what I hold evil, And chose what I do not want.

יב וּמָנִיתִי אֶתְכֶם לַחֶרֶב וְכֻלְּכֶם לַטֶּבַח תִּכְרָעוּ יַעַן קָרָאתִי וְלֹא עֲנִיתֶם דִּבַּרְתִּי וְלֹא שְׁמַעְתֶּם וַתַּעֲשׂוּ הָרַע בְּעֵינַי וּבַאֲשֶׁר לֹא־חָפַצְתִּי בְּחַרְתֶּם:

¹³ Assuredly, thus said *Hashem*: My servants shall eat, and you shall hunger; My servants shall drink, and you shall thirst; My servants shall rejoice, and you shall be shamed;

יג לָכֵן כֹּה־אָמַר אֲדֹנָי יהוה הִנֵּה עֲבָדַי יֹאכֵלוּ וְאַתֶּם תִּרְעָבוּ הִנֵּה עֲבָדַי יִשְׁתּוּ וְאַתֶּם תִּצְמָאוּ הִנֵּה עֲבָדַי יִשְׂמָחוּ וְאַתֶּם תֵּבֹשׁוּ:

¹⁴ My servants shall shout in gladness, And you shall cry out in anguish, Howling in heartbreak.

יד הִנֵּה עֲבָדַי יָרֹנּוּ מִטּוּב לֵב וְאַתֶּם תִּצְעֲקוּ מִכְּאֵב לֵב וּמִשֵּׁבֶר רוּחַ תְּיֵלִילוּ:

¹⁵ You shall leave behind a name By which My chosen ones shall curse: "So may *Hashem* slay you!" But His servants shall be given a different name.

טו וְהִנַּחְתֶּם שִׁמְכֶם לִשְׁבוּעָה לִבְחִירַי וֶהֱמִיתְךָ אֲדֹנָי יהוה וְלַעֲבָדָיו יִקְרָא שֵׁם אַחֵר:

¹⁶ For whoever blesses himself in the land Shall bless himself by the true *Hashem*; And whoever swears in the land Shall swear by the true *Hashem*. The former troubles shall be forgotten, Shall be hidden from My eyes.

טז אֲשֶׁר הַמִּתְבָּרֵךְ בָּאָרֶץ יִתְבָּרֵךְ בֵּאלֹהֵי אָמֵן וְהַנִּשְׁבָּע בָּאָרֶץ יִשָּׁבַע בֵּאלֹהֵי אָמֵן כִּי נִשְׁכְּחוּ הַצָּרוֹת הָרִאשֹׁנוֹת וְכִי נִסְתְּרוּ מֵעֵינָי:

¹⁷ For behold! I am creating A new heaven and a new earth; The former things shall not be remembered, They shall never come to mind.

יז כִּי־הִנְנִי בוֹרֵא שָׁמַיִם חֲדָשִׁים וָאָרֶץ חֲדָשָׁה וְלֹא תִזָּכַרְנָה הָרִאשֹׁנוֹת וְלֹא תַעֲלֶינָה עַל־לֵב:

¹⁸ Be glad, then, and rejoice forever In what I am creating. For I shall create *Yerushalayim* as a joy, And her people as a delight;

יח כִּי־אִם־שִׂישׂוּ וְגִילוּ עֲדֵי־עַד אֲשֶׁר אֲנִי בוֹרֵא כִּי הִנְנִי בוֹרֵא אֶת־יְרוּשָׁלַ͏ִם גִּילָה וְעַמָּהּ מָשׂוֹשׂ:

¹⁹ And I will rejoice in *Yerushalayim* And delight in her people. Never again shall be heard there The sounds of weeping and wailing.

יט וְגַלְתִּי בִירוּשָׁלַ͏ִם וְשַׂשְׂתִּי בְעַמִּי וְלֹא־יִשָּׁמַע בָּהּ עוֹד קוֹל בְּכִי וְקוֹל זְעָקָה:

v'-gal-TEE vee-ru-sha-LA-im v'-sas-TEE v'-a-MEE v'-lo
yi-sha-MA BAH OD KOL b'-KHEE v'-KOL z'-a-KAH

²⁰ No more shall there be an infant or graybeard Who does not live out his days. He who dies at a hundred years Shall be reckoned a youth, And he who fails to reach a hundred Shall be reckoned accursed.

כ לֹא־יִהְיֶה מִשָּׁם עוֹד עוּל יָמִים וְזָקֵן אֲשֶׁר לֹא־יְמַלֵּא אֶת־יָמָיו כִּי הַנַּעַר בֶּן־מֵאָה שָׁנָה יָמוּת וְהַחוֹטֶא בֶּן־מֵאָה שָׁנָה יְקֻלָּל:

65:19 And I will rejoice in *Yerushalayim*, and delight in her people *Yeshayahu's* vision of the redemption is a natural one. As the next verse states, there will be death, and people will still sin. However, the people will dwell safely in their land. They will live for an entire lifespan (verse 20), build houses and plant fields and vineyards (verse 21), and live without fear of invasion and exile. For this alone, *Hashem* rejoices with *Yerushalayim* and the People of Israel.

A street in the Yemin Moshe neighborhood of *Yerushalayim*

Isaiah

21 They shall build houses and dwell in them, They shall plant vineyards and enjoy their fruit.

כא וּבָנוּ בָתִּים וְיָשָׁבוּ וְנָטְעוּ כְרָמִים וְאָכְלוּ פִּרְיָם:

22 They shall not build for others to dwell in, Or plant for others to enjoy. For the days of My people shall be As long as the days of a tree, My chosen ones shall outlive The work of their hands.

כב לֹא יִבְנוּ וְאַחֵר יֵשֵׁב לֹא יִטְּעוּ וְאַחֵר יֹאכֵל כִּי־כִימֵי הָעֵץ יְמֵי עַמִּי וּמַעֲשֵׂה יְדֵיהֶם יְבַלּוּ בְחִירָי:

23 They shall not toil to no purpose; They shall not bear children for terror, But they shall be a people blessed by *Hashem*, And their offspring shall remain with them.

כג לֹא יִיגְעוּ לָרִיק וְלֹא יֵלְדוּ לַבֶּהָלָה כִּי זֶרַע בְּרוּכֵי יְהֹוָה הֵמָּה וְצֶאֱצָאֵיהֶם אִתָּם:

24 Before they pray, I will answer; While they are still speaking, I will respond.

כד וְהָיָה טֶרֶם־יִקְרָאוּ וַאֲנִי אֶעֱנֶה עוֹד הֵם מְדַבְּרִים וַאֲנִי אֶשְׁמָע:

25 The wolf and the lamb shall graze together, And the lion shall eat straw like the ox, And the serpent's food shall be earth. In all My sacred mount Nothing evil or vile shall be done – said *Hashem*.

כה זְאֵב וְטָלֶה יִרְעוּ כְאֶחָד וְאַרְיֵה כַּבָּקָר יֹאכַל־תֶּבֶן וְנָחָשׁ עָפָר לַחְמוֹ לֹא־יָרֵעוּ וְלֹא־יַשְׁחִיתוּ בְּכָל־הַר קָדְשִׁי אָמַר יְהֹוָה:

66 1 Thus said *Hashem*: The heaven is My throne And the earth is My footstool: Where could you build a house for Me, What place could serve as My abode?

סו א כֹּה אָמַר יְהֹוָה הַשָּׁמַיִם כִּסְאִי וְהָאָרֶץ הֲדֹם רַגְלָי אֵי־זֶה בַיִת אֲשֶׁר תִּבְנוּ־לִי וְאֵי־זֶה מָקוֹם מְנוּחָתִי:

2 All this was made by My hand, And thus it all came into being – declares *Hashem*. Yet to such a one I look: To the poor and brokenhearted, Who is concerned about My word.

ב וְאֶת־כָּל־אֵלֶּה יָדִי עָשָׂתָה וַיִּהְיוּ כָל־אֵלֶּה נְאֻם־יְהֹוָה וְאֶל־זֶה אַבִּיט אֶל־עָנִי וּנְכֵה־רוּחַ וְחָרֵד עַל־דְּבָרִי:

3 As for those who slaughter oxen and slay humans, Who sacrifice sheep and immolate dogs, Who present as oblation the blood of swine, Who offer incense and worship false gods – Just as they have chosen their ways And take pleasure in their abominations,

ג שׁוֹחֵט הַשּׁוֹר מַכֵּה־אִישׁ זוֹבֵחַ הַשֶּׂה עֹרֵף כֶּלֶב מַעֲלֵה מִנְחָה דַּם־חֲזִיר מַזְכִּיר לְבֹנָה מְבָרֵךְ אָוֶן גַּם־הֵמָּה בָּחֲרוּ בְּדַרְכֵיהֶם וּבְשִׁקּוּצֵיהֶם נַפְשָׁם חָפֵצָה:

4 So will I choose to mock them, To bring on them the very thing they dread. For I called and none responded, I spoke and none paid heed. They did what I deem evil And chose what I do not want.

ד גַּם־אֲנִי אֶבְחַר בְּתַעֲלוּלֵיהֶם וּמְגוּרֹתָם אָבִיא לָהֶם יַעַן קָרָאתִי וְאֵין עוֹנֶה דִּבַּרְתִּי וְלֹא שָׁמֵעוּ וַיַּעֲשׂוּ הָרַע בְּעֵינַי וּבַאֲשֶׁר לֹא־חָפַצְתִּי בָּחָרוּ:

5 Hear the word of *Hashem*, You who are concerned about His word! Your kinsmen who hate you, Who spurn you because of Me, are saying, "Let *Hashem* manifest His Presence, So that we may look upon your joy." But theirs shall be the shame.

ה שִׁמְעוּ דְּבַר־יְהֹוָה הַחֲרֵדִים אֶל־דְּבָרוֹ אָמְרוּ אֲחֵיכֶם שֹׂנְאֵיכֶם מְנַדֵּיכֶם לְמַעַן שְׁמִי יִכְבַּד יְהֹוָה וְנִרְאֶה בְשִׂמְחַתְכֶם וְהֵם יֵבֹשׁוּ:

6 Hark, tumult from the city, Thunder from the Temple! It is the thunder of *Hashem* As He deals retribution to His foes.

ו קוֹל שָׁאוֹן מֵעִיר קוֹל מֵהֵיכָל קוֹל יְהֹוָה מְשַׁלֵּם גְּמוּל לְאֹיְבָיו:

7 Before she labored, she was delivered; Before her pangs came, she bore a son.

ז בְּטֶרֶם תָּחִיל יָלָדָה בְּטֶרֶם יָבוֹא חֵבֶל לָהּ וְהִמְלִיטָה זָכָר:

8 Who ever heard the like? Who ever witnessed such events? Can a land pass through travail In a single day? Or is a nation born All at once? Yet *Tzion* travailed And at once bore her children!

ח מִי־שָׁמַע כָּזֹאת מִי רָאָה כָּאֵלֶּה הֲיוּחַל אֶרֶץ בְּיוֹם אֶחָד אִם־יִוָּלֵד גּוֹי פַּעַם אֶחָת כִּי־חָלָה גַּם־יָלְדָה צִיּוֹן אֶת־בָּנֶיהָ:

9 Shall I who bring on labor not bring about birth? – says *Hashem*. Shall I who cause birth shut the womb? – said your God.

ט הַאֲנִי אַשְׁבִּיר וְלֹא אוֹלִיד יֹאמַר יְהֹוָה אִם־אֲנִי הַמּוֹלִיד וְעָצַרְתִּי אָמַר אֱלֹהָיִךְ:

10 Rejoice with *Yerushalayim* and be glad for her, All you who love her! Join in her jubilation, All you who mourned over her –

י שִׂמְחוּ אֶת־יְרוּשָׁלַ͏ִם וְגִילוּ בָהּ כָּל־אֹהֲבֶיהָ שִׂישׂוּ אִתָּהּ מָשׂוֹשׂ כָּל־הַמִּתְאַבְּלִים עָלֶיהָ:

11 That you may suck from her breast Consolation to the full, That you may draw from her bosom Glory to your delight.

יא לְמַעַן תִּינְקוּ וּשְׂבַעְתֶּם מִשֹּׁד תַּנְחֻמֶיהָ לְמַעַן תָּמֹצּוּ וְהִתְעַנַּגְתֶּם מִזִּיז כְּבוֹדָהּ:

12 For thus said *Hashem*: I will extend to her Prosperity like a stream, The wealth of nations Like a wadi in flood; And you shall drink of it. You shall be carried on shoulders And dandled upon knees.

יב כִּי־כֹה אָמַר יְהֹוָה הִנְנִי נֹטֶה־אֵלֶיהָ כְּנָהָר שָׁלוֹם וּכְנַחַל שׁוֹטֵף כְּבוֹד גּוֹיִם וִינַקְתֶּם עַל־צַד תִּנָּשֵׂאוּ וְעַל־בִּרְכַּיִם תְּשָׁעֳשָׁעוּ:

kee KHOH a-MAR a-do-NAI hi-n'-NEE no-teh ay-LE-ha k'-na-HAR sha-LOM ukh-NA-khal sho-TAYF k'-VOD go-YIM vee-nak-TEM al TZAD ti-na-SAY-u v'-al bir-KA-yim t'-sha-o-SHA-u

13 As a mother comforts her son So I will comfort you; You shall find comfort in *Yerushalayim*.

יג כְּאִישׁ אֲשֶׁר אִמּוֹ תְּנַחֲמֶנּוּ כֵּן אָנֹכִי אֲנַחֶמְכֶם וּבִירוּשָׁלַ͏ִם תְּנֻחָמוּ:

14 You shall see and your heart shall rejoice, Your limbs shall flourish like grass. The power of *Hashem* shall be revealed In behalf of His servants; But He shall rage against His foes.

יד וּרְאִיתֶם וְשָׂשׂ לִבְּכֶם וְעַצְמוֹתֵיכֶם כַּדֶּשֶׁא תִפְרַחְנָה וְנוֹדְעָה יַד־יְהֹוָה אֶת־עֲבָדָיו וְזָעַם אֶת־אֹיְבָיו:

15 See, *Hashem* is coming with fire – His chariots are like a whirlwind – To vent His anger in fury, His rebuke in flaming fire.

טו כִּי־הִנֵּה יְהֹוָה בָּאֵשׁ יָבוֹא וְכַסּוּפָה מַרְכְּבֹתָיו לְהָשִׁיב בְּחֵמָה אַפּוֹ וְגַעֲרָתוֹ בְּלַהֲבֵי־אֵשׁ:

16 For with fire will *Hashem* contend, With His sword, against all flesh; And many shall be the slain of *Hashem*.

טז כִּי בָאֵשׁ יְהֹוָה נִשְׁפָּט וּבְחַרְבּוֹ אֶת־כָּל־בָּשָׂר וְרַבּוּ חַלְלֵי יְהֹוָה:

66:12 I will extend to her prosperity like a stream
In this final chapter of *Yeshayahu*, the prophet assures the Jewish people that *Hashem* will extend *shalom* (שלום) upon them, and that all the nations will come forth with blessings like a torrent or river sweeping effortlessly along. The Hebrew word *shalom* is usually understood to mean 'peace,' but it is translated here as 'prosperity.' Jewish tradition (*Mishna Uktzin*) teaches that peace is like a vessel that holds all of the other precious blessings in our lives. The blessing of peace is the ultimate blessing, since all the other blessings of the world are contained within it.

The *Yarden* (Jordan River)

¹⁷ Those who sanctify and purify themselves to enter the groves, imitating one in the center, eating the flesh of the swine, the reptile, and the mouse, shall one and all come to an end – declares *Hashem*.

יז הַמִּתְקַדְּשִׁים וְהַמִּטַּהֲרִים אֶל־הַגַּנּוֹת אַחַר אחד [אַחַת] בַּתָּוֶךְ אֹכְלֵי בְּשַׂר הַחֲזִיר וְהַשֶּׁקֶץ וְהָעַכְבָּר יַחְדָּו יָסֻפוּ נְאֻם־יְהֹוָה:

¹⁸ For I [know] their deeds and purposes. [The time] has come to gather all the nations and tongues; they shall come and behold My glory.

יח וְאָנֹכִי מַעֲשֵׂיהֶם וּמַחְשְׁבֹתֵיהֶם בָּאָה לְקַבֵּץ אֶת־כָּל־הַגּוֹיִם וְהַלְּשֹׁנוֹת וּבָאוּ וְרָאוּ אֶת־כְּבוֹדִי:

¹⁹ I will set a sign among them, and send from them survivors to the nations: to Tarshish, Pul, and Lud – that draw the bow – to Tubal, Javan, and the distant coasts, that have never heard My fame nor beheld My glory. They shall declare My glory among these nations.

יט וְשַׂמְתִּי בָהֶם אוֹת וְשִׁלַּחְתִּי מֵהֶם פְּלֵיטִים אֶל־הַגּוֹיִם תַּרְשִׁישׁ פּוּל וְלוּד מֹשְׁכֵי קֶשֶׁת תֻּבַל וְיָוָן הָאִיִּים הָרְחֹקִים אֲשֶׁר לֹא־שָׁמְעוּ אֶת־שִׁמְעִי וְלֹא־רָאוּ אֶת־כְּבוֹדִי וְהִגִּידוּ אֶת־כְּבוֹדִי בַּגּוֹיִם:

²⁰ And out of all the nations, said *Hashem*, they shall bring all your brothers on horses, in chariots and drays, on mules and dromedaries, to *Yerushalayim* My holy mountain as an offering to *Hashem* – just as the Israelites bring an offering in a pure vessel to the House of *Hashem*.

כ וְהֵבִיאוּ אֶת־כָּל־אֲחֵיכֶם מִכָּל־הַגּוֹיִם מִנְחָה לַיהֹוָה בַּסּוּסִים וּבָרֶכֶב וּבַצַּבִּים וּבַפְּרָדִים וּבַכִּרְכָּרוֹת עַל הַר קָדְשִׁי יְרוּשָׁלַ‍ִם אָמַר יְהֹוָה כַּאֲשֶׁר יָבִיאוּ בְנֵי יִשְׂרָאֵל אֶת־הַמִּנְחָה בִּכְלִי טָהוֹר בֵּית יְהֹוָה:

²¹ And from them likewise I will take some to be levitical *Kohanim*, said *Hashem*.

כא וְגַם־מֵהֶם אֶקַּח לַכֹּהֲנִים לַלְוִיִּם אָמַר יְהֹוָה:

²² For as the new heaven and the new earth Which I will make Shall endure by My will – declares *Hashem* – So shall your seed and your name endure.

כב כִּי כַאֲשֶׁר הַשָּׁמַיִם הַחֲדָשִׁים וְהָאָרֶץ הַחֲדָשָׁה אֲשֶׁר אֲנִי עֹשֶׂה עֹמְדִים לְפָנַי נְאֻם־יְהֹוָה כֵּן יַעֲמֹד זַרְעֲכֶם וְשִׁמְכֶם:

²³ And new moon after new moon, And *Shabbat* after *Shabbat*, All flesh shall come to worship Me – said *Hashem*.

כג וְהָיָה מִדֵּי־חֹדֶשׁ בְּחָדְשׁוֹ וּמִדֵּי שַׁבָּת בְּשַׁבַּתּוֹ יָבוֹא כָל־בָּשָׂר לְהִשְׁתַּחֲוֹת לְפָנַי אָמַר יְהֹוָה:

²⁴ They shall go out and gaze On the corpses of the men who rebelled against Me: Their worms shall not die, Nor their fire be quenched; They shall be a horror To all flesh. And new moon after new moon, And *Shabbat* after *Shabbat*, All flesh shall come to worship Me – said *Hashem*.

כד וְיָצְאוּ וְרָאוּ בְּפִגְרֵי הָאֲנָשִׁים הַפֹּשְׁעִים בִּי כִּי תוֹלַעְתָּם לֹא תָמוּת וְאִשָּׁם לֹא תִכְבֶּה וְהָיוּ דֵרָאוֹן לְכָל־בָּשָׂר:

Isaiah

118

List of Transliterated Words in *The Israel Bible*

The following is a list of nouns which have been transliterated into Hebrew in the English translation and commentary of *The Israel Bible*:

Hebrew Name	English Name	Pronunciation	Hebrew
Achan	Achan	a-KHAN	עָכָן
Achav	Ahab	akh-AV	אַחְאָב
Achaz	Ahaz	a-KHAZ	אָחָז
Achazyahu	Ahaziah	a-khaz-YA-hu	אֲחַזְיָהוּ
Achiezer	Ahiezer	a-khee-E-zer	אֲחִיעֶזֶר
Achihud	Ahihud	a-khee-HUD	אֲחִיהוּד
Achikam	Ahikam	a-khee-KAM	אֲחִיקָם
Achilud	Ahilud	a-khee-LUD	אֲחִילוּד
Achimelech	Ahimelech	a-khee-ME-lekh	אֲחִימֶלֶךְ
Achira	Ahira	a-khee-RA	אֲחִירַע
Achisamach	Ahisamach	a-khee-sa-MAKH	אֲחִיסָמָךְ
Achitofel	Ahithophel	a-khee-TO-fel	אֲחִיתֹפֶל
Achituv	Ahitub	a-khee-TUV	אֲחִיטוּב
Achiya	Ahijah	a-khi-YAH	אֲחִיָּה
Adam	Adam	a-DAM	אָדָם
Adar	Adar	a-DAR	אֲדָר
Adoniyahu	Adonijah	a-do-ni-YA-hu	אֲדֹנִיָּהוּ
Adulam	Adullam	a-du-LAM	עֲדֻלָּם
Agur	Agur	a-GUR	אָגוּר
Aharon	Aaron	a-ha-RON	אַהֲרֹן
Amasa	Amasa	a-ma-SA	עֲמָשָׂא
Amatzya	Amaziah	a-matz-YAH	אֲמַצְיָה
Amen	Amen	a-MAYN	אָמֵן
Amiel	Ammiel	a-mee-AYL	עַמִּיאֵל
Aminadav	Amminadab	a-mee-na-DAV	עַמִּינָדָב
Amitai	Amittai	a-mi-TAI	אֲמִתַּי
Amnon	Amnon	am-NON	אַמְנֹן

Hebrew Name	English Name	Pronunciation	Hebrew
Amon	Amon	a-MON	אָמוֹן
Amos	Amos	a-MOS	עָמוֹס
Amotz	Amoz	a-MOTZ	אָמוֹץ
Amram	Amram	am-RAM	עַמְרָם
Anatot	Anathoth	a-na-TOT	עֲנָתוֹת
Aron	Ark	a-RON	אָרוֹן
Aron HaBrit	Ark of the Covenant	a-RON ha-b'-REET	אָרוֹן הַבְּרִית
Arpachshad	Arpachshad	ar-pakh-SHAD	אַרְפַּכְשָׁד
Asa	Asa	a-SA	אָסָא
Asael	Asahel	a-sah-AYL	עֲשָׂהאֵל
Asaf	Asaph	a-SAF	אָסָף
Ashdod	Ashdod	ash-DOD	אַשְׁדּוֹד
Asher	Asher	a-SHAYR	אָשֵׁר
Ashkelon	Ashkelon	ash-k'-LON	אַשְׁקְלוֹן
Atalya	Athaliah	a-tal-YAH	עֲתַלְיָה
Avdon	Abdon	av-DON	עַבְדּוֹן
Avichayil	Abihail	a-vee-KHA-yil	אֲבִיחַיִל
Avidan	Abidan	a-vee-DAN	אֲבִידָן
Avigail	Abigail	a-vee-GA-yil	אֲבִיגַיִל
Avihu	Abihu	a-vee-HU	אֲבִיהוּא
Avimelech	Abimelech	a-vee-ME-lekh	אֲבִימֶלֶךְ
Avinadav	Abinadab	a-vee-na-DAV	אֲבִינָדָב
Aviram	Abiram	a-vee-RAM	אֲבִירָם
Avishai	Abishai	a-vee-SHAI	אֲבִישַׁי
Aviya	Abijah	a-vi-YAH	אֲבִיָּה
Aviyam	Abijam	a-vi-YAM	אֲבִיָם
Avner	Abner	av-NAYR	אַבְנֵר
Avraham	Abraham	av-ra-HAM	אַבְרָהָם
Avram	Abram	av-RAM	אַבְרָם
Avshalom	Absalom	av-sha-LOM	אַבְשָׁלוֹם
Azarya	Azariah	a-zar-YAH	עֲזַרְיָה
Azeika	Azekah	a-zay-KAH	עֲזֵקָה
Azza	Gaza	a-ZAH	עַזָּה

Hebrew Name	English Name	Pronunciation	Hebrew
B'nei Yisrael	The Children of Israel	b'-NAY yis-ra-AYL	בְּנֵי יִשְׂרָאֵל
Barak	Barak	ba-rakh-AYL	בָּרָק
Baruch	Baruch	ba-RUKH	בָּרוּךְ
Barzilai	Barzillai	bar-zi-LAI	בַּרְזִלַּי
Basha	Baasa	ba-SHA	בַּעְשָׁא
Batsheva	Bath-sheba	bat-SHE-va	בַּת־שֶׁבַע
Be'er Sheva	Beer-sheba	b'-AYR SHE-va	בְּאֵר שֶׁבַע
Be'eri	Beeri	b'-ay-REE	בְּאֵרִי
Beit Aven	Beth-aven	bayt A-ven	בֵּית אָוֶן
Beit El	Beth-el	bayt el	בֵּית אֵל
Beit Hamikdash	Temple	bayt ha-mik-DASH	בֵּית הַמִּקְדָּשׁ
Beit Lechem	Beth-lehem	bayt LE-khem	בֵּית לֶחֶם
Beit Shean	Beth-shean	bayt sh'-AN	בֵּית שְׁאָן
Beit Shemesh	Beth-shemesh	bayt SHE-mesh	בֵּית שֶׁמֶשׁ
Berechya	Berechiah	be-rekh-YAH	בֶּרֶכְיָה
Betzalel	Bezalel	b'-tzal-AYL	בְּצַלְאֵל
Bilha	Bilhah	bil-HAH	בִּלְהָה
Binyamin	Benjamin	bin-ya-MIN	בִּנְיָמִין
Boaz	Boaz	BO-az	בֹּעַז
Buki	Bukki	bu-KEE	בֻּקִּי
Buzi	Buzi	bu-ZEE	בּוּזִי
Carmel	Carmel	kar-MEL	כַּרְמֶל
Chachalya	Hacaliah	kha-khal-YAH	חֲכַלְיָה
Chagai	Haggai	kha-GAI	חַגַּי
Chana	Hannah	kha-NAH	חַנָּה
Chanamel	Hanamel	kha-nam-AYL	חֲנַמְאֵל
Chanani	Hanani	kha-NA-nee	חֲנָנִי
Chananya	Hananiah	kha-nan-YAH	חֲנַנְיָה
Chaniel	Hanniel	kha-nee-AYL	חַנִּיאֵל
Chanoch	Enoch	kha-NOKH	חֲנוֹךְ
Chava	Eve	kha-VAH	חַוָּה
Chavakuk	Habakkuk	kha-va-KUK	חֲבַקּוּק
Chermon	Hermon	kher-MON	חֶרְמוֹן

121

Hebrew Name	English Name	Pronunciation	Hebrew
Chetzron	Hezron	khetz-RON	חֶצְרוֹן
Chever	Heber	KHE-ver	חֶבֶר
Chevron	Hebron	khev-RON	חֶבְרוֹן
Chilkiyahu	Hilkiah	khil-ki-YA-hu	חִלְקִיָּהוּ
Chizkiyahu	Hezekiah	khiz-ki-YA-hu	חִזְקִיָּהוּ
Chofni	Hophni	khof-NEE	חָפְנִי
Chogla	Hoglah	khog-LAH	חָגְלָה
Chulda	Hulda	khul-DAH	חֻלְדָּה
Chur	Hur	Khur	חוּר
Dan	Dan	Dan	דָּן
Daniel	Daniel	da-ni-YAYL	דָּנִיֵּאל
Datan	Dathan	da-TAN	דָּתָן
David	David	da-VID	דָּוִד
Devora	Deborah	d'-vo-RAH	דְּבוֹרָה
Dina	Dinah	DEE-nah	דִּינָה
Doeg Ha'adomi	Doeg the Edomite	do-AYG ha-a-do-MEE	דּוֹאֵג הָאֲדֹמִי
Efraim	Ephraim	ef-RA-yim	אֶפְרַיִם
Efrat	Ephrat	ef-RAT	אֶפְרָתָה
Efrat	Ephrathah	ef-RA-tah	אֶפְרָתָה
Ehud	Ehud	ay-HUD	אֵהוּד
Eila	Elah	AY-lah	אֵלָה
Eilon	Elon	ay-LON	אֵילוֹן
Ein Gedi	En-gedi	ayn GE-dee	עֵין גֶּדִי
Elazar	Eleazar	el-a-ZAR	אֶלְעָזָר
Elchanan	Elhanan	el-kha-NAN	אֶלְחָנָן
Eli	Eli	ay-LEE	עֵלִי
Eliav	Eliab	e-lee-AV	אֱלִיאָב
Elidad	Elidad	e-lee-DAD	אֱלִידָד
Eliezer	Eliezer	e-lee-E-zer	אֱלִיעֶזֶר
Elimelech	Elimelech	e-lee-ME-lekh	אֱלִימֶלֶךְ
Elisha	Elisha	e-lee-SHA	אֱלִישָׁע
Elishama	Elishama	e-lee-sha-MA	אֱלִישָׁמָע
Elisheva	Elisheba	e-lee-SHE-va	אֱלִישֶׁבַע

Hebrew Name	English Name	Pronunciation	Hebrew
Elitzafan	Eli-zaphan	e-lee-tza-FAN	אֱלִיצָפָן
Elitzur	Elizur	e-lee-TZUR	אֱלִיצוּר
Eliyahu	Elijah	ay-li-YA-hu	אֵלִיָּהוּ
Elkana	Elkanah	el-ka-NAH	אֶלְקָנָה
Elyasaf	Eliasaph	el-ya-SAF	אֶלְיָסָף
Elyashiv	Eliashib	el-ya-SHEEV	אֶלְיָשִׁיב
Enosh	Enosh	e-NOSH	אֱנוֹשׁ
Er	Er	ayr	עֵר
Eshtaol	Eshtaol	esh-ta-OL	אֶשְׁתָּאֹל
Esther	Esther	es-TAYR	אֶסְתֵּר
Eved Melech	Ebed-melech	E-ved ME-lekh	עֶבֶד־מֶלֶךְ
Even Ha-Ezer	Eben-Ezer	E-ven ha-E-zer	אֶבֶן הָעֵזֶר
Ever	Eber	AY-ver	עֵבֶר
Evyatar	Abiathar	ev-ya-TAR	אֶבְיָתָר
Ezra	Ezra	ez-RA	עֶזְרָא
Gad	Gad	gad	גָּד
Gadi	Gaddi	ga-DEE	גַּדִּי
Gadiel	Gaddiel	ga-dee-AYL	גַּדִּיאֵל
Gamliel	Gamaliel	gam-lee-AYL	גַּמְלִיאֵל
Gedalia	Gedaliah	g'-dal-YA (hu)	גְּדַלְיָהוּ
Gedera	Gederah	g'-day-RAH	גְּדֵרָה
Gershom	Gershom	gay-r'-SHOM	גֵּרְשֹׁם
Gershon	Gershon	gay-r'-SHON	גֵּרְשׁוֹן
Geshem	Geshem	GE-shem	גֶּשֶׁם
Geuel	Geuel	g'-u-AYL	גְּאוּאֵל
Gidon	Gideon	gid-ON	גִּדְעוֹן
Gilad	Gilead	gil-AD	גִּלְעָד
Gilgal	Gilgal	gil-GAL	גִּלְגָּל
Giva	Gibeah	giv-AH	גִּבְעָה
Givon	Gibeon	giv-ON	גִּבְעוֹן
Hadassa	Hadassah	ha-da-SAH	הֲדַסָּה
Har Eival	Mount Ebal	ay-VAL	הַר עֵיבָל
Har Gerizim	Mount Gerizim	g'-ri-ZEEM	הַר גְּרִזִים

Hebrew Name	English Name	Pronunciation	Hebrew
Har HaBayit	Temple Mount	har ha-BA-yit	הַר הַבַּיִת
Har HaZeitim	the Mount of Olives	har ha-zay-TEEM	הַר הַזֵּיתִים
Hashem	Lord/God		
Hayman	Heman	hay-MAN	הֵימָן
Hoshea	Hosea	ho-SHAY-a	הוֹשֵׁעַ
Ido	Iddo	i-DO	עִדּוֹ
Imanu-El	Immanuel	i-MA-nu ayl	עִמָּנוּ אֵל
Ish-boshet	Ish-bosheth	eesh BO-shet	אִישׁ־בֹּשֶׁת
Itamar	Ithamar	ee-ta-MAR	אִיתָמָר
Itiel	Ithiel	ee-tee-AYL	אִיתִיאֵל
Ivtzan	Ibzan	iv-TZAN	אִבְצָן
Iyov	Job	i-YOV	אִיּוֹב
Kadmiel	Kadmiel	kad-mee-AYL	קַדְמִיאֵל
Kalev	Caleb	ka-LAYV	כָּלֵב
Keesh	Kish	keesh	קִישׁ
Kehat	Kohath	k'-HAT	קְהָת
Keinan	Kenan	kay-NAN	קֵינָן
Kemuel	Kemuel	k'-mu-AYL	קְמוּאֵל
Keruvim	Cherubim	k'-ru-VEEM	כְּרוּבִים
Kilyon	Chilion	kil-YON	כִּלְיוֹן
Kiryat Arba	Kiriath-arba	keer-YAT AR-bah	קִרְיַת אַרְבַּע
Kiryat Sefer	Kiriath-sepher	keer-YAT SAY-fer	קִרְיַת־סֵפֶר
Kiryat Ye'arim	Kiriath-jearim	keer-YAT y'-a-REEM	קִרְיַת יְעָרִים
Kislev	Chislev	kis-LAYV	כִּסְלֵו
Kohanim	Priests	ko-ha-NEEM	כֹּהֲנִים
Kohelet	Koheleth	ko-HE-let	קֹהֶלֶת
Kohen	Priest	ko-HAYN	כֹּהֵן
Kohen Gadol	High Priest	ko-HAYN ga-DOL	כֹּהֵן גָּדוֹל
Korach	Korah	KO-rakh	קֹרַח
Kushi	Cushi	ku-SHEE	כּוּשִׁי
Lachish	Lachish	la-KHEESH	לָכִישׁ
Leah	Leah	lay-AH	לֵאָה
Lemech	Lamech	LE-mekh	לֶמֶךְ

Hebrew Name	English Name	Pronunciation	Hebrew
Lemuel	Lemuel	l'-mu-AYL	לְמוֹאֵל
Levi	Levi	lay-VEE	לֵוִי
Leviim	Levites	l'-vee-IM	לְוִיִּם
Machla	Mahlah	makh-LAH	מַחְלָה
Machlon	Mahlon	makh-LON	מַחְלוֹן
Machseya	Mahseiah	makh-say-YAH	מַחְסֵיָה
Malachi	Malachi	mal-a-KHEE	מַלְאָכִי
Manoach	Manoah	ma-NO-akh	מָנוֹחַ
Mashiach	Messiah	ma-SHEE-akh	מָשִׁיחַ
Mefiboshet	Mephibosheth	m'-fee-VO-shet	מְפִיבשֶׁת
Mehalalel	Mahalalel	ma-ha-lal-AYL	מַהֲלַלְאֵל
Menachem	Menahem	m'-na-KHAYM	מְנַחֵם
Menashe	Menasseh	m'-na-SHEH	מְנַשֶּׁה
Menorah	Candlestick	m'-no-RAH	מְנֹרָה
Merari	Merari	m'-ra-REE	מְרָרִי
Metushelach	Methusaleh	m'-tu-SHE-lakh	מְתוּשֶׁלַח
Micha	Micah	mee-KHAH	מִיכָה
Michael	Michael	mee-kha-AYL	מִיכָאֵל
Michaihu	Micaiah	mee-KHAI-hu	מִיכָיְהוּ
Michal	Michal	mee-KHAL	מִיכַל
Milka	Milcah	mil-KAH	מִלְכָּה
Miriam	Miriam	mir-YAM	מִרְיָם
Mishael	Mishael	mee-sha-AYL	מִישָׁאֵל
Mishkan	Tabernacle	mish-KAN	מִשְׁכָּן
Mitzpa	Mizpah	mitz-PAH	מִצְפָּה
Mizbayach	Altar	miz-BAY-akh	מִזְבֵּחַ
Mordechai	Mordecai	mor-d'-KHAI	מָרְדְּכַי
Moriah	Moriah	mo-ri-YAH	מוֹרִיָּה
Moshe	Moses	mo-SHEH	משֶׁה
Nachbi	Nahbi	nakh-BEE	נַחְבִּי
Nachor	Nahor	na-KHOR	נָחוֹר
Nachshon	Nahshon	nakh-SHON	נַחְשׁוֹן
Nachum	Nahum	na-KHUM	נַחוּם

Hebrew Name	English Name	Pronunciation	Hebrew
Nadav	Nadab	na-DAV	נָדָב
Naftali	Naphtali	naf-ta-LEE	נַפְתָּלִי
Naomi	Naomi	na-o-MEE	נָעֳמִי
Natan	Nathan	na-TAN	נָתָן
Naval	Nabal	na-VAL	נָבָל
Navi	Prophet	na-VEE	נָבִיא
Navot	Naboth	na-VAL	נָבָל
Nechemya	Nehemiah	n'-khem-YAH	נְחֶמְיָה
Negev	Negeb	NE-gev	נֶגֶב
Nerya	Neriah	nay-ri-YAH	נֵרִיָּה
Netanel	Nethanel	n'-tan-AYL	נְתַנְאֵל
Neviah	Prophetess	n'-vee-AH	גְּבִיאָה
Neviim	Prophets	n'-vee-EEM	גְּבִיאִים
Nisan	Nisan	nee-SAN	נִיסָן
Noa	Noah	no-AH	נֹעָה
Noach	Noah	NO-akh	נֹחַ
Nov	Nob	nov	נֹב
Nun	Nun	nun	נוּן
Oded	Oded	o-DAYD	עוֹדֵד
Ohola	Oholah	a-ho-LAH	אָהֳלָה
Oholiav	Oholiab	o-ha-lee-AV	אָהֳלִיאָב
Oholiva	Oholibah	a-ho-lee-VAH	אָהֳלִיבָה
Omri	Omri	om-REE	עָמְרִי
Onan	Onan	o-NAN	אוֹנָן
Otniel	Othniel	ot-nee-AYL	עָתְנִיאֵל
Ovadya	Obadiah	o-vad-YAH	עֹבַדְיָה
Oved	Obed	o-VAYD	עוֹבֵד
Oved Edom	Obed Edom	o-VAYD e-DOM	עוֹבֵד אֱדוֹם
Pagiel	Pagiel	pag-ee-AYL	פַּגְעִיאֵל
Palti	Palti	pal-TEE	פַּלְטִי
Paltiel	Paltiel	pal-tee-AYL	פַּלְטִיאֵל
Pekach	Pekah	PE-kakh	פֶּקַח
Pedael	Pedahel	p'-da-AYL	פְּדַהְאֵל

126

Hebrew Name	English Name	Pronunciation	Hebrew
Pekachya	Pekahiah	p'-kakh-YAH	פְּקַחְיָה
Peleg	Peleg	PE-leg	פֶּלֶג
Penina	Peninnah	p'-ni-NAH	פְּנִנָּה
Peretz	Perez	PE-retz	פֶּרֶץ
Petuel	Pethuel	p'-tu-AYL	פְּתוּאֵל
Pinchas	Phinehas	peen-KHAS	פִּינְחָס
Rachel	Rachel	ra-KHAYL	רָחֵל
Ram	Ram	ram	רָם
Rama	Ramah	ra-MAH	רָמָה
Re'u	Reu	r'-U	רְעוּ
Rechovam	Rehoboam	r'-khav-AM	רְחַבְעָם
Reuven	Reuben	r'-u-VAYN	רְאוּבֵן
Rivka	Rebecca	riv-KAH	רִבְקָה
Rut	Ruth	rut	רוּת
Salma	Salmon/Salmah	sal-MAH	שַׂלְמָה
Salmon	Salmon	sal-MON	שַׂלְמוֹן
Sara	Sarah	sa-RAH	שָׂרָה
Sarai	Sarai	sa-RAI	שָׂרַי
Selah	Selah	SE-lah	סֶלָה
Seraya	Seraiah	s'-ra-YAH	שְׂרָיָה
Serug	Serug	s'-RUG	שְׂרוּג
Setur	Sethur	s'-TUR	סְתוּר
Shaarayim	Shaaraim	sha-a-RA-yim	שַׁעֲרַיִם
Shabbat	Sabbath	sha-BAT	שַׁבַּת
Shabbatot	Sabbaths	sha-ba-TOT	שַׁבָּתוֹת
Shafan	Shaphan	sha-FAN	שָׁפָן
Shafat	Shaphat	sha-FAT	שָׁפָט
Shalem	Salem	sha-LAYM	שָׁלֵם
Shalum	Shallum	sha-LUM	שַׁלּוּם
Shamgar	Shamgar	sham-GAR	שַׁמְגַּר
Shamua	Shammua	sha-MU-a	שַׁמּוּעַ
Shaul	Saul	sha-UL	שָׁאוּל
Shealtiel	Shealtiel	sh'-al-tee-AYL	שְׁאַלְתִּיאֵל

Hebrew Name	English Name	Pronunciation	Hebrew
Shear Yashuv	Shear-Jashub	sh'-AR ya-SHUV	שְׁאָר יָשׁוּב
Shechanya	Shecaniah	sh'-khan-YAH	שְׁכַנְיָה
Shechem	Shechem	sh'-KHEM	שְׁכֶם
Sheila	Shelah	shay-LAH	שֵׁלָה
Shelach	Shelah	SHE-lakh	שֶׁלַח
Shelumiel	Shelumiel	sh'-lu-mee-AYL	שְׁלֻמִיאֵל
Shem	Shem	Shaym	שֵׁם
Shemaya	Shemaiah	sh'-ma-YAH	שְׁמַעְיָה
Sheshbatzar	Sheshbazzar	shaysh-ba-TZAR	שֶׁשְׁבַּצַּר
Shet	Seth	Shayt	שֵׁת
Shevat	Shebat	sh'-VAT	שְׁבָט
Shilo	Shiloh	shi-LOH	שִׁלֹה
Shim'i	Shimei	shim-EE	שִׁמְעִי
Shimon	Simeon	shim-ON	שִׁמְעוֹן
Shimshon	Samson	shim-SHON	שִׁמְשׁוֹן
Shlomo	Solomon	sh'-lo-MOH	שְׁלֹמֹה
Shmuel	Samuel	sh'-mu-AYL	שְׁמוּאֵל
Shofar	Horn	sho-FAR	שׁוֹפָר
Shofarot	Horns	sho-fa-ROT	שׁוֹפָרוֹת
Shomron	Samaria	sho-m'-RON	שֹׁמְרוֹן
Sivan	Sivan	see-VAN	סִיוָן
Tamar	Tamar	ta-MAR	תָּמָר
Tanakh	Hebrew Bible	ta-NAKH	תַּנַ"ךְ
Tapuach	Tappuah	ta-PU-akh	תַּפּוּחַ
Tavor	Tabor	ta-VOR	תָּבוֹר
Tekoa	Tekoa	t'-KO-a	תְּקוֹעָה
Terach	Terah	TE-rakh	תֶּרַח
Teveria	Tiberias	t'-ver-YAH	טְבֶרְיָה
Tevet	Tebeth	tay-VAYT	טֵבֵת
Tirtza	Tirzah	tir-TZAH	תִּרְצָה
Tola	Tola	to-LA	תּוֹלָע
Tzadok	Zadok	tza-DOK	צָדוֹק
Tzefanya	Zephaniah	tz'-fan-YAH	צְפַנְיָה

Hebrew Name	English Name	Pronunciation	Hebrew
Tzelofchad	Zelophehad	tz'-lo-f-KHAD	צְלָפְחָד
Tzeruya	Zeruiah	tz'-ru-YAH	צְרוּיָה
Tzfat	Safed	tz'-FAT	צְפַת
Tzidkiyahu	Zedekiah	tzid-ki-YA-hu	צִדְקִיָּהוּ
Tziklag	Ziklag	tzi-k'-LAG	צִקְלַג
Tzion	Zion	tzi-YON	צִיּוֹן
Tzipora	Zipporah	tzi-po-RAH	צִפֹּרָה
Tzora	Zorah	tzor-AH	צָרְעָה
Tzuriel	Zuriel	tzu-ree-AYL	צוּרִיאֵל
Ukal	Ucal	u-KAL	אֻכָל
Uri	Uri	u-REE	אוּרִי
Uriya	Uriah	u-ri-YAH	אוּרִיָּה
Utz	Uz	Utz	עוּץ
Uzziyahu	Uzziah	u-zi-YA-hu	עֻזִּיָּהוּ
Yaakov	Jacob	ya-a-KOV	יַעֲקֹב
Yachaziel	Jahaziel	ya-kha-zee-AYL	יַחֲזִיאֵל
Yael	Jael	ya-AYL	יָעֵל
Yaffo	Joppa/Jaffa	ya-FO	יָפוֹ
Yair	Jair	ya-EER	יָאִיר
Yakeh	Jakeh	ya-KEH	יָקֶה
Yarden	Jordan	yar-DAYN	יַרְדֵּן
Yarmut	Jarmuth	yar-MUT	יַרְמוּת
Yechezkel	Ezekiel	y'-khez-KAYL	יְחֶזְקֵאל
Yechiel	Jehiel	y'-khee-AYL	יְחִיאֵל
Yechonya	Jeconiah	y'-khon-YAH	יְכָנְיָה
Yedutun	Jeduthun	y'-du-TUN	יְדוּתוּן
Yehoachaz	Jehoahaz	y'-ho-a-KHAZ	יְהוֹאָחָז
Yehoash	Jehoash	y'-ho-ASH	יְהוֹאָשׁ
Yehochanan	Jehohanan	y'-ho-kha-NAN	יְהוֹחָנָן
Yehonatan	Jonathan	y'-ho-na-TAN	יְהוֹנָתָן
Yehoram	Jehoram	y'-ho-RAM	יְהוֹרָם
Yehoshafat	Jehoshaphat	y'-ho-sha-FAT	יְהוֹשָׁפָט
Yehoshavat	Jehoshabeath	y'-ho-shav-AT	יְהוֹשַׁבְעַת

Hebrew Name	English Name	Pronunciation	Hebrew
Yehosheva	Jehosheba	y-ho-SHE-va	יְהוֹשֶׁבַע
Yehoshua	Joshua	y'-ho-SHU-a	יְהוֹשֻׁעַ
Yehotzadak	Jehozadak	y'-ho-tza-DAK	יְהוֹצָדָק
Yehoyachin	Jehoiachin	y'-ho-ya-KHEEN	יְהוֹיָכִין
Yehoyada	Jehoiada	y'-ho-ya-DA	יְהוֹיָדָע
Yehoyakim	Jehoiakim	y'-ho-ya-KEEM	יְהוֹיָקִים
Yehu	Jehu	yay-HU	יֵהוּא
Yehuda	Judah	y'-hu-DAH	יְהוּדָה
Yehudi	Jew	y'-hu-DEE	יְהוּדִי
Yehudim	Jews	y'-hu-DEEM	יְהוּדִים
Yered	Jared	YE-red	יֶרֶד
Yericho	Jericho	y'-ree-KHO	יְרִיחוֹ
Yerovam	Jeroboam	ya-rov-AM	יָרָבְעָם
Yerubaal	Jerubbaal	y'-ru-BA-al	יְרֻבַּעַל
Yerushalayim	Jerusalem	y'-ru-sha-LA-yim	יְרוּשָׁלַיִם
Yeshayahu	Isaiah	y'-sha-YA-hu	יְשַׁעְיָהוּ
Yeshua	Jeshua	yay-SHU-a	יֵשׁוּעַ
Yiftach	Jephthah	yif-TAKH	יִפְתָּח
Yigal	Igal	yig-AL	יִגְאָל
Yirmiyahu	Jeremiah	yir-m'-YA-hu	יִרְמְיָהוּ
Yishai	Jesse	yi-SHAI	יִשַׁי
Yisrael	Israel	yis-ra-AYL	יִשְׂרָאֵל
Yissachar	Issachar	yi-sa-KHAR	יִשָּׂשׁכָר
Yitzchak	Issac	yitz-KHAK	יִצְחָק
Yizrael	Jezreel	yiz-r'-EL	יִזְרְעָאל
Yoash	Joash	yo-ASH	יוֹאָשׁ
Yoav	Joab	yo-AV	יוֹאָב
Yochanan	Johanan	yo-kha-NAN	יוֹחָנָן
Yocheved	Jochebed	yo-KHE-ved	יוֹכֶבֶד
Yoel	Joel	yo-AYL	יוֹאֵל
Yona	Jonah	yo-NAH	יוֹנָה
Yonadav	Jonadab	yo-na-DAV	יוֹנָדָב
Yonatan	Jonathan	yo-na-TAN	יוֹנָתָן

Hebrew Name	English Name	Pronunciation	Hebrew
Yoram	Joram	yo-RAM	יוֹרָם
Yosef	Joseph	yo-SAYF	יוֹסֵף
Yoshiyahu	Josiah	yo-shi-YA-hu	יאשִׁיָּהוּ
Yotam	Jotham	yo-TAM	יוֹתָם
Yotzadak	Jozadak	yo-tza-DAK	יוֹצָדָק
Yozavad	Jozabad	yo-za-VAD	יוֹזָבָד
Zanoach	Zanoah	za-NO-akh	זָנוֹחַ
Zecharya	Zechariah	z'-khar-YAH	זְכַרְיָה
Zerach	Zerah	ZE-rakh	זֶרַח
Zerubavel	Zerubbabel	z'-ru-ba-VEL	זְרֻבָּבֶל
Zevulun	Zebulun	z'-vu-LUN	זְבוּלֻן
Zilpa	Zilpah	zil-PAH	זִלְפָּה
Zimri	Zimri	zim-REE	זִמְרִי

Jewish Holidays

Chanukah	Hanukkah	kha-nu-KAH	חֲנוּכָּה
Pesach	Passover	PE-sakh	פֶּסַח
Purim	Purim	pu-REEM	פּוּרִים
Rosh Hashana	Jewish New Year	rosh ha-sha-NAH	ראש הַשָּׁנָה
Shavuot	Feast of Weeks	sha-vu-OT	שָׁבוּעוֹת
Shemini Atzeret	Eight Day of Assembly	sh'-mee-NEE a-TZE-ret	שְׁמִינִי עֲצֶרֶת
Sukkot	Feast of Tabernacles	su-KOT	סֻכּוֹת
Yom Kippur	Day of Atonement	yom kee-PUR	יום כִּיפוּר

Biblical Measurements

Amah	Cubit	a-MAH	אַמָּה
Amot	Cubits	a-MOT	אַמוֹת
Bat	Bath	bat	בַּת
Batim	Baths	ba-TEEM	בַּתִּים
Beka	half-shekel	BE-ka	בֶּקַע
Chomarim	Homers	kho-ma-REEM	חֲמָרִים
Chomer	Homer	KHO-mer	חֹמֶר
Efah	Ephah	ay-FAH	אֵיפָה
Geira	Gerah	gay-RAH	גֵּרָה

Hebrew Name	English Name	Pronunciation	Hebrew
Gomed	Gomed	GO- med	גֹּמֶד
Hin	Hin	heen	הִין
Kav	kab	kav	קַב
Kesita	kesitah	k'-see-TAH	קְשִׂיטָה
Kikar	talent	ki-KAR	כִּכָּר
Kikarim	talents	ki-ka-RIM	כִּכָּרִים
Kor	kor	kor	כֹּר
Letek	lethech	LE-tek	לֶתֶךְ
Log	Log	log	לֹג
Maneh	Mina	ma-NEH	מָנֶה
Manim	Minas	ma-NEEM	מָנִים
Omer	Omer	O-mer	עֹמֶר
Pim	Pim	peem	פִּים
Se'ah	Seah	say-AH	סְאָה
Se'eem	Seahs	s'-EEM	סְאִים
Shekalim	Shekels	sh'-ka-LEEM	שְׁקָלִים
Shekel	Shekel	SHE-kel	שֶׁקֶל
Tefach	Handbreadth	TE-fakh	טֶפַח
Zeret	Span	ZE-ret	זֶרֶת

Photo Credits

1:9 pokku/Shutterstock.com, **2:3** Courtesy of Israel365, **3:4** Lenar Musin/Shutterstock.com, **4:2** kavram/Shutterstock.com, **5:1** Gal Eitan Photographer/Shutterstock.com, **6:1** Mikhail Semenov/Shutterstock.com, **7:3** Ranbar at Hebrew Wikipedia, CC BY-SA 2.5 <https://creativecommons.org/licenses/by-sa/2.5>, via Wikimedia Commons, **8:18** Andrew Shiva via Wikimedia Commons, **9:5** Africa Studio/Shutterstock.com, **10:5** Joshua Haviv/Shutterstock.com, **11:12** Moshe Milner, Government Press Office (Israel), **12:5** Protasov AN/Shutterstock.com, **14:14** Protasov AN/Shutterstock.com, **15:5** Roniuru/Shutterstock.com, **16:5** Irina Opachevsky/Shutterstock.com, **17:7** Moshe Milner, Government Press Office (Israel), **18:3** Noam Armonn/Shutterstock.com, **19:18** blueeyes/Shutterstock.com, **20:2** Liron-Afuta/Shutterstock.com, **21:5** denisgo/Shutterstock.com, **22:11** Tamar Hayardeni via Wikimedia Commons, **23:9** Hitman Sharon/Shutterstock.com, **24:5** Idan Ben Haim/Shutterstock.com, **25:8** El Ágora, CC BY-SA 3.0 <https://creativecommons.org/licenses/by-sa/3.0>, via Wikimedia Commons, **27:6** Amos Ben Gershom Government Press Office (Israel), **28:16** Thais29/Shutterstock.com, **28:25** Amos Ben Gershom Government Press Office (Israel), **29:13** mikhail/Shutterstock.com, **30:18** Zhukovskyi/Shutterstock.com, **31:9** Fat Jackey/Shutterstock.com, **32:18** Idan Ben Haim/Shutterstock.com, **33:5** Courtesy of Israel365, **34:16** zeevveez via flickr.com https://www.flickr.com/photos/zeevveez/3821689983/, **36:7** G Allen Penton/Shutterstock.com, **37:20** MWPHOTOS55/Shutterstock.com, **38:1** TaliV/Shutterstock.com, **39:8** mikhail/Shutterstock.com, **40:1** Danita Delimont/Shutterstock.com, **41:8** kavram/Shutterstock.com, **42:6** Government Press Office (Israel), **43:1** By מידע אין – The Palmach Archive via the PikiWiki – Israel free image collection project, Public Domain, https://commons.wikimedia.org/w/index.php?curid=20336470, **44:3** John Theodor/Shutterstock.com, **45:4** Prioryman, CC BY-SA 3.0 <https://creativecommons.org/licenses/by-sa/3.0>, via Wikimedia Commons, **46:13** Leonid Andronov/Shutterstock.com, **48:22** Courtesy of Nefesh B'Nefesh, **49:15** Inna Reznik/Shutterstock.com, **50:1** IVASHstudio/Shutterstock.com, **51:3** Prostav AN/Shutterstock.com, **53:12** Ms. Li/Shutterstock.com, **55:6** Fat Jackey/Shutterstock.com, **56:5** David Shankbone via Wikimedia Commons, **57:19** mikhail/Shutterstock.com, **58:14** By Daryag – Own work, CC BY-SA 4.0, https://commons.wikimedia.org/w/index.php?curid=57166594, **59:20** alefbet/Shutterstock.com, **60:1** SJ Travel Photo and Video/Shutterstock.com, **61:5** Courtesy of Israel365, **61:10** TI/Shutterstock.com, **62:2** Aleksandra H. Kossowska/Shutterstock.com, **63:16** Astakhova Natasha/Shutterstock.com, **64:7** J. Lee – Jeffrey's Photos/Shutterstock.com, **65:19** Alon Adika/Shutterstock.com, **66:12** SoloTanja/Shutterstock.com

Map of Modern-Day Israel and its Neighbors

The following is a map of modern-day Israel and the surrounding countries

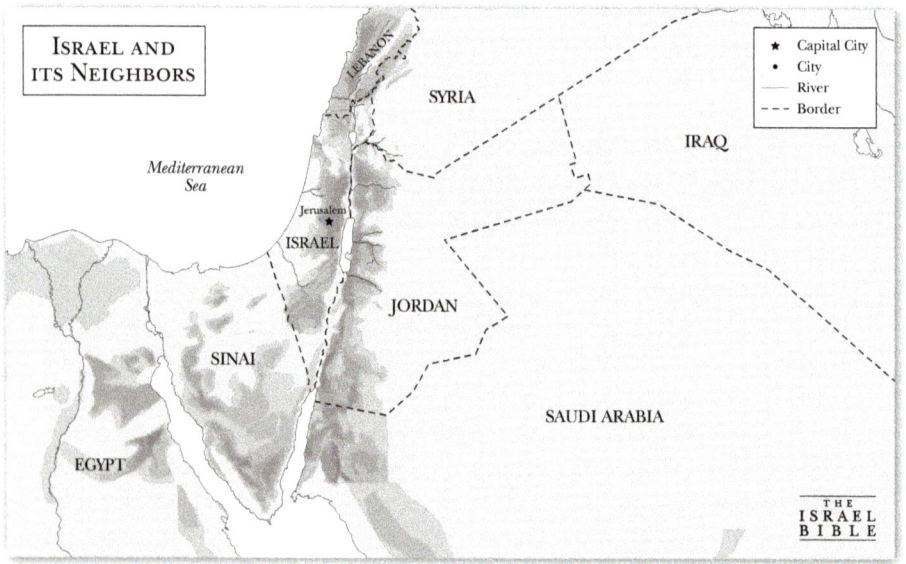

NOTES

NOTES

NOTES

NOTES

NOTES

For more inspiring commentary,
interactive maps, educational videos,
vivid photographs and more,
please visit our website

www.TheIsraelBible.com

THE
ISRAEL
BIBLE